WORKING YET POOR

This open access book explores the EU regulatory framework to measure in-work poverty and reduce its impact on different groups of workers in the labour market. Its innovative approach links the enhancement of social rights with the full realisation of EU citizenship entitlements and values.

For almost two decades, EU countries have experienced rampant inequalities as well as the varied spread of in-work poverty, both around Europe and within national labour markets. Without the realistic prospect of EU citizens earning a decent living, the substantive content of EU citizenship itself could be put in jeopardy.

Following an in-depth scrutiny of the main policy options at EU and national level to reduce the number of working poor, this invaluable resource provides a theoretical reflection on the role of legislation and socio-fiscal welfare in contemporary labour markets.

The publication of this book has been possible thanks to the funding received from the European Union's Horizon 2020 research and innovation programme under grant agreement No 870619. The content of this book reflects only the authors' view, and the Research Executive Agency is not responsible for any use that may be made of the information it contains.

Working Yet Poor

Challenges to EU Social Citizenship

Edited by
Luca Ratti
and
Paul Schoukens

·HART·
OXFORD · LONDON · NEW YORK · NEW DELHI · SYDNEY

HART PUBLISHING

Bloomsbury Publishing Plc

Kemp House, Chawley Park, Cumnor Hill, Oxford, OX2 9PH, UK

1385 Broadway, New York, NY 10018, USA

29 Earlsfort Terrace, Dublin 2, Ireland

HART PUBLISHING, the Hart/Stag logo, BLOOMSBURY and the Diana logo are
trademarks of Bloomsbury Publishing Plc

First published in Great Britain 2023

A catalogue record for this book is available from the British Library.

A catalogue record for this book is available from the Library of Congress.

Library of Congress Control Number: 2023943765

ISBN: HB: 978-1-50996-654-7
       ePDF: 978-1-50996-656-1
       ePub: 978-1-50996-655-4

Typeset by Compuscript Ltd, Shannon

To find out more about our authors and books visit www.hartpublishing.co.uk.
Here you will find extracts, author information, details of forthcoming events
and the option to sign up for our newsletters.

FOREWORD: THE CHALLENGE OF COMBATING IN-WORK POVERTY

I am grateful to Luca Ratti and Paul Schoukens for providing me with an opportunity to explain why this book is important, and why it deserves to become an important source of inspiration for further initiatives to combat in-work poverty.

The European Union defines the working poor as people who are employed (having held a job for at least seven months during the reference year) but whose incomes are below 60 per cent of the national median equivalised disposable income.[1] In 2017, the working poor in the European Union thus defined constituted 10 per cent of the active working population, up from 8 per cent 10 years before;[2] by 2022, the latest year for which data are available, the figure for the EU-27 was 8.5 per cent of the employed population, with wide variations ranging from 14.3 per cent for Romania and 2.5 per cent in Finland.

In other terms, almost one in 10 workers in the EU are paid wages that do not protect from being at risk of poverty. The cost-of-living crisis only adds to the urgency of addressing this situation: while annual inflation reached its highest ever level in the EU in 2022, more than tripling to 9.2 per cent, wages lagged far behind, up just 4.4 per cent.

The authors set themselves the challenge of addressing the causes of this phenomenon, and of proposing solutions. The research presented in this book does not remain at this highly general level, however. Instead, it focuses on four groups that are particularly at risk – what the authors call 'Vulnerable and Underrepresented Groups'. These are (1) low- or unskilled employees employed in low-wage sectors, who are disproportionately at risk of poverty despite having standard employment contracts; (2) self-employed, particularly bogus self-employed and solo (economically dependent) self-employed; (3) workers under non-standard employment contracts (including in particular temporary agency workers, part-time workers and workers with a fixed-term contract); and (4) casual and platform workers. This approach is particularly fruitful, because it allows the identification of factors explaining in-work poverty specific to each of these categories, which therefore may call for distinct regulatory or policy responses. For instance, the adoption of Directive (EU) 2022/2041 of 19 October 2022

---

[1] Eurofound, *Working poor* (29 November 2022). The equivalised disposable income represents the amount of money that an individual or household earns after taxes and other deductions have been taken out, adjusted for the size and composition of the household.

[2] Eurofound, *In-work poverty in the EU* (Eurofound, 2017) 5.

on adequate minimum wages in the European Union, despite its potentially significant contribution to protecting workers from in-work poverty,[3] will provide little solace to platform workers misclassified as 'self-employed'; and it will not provide temporary agency workers or workers on fixed-term contracts with the kind of long-term income security that they need to plan their lives and take control of their future: other regulatory initiatives are needed for these categories of workers.

At the same time, certain structural developments affect the world of work in general, and explain the persistence of in-work poverty in the EU. Globalisation has made the situation of the least qualified workers in rich countries more fragile, by weakening the bargaining position of unions faced with the threat of outsourcing production to low-wage jurisdictions. The automation of work, now magnified by the rise of artificial intelligence, threatens whole segments of the workforce, and workers who fear they may become redundant will easily be pressured into making concessions on wages. Globally, automation may lead to up to 890 million jobs being lost by 2030,[4] and to 1.1 billion jobs, about a third of total employment, changing radically as individual tasks are automated, with the risk that workers unable to acquire new skills will be left behind.[5] Technological advances also facilitate the outsourcing of services such as accounting, translation, editing, data entry, completing surveys, tagging photos or business consulting, to workers operating from countries where wages are low, and who can compete with workers in the EU with low levels of qualification: the average hourly wage of the workers on web-based platforms is US$3.4, and half of them earn less than US$2.1 per hour.[6] In effect, such forms of outsourcing result in the export of labour without the migration of those providing it: it is as if the labour supply in rich countries suddenly expanded dramatically.[7]

Labour law itself has not been immune from such pressures. Work has been made more flexible in a desperate quest to increase the rate of employment (the Europe 2020 target is that 75 of the working age population should be at work). This quest however has led not to a reduction of poverty,[8] but instead to the

---

[3] Directive (EU) 2022/2041 of the European Parliament and of the Council of 19 October 2022 on adequate minimum wages in the European Union [2022] OJ L 275/33. Directive 2022/2041 provides that the EU Member States will set, and regularly update, minimum wages, based on four criteria: purchasing power; the general level of wages and their distribution; the growth rate of wages; and long-term national productivity levels and developments. The EU Member States are therefore expected to define minimum wage not only in absolute terms, based on cost-of-living, but also in relative terms, relying in that regard on reference values commonly used at international level such as 60 per cent of the gross median wage and 50 per cent of the gross average wage.

[4] McKinsey Global Institute, 'Jobs lost, jobs gained: workforce transitions in a time of automation' (2017) 2.

[5] OECD, *The Future of Work: OECD Employment Outlook 2019* (Paris, OECD Publishing, 2019) 3.

[6] ILO, *World Employment and Social Outlook: Trends 2021* (Geneva, ILO, 2021) 23.

[7] G Standing, *The Precariat: The New Dangerous Class* (London, Tauris, 2021) viii–ix.

[8] See I Marx, P Vandebroucke and G Verbist, 'Can higher employment levels bring down relative income poverty in the EU? Regression-based simulations of the Europe 2020 target' (2012) 22(5) *Journal of European Social Policy* 472.

growth of precarious forms of employment.[9] Corporate strategies associated with post-Fordist economic restructuring (externalising, downsizing, outsourcing and subcontracting) lead to what has been called 'informalisation from above': starting in the 1980s, production increasingly has been decentralised towards smaller-scale and more flexible economic units, with many more menial tasks (such as cleaning or transportation) being outsourced to sub-contractors, leading to the growth of non-standard or atypical jobs characterised by hourly wages and few benefits, or even piece-rate jobs with no benefits.[10] In many non-standard forms of employment, working schedules are either unpredictable (permanently changing on short notice) or inflexible (not subject to negotiation), or both (with non-negotiable sudden changes). This worsens the impacts of poverty-induced time deficits: individuals facing such schedules cannot combine multiple jobs, especially when they commute long distances, nor perform other tasks such as taking care of other family members; and it is difficult for them to seek training to improve their qualifications. Poverty-induced time deficits perpetuate the cycle of poverty, as individuals have limited opportunities to improve their economic situation due to time constraints.

These trends are made worse by inter-jurisdictional competition within the EU. Member States' choices in setting wages and levels of social contributions are still driven by the perception that any increase in wages or social contributions could negatively affect their external cost competitiveness and reduce their attractiveness to potential investors in the most labour-intensive segments of the industry, thereby resulting in increased unemployment. Yet there is little to no evidence of a negative impact of minimum wages on unemployment.[11] Instead, the International Labour Organization (ILO) has shown that in fact minimum wages can contribute to higher labour productivity, both at the enterprise level and across the economy, which can in turn strengthen competitiveness.[12] There is also evidence that, contrary to the fears expressed by certain conservative groups, the indexation of wages to the consumer price index (as has been the case for a number of years in Belgium, Cyprus and Luxembourg[13]) will not lead to a wage-price spiral, threatening jobs. In fact, such indexation systems (the development of which is now encouraged by the 2022 directive on adequate minimum wages in the European Union) supports the purchasing power of the middle classes,

---

[9] ILO, *Non-Standard Employment around the World: Understanding Challenges, Shaping Prospects – Key Findings* (Geneva, ILO, 2016).

[10] MA Chen, 'The Informal Economy: Definitions, Theories and Policies' WIEGO Working Paper No 1 (2012).

[11] P Heimberger, 'Does employment protection affect unemployment? A meta-analysis' Oxford Economic Papers, 28 November 2020 doi.org/10.1093/oep/gpaa037.

[12] ILO, *Minimum Wage Policy Guide* 75, www.ilo.org/wcmsp5/groups/public/---ed_protect/---protrav/---travail/documents/publication/wcms_508566.pdf.

[13] Belgium and Cyprus rely on the national Consumer Price Index (CPI); in Luxembourg the Health Index is used, thus excluding alcohol, tobacco and petrol (but including heating fuel, gas and electricity).

improving the resilience of the economy in times of crisis. And comparative studies have shown that fears of a wage-price spiral are ill-founded, especially under circumstances of imported inflation.[14]

Finally, the failure to allow asylum-seekers or undocumented migrants access to regular employment may also lead to forms of exploitation that, again, will make the situation of workers across whole sectors, particularly construction and agriculture, more fragile. In 2012, the Special Rapporteur on the human rights of migrants, François Crépeau, reported that during his official visit to Italy, he met with 'numerous irregular migrants working in informal sectors, many of whom were being exploited by unscrupulous employers, who appeared to enjoy total impunity. Employers appear to exploit the fact of the migrants' irregular status by requiring them to undertake strenuous physical labour for long hours, and often paid far below the minimum wages, or not at all'.[15] This will come as no surprise to anyone familiar with the situation of migrants in the EU. While the Employers' Sanctions Directive[16] prohibiting the employment of irregular migrants should allow the worst forms of exploitation to be combated, the implementation remains uneven across Member States, not least because the exploitation of undocumented migrant workers in certain sectors is seen as benefiting the local economy. Providing these migrants with access to regular employment would not only ensure a better protection against abuse, but it is also a requirement of international human rights law: in addition to the right to self-employment, which is guaranteed to all refugees under the 1951 Geneva Convention relating to the Status of Refugees, any difference in treatment based on residency status in access to employment would require justification under the International Covenant on Economic, Social and Cultural Rights; indeed, the Committee on Economic, Social and Cultural Rights has specifically reminded the States parties to the Covenant that employment can be an 'important channel for integration within the host country and will reduce the dependence of refugees or migrants on public support or private charity'.[17]

Globalisation, automation, flexibilisation, casualisation, inter-jurisdictional competition, and finally, in certain sectors, exploitation of irregularly staying migrants: these structural factors matter. Contrary to what is assumed in certain

---

[14] J Alvarez et al, 'Wage-Price Spirals: What is the Historical Evidence?' IMF Working Paper 22/221 (2022) (based on a review of 79 episodes of 'wage-price spirals' in advanced economies between 1973 and 2017, and 100 episodes in the manufacturing sector using a narrower but more widely available wage concept). This conclusion is further supported by the International Monetary Fund's 2022 *World Economic Outlook*, examining 22 situations in advanced economies over the past 50 years with conditions similar to 2021 when price inflation was rising (IMF, *World Economic Outlook: Countering the Cost-of-Living Crisis* (October 2022), ch 2).

[15] UN doc A/HRC/23/46/Add.3 (2012), para 87.

[16] Directive 2009/52/EC of the European Parliament and of the Council of 18 June 2009 providing for minimum standards on sanctions and measures against employers of illegally staying third-country nationals [2009] OJ L 168/24.

[17] Committee on Economic, Social and Cultural Rights, 'Duties of States towards migrants and refugees under the International Covenant on Economic, Social and Cultural Rights', UN doc E/C.12/2017/1 (13 March 2017), para 6.

neoclassical theories of the employment market, wages are not the result of supply and demand curves meeting at some equilibrium point. They are the result of a bargaining process, in which unions and employers each seek to coerce the other party into making certain concessions, in what Robert Lee Hale called the economy's system of power.[18] This is also why the growth of job guarantee schemes, as illustrated for instance by *Territoires zero chômeurs longue durée* in France (now covering 58 municipalities) or by the *Kinofelis* programme set up in Greece as part of the response to the debt crisis in 2011 (which offered eight months of employment to 45,000 participants by 2017),[19] could be game-changers in the future. For workers facing exploitative employers, a job guarantee programme subsidised through the public purse may constitute a fall-back option, strengthening their bargaining position, and allowing them to claim a right to decent work – and if they are in informal work because of an unwillingness of the employer to declare them in order to circumvent protective legislation or to avoid paying social contributions, to seek formalisation. Where the employment provided under the job guarantee programme includes paid leave, pension contribution, health insurance and childcare subsidy, or where it pays a wage above the minimum wage, it raises the bar across the whole economy.[20]

One final remark may be in order. When official statistics speak of one in 10 workers in the EU being at risk of poverty, they do not mean that all these workers face extreme material deprivation: the 'at-risk-of-poverty' measure is, for the most part, a measure of wage inequality. The discussion about in-work poverty therefore should not only be a discussion about the minimum wage corresponding to a living wage, but also a discussion about the fairness of wage scales.

This is also a requirement of human rights law. In addition to having a right to a 'living wage', workers have a right to 'fair wages'.[21] The orthodox interpretation of this requirement is that wages should reflect 'not only the output of the work but also the responsibilities of the worker, the level of skill and education required to perform the work, the impact of the work on the health and safety of the worker, specific hardships related to the work and the impact on the worker's personal and family life'.[22] In practice however, the levels of wages are the result of bargaining processes in which most workers, or the unions representing them in collective bargaining, are in a weak position from which to negotiate better wages. This is the result of the constellation of structural factors described above. Only by strengthening unions and protecting the right to collective bargaining will it be possible to uphold the right to a fair remuneration.

---

[18] See in particular Robert Lee Hale, 'Coercion and Distribution in a Supposedly Non-Coercive State' (1923) 38 *Political Science Quarterly* 470.

[19] ILO, 'The Right to Work Now Lessons from Kinofelis: the Greek public employment programme' (19 March 2018) 2.

[20] P Tcherneva, *The Case for a Job Guarantee* (Cambridge, Polity, 2020) 83.

[21] International Covenant on Economic, Social and Cultural Rights, Art 7(a)(i).

[22] E/C.12/GC/23, para 10.

Another and more fundamental problem is that the bargaining position of workers depends in part on what the end purchaser of the good or service provided will pay. However, as illustrated by the case of unpaid care workers,[23] the most important contributions of work to overall well-being are not necessarily in the added monetary value it creates. Workers performing essential functions on which society depends are typically underpaid, because their contributions are insufficiently valued, and because the services they provide have the nature of a public good, for which the beneficiaries are unwilling or unable to pay. These workers moreover provide services that serve communities, including people living in poverty, who cannot afford to pay for such services: as a result of how work is currently valued in the labour market, the more the work serves the needs of the poor, the less well it will be remunerated.

The low remuneration of workers providing care can also be attributed to the fact that many of their tasks were traditionally performed by women within households and communities, without remuneration; even once these tasks were paid for, the wages were set at a low level, reflecting such a lack of recognition of the value to society of the work of reproduction (as contrasted with production).[24] The activities of domestic workers, for instance – such as cooking, cleaning, washing and caregiving – are undervalued both because they are often considered 'unproductive'[25] and because they have traditionally been assumed by women – whereas they are a valuable and necessary labour which the functioning of communities and entire economies depend on.[26]

This should not be allowed to continue. In order to be 'fair', the remuneration should reflect not only the economic value created by the worker, but also the contribution to society of the work performed.[27] Prospective workers otherwise will seek the kind of training, and workers will provide the goods and services, that serve not the needs of the community, and particularly those of low-income groups, but those of the most affluent only. Thus, instead of making phones that last for many years and can be easily repaired, engineers will plan their phones so that they will have to be replaced with an even smarter version within 20 months; instead of designing schemes to help people in poverty, economists will become

---

[23] UN doc A/68/293.

[24] B Palier, 'Pourquoi les personnes occupant un emploi "essentiel" sont-elles si mal payées?" Sciences Po LIEPP Working Paper no 116 (2020).

[25] ILO, 'Social protection for domestic workers: Key policy trends and statistics' (Geneva, ILO, 2016) 5.

[26] ILO, *Minimum Wage Policy Guide: Chapter 8 – Minimum wages for domestic workers* 3–4; P Bamu-Chipunza, 'Promoting Decent Work for Domestic Workers: Lessons from Five Countries' WIEGO Resource Document No 8 (Manchester, WIEGO, 2018).

[27] N Bueno, 'From Productive Work to Capability-Enhancing Work: Implications for Labour Law and Policy' (2022) 23(3) *Journal of Human Development and Capabilities* 366; E Dermine and D Dumont, 'A Renewed Critical Perspective on Social Law: Disentangling Its Ambivalent Relationship with Productivism' (2022) 38(3) *International Journal of Comparative Labour Law and Industrial Relations* 267.

traders; instead of building low-cost social housing, architects will aim at building mansions for the ultra-rich; and so on. The result is not only that the incentives are distorted against serving the needs of the poorest groups within society, and that an enormous human potential is wasted while it could serve societal needs, it is also that, since goods or services for these groups are undersupplied, their prices may increase, resulting in an artificial scarcity.

To remedy this, work that is of higher societal value should be better remunerated. In a study on the jobs that the Covid-19 pandemic showed to be 'essential', the ILO found that 'essential workers' earn, on average, 26 per cent less than other workers, and that only two thirds of the gap could be explained by differences in education and experience.[28] In other terms, the workers providing the most vital services to society, in areas such as food production and retail, healthcare, cleaning and sanitation, or transport, are underpaid.

This is not inevitable. States could draw up a list of goods and services the provision of which is essential and of high societal value, and ensure that the workers involved in such provision are paid fair wages (beyond the minimum wage allowing the meet basic needs); they could also, conversely, draw up a list of professions that are currently highly paid despite their negative externalities (such as those of traders encouraging speculation on financial markets, workers involved in the extraction of fossil energy, in pesticides production, in plastic production, or in the tobacco industry, or workers in the advertising industry), and cap high remunerations in those sectors. In order for these mandates to be economically viable in the private for-profit sector, tax incentives and subsidies could be provided, compensating for the increased costs of labour in the sectors that society seeks to support, while at the same time higher income taxes would penalise the excessively high remuneration of professions causing high negative externalities.

What is needed to combat in-work poverty is more political imagination, and audacity. I welcome this book as a major contribution to the discussion on why we still have almost 20 million workers at risk of poverty in the EU. I have no doubt that this comparative research will continue to influence debates in the next few years on what needs to be done to address it. The authors should be commended for providing us with the robust scientific basis on which these debates can now be grounded.

Olivier De Schutter
United Nations Special Rapporteur on
extreme poverty and human rights

---

[28] ILO, *World Employment and Social Outlook 2023: The Value of Essential Work* (Geneva, ILO, 2023) 62.

CONTENTS

PART III
ADDRESSING IN-WORK POVERTY

PART IV
IDENTIFYING NEW PATHWAYS FOR FURTHER RESEARCH

LIST OF CONTRIBUTORS

Luca Ratti (editor) is an Associate Professor of European and Comparative Labour Law and Director of the Master in European Law (I year) at the University of Luxembourg. He was previously Senior Researcher and Adjunct Professor of Labour Law and Social Security at the University of Bologna, where he also obtained his Doctorate. From 2020 to 2023 he coordinated the Working, Yet Poor (WorkYP) project. He currently holds a Jean Monnet Chair in European labour law on Sustainability of the European Social Model (2022–2025).

Paul Schoukens (editor) is Professor of Social Security Law (Comparative, International, and European) at the KU Leuven. He heads the department of social law in the Faculty of Law. As from March 2015 he has held the Instituut Gak chair International and European Social Security Law at Tilburg University. In 2013, he became Secretary-General of the European Institute of Social Security, an international scientific network of persons professionally active in the fields of social security and social protection.

Ane Aranguiz is an Assistant Professor in European Labour and Social Security Law at the Private, Business and Labour Law Department of Tilburg Law School. Her research focuses on European social law with an interest in poverty, social exclusion, labour precarity and human rights. She is also a guest professor at the Faculty of Law of the University of Antwerp and the Faculty of Law of the Université Libre de Bruxelles, where she teaches international labour and social law.

Marta Capesciotti is a Researcher with a specific focus on fundamental rights and migration law. She graduated in international cooperation and development at the 'Sapienza' University of Rome and has a PhD in Law and Economics from the 'Sapienza' University of Rome and in Constitutional Law from the University of Granada on the right to housing and social housing of third-country citizens living in Italy and Spain. She also has an MSc in Gender Equality and Diversity Management. Since 2016 she has been working at the 'Fondazione Giacomo Brodolini' (Rome) on fundamental rights, non-discrimination legislation, gender-based violence, protection of crime victims, gender equality, migration policies and rights of persons with disabilities, mainly coordinating and implementing reporting activities and fieldwork research for the Fundamental Rights Agency (FRA) of the European Union. She has also supported the research activities carried out by Fondazione for the European Institute for Gender Equality (EIGE) and for the Scientific Analysis and Advice on Gender Equality in the EU (SAAGE) network.

Eleni De Becker is a Professor (Free University Brussels) and a substitute professor (KU Leuven) in (EU, comparative and national) social security law. Eleni focuses on fundamental social rights from a comparative, international and European perspective, as well as the social security protection for atypical workers and the role of the EU. In the framework of the Working, Yet Poor project, Eleni was responsible for the comparative analysis of the social security protection offered to the four Vulnerable and Underrepresented Persons groups in the seven selected EU Member States. Recently, she has also advised both Belgian and Dutch social security institutions on matters of social security.

Alexander Dockx graduated cum laude from KU Leuven and is currently a legal advisor for the Flemish minister of Well-being, Health and Family. There he specialises in youth policy, privacy and data protection. Additionally, he is connected to the KU Leuven Institute of Social Law, where he previously researched European systems of socio-fiscal welfare and lectured on legal writing techniques. He is interested in policy making and socio-economic issues, being involved in political organisations based in both the Leuven and Brussels regions, as well as procedural law, in which he has also been published.

Antonio Garcia-Muñoz Alhambra is Postdoctoral Researcher at the University of Luxembourg. He has worked in several Universities on topics related to Social Europe, with a focus on EU level social dialogue and collective bargaining and has been involved in several European research projects. Currently he is exploring the role of labour law in the production of in-work poverty and other instances of vulnerability; the regulation of telework, including the right to disconnect; and the relations between labour law, economic growth and sustainability in the EU and beyond.

Dalila Ghaliani is a lawyer with 20 years of experience in monitoring a range of issues related to the social dimension of the EU, including employment, in-work poverty, social protection, minimum income, job quality and digitalisation, notably under the scope of gender equality. As Senior Researcher at the European social Observatory (OSE), she has conducted several studies for EU institutions and has been involved in several EU research projects. In the framework of her research on in-work-poverty she co-authored a synthesis report for the European Social Policy Network (ESPN) of the European Commission.

Ann-Christine 'Ankie' Hartzén is a Senior Lecturer in labour law at the Department of Business Law, Lund University. Her current research is dedicated to platform work focusing the intersection between labour law and social security law as well as the development and interaction between EU-law and national level systems of industrial relations. She holds a deep interest for Social Europe and previous publications cover issues such as in-work poverty, the European Social Dialogue, European integration and solidarity, as well as system theory implications for socio-legal method.

Christina Hiessl is Professor of Labour Law at KU Leuven, Invited Professor of Social Welfare at Yonsei University, and Consulting Expert of the European Commission's Centre of Expertise in the Field of Labour Law (ECE). She has worked and/or studied in eight countries, focusing on comparative social law and policy research. In the framework of her research on in-work poverty, she has guest-edited two multiple-author special issues of academic journals and provided policy advice for recent reforms in Germany.

Mijke Houwerzijl is a Full Professor of Labour Law at Tilburg University (since 2011). Previously, she was also an endowed Professor of European and comparative labour law at the University of Groningen (2010–2020). She lectures and has published widely on issues related to Dutch and European labour law and social security law, with an emphasis on legal aspects of transnational labour mobility and flexible labour relationships, such as temporary agency work and online platform work.

Korina Kominou is a social policy researcher at the European Social Observatory. Her research work and scientific interests cover topics on labour market inequalities, unemployment, EU social dialogue, in-work poverty and the effective implementation of the European Pillar of Social Rights. She has been a researcher and scientific collaborator at the Center of Social Policy and Morphology and in the Center in Gender Studies of Panteion University of Social and Political Sciences of Greece (Athens) for several years researching among others social and gender inequalities topics.

Giulia Marchi is a Postdoctoral Researcher at the University of Bologna, Italy, where she worked on the Horizon 2020 Project 'Working, Yet Poor'. She obtained her PhD at the University of Milan-Statale. Her research explores social clauses and protections for employees in outsourcing processes in the field of Italian and EU labour law and the right to fair and adequate wage.

Roberta Paoletti is a Researcher on Gender equality with a focus on EU level policy. She has a PhD in Philosophical Anthropology from the University of Palermo (visiting researcher at Freie Universitaet in Berlin). MSc in Gender Equality and Diversity Management. Scientific Coordinator for the Master's Degree 'Studi e politiche di genere' at Roma Tre University. During the legislature 2014–2019, she was in charge of gender mainstreaming network and responsible for the legislative work of FEMM (Women's Rights and Gender Equality) and INTA (International Trade) Committees at the European Parliament.

Ramón Peña-Casas is a sociologist with a strong expertise in socioeconomic analysis. He is a Senior Research Fellow at the European Social Observatory (OSE) since 2000. In this context, he has been involved in several EU research projects. His areas of interest include the assessment and comparative analysis of EU Member States regarding socio-economic issues that cut across the various areas of the EU social dimension: poverty and social exclusion; in-work poverty, social protection, social assistance and minimum income; job quality; precariousness of employment, flexicurity, working conditions and social dialogue. In relation to in-work poverty in Europe he has notably co-edited an academic book on the topic as well as a synthesis report for the European Social Policy Network (ESPN) of the European Commission.

Vincenzo Pietrogiovanni is an Associate Professor of Labour Law at the Department of Law at SDU – University of Southern Denmark, and he is also affiliated with the Department of Business Law at Lund University. He holds a PhD in Labour Law from the University of Bari. His current research focuses on AI and work; minimum wages; labour law implications of climate change adaptation and mitigation policies; collective labour freedoms; and fundamental rights at work. He teaches courses on anti-discrimination law, EU labour law and international and comparative labour law.

TABLE OF CASES

Case Law

ILO Committee on Freedom of Association

National Courts

TABLE OF LEGISLATION

International Law

National legislation

Introduction

LUCA RATTI AND PAUL SCHOUKENS

It was late 2018 when we as a group of European lawyers started realising that a relatively new phenomenon was severely affecting the normal functioning of labour markets across the EU. In-work poverty was rampant in most EU countries. Yet, significant differences existed amongst them in terms of in-work poverty levels and the composition of the workforce affected. Even neighbouring countries, or those with a similar economic structure, presented marked discrepancies. Certainly, in-work poverty was significantly more widespread in 2018 than in the previous decade.

An observation of such an emerging trend came with two assumptions to test and, perhaps, falsify.

The first one concerned the unequal spread of in-work poverty across the labour market, since in-work poverty was disproportionately affecting low-skilled workers and economic sectors with a high number of low-wage workers, self employed, flexible and atypical workers, as well as casual and platform workers. We decided to analyse their situation grouping them into clusters, and we identified four such clusters of Vulnerable and Under-represented Persons. We named them VUPs – as opposed to VIPs – and we continued to examine in-work poverty using the VUP Groups as an analytical tool to see what legal and policy implications could be derived. Throughout this book, the reader will find constant reference to such VUP Groups as an innovative analytical tool to concentrate the legal analysis (and elaborate targeted policy responses) precisely on those who are most affected by in-work poverty in the European context.

The second assumption was that being 'working poor' risks undermining the place of an individual vis-à-vis the society they are embedded in, so that their status as citizens of the EU deteriorates. Not only did this called to be repaired, but above all it required a re-conceptualisation of the very concept of EU citizenship, which is currently derivative and lacks any substantive content in terms of social entitlements. Re-thinking EU social citizenship is therefore possible, and much needed.

Based on an amazing consortium of nine universities (Luxembourg, Leuven, Bologna, Frankfurt, Gdansk, Lund, Rotterdam, Tilburg, and Utrecht) and three social rights institutions (OSE (*Observatoire Social Européen*), EAPN European Anti-Poverty Network, and FGB (*Fondazione Giacomo Brodolini*)) coordinated by the University of Luxembourg, the Working, Yet Poor (WorkYP) project found its way thanks to the generous funding received from the EU research and innovation programme Horizon 2020. The project's activities were carried out between February 2020 and January 2023. The main findings of the project were presented at the WorkYP final international conference held in Brussels in January 2023, opened by Mr Nicolas Schmit (EU Commissioner for Jobs and Social Rights) and Professor Olivier de Schutter (UN Rapporteur on Human Rights and Extreme Poverty). More than 200 people attended the final conference, including academics, social partners, policy makers, NGOs and grassroots campaigners, and ordinary citizens having experienced poverty and in-work poverty.

During the three years of its lifespan, the WorkYP project produced impressive outputs, including 29 deliverables, more than 3,000 pages written, a first book published in 2022 (L Ratti (ed), *In-Work Poverty in Europe. Vulnerable and Underrepresented Persons in a Comparative Perspective* (Wolters Kluwer 2022)), around 40 scientific contributions in top class journals at European and national level, five special issues of scientific journals, and five project newsletters.

Those three years have seen the emergence of both previously existing and completely new challenges from a legal, economic, statistical and sociological perspective.

The WorkYP researchers were confronted with the lack of on-time/updated data, a wide variety of legal regimes, and fragmented social security systems. The project also faced the limits of the current statistical indicators of in-work poverty and, in some of the countries investigated, the absence of political and social awareness about this issue.

Several challenges are on the horizon, including responding to demographic change and the future structure of EU societies, developing a longitudinal and lifetime perspective on in-work poverty, carrying out a proper assessment of the impact of the Covid-19 pandemic crisis, and elaborating new indicators of in-work poverty that will be able to integrate more detailed information, such as the migrant/non-migrant variable and the unemployed/underemployed continuum.

This book intends to address some of these challenges and project them towards a future research agenda – one which is capable of grasping the societal changes triggered by the recent crises and finding the most suitable legal responses to them. As will become clear after reading the 11 chapters of this book, a legal approach to in-work poverty confirms the need to adopt a holistic perspective, providing policy responses that function in connection with existing labour law institutions and which recognise the essential function of major stakeholders, particularly social partners.

The book is structured as follows.

In chapter one, Antonio García-Muñoz Alhambra sets the scene by focusing on how in-work poverty is defined and measured in the European context, and outlines its main determinants at individual, household, and institutional level. He provides an account of the increasing attention paid by EU institutions to the rampant levels of in-work poverty, culminating with the European Pillar of Social Rights (EPSR) and its action plan.

Chapter two by Christina Hiessl provides a comparative overview on the four VUP Groups across the seven countries that have been investigated by the WorkYP project, namely Germany, the Netherlands, Belgium, Luxembourg, Poland, Italy and Sweden. The chapter discusses the role of activation policies, training, minimum wages, and social benefits including income support measures. Hiessl's conclusion is that policy approaches at national level are not exclusively meant as protective measures but are the result of a policy mix which consider a wide array of social risks related to the most vulnerable workers in the labour market.

In chapter three, Mijke Houwerzijl provides an overview of EU law's attitude towards the regulation of the four VUP Groups considered by the WorkYP Project, focusing in particular on the recent EU directive on adequate minimum wages on VUP Group 1 and the three directives on atypical work on VUP Group 3. She furthermore highlights the still undeveloped approach regarding self-employment (VUP Group 2) as well as casual and platform work (VUP Group 4), on which the regulatory initiative is still ongoing. Her conclusion argues that EU harmonisation should be operationalised through the horizontal social clause (Article 9 of the Treaty on the Functioning of the European Union) streamlining social protection across all European policy areas.

Chapter four by Marta Capesciotti and Roberta Paoletti unveils the 'gender paradox' in in-work poverty, in which women's situation is often hidden by the fact that they are second breadwinner and therefore do not emerge from in-work poverty statistics. They furthermore articulate horizontal and vertical segregation as crucial aspects to countering this gender paradox.

In chapter five, Ane Aranguiz explores the idea of an EU social citizenship that is relevant for all and not only for persons who benefit from the protection granted by the EU rules on free movement for workers and professionally active persons. She starts first with the concept of citizenship when it was launched by the EU. She departs from the common underpinning of a value-based 'civitas' among Europeans and the rationale and mandates of the EU as a normative foundation to argue in favour of a more complete citizenship that entails a social dimension as well. She also elaborates on how this idea fits in a multitiered network of citizens, in which the EU plays primarily a complementary role. The chapter ends by relating social citizenship to the EPSR and how this can be used to develop further social action on the European level to combat in-work poverty.

Chapter six by Giulia Marchi provides a compelling analysis of the many concepts associated with wages, including fair and adequate wage, living wage and minimum wage. She considers the EU Directive on adequate minimum wages (Directive 2022/2041) in the context of the recent policy initiatives prompted by the EPSR and argues for the introduction of more accurate indicators on in-work poverty that may consider relative and absolute criteria together, with a view to appropriately assessing the adequacy of wages.

Chapter seven by Eleni De Becker analyses the social security systems regarding their adequacy when providing income replacement benefits for the VUP Groups. Social security systems in EU Member States still largely rely on their traditional design, based on workers with a full-time contract of indefinite duration. This traditional approach in national social security systems does not, however, seem well equipped to deal with the situation of non-standard work and the higher risk of in-work poverty for non-standard workers. The question therefore arises what protection national social security systems currently provide for the in-work poor and if and how such systems should be adapted to provide adequate and sufficient protection for all types of workers. This comparative report on social security tries to answer these questions and focuses on the level of protection provided in case of unemployment and sickness by the selected EU Member States' social security schemes for each VUP Group. The aim of the report is not only to map the level of social protection coverage, but also to look at (possible) impediments in the design of the selected national social security schemes for the VUP Groups.

In chapter eight Ramón Peña-Casas, Dalila Ghailani and Korina Kominou aim to make general policy recommendations for the European Union to tackle in-work poverty, building on the main findings of the WorkYP project, and considering the European Pillar of Social Rights (EPSR) principles as the main reference framework. With their findings, the ambition of the authors is to enhance an effective EU social citizenship. The chapter is structured around five lines of action: how the assessment of in-work poverty in the EU social indicators framework can be improved; how in-work poverty as a cross-sectional concern into all EU socio-economic policies and purposes can be more effectively mainstreamed; how access of low-skilled workers and non-standard workers to learning and training can be improved; how access to social protection for vulnerable workers can be developed; and how a participatory social dialogue on in-work poverty in the EU can be revived and further stimulated.

In chapter nine, Ann-Christine Hartzén and Vincenzo Pietrogiovanni examine the role of social partners in addressing in-work poverty across the seven countries investigated. They highlight how the phenomenon penetrated into social partners' discourse, particularly on the employees' side. They conclusively suggest possible pathways to further embed concrete strategies in social partners' action and the way these may influence policy making.

Chapter ten by Paul Schoukens, Alexander Dockx and Eleni De Becker offers an analysis of socio-fiscal welfare and its relationship with traditional social security schemes. They focus on its possible significance for supporting social security in achieving its goals of safeguarding living standards and combating poverty. The chapter concludes by looking at how the EU could integrate socio-fiscal welfare into its current monitoring of national social security and poverty (plans).

The book concludes with chapter eleven by Luca Ratti, who focuses on the role of legislation to address the many issues relating to in-work poverty. He argues that instead of aiming to reduce in-work poverty, the law has frequently contributed to structuralise it, which emerges now as an endemic characteristic of contemporary labour markets.

PART I

Setting the Scene: In-work Poverty in the EU

1

Conceptualisation: In-work Poverty and its Determinants

ANTONIO GARCÍA-MUÑOZ ALHAMBRA

I. Introduction

What does it mean to be working poor in the EU? Who are the 'working poor' in this region of the world? Why are some workers 'at risk of poverty' and what can be done to avoid this situation? Answering these questions demands an accurate understanding of how in-work poverty is conceptualised and measured. These are mutually dependent questions, that cannot be separated. The same goes for our perception of what exactly the drivers are behind in-work poverty, and what their relative importance is. This chapter seeks to advance some answers to the above questions by presenting the concept of in-work poverty and explaining how we measure it. It also describes and assesses some of the reasons that favour its existence and expansion. Finally, it engages with the context in which in-work poverty occurs in the EU in an attempt to better understand the meaning and impact of this phenomenon in our societies.

The working poor in the EU, according to Eurostat, amounted to 8.9 per cent of the employed population in 2021.[1] This means that almost one in every ten EU workers experienced poverty. Most readers will agree that this is bad news. Probably, they will also ask themselves how this is possible. How can it be that so many people are experiencing poverty despite being at work?

This is a legitimate question, since in our societies we traditionally associate poverty with situations of worklessness, such as unemployment, illness or similar. Work, on the contrary, is perceived as a shield against poverty. The fact that workers, at least a great number of them, also may experience poverty, is seen therefore as an anomaly, a sign that something is not as it should be.[2] After all, 'the working

---

[1] Eurostat, *In-work at-risk-of-poverty rate by age and sex – EU-SILC survey* (online data code: ILC_IW01).

[2] However, outside the EU, particularly in the global south, the perception may be different, since the idea that work protects from poverty has probably never corresponded to the reality.

poor presumably play by the rules, and the normative expectation is that work should – if only for moral reasons – be rewarded with an above-poverty standard of living'.[3] But the fact is that the concept of in-work poverty is more complex than it appears. It describes a multidimensional reality. It is not all about having a work or even a decent wage – the type of household in which the worker lives is also very relevant. To understand why this is so, it is absolutely necessary to engage with indicators and how they measure in-work poverty. In the present chapter, the focus is on the most important of such indicators in the EU: the *in-work at-risk-of poverty* indicator.

Finally, the concept of in-work poverty is influenced by the broader societal, legal and economic context in which it takes place. How in-work poverty is constructed as a category is influenced by this context, which in turn gives meaning to the reality it helps to construct. Only by taking the context seriously, can we correctly understand the impact of in-work poverty in the EU. To this end, this chapter will attempt to understand why in-work poverty has (re-)emerged recently as a social and policy problem in Europe and what this says about the current evolution of EU labour markets and societies.

For the purposes of the present book, it is also necessary to refer to one analytical concept that has been used throughout the Working, Yet Poor (WorkYP) project: the idea of VUP groups (for Vulnerable and Underrepresented Persons). This concept groups together different clusters of workers that are in a particularly vulnerable position in the labour market. The following clusters of vulnerable and underrepresented persons have been identified: (1) VUP Group 1 – low- or unskilled employees with standard employment contracts employed in poor sectors (defined as those sectors where more than 20 per cent of workers earn wages that are two-thirds or less of the national median gross hourly earnings); (2) VUP Group 2 – self-employed, particularly bogus self-employed and solo (economically dependent) self-employed; (3) VUP Group 3 – flexible employed persons (ie temporary agency workers, part-time workers and workers with a fixed-term contract); and (4) VUP Group 4 – casual and platform workers.[4] Focusing the analysis of in-work poverty on these disadvantaged groups allows for a more detailed and tailored approach to the needs and legal problems experienced by those who are, according to available statistics, at a higher risk of being working poor.

---

[3] B Thiede, D Lichter and S Sanders, 'America's Working Poor: Conceptualization, Measurement and New Estimates' (2015) 42(3) *Work and Occupations* 270. This may be after all just a normative expectation based, on the one hand, in the very particular experience of Western societies in the second half of the twentieth century and, on the other, on the assumption that the wage fully compensates the reproduction of the workers' labour-power. See more details on a critique of this assumption in section IV.

[4] A detailed description of these VUP Groups is found in L Ratti, A García-Muñoz and V Vergnat, 'The challenge of defining, measuring and overcoming in-work poverty in Europe: an introduction' in L Ratti (ed), *In-work Poverty in Europe. Vulnerable and Under-Represented Persons in a Comparative Perspective* (London, Wolters Kluwer, 2022).

The chapter develops as follows. Section II introduces the concept of in-work poverty, explaining how it is measured in the EU. It is subdivided in two parts. In section II.A, after discussing the main elements of the concept, a brief comparison on how different countries and organisations measure in-work poverty helps to put the EU approach in perspective. Then follows a detailed analysis of the EU indicators, highlighting their rationale, strengths, problems and limitations with a focus in the *in-work at-risk-of-poverty* indicator. Section II.B consists of an analysis of apparently paradoxical statistical results, such as the weak correlation between in-work poverty and low salaries or the fact that, whereas women are in a more precarious position in the labour market, there is nevertheless a higher risk of in-work poverty for men. To focus on these apparent paradoxes is very useful in order to understand the limitations of existing indicators. Section III delves into the causes and determinants of in-work poverty in the EU. To do so, it reviews a number of empirical and doctrinal contributions, offering a picture of the complex and intertwined factors shaping in-work poverty. Finally, section IV puts in-work poverty in the EU in its broader context, in an attempt to shed light on the reasons for its recent visibility and formulation as a policy concern. The conclusion summarises the main ideas of the chapter.

II. The Concept of In-work Poverty

A. The Concept and Measurement of In-work Poverty, and their Limitations

Our conceptualisation of in-work poverty is strongly connected to how we measure it. These two questions are interlinked, and that is the reason why they are addressed simultaneously in this section.

In any conceptualisation of in-work poverty two different components emerge: work and poverty. Therefore, all attempts to define in-work poverty are confronted with the same basic problems regarding these two elements. It is necessary to clarify, first, who is to be considered 'in work'; second, when such working persons are to be considered poor.

On the first question, it is advisable to proceed in two steps. First, it must be established who qualifies as a 'worker'. Second, within this group of potential workers, it is necessary to identify who are actually working, ie 'in work'.[5]

The first step is, therefore, the problem of defining the 'working population'. There are some groups of people who, due to different reasons, are not expected to work or even are not eligible to work even if they would like to do so. These

---

[5] H Lohmann, 'The concept and measurement of in-work poverty' in H Lohmann and I Marx (eds), *Handbook on In-Work Poverty* (Cheltenham, Edward Elgar, 2019) 14.

persons, consequently, do not qualify as workers and are therefore not counted as part of the working population. In our societies, the most important criterion to differentiate between groups of people able and unable to work is age. The application of the age criterion to decide who should and can work results in some parts of the population being left outside the group of 'workers'. Those making up the 'non-working' population are normally the elderly and children.[6] It is possible to find some other, if more marginal, excluded groups defined by other reasons different to age, like those defined by education, illness or disability.[7] In any case, there is no universal agreement on how to define the 'working population'.

In a second step the aim is to differentiate, within all those belonging to the working population, between those who are actually working and those who are not, such as, for example, the unemployed (although in the case of US those looking for jobs during a period of time are also considered as 'in work'). First, what is to be 'working' must be defined. Not all human activities will qualify as 'work' for the purposes of defining in-work poverty; not even many activities that are socially necessary and create value, such as, for instance, care work within the household. Normally, when we refer to in-work poverty, there is an implicit understanding that we are referring to 'employment' or 'paid work'.[8] Second, it must be decided when someone is 'at work' or, on the contrary, 'not at work'. In this point, there are divergences between indicators worldwide. For instance, in the case of the International Labour Organization (ILO), for the purposes of measuring in-work poverty, a person is at work when that person has been working for at least one hour in a reference period of one week.[9] In the US, the Bureau of Labour Statistics (BLS) includes as workers those who have been active at least 27 weeks (working, but also those looking for a job) within a reference period of one year.[10] In the EU, those who are 'in work' are all persons who declare to be employed 'for more than half the total number of months … during the income reference period'.[11]

---

[6] M Kim, 'The working poor: Lousy jobs or lazy workers?' (1998) 32(1) *Journal of Economic Issues* 71.

[7] Lohmann (n 5) 14.

[8] In-work poverty research differentiates between employment, defined as 'the production of goods or provision of services for pay or profit' and other forms of work, such as own-use production, unpaid trainee work, volunteer work, etc, as defined in the work of the International Conference of Labour Statisticians. See on this point Lohmann (n 5).

[9] Under this definition almost everyone who has even a small amount of work is working. Therefore, being unemployed will only occur when someone works zero hours. See unstats.un.org/sdgs/metadata/files/Metadata-01-01-01b.pdf (last visited 27 February 2023).

[10] See the BLS report, 'A profile of the working poor, 2019' (2021), in particular the section 'concepts and definitions'. Available at www.bls.gov/opub/reports/working-poor/2019/home.htm#technical-notes (last visited 27 February 2023).

[11] This is, therefore, a rather strict definition of 'in-work'. Consequently, a large part of the population with low work intensity will not be taken into account in the measurement of in-work poverty in the EU. See the methodology applied for the computation of the statistical indicator pertinent to the subject area of in-work poverty (ilc_iw) ec.europa.eu/eurostat/statistics-explained/index.php?title=EU_statistics_on_income_and_living_conditions_(EU-SILC)_methodology_-_in-work_poverty (last visited 27 February 2023); L Bardone and A-C Guio, *In-work poverty – New commonly agreed indicators at the EU level* (Luxembourg, Eurostat, Statistics in Focus, 5/2005, 2).

On the second question, ie when a person 'in work' is considered to be poor, there are several aspects to consider. First, the concept of poverty can be constructed as relative or absolute. Absolute poverty refers to a situation where the level of resources is too low to sustain life. This concept is therefore based on the idea of a basic level of material invariable needs.[12] On the contrary, a relative concept of poverty considers a level of resources that refers to what is acceptable and normal in a given society, and is therefore not strictly limited to basic material needs. This concept is based on the idea of a standard of living in a specific society.[13]

Whereas the latter approach is more common in richer countries, an absolute approach is more common in poorer countries,[14] although in US the Bureau of Labor Statistics (BLS) also uses an absolute approach, if adapted to the size of the family unit and the number of children.[15] In both approaches, however, it is still necessary to define a poverty threshold. In defining absolute poverty, the ILO, for instance, establishes different thresholds for extreme poverty (US\$ 1.90 ppp) and moderate poverty (between US\$ 1.90 and 3.10 ppp).[16] Eurostat, using a relative concept of poverty instead, establishes the poverty threshold at 60 per cent of the national household median equivalised disposable income level. 'Equivalised' means that a methodology is applied to account for differences in size and composition of the households, whereas 'disposable' means that it considers income after transfers and taxes.

A second important aspect is that while the unit of analysis of in-work poverty is the individual, resources, as well as the poverty status, tend to be measured at the family household level.[17] This means that the composition of the household, as well as its size and the work intensity thereof, become relevant to determine whether an individual is experiencing poverty.[18] The methods used to incorporate differences in the size and composition of the households to the measurement also differ.[19] Eurostat uses the 'modified' equivalence scale developed by the OECD,[20]

---

[12] Lohmann (n 5) 10.

[13] For instance, the European Commission defines poverty as follows: 'people are said to be living in poverty if their income and resources are so inadequate as to preclude them from having a standard of living considered acceptable in the society in which they live'. European Commission, *Joint Report on Social Exclusion 2004* (Luxembourg, Publications Office of the European Union, 2004).

[14] M Ravallion, C Shaohua and P Sangraula, 'Dollar a day revisited' (2009) 23(2) *World Bank Economic Review* 163–84.

[15] See J Semega et al, *Income and Poverty in the United States: 2019* (US Census Bureau, issued 2020, revised 2021).

[16] ILOStat, *The working poor or how a job is no guarantee of decent living conditions*, available www.ilo.org/wcmsp5/groups/public/---dgreports/---stat/documents/publication/wcms_696387.pdf (last visited 27 February 2023). The values provided refer to purchase power (ppp).

[17] Lohmann (n 5) 13.

[18] Eurofound, *In-work poverty in the EU* (Luxembourg, Publications Office of the European Union, 2017) 6.

[19] Lohmann (n 5) 13.

[20] Eurostat adopted in the late 1990s the so-called 'OECD-modified equivalence scale'. This scale assigns a value of 1 to the household head, of 0.5 to each additional adult member and of 0.3 to each child. United Nations, *Canberra Group Handbook on Household Income Statistics. Second edition 2011* (Geneva, 2011) 69.

whereas for instance the US Census Bureau provides different poverty thresholds that vary with the family size and composition. Although there are some good reasons to measure poverty at household level, such as the fact that individuals do not live in isolation, the existence of solidarity, and economies of scale within households, the household dimension also introduces important distortions. This is key to understand apparently paradoxical data connected to in-work poverty levels in the EU, such as the higher prevalence of in-work poverty among men or the rather weak correlation between poverty and low wages (see section II.B).

Finally, measures of in-work poverty refer to income or consumption at household or family level. To calculate income, complex methodologies have been developed. The EU-SILC, on which the EU indicator *in-work at-risk-of-poverty* relies, contains information on income from employment, property, and transfers received and paid (including taxes), but not all of these components are measured, and some other information that could be relevant, such as employer's social insurance contributions or information on the value of the owner-occupied housing services, are not included.[21]

As evidenced in the preceding paragraphs, the measurement of in-work poverty is a thorny endeavour, complicated by a number of questions and lack of agreement in many aspects on how to address this issue. There are many proposals to measure in-work poverty worldwide, which results on a 'definitional chaos'.[22] Furthermore, this chaos is not without practical consequences. Research shows that the choices made in the definitions have strong impact on the results on in-work poverty that the different indicators project, as well as in our perception of the problem.[23] For instance, using a more demanding criterion to define who is at employment will result in a bigger group of workers in less-stable employed arrangements excluded from the statistics, which in turn results in lower levels of in-work poverty and a different gender composition of the working poor.[24] Likewise, leaving the unemployed outside the definition of a worker could lead to the perception that after a crisis, if the number of unemployed has increased, the level of in-work poverty has decreased, which obviously could lead to the false conclusion that the economic situation of workers is improving.[25]

Another issue is that measuring in-work poverty by income can be criticised. The idea behind this critique is that the well-being of a person is dependent on many dimensions of human life. An exclusive focus on income is, therefore, a

[21] Lohmann (n 5), 13.
[22] E Crettaz, 'A state-of-the-art review of working poverty in advanced economies: theoretical models, measurement issues and risk groups' (2013) 23(4) *Journal of European Social Policy* 347–62. The diversity of proposals further complicates comparability.
[23] S Ponthieux, 'Assessing and analysing in-work poverty risk' in A Atkinson and E Marlier (eds), *Income and Living conditions in Europe* (Luxembourg, Publications Office of the European Union, 2010); E Crettaz, 'Poverty and material deprivation among European workers in times of crisis' (2015) 24 *International Journal of Social Welfare* 312–23; Thiede, Lichter and Sanders (n 3); Lohmann (n 5).
[24] Lohmann (n 5) 15.
[25] Ratti, García-Muñoz and Vergnat (n 4) 12.

narrow perception of what poverty means. Other dimensions, such as housing, education, life expectancy or social life should be taken into account.[26] To meet this critique, alternative indicators of poverty have developed over time.[27] Limiting ourselves to list here those who are used by Eurostat, we find indicators such as the *material deprivation index*, the *severe material deprivation*, the *social and material deprivation index* and indicators on work intensity of households, such as *people living in households with very low work intensity*.

Both the *material deprivation* and the *severe material deprivation* indicators are absolute approaches to the measurement of poverty. These are defined by reference to the 'enforced inability' to afford a number of items that are considered 'desirable or even necessary for a decent life'.[28] This inability is, once more, considered at household level. The key idea behind the concept of deprivation is that it affects the capacity to live with dignity.[29] The Social Protection Committee of the European Commission has defined the 'material deprivation rate' as the share of population not able to afford at least three out of a list of nine items. In the case of severe material deprivation, the focus is on those who cannot afford at least four out nine.[30] The difficulty remains, however, to define such a list of items.

Considering the limitations of the *material deprivation index*, some alternatives have been developed. The most important of such alternatives, proposing a statistically more accurate and adequate index to measure material deprivation in Europe is the *social and material deprivation index*.[31] The added value of this indicator is that it considers social items, thus reflecting the ability to participate in the social life of the community.[32]

---

[26] E Ferragina, M Tomlinson and R Walker, *Poverty, participation and choice. The legacy of Peter Townsend* (York, Josef Rowntree Foundation Report, 2013); A Sen, *Inequality Re-examined* (Cambridge MA, Harvard University Press, 1992).

[27] A Swigost, 'Approaches towards social deprivation: reviewing measurement methods' (2017) 38 *Bulletin of Geography. Socio-economic Series* 131–41.

[28] Eurostat, 'Glossary: material deprivation' *Statistics explained*, 2021. Available at ec.europa.eu/eurostat/statistics-explained/index.php?title=Glossary:Material_deprivation#:~:text=Material%20deprivation%20refers%20to%20a,adequate%20heating%20of%20a%20dwelling%2C (last visited 27 February 2023).

[29] P Townsend, 'Deprivation' (1987) 16(2) *Journal of Social Policy* 125–46.

[30] These items are: (1) to pay rent or utility bills; (2) to keep the home adequately warm; (3) to face unexpected expenses; (4) to eat meat, fish or a protein equivalent every second day; (5) to have a week's holiday away from home; (6) having a car; (7) having a washing machine; (8) having a colour TV; (9) having a telephone. See Social Protection Committee – Indicators subgroup, *Portfolio of EU social indicators for the monitoring of progress towards the EU objectives for social protection and social inclusion: 2015 update* (Luxembourg, Publications Office of the European Union, 2015).

[31] AC Guio, D Gordon and E Marlier, 'Measuring material deprivation in the EU: indicators for the whole population and child-specific indicators', Eurostat methodologies and working papers (Luxembourg, Publications Office of the European Union, 2012): AC Guio, E Marlier, and M Pomati, 'Improving the measurement of material deprivation at the European Union level' (2016) 26(3) *Journal of European Social Policy* 219–333.

[32] To this end, this indicator, that mixes items measured at individual level and others measured at household level, establishes a list of 13 items, including variables related to community life, such as having regular leisure activities, get together with friends/family for a drink or meal at least once per month or have internet connection. A person will experience social and material deprivation when that person cannot afford at least 5 out of the 13 items.

On their part, the indexes measuring work intensity aim at integrating employment into the analysis of socially disadvantaged households.[33] These are constructed comparing the total number of months of effective work of all individuals of working age in a household with the theoretical number of months that could be worked by them. When the effective time spent working is less than 20 per cent of the potential for the household, this is considered a *very low work intensity* or *quasi-joblessness* household, whereas the Eurostat indicator of *people living in households with very low work intensity* refers to the proportion of persons under 60 years old living in a *quasi-joblessness* household.[34]

To conclude, and focusing our attention more specifically on the EU, we can highlight the following ideas. In the EU, the most important indicator to measure in-work poverty is the *in-work at-risk-of-poverty* indicator. In this indicator, those 'in work' are defined as all the persons aged 18 and above who declared to be at work for at least seven months in the last reference year. The indicator measures equivalised disposable income at household level. Equivalised means that a methodology is applied to account for differences in size and composition in the households, whereas disposable means that it takes into account incomes after transfers and taxes. The poverty threshold is met when the yearly equivalised disposable income is below 60 per cent of the national household median income level. This indicator is, therefore, based upon a relative concept of in-work poverty. Poverty, therefore, is not conceptualised only, or mostly, as a problem of access to basic material resources to cover pure physiological needs, but on a broader conception of dignity and participation in the community. This results in a country-specific indicator: since the measurement focuses on a level of income relative to a national median, the resulting levels of in-work poverty may have a very different meaning in two different countries. In other words, two households with the same level of equivalised disposable income in different countries can be categorised as poor in one country and not in the other. This means also that the *in-work at-risk-of-poverty* indicator is not suitable for comparisons across countries. But this is not the only shortcoming of the indicator. Since the indicator is built using data from the EU-SILC survey, the immanent limitations of such surveys need to be kept in mind. Indeed, such surveys do not cover the whole population (homeless people or those living in institutions remain excluded), the data may suffer from measurement errors, there is always a gap between the data and reality,[35] etc. It is partly to overcome some of these limitations that other indicators, such as the above-described

---

[33] Ratti, García-Muñoz and Vergnat (n 4) 14.

[34] T Ward and E Ozdemir, 'Measuring low work intensity – an analysis of the indicator', ImPRovE Working Papers 13/09, Herman Deleeck Centre for Social Policy, University of Antwerp (2013).

[35] To avoid this temporal gap, *nowcasting* methods to determine the current value of indicators based on past values and applying assumptions of changes in demographics, the labour market and macroeconomic conditions have been developed. See J Navicke, O Rastrigina and H Sutherland, 'Nowcasting Indicators of Poverty Risk in the European Union: A Microsimulation Approach' (2014) 119(1) *Social Indicators Research* 101.

material deprivation index, social and material deprivation index and indicators on work intensity of households, such as *people living in households with very low work intensity* should be used in combination with the *in-work at-risk-of-poverty* indicator to obtain a more detailed and accurate picture of the working poor. Ideally, all these indicators should be considered simultaneously. This would result in a dashboard of indicators on the question of in-work poverty, projecting a more accurate picture of who the working poor are.

B. In-work Poverty, Low Wages and the Gender Paradox

As advanced in the previous section, statistical data on in-work poverty shows, among other issues, two somewhat counter-intuitive results: the low correlation between low salaries and in-work poverty, on the one hand, and the lower levels of in-work poverty for women, on the other.

The weak correlation between in-work poverty and low salaries is a well-established fact in research on the topic.[36] Low wages are defined in the EU independently of poverty. They indicate a relative position in terms of earnings in the labour market, since workers on low wages are all those falling below a low-pay threshold that is set at two-thirds of the median earnings.[37] A decade ago, Maître et al showed that, in the EU, the poverty rate of low-wage workers was around 13 per cent. This means that, independently of the fact that poverty levels for workers with higher salaries was lower, still over 80 per cent of low-wage workers were not poor.[38] This is indeed confirmed in later studies, where a large gap between low-wage levels and in-work poverty levels is described (being low wage levels higher than in-work poverty).[39]

As explained by Lohmann, this weak correlation can be better understood when the household dimension of in-work poverty is considered: whereas low-wage work is an individual concept, in-work poverty refers 'to individuals sharing resources within households'. It seems that a large part of the impact of low salaries is 'neutralized by the redistribution of incomes and/or the household

---

[36] See, among others, W Salverda, 'Low drivers and their drivers in relation to in-work poverty' in H Lohmann and I Marx (eds), *Handbook on In-Work Poverty* (Cheltenham, Edward Elgar, 2019) 28–29; I Marx and G Verbist, 'Low-paid work and poverty: a cross-country perspective' in S Bazen, M Gregory and W Salverda (eds), *Low-wage employment in Europe* (Cheltenham; Edward Elgar, 1998), 63–85; R Buckhauser and J Sabia, 'The effectiveness of minimum wage increases in reducing poverty: Past, present and future' (2007) 25(2) *Contemporary Economic Policy* 262. Our own results in the project 'Working, Yet Poor' show that low-wage workers, although experiencing a higher risk of in-work poverty than the average employed population, are much better protected (when having an indefinite contract) than other vulnerable groups of workers.

[37] As Salverda explains, this threshold 'seems to hark back to the idea of a living wage based on the Council of Europe's European Social Charter of 1968, that was operationalized as 68 per cent of average gross employee income'. Salverda (n 36) 27.

[38] B Maître, T Nolan and Ch Whelan, 'Low-pay, in-work poverty and economic vulnerability: a comparative analysis using EU-SILC' (2012) 80(1) *The Manchester School* 107.

[39] Salverda (n 36) 28.

combination of individual earnings, implying that most low-paid employees are members of a non-poor household'.[40] How the social and labour market conditions have changed and evolved in the last decades also helps to explain this apparent paradox. Family structures have greatly changed and are nowadays more diverse. Women have incorporated massively to the paid work and the labour market itself has diversified, with multiple and different work arrangements coexisting. This has resulted in a complex link between low salaries and in-work poverty, far from the more straightforward relation found when a male breadwinner model is dominant.[41] The size and composition of the household, ie, the number of other earners as well as the number of dependants are thus considered a more important factor than individual earnings in explaining the risk of in-work poverty.[42] Furthermore, the social and tax systems play also a decisive role, further contributing to the lack of correlation between low salaries and in-work poverty.

A closely related issue is that of the gender differences that can be observed in low-wage work (where women are the majority) and in-work poverty (affecting more men). Here, again, the household dimension is crucial. Measuring in-work poverty combining the individual and household dimension is problematic from a gender perspective. And this is so because the measurement of poverty at household level rests on the assumption of income pooling, ie the idea that within a household all the incomes are pooled and shared so the well-being of all the household members is equal.[43] However, empirical research shows that this assumption does not correspond to the reality of the majority of households.[44] Therefore, this assumption, that neglects the reality of intra-household inequality, results, as Ponthieux puts it, in a 'biased assessment of women's poverty'.[45] Indeed, research applying gender-sensitive methodologies to measure poverty that depart from the assumption of income pooling show higher levels of in-work poverty for women and lower level for men.[46]

If the household dimension makes it difficult, as we have seen, to establish a link between work and poverty, this is even more the case for women. This situation results in the so-called 'gender paradox': even though women are in a less favourable position than men in the labour market, and despite the existence of a

[40] ibid 29.
[41] Lohmann (n 5) 8. The departure from the breadwinner model will also explain why in-work poverty is no longer 'merely a situation where a working household head is unable to provide for their family'. I Airio, *Change of norm? In-work poverty in a comparative perspective* (2008) 92 *Studies in Social Security and Health, Kela Research Department* 12.
[42] B Maître, T Nolan and Ch Whelan, 'Low pay, in-work poverty and economic vulnerability' in H Lohmann and I Marx (eds), *Handbook on In-Work Poverty* (Cheltenham, Edward Elgar, 2019) 124.
[43] S Ponthieux, 'Gender and in-work poverty' in H Lohmann and I Marx (eds), *Handbook on In-Work Poverty* (Cheltenham, Edward Elgar, 2019) 70.
[44] S Ponthieux, 'Income pooling and equal sharing within the household – what can we learn from the 2010 EU-SILC module?', Eurostat Methodologies and working papers (2013).
[45] Ponthieux (n 43).
[46] S Ponthieux and D Meurs, 'Gender inequality' in A Atkinson and F Bourguignon (eds), *Handbook of income distribution*, Vol 2 (Amsterdam, Elsevier, 2015) 981–1146.

pay gap, they are not at higher risk of experiencing in-work poverty than men.[47] This gender paradox is the outcome of 'an approach to individual poverty based on household income in a context of gender inequality that the household itself conceals'.[48] As a result, the disadvantage that women experience in the labour market does not translate into poverty as often as it could be expected. These results are very similar to the gap observed in low pay and poverty for women,[49] where it has also been observed that 'individual low pay translates into household poverty to a different degree for men and women'.[50]

The key is to understand that men and women are not in an equal position in the labour market and that this inequality is itself linked to the gender division of work within households.[51] Therefore the household dimension is simultaneously shaping gender inequality in terms of work participation and partly compensating it, by assuming pooling of resources, in terms of poverty.[52] The reasons for these inequalities are to be found in family circumstances and how they impact differently on men and women, in particular parenthood, which has on average a negative impact on women's employment and incomes whereas it seems that it does not impact men.[53] The same goes for the distribution of work within households: in couple households, quite often one of the members of the couple, normally the woman, either is not at work or is a 'secondary earner', ready to accept more precarious work arrangements.[54]

To avoid the problems that the existing measurement of poverty causes from a gender perspective and develop a more gender-sensitive approach to in-work poverty, alternative methodologies to measure in-work poverty have been developed. These have in common that the focus of the measurement is on the individual, thus avoiding the distortions introduced by the household dimension. Proposals are varied. Some suggest measuring income based on individual earnings and individualised household incomes components.[55] Others propose to measure 'poverty in earned income' defined at the individual level. This second

---

[47] Inequality between men and women in the labour market is well established. First, 'in-work' rates are lower for women than for men in almost all EU countries. Second, women are overrepresented in part-time work. Third, women are overrepresented at the lower end of the wage distribution. Ponthieux (n 43).

[48] ibid 75.

[49] See JC Gornick and M Jäntti, 'Women, poverty and social policy regimes: a cross-national analysis', LIS working paper no 534 (2010).

[50] K Gardiner and J Millar, 'How low-paid employees avoid poverty: an analysis by family type and household structure' (2006) 35(3) *Journal of Social Policy* 357.

[51] Ponthieux (n 43) 75.

[52] ibid 76.

[53] A review of research on gender inequality in employment and earnings and the role of the family status in women's labour participation and earnings in Ponthieux and Meurs (n 46).

[54] Ponthieux (n 43) 79.

[55] R Peña-Casas and D Ghailani, 'Towards individualizing gender in-work poverty risks' in N Fraser, R Gutierrez and R Peña-Casas (eds), *Working Poverty in Europe: A Comparative Approach* (London and New York, Palgrave Macmillan, 2011), 202–31; D Meulders and S O'Dorchai, 'Revisiting poverty measures towards individualization', ULB-Dulbea Working Paper, no 10-03 (2010).

approach consists in considering workers individually (ie as if they were living alone) and measuring their incomes including only the earnings they get from their economic activity.[56] Invariably, the results of applying such methodologies show higher levels of in-work poverty for women than those measuring poverty at household level.

III. Determinants of In-work Poverty

Which are the most relevant causes of the occurrence and reproduction of in-work poverty in the EU? In-work poverty being a complex and multidimensional phenomenon, many factors have an influence. Some of them, and their prevalence, are closely connected to how we measure in-work poverty, whereas others, for the same reason, may remain out of sight. For descriptive purposes, existing research tends to group the different causes into individual, household and institutional drivers.[57]

Individual drivers refer to two different groups of causes: those linked to the employment situation of individuals and those connected to socio-demographic characteristics. We have seen that, given the hybrid nature of in-work poverty and the measurement of poverty at household level, it is not easy to establish clear links between individual characteristics and poverty. Still, there are some circumstances affecting the individual worker that appear in statistics as 'risk factors', since workers with such conditions are at a higher risk of poverty.

Among the first group, the employment-related causes, wage levels and type of contract are the most relevant. Although, as we have seen in section II.B, there is a low correlation between low salaries and in-work poverty, low-wage workers are still at a higher risk of in-work poverty than the average worker. As for the type of contract, statistics show that temporary and part-time workers are at a higher risk of in-work poverty than those with indefinite and full-time contracts.[58] Continuity of work and work intensity therefore seem to be problematic. Part-time workers, and also temporary workers, can face additional difficulties due to obstacles to access social benefits due to eligibility criteria based on the number of effective hours at work or other criteria disadvantageous to them.[59] Likewise,

---

[56] S Ponthieux, 'The working poor as a statistical category: methodological difficulties and exploration of a notion of poverty in earned income', Insee Working Paper no 0902 (2009).

[57] For instance, Eurofound groups the drivers of in-work poverty in just two categories: individual and household drivers, whereas a recent study of the European Social Policy Networks adds the third category of institutional drivers. See, respectively, Eurofound (n 17) and R Peña-Casas et al, *In-work poverty in Europe. A study of national policies* (Brussels, European Social Policy Network, 2019).

[58] J Horemans, 'Atypical employment and in-work poverty' in H Lohmann and I Marx (eds), *Handbook on In-Work Poverty* (Cheltenham, Edward Elgar, 2019) 150.

[59] J Horemans and I Marx, 'In-work poverty in times of crisis: do part-timers fare worse?', ImPRovE Working Papers 13/14, Herman Deleeck Centre for Social Policy, University of Antwerp (2013); OECD, *How good is part-time work?* Employment Outlook 2010 (Paris, OECD Publishing, 2010).

the self-employed also experience higher risk of in-work poverty in most EU Member States, although data referring to this group must be considered with caution.[60]

All these data seem to indicate that the work situation is relevant for the risk of in-work poverty, with the most precarious workers being in a worse situation.[61] However, and for the same reasons discussed in section II.B, the household dimension somehow blurs the links between poverty and individual employment status. When attention turns to the employment situation of the different members of the household, a different picture emerges, with non-standard employment having an impact on poverty through its increase in households where all workers are non-standard.[62]

Socio-demographic characteristics refer to aspects such as the level of education, gender, age and migrant background. Statistically, educational level is the most relevant of the socio-demographic characteristics associated with in-work poverty. The higher the level of education, the lower the in-work poverty risk.[63] Second in relevance is the country of birth: those born abroad are at a higher risk of in-work poverty than native populations. This is, in turn, connected to the position in the labour market of migrants: research shows that part-time and temporary work is more widespread among foreign-born workers, who tend to be overrepresented in elementary occupations,[64] very often in the low-wage sectors of the economy.[65] Other aspects linked to the condition of migrant or minority, such as discrimination and its impact on in-work poverty, remain understudied in the EU.[66]

Age and gender, on the contrary, are less relevant in connection to in-work poverty levels,[67] although being young represents a disadvantageous condition, since young people at the beginning of their careers are overrepresented in unstable jobs.[68] As for gender, we have already explained why and how existing statistics of in-work poverty 'hide' female poverty behind the household model under the pooling assumption. Lastly, intersectionality is also relevant for this group of

---

[60] In particular, data referring to income, since there is a risk of underestimation of income by the self-employed population in surveys. See Peña-Casas et al (n 57) 33; Crettaz (n 21).

[61] Particularly worrying are in-work poverty levels of those on temporary contracts working part-time, as the data of the national reports of the *Working, yet poor* research project show.

[62] See on this OECD, *Non-standard work, job polarisation and inequality. In It Together: Why Less Inequality Benefits All* (Paris, OECD Publishing, 2015).

[63] Ratti, García-Muñoz and Vergnat (n 4) 5.

[64] Eurofound (n 18) 8.

[65] E Crettaz, 'In-work poverty among migrants' in H Lohmann and I Marx (eds), *Handbook on In-Work Poverty* (Cheltenham, Edward Elgar, 2019) 89.

[66] E Crettaz, 'Working Poverty among Immigrants and 'Ethnic Minorities': Theoretical Framework and Empirical Evidence across Welfare Regimes', University of Neuchâtel, MAPS Working Papers Series 3/2011.

[67] Peña-Casas et al (n 57) 26.

[68] M Filandri and E Struffolino, 'Individual and household in-work poverty in Europe: understanding the role of labour market characteristics' (2019) 21(1) *European Societies* 135.

causes: when two or more 'risk factors' accumulate in the same person, the risk of in-work poverty increases.[69]

The second group of drivers focuses on aspects linked to the household dimension. These have proved to be very relevant in defining in-work poverty levels. The size and composition of the household on the one hand, and work intensity on the other, are the main factors to be considered. Indeed, household composition seems to be extremely important in connection to in-work poverty. Research shows that the risk of in-work poverty is much higher for particular types of households. In particular, people living in a household with children experience a higher risk of in-work poverty, with single parent households with children being the type experiencing the highest risk.[70] On the contrary, households with two adults without children experience much lower risk of in-work poverty.[71] Recent trends and changes in family structures are, therefore, relevant to understand the recent evolution of in-work poverty rates.[72]

Work intensity at household level is also relevant. It can be defined as the ratio resulting from comparing the total number of months that all working-age members of the household have worked during the income reference year with the maximum number of months that those members could have potentially worked in the same period.[73] The relation between the household's work intensity and the individual risk of in-work poverty is inversely proportional: the lower the overall level of work intensity in the household, the higher the poverty risk of the worker living in that household.[74] As described in section II.B, work intensity has a gender dimension: women are more often second earners and are overrepresented in part-time work. Institutional and cultural factors play a role. The still prevalent gender division of labour tends to favour that women dedicate more time to take care of children. Likewise, the availability and affordability of childcare or access to flexible work arrangements can have an important impact on women's work intensity.[75] Interestingly, the contribution of second earners to household income serves as an important factor to prevent in-work poverty, particularly in the case of individuals with precarious employment characteristics.[76]

[69] Peña-Casas et al (n 57) 25.
[70] R Nieuwenhuis and L.C. Maldonado, 'Single-parent families and in-work poverty', in H Lohmann and I Marx (eds), *Handbook on In-Work Poverty* (Cheltenham, Edward Elgar, 2019) 171.
[71] Peña-Casas et al (n 57) 39.
[72] B Thiede, S Sanders and D Lichter, 'Demographic drivers of in-work poverty', in H Lohmann and I Marx (eds), *Handbook on In-Work Poverty* (Cheltenham, Edward Elgar, 2019) 109. For a review of quantitative evidence on in-work poverty and family demographic processes in the EU (including other OECD countries) see A Polizzi, E Struffolino and Z Van Winkle, 'Family demographic processes and in-work poverty: A systematic review' (2022) *Advances in Life Course Research* 52.
[73] Eurostat, 'Glossary: persons living in households with low work intensity.' *Statistics explained*, 2021. Available at ec.europa.eu/eurostat/statistics-explained/index.php?title=Glossary:Persons_living_in_households_with_low_work_intensity (last visited 27 February 2023).
[74] Peña-Casas et al (n 57) 40.
[75] Eurofound (n 18) 10.
[76] H Jara Tamayo and D Popova, 'Second Earners and In-work Poverty in Europe' (2021) 50(3) *Journal of Social Policy* 488.

Finally, a third group of drivers, often referred to as 'institutional' factors, can be distinguished. This would include a varied array of aspects with an incidence on in-work poverty levels, such as social transfers; taxation; the possibility for workers to opt-out of the labour market when wages or working conditions are not satisfactory;[77] the levels of employment protection; and the existence and functioning of labour market institutions, such as wage-setting mechanisms, minimum wage legislation or collective bargaining, and so on.[78] The European Parliament adds to these lack of affordable housing and technological change.[79]

IV. The In-work Poor in the EU: A Contextual Approach

The context in which in-work poverty occurs is decisive in the way it is understood, conceptualised and measured. It is not possible, however, to develop here a comprehensive or exhaustive description of decades of economic, legal and societal changes in the EU. Therefore, I limit myself here to highlighting some of the most relevant of such changes, outlining the main lines of the current context in the EU and the recent policy debates on in-work poverty.

As Crettaz wrote in 2013, few authors offer specific theoretical models explaining the (re-)emergence of in-work poverty, particularly in Europe. This is still the case today. Probably the most successful attempts to develop such models are variations of the 'unified theory' developed in labour economics. Such approaches focus on 'the interplay between macroeconomic shocks – globalization, deindustrialization and technological changes in particular – and national institutional contexts'.[80] The main conclusion in this strand of research is that while macroeconomic shocks affected all industrialised countries, diverse national institutional reactions to these made a difference in terms of in-work poverty.[81] Variations of

---

[77] From a policy perspective, in-work poverty is connected to labour market and social policies, which have been characterised in the last decades in the EU by a strong focus on activation policies, ie measures targeted at reintegrating the unemployed into the labour market. It is not possible to develop this point in this chapter, but there is a strand of interesting research on how active labour market policies are linked to in-work poverty. This research suggests that activation policies often result in a shift from poor unemployed into working poor, mostly due to strict conditionality of welfare benefits and a high degree of commodification of labour forcing the unemployed to accept jobs regardless of pay levels and type of contract. See, among many others, D Seikel and D Spannagel, 'Activation and in-work poverty' in H Lohmann and I Marx (eds), *Handbook on In-Work Poverty* (Cheltenham, Edward Elgar, 2019) 245–60.

[78] See in detail Eurofound (n 18).

[79] European Parliament, *Resolution of 10 February 2021 on reducing inequalities with a special focus on in-work poverty* (2019/2188 (INI)).

[80] Crettaz (n 22) 349.

[81] In particular this strand of research concluded that while in the US the flexible approach to labour market regulation resulted in greater inequality but lower unemployment levels, the more 'rigid' European approach prevented such increase in inequality, but at the price of an increase in unemployment levels. Crettaz (n 22) 349.

these theories focus on the role of globalisation and the international, north–south divide, in the organisation of production, trade and labour. In this description the new world economy resulting from globalisation would combine with rapid technological change in generating dynamics which impact disproportionately on the working conditions of low-skilled workers in advanced economies.[82] Yet another strand of research, closely related to the other two, focuses more in particular in the role of welfare states, particularly in comparative perspective. In these studies, attention is devoted to the role of various 'welfare regimes' on income distribution and employment levels,[83] or even more specifically to the impact of welfare states and social transfers on income inequality and material deprivation.[84] However, very few of these studies focus specifically on the impact of welfare states' models on in-work poverty.[85]

An example of contextual approach that builds on the described theoretical models but goes one step beyond can be found in the work of Pradella.[86] In her work, Pradella contextualises in-work poverty in the EU by adopting a (critical) political economy perspective. This helps to understand, for instance, the impact of the 2008 crisis on employment levels, social exclusion and poverty (including in-work poverty) and, more importantly, the European management of the crisis, with its focus on austerity and structural adjustments policies. It also helps to explain the long-identified contradictions between economic and social policies at EU level.

In her analysis, Pradella brings in the international dimension of the working-poor phenomenon, situating the EU in a changing geography of global production. Without going into full details here, she describes a process of de-industrialisation and change of economic model with multiple and interrelated causes and consequences that favours the emergence of high levels of in-work poverty. The root of the problem is to be found in the relocation of industrial production out of Western Europe, already seen in the 1970s, driven by dropping profitability levels, together with a subsequent growth model during the neoliberal era that has been dependent on credit bubbles.[87] The EU integration process, which has

[82] F Nielsen and AS Alderson, 'Globalization and the Great U-Turn: Income Inequality Trends in 16 OECD Countries' (2002) 107(5) *American Journal of Sociology* 1244; G Esping-Andersen, *Social Foundations of Postindustrial Economies* (Oxford, Oxford University Press, 2019).

[83] B Parlier, *A Long Goodbye to Bismarck? The Politics of Welfare Reform in Continental Europe* (Amsterdam, Amsterdam University Press, 2010).

[84] K Nelson, 'Counteracting Material Deprivation: The Role of Social Assistance in Europe' (2012) 22(2) *Journal of European Social Policy* 148–63.

[85] Two examples of such studies are the books by Andress and Lohmann and Fraser, Gutiérrez and Peña-Casas. See H.J Andress and H Lohmann, *The Working Poor in Europe: Employment, Poverty and Globalisation* (Cheltenham, Edward Elgar Publishing, 2008); N Fraser, R Gutiérrez and R Peña-Casas, *Working Poverty in Europe. A Comparative Approach* (London and New York, Palgrave Macmillan, 2011).

[86] L Pradella, 'The working poor in Western Europe: labor, poverty, and global capitalism' (2015) 13 *Comparative European Politics* 596. See in particular L Pradella, 'The international political economy of the working poor in Western Europe' in H Lohmann and I Marx (eds), *Handbook on In-Work Poverty* (Cheltenham, Edward Elgar, 2019) 277–94.

[87] A Callinicos, *Bonfire of Illusions: The Twin Crises of the Neoliberal World* (Cambridge, Polity Press, 2010).

accelerated since the 1980s, the EU enlargements to the east in the early 2000s[88] and the associated increase in labour mobility, and external factors affecting the global organisation of the economy, such as the integration of China in the World Trade Organization (WTO) in 2001, are also important events in this process.[89] Also, the introduction of a European common currency, the euro, has been functional to a process of capital internationalisation, in a context of an unprecedented expansion of the global reserve 'army' of labour.[90] The 2008 economic crisis accelerated the global shift of production towards East Asia, while there was a sharp fall in the profit margins of non-financial corporations in the eurozone in the onset of the crisis.[91] Within the EU, a process of economic specialisation and differentiation between the different Member States, particularly between the north and the south, led to imbalances that became visible during the eurozone crisis. This specialisation and polarisation of the EU productive structure helps to explain differences in de-industrialisation processes in different Member States.[92] This de-industrialisation has unleashed a number of processes, such as the emergence of flexible and atypical employment relations.[93] This, in turn, has weakened the power of organised labour, easing the implementation of austerity and structural adjustment programmes.[94] To sum up, all these interrelated events and developments have resulted in a combination of 'industrial upgrading in emerging countries and falling profitability' (within the EU) that 'is putting increasing pressure on wages, working conditions and welfare spending in the EU'.[95] To this macro-perspective, one should add the impact of the latest developments, such as the Covid-19 pandemic crisis in 2020 and the cost-of-living crisis that followed.

Together with this macro-perspective,[96] other strands of research focus in more meso- and micro-level questions. These are complementary perspectives that add to the context and its complexity. For instance, research on the role of

---

[88] In East-Central Europe the neoliberal transition to a capitalist economy was characterised by a series of common features: increasing labour market segmentation, precarisation and non-participation underpinned the deregulation of labour market and welfare systems, contributing to the emergence of the relatively new phenomenon of the working poor. A Smith et al, 'The emergence of a working poor: labor markets, neoliberalisation and diverse economies in post-socialist cities' (2008) 40(2) *Antipode* 283.

[89] Pradella, 'The international political economy of the working poor' (n 86) 282.

[90] JB Foster, R McChesney and RJ Jonna, 'The global reserve army of labor and the new imperialism' (2011) 63(6) *Monthly Review* 1.

[91] Pradella, 'The international political economy of the working poor' (n 86) 284.

[92] ibid.

[93] Eurofound, *Upgrading or Polarization? Long-Term and Global Shifts in the Employment Structure: European Jobs Monitor 2015* (Luxembourg, Publications Office of the European Union, 2015).

[94] Pradella, 'The international political economy of the working poor' (n 86) 285.

[95] ibid.

[96] Although for reasons of space I cannot fully engage with her arguments, Pradella adds to the described 'international dimension of the working poor' an interesting critique of some of the presumptions of in-work poverty research, challenging the very conceptualisation of this phenomenon. Her critique rests on the idea that the trend towards increasing levels of in-work poverty is the logical consequence of the development of capitalist production relations on a global scale. She questions the

active labour market policies and reforms in the social security and labour law domains to implement a 'workforce' model have produced interesting results that help explain the increase of in-work poverty levels in the EU.[97] Finally, research on the impact of demographics and social change in family patterns is of the utmost importance.[98]

In this context, in-work poverty has recently become a concern for EU policy makers and features high on the EU policy agenda. A crucial first step in this process was the adoption, in 2003, of a specific indicator to measure in-work poverty, by introducing the *in-work at-risk-of-poverty* as part of the EU social indicators.[99] Before, in-work poverty was not distinguished at policy level in the EU from the overall goal to reduce poverty. Indeed, one of the headline targets of the EU 2020 strategy was to reduce the number of poor by at least 20 million, identifying the unemployed as a particularly vulnerable group. Therefore, one of the main policy priorities in the last decades, particularly in the aftermath of the 2008 crisis, was that of employment creation, without paying much attention to the impact of these policies on in-work poverty.[100] It is necessary to wait until the adoption, in 2017, of the European Pillar of Social Rights (EPSR), to see a qualitative change in the EU approach towards in-work poverty. Indeed, with the EPSR, in-work poverty has been recognised for the first time as one of the problems that the EU social agenda must address.[101] Furthermore, the Action Plan elaborated by the Commission to implement the EPSR establishes the objective of reducing the number of people at risk of poverty or social exclusion (by at least 15 million by 2030).[102] A number of legislative initiatives has been adopted or presented that may go in the right direction to tackle in-work poverty. Among these, the Directive on adequate minimum wages may be a game changer. Similarly, the proposal for a Directive on improving the working conditions of platform workers is to be welcomed.[103] This may well be a moment of re-balancing between economic and social goals in EU policy that could work as a sort of 'counter-movement' on the above-described context with the potential to improve the position of the most precarious groups of workers, protecting them from poverty.

---

assumption that wages represent a full compensation to the workers for the work performed, highlighting, on the contrary, the structural role that impoverishment plays in accumulation, which is one of the compulsions of a capitalist economy.

[97] Seikel and Spannagel (n 77).

[98] See Jara Tamayo and Popova (n 76); B Thiede, S Sanders and D Lichter (n 71); Polizzi, Struffolino and Van Winkle (n 71).

[99] I Marx and B Nolan, 'In-work poverty', GINI discussion paper 51 (2012) 11.

[100] Ratti, García-Muñoz and Vergnat (n 4) 8.

[101] In particular, Arts 6 and 12 of the EPSR are directly relevant for in-work poverty. Furthermore, indirectly several other principles in the EPSR, such as equal opportunities, access to the labour market, fair working conditions, social protection and inclusion are also relevant to in-work poverty.

[102] European Commission, 'The European Pillar of Social Rights Action Plan', SWD (2021) 46 final.

[103] European Commission, 'Proposal for a directive of the European Parliament and of the Council on improving working conditions in platform work', COM (2021) 762 final.

V. Conclusions

This chapter described the main elements that need to be considered when thinking about in-work poverty and its meaning. A serious approach to the concept of in-work poverty needs to engage with the problems arising from its measurement. The measurement of in-work poverty is a complex endeavour that needs to answer several questions concerning its main two elements: work and poverty. To define work, it is necessary to define the working population and those who, within this group, are 'in-work'. To define poverty, a number of decisions concerning how to measure it need to be taken. Poverty can be measured adopting an absolute or relative approach, and poverty thresholds need to be defined. Finally, poverty can be measured at individual or household level. The decisions taken in all these points are crucial for the perception of the problems and, therefore, its definition and concept.

In existing indicators, particularly in the reference indicator in the EU, the *in-work at-risk-of-poverty* rate, the adoption of an hybrid concept of in-work poverty that combines the individual position of workers in the labour market with the measurement of poverty at household level introduces important distortions, the most important of which are the weakening of the link between wages and poverty and the hiding of working poor women behind the household dimensions and its main assumption, ie the pooling of resources.

Defined as a relative approach to in-work poverty that measures equivalised disposable income at household level, the statistical information generated by the *in-work at-risk-of-poverty* rate shows an array of different 'risk factors' or determinants of in-work poverty. These can be grouped for descriptive purposes in individual, household and institutional factors, each of them composed of several causes that are often intertwined.

However, the crude statistical information and the description of 'risk factors' should not hide the 'bigger picture' in which in-work poverty takes place. Although a theoretical model describing this bigger context that could explain the (re)emergence of in-work poverty remains somehow underdeveloped, existing attempts show a complex landscape of economic, social and legal changes, mutually influencing each other. From a western European perspective, the process of de-industrialisation and the resulting re-ordering of the world and European economies since the 1970s is crucial to explain the rising in-work poverty level. In this broad context, the process of European integration is part of the forces behind the recent evolution of European economies and labour markets. At the same time, the recent attention at EU level to in-work poverty and its inclusion in the EPSR, as well as the adoption of some, even if limited, initiatives that could help to tackle in-work poverty levels, need to be acknowledged.

2

In-work Poverty Across EU Countries: A Comparative Analysis of Regulatory Approaches

CHRISTINA HIESSL

I. Introduction

In-work poverty as described in chapter one is a symptom, not a diagnosis. It is moreover not an isolated phenomenon, but one that appears on the fringes of more general questions of the availability of resources and opportunities within a given society, and their distribution among the human beings of which it is composed. The indicators used are highly sensitive to aspects which have little to do with how well such distribution is organised by the legal system. For instance, as concerns severe material deprivation, the inherent normativity of attempts to define what is necessary for a dignified life is illustrated by the Council of Ministers' Social Protection Committee's decision in 2021 to significantly redefine the elements measured, and to rename the indicator to 'severe material *and social* deprivation'.[1] At-risk-of-poverty rates in turn suffer from a characteristic inherent in all relative indicators, namely that the calculation is effectively just as sensitive to 'out-of-work wealthiness' as it is to in-work poverty, resulting in counter-intuitively high rates in countries such as Luxembourg.

All of this illustrates the inherent limitations of any attempt to provide an analysis of the regulatory choices capable of influencing the occurrence of in-work poverty. More than that, the sheer extent of areas of regulation which may be of relevance makes it illusory to elaborate a 'full picture' of such regulatory choices. Finally, just as for the phenomenon itself, it is impossible to view the approaches to address in-work poverty in isolation. After all, approaches capable of reducing in-work poverty may have adverse side effects, eg in relation to labour market

---

[1] For an overview of the elements of the new indicator and their consideration in the calculation, see Eurostat, *Glossary: Severe material and social deprivation rate*, ec.europa.eu/eurostat/statistics-explained/index.php?curid=99141&oldid=534257 (last accessed 19 February 2023).

participation and out-of-work poverty, so that their potential to improve social welfare in a society overall needs to be scrutinised.

In light of these challenges, the cross-country comparative analysis undertaken in the framework of the Working, Yet Poor (WorkYP) project tried to walk the line between oversimplifying (presenting isolated measures as 'the solution' to in-work poverty) and over-including (risking making it impossible to discern any conclusions in regard to concrete policy measures). One of the key choices flowing from these considerations was to focus the analysis mainly on social security, labour law, collective bargaining and labour market policies. Another was to largely limit it to the exploration of approaches in seven countries, all of which represent one or more particularly distinctive policy features in their approach to in-work poverty: Belgium, Germany, Italy, Luxembourg, the Netherlands, Poland and Sweden. The analysis is thus inherently limited in terms of the consideration of measures belonging to other policy fields or employed outside the chosen country sample. At least in regard to the latter, multi-country datasets providing overviews of empirical outcomes and (simplified) regulatory structures have been consulted to gain an idea of the actual representativeness of the countries included in the analysis. Finally, the discussion of outcomes for in-work poverty has been approached with a keen awareness of potential side effects which may compromise the desirability of certain measures if the aim is to improve social welfare overall.

With this in mind, the present chapter aims to give an insight into pathways to avoiding or alleviating in-work poverty through the comparative assessment of the seven legal systems in their development over time. It should be noted at the outset that, within the available space, only a selection of outcomes can be highlighted. Details on the aspects of regulation at issue and their consideration in the comparative analysis can be found in the reports submitted as Deliverables 3.2, 3.4 and 3.5 of the WorkYP project.[2] In what follows, a brief reference to the most pertinent empirical findings (section II) will be followed by a discussion of the scope of protective regulation (section III) and a structured overview of policies (a) aiming to foster employability (section IV), (b) determining levels of remuneration from work (section V), and (c) concerning the provision of social benefits (section VI). Section VII offers some tentative conclusions on the status quo and sets the scene for a more result-oriented discussion of the way forward, which will be provided in Part III of the present book.

II. Insights from Empirical Data

Paid labour stands out across countries as the overriding major pathway to avoiding poverty. Cross-European statistics researching poverty levels for different

---

[2] Available at workingyetpoor.eu/deliverables.

groups leave no doubt in this regard. In-work poverty rates of around 9 per cent across the EU in 2019[3] compare to poverty rates close to 50 per cent for the unemployed and almost 30 per cent for the economically inactive.[4]

As long as such a clear relationship between work and poverty reduction can be assumed to hold true in general, a pivotal element in any strategy to alleviate poverty may reasonably be assumed boost labour market participation. Yet, the development of indicators over a period of relative stability and economic growth (between the global financial crisis and the Covid-19 pandemic crisis)[5] indicate that moving more people into employment has not resulted in a reduction of poverty rates – pointing to the fact that, for many, out-of-work poverty has been replaced by in-work poverty. In other words, the emergence and persistence of vulnerable groups who fail to escape poverty through work evidences that work participation may be a necessary, but not necessarily sufficient element to lift households out of poverty.

The following three sections attempt to do justice to this necessity of a combined consideration of measures aiming to ensure that work is available, adequately paid, and where necessary complemented by income from social benefits.

III. Scope of Labour Law, Social Security and Labour Market Policies

Any exploration of the potential of policy measures to address in work poverty needs to start from a critical review of the scope of those measures, notably as regards the coverage of the Vulnerable and Underrepresented Persons (VUP) Groups as defined in the preceding chapter. Beyond the specific exclusions existing for some groups of employees (eg small-scale work or work in private households), this most notably concerns workers classified as self-employed.

In all of the countries studied, at least the application of labour law is largely dependent on a worker's categorisation as an employee. While a discussion of variations in national concepts of employee status would be beyond the scope of the present contribution,[6] such categorisation effectively entails at least elements of personal work for another, remuneration and subordination. What does seem

---

[3] Although, at the time of writing, Eurostat data for 2020 and (partly) 2021 are available, this report will essentially refer to the numbers of 2019. This is to avoid basing conclusions on the exceptional social and labour market situation emerging in the context of the Covid-19 crisis, which partly also affected the quality and continuity of data collection.

[4] See Eurostat data at https://ec.europa.eu/eurostat/databrowser/view/ILC_LI04__custom_2223204/default/table?lang=en (last accessed 19 February 2023).

[5] See Eurostat data at ec.europa.eu/eurostat/statistics-explained/index.php?oldid=476638 (last accessed 19 February 2023).

[6] For a detailed analysis, see C Hiessl, 'Case Law on the Classification of Platform Workers: Cross-European Comparative Analysis and Tentative Conclusions' (2022) 42(2) *Comparative Labour Law & Policy Journal* 465–518.

important to note, though, is the perhaps disillusioningly limited impact of a sophisticated design of this concept on the actual likelihood of vulnerable groups to forego protections. Suffice it to note that the Netherlands, the very country which stands out by operating a broadly conceived legal presumption of employee status, has seen a highly atypical rise of self-employment (contrary to falling trends virtually all across the EU), and notably a spike in solo self-employment in recent years. This indicates that adverse incentives and lax enforcement may subvert the most sophisticated legislative design, but also trigger bold steps by the courts to halt the development – considering that Dutch law has probably seen the most remarkable jurisprudential developments of the concept of employee in recent years, including by the Supreme Court's finding of absolute primacy of facts[7] and the case law which has brought a uniquely broad range of platform workers under the protection of labour law.[8]

By the same token, the Italian case suggests that bold legislative action may emerge as a response to the evasion of the employment relationship. Thus, while the proportion of the self-employed in the workforce in Italy continues to be the second highest in the EU,[9] a unique, layered set of protections has been created for self-employed individuals who are not subject to subordination, but nonetheless in a weaker bargaining position vis-à-vis their clients. Thereby, a considerable share of the self-employed comes either under rules which extend protections originally conceived for employees or under tailor-made protections against abuse by clients. In the other countries studied, the extension of provisions of labour law to the self-employed is rather exceptional and generally restricted to individual provisions and rather narrowly defined subgroups of the self-employed. The area most frequently subject to such extensions concerns access to special procedures (eg labour courts).

As regards collective bargaining rights, the inclusion of the self-employed – as basically required by international case law in relation to the International Labour Organization (ILO)'s fundamental conventions[10] – continues to be subject to be limited in two ways across countries. First, this relates to the applicability of rules specifically aiming at the regulation of collective bargaining – eg regarding the legal effect of agreements, or the rights and protections of representatives. Those rules are often formulated or have at least been traditionally interpreted as covering only dependent employees. Second, notably in recent years the question of the compatibility of collective bargaining for the self-employed with competition law has cast doubts on the degree to which certain or all self-employed workers might need to be excluded. The latter issue may be alleviated, though probably not solved, by the publication of the European Commission's Guidelines on the

[7] *X v Gemeente Amsterdam*, HR 6 nov 2020, ECLI:NL:HR:2020:1746.
[8] Hiessl (n 6) subsection 1.10.
[9] See Eurostat data at ec.europa.eu/eurostat/databrowser/view/LFST_HHSETY/default/table?lang=en (last accessed 19 February 2023).
[10] See eg ILO Committee on Freedom of Association (2001) Report No 326, Case No 2013, para 416.

application of EU competition law to collective agreements regarding the working conditions of solo self-employed persons.[11]

The notion of employee for purposes of social security tends to be largely or entirely equivalent to the distinction in the field of labour law. Additionally, especially in countries where collective agreements tend to stipulate considerable additional benefits, which improve the level of social security enjoyed by the employees covered, the unequal protection of different groups of workers may be much more pronounced in practice than suggested by legal provisions. As described for Germany – which practices the most far-going exclusion of the self-employed from mandatory social insurance – participation in voluntary insurance very rarely results in significant rates of coverage, most notably for those who might be most in need of it. Where the law allows certain groups to opt out of insurance, this option is frequently used by a majority (eg 80 per cent of German mini-jobbers).

Finally, labour market policies appear to be increasing their scope in many countries, moving from a traditional focus on unemployed recipients of insurance benefits towards expanding programmes for young labour market entrants, jobseekers without benefit entitlements, but notably also the working poor whose current labour market activity is insufficient to keep them and their families out of poverty.

IV. Policies and Instruments to Foster Employability

A. The Role of ALMPs and VET Policies

Systems regulating vocational education and training (VET) and active labour market policies (ALMPs) have a crucial potential to enable and encourage as many workers as possible to obtain relevant skills and find employment that matches their level of qualification. Skills are immediately related to the degree to which an employee appears 'replaceable' for a company, which affects both the stability of their employment situation and their bargaining power in relation to the level of remuneration. Public labour market policies, including ALMPs, are a constantly changing legal matter, much more so than workers' entitlements vis-à-vis employers. This is also the only area in which an overall expansive tendency can be observed with a view to recent and ongoing innovations in all of the countries studied.

---

[11] European Commission's Guidelines on the application of EU competition law to collective agreements regarding the working conditions of solo self-employed persons (2022/C 374/02). For a discussion, see C Hiessl, 'Collective Bargaining for the Self-employed: How to Square EU Competition Law with Fundamental Labour Rights?' (2022) 9 *EU Law Live* Weekend Edition No 111, 16–26.

In all countries, detailed statutory and administrative provisions set out a general framework for mandatory and discretionary measures for jobseekers and – at times – employees, as well as various programmes for specific groups such as parents, migrants, young or older jobseekers, or the disabled. In Sweden, the PES (public employment services) are obliged to prioritise those facing particular difficulties. This may be an important precaution against tendencies (reported for several countries) of targeting discretionary measures at those with already better chances of re-employment, which enables the office's staff to report the intervention as a success.

Specifically with a view to the disabled, national law as described in this section generally establishes a threshold marking the degree of disability which exempts the beneficiary from the obligation of making efforts to secure their livelihood by labour market participation. The flipside of an exemption from job-search conditionality for benefit receipt based on a finding of permanent incapacity to work is usually the exclusion from the right to support by various ALMPs. For the Netherlands, half of the individuals excluded in this way have been found involved in work at least to a certain degree. Apart from the disabled, access to ALMPs is often restricted for jobseekers who are not or no longer entitled to unemployment insurance benefits, but whose household income or assets are still above the threshold for an entitlement to means-tested benefits. With a view to the eligibility conditions and coverage rates as described in section IV.B, this is likely to concern a significant number of jobseekers (especially in countries such as Poland, but less so in Belgium, for example). Additionally, measures of support by the PES are unlikely to reach those reluctant to take up benefits (which in Germany is estimated to be the case for about half of all households basically entitled to means-tested benefits).

B. Training

All countries studied pursue an approach to vocational training which entails both out-of-work and – increasingly – in-work support, so as to foster up- and re-skilling. These policies ideally address both the macroeconomic need of addressing current and predicted skills shortages in certain sectors and the social policy aim of enabling workers to enhance their employability as a central component of avoiding poverty in and out of work.

i. *Out-of-work Support*

In all countries studied, the law or administrative guidelines stipulate an individual assessment of each beneficiary registering with the PES, so as to identify those for whom support measures beyond job matching assistance seems reasonable and necessary (and affordable with a view to the current budget situation). Several country reports refer to general rules regarding the allocation of ALMP measures focusing on VET and skills enhancement.

Several country reports refer to differences regarding the support granted to beneficiaries depending on the type of benefit they are entitled to. Such differences often reflect an assumption that the needs and resources of recipients of insurance-based benefits – who have thus usually lost their employment in the (recent) past – are different from those of claimants for second-tier (usually means-tested) benefits. Generally, this is reinforced by institutional separation between the authorities in charge of beneficiaries of insurance-based benefits on the one hand and those of last-resort benefit types on the other – although past reforms have strengthened institutional cooperation, for example in Germany and the Netherlands. For countries such as Belgium, Germany and Italy, the federal legislator lacks the competence to create a comprehensive uniform design for means-tested social assistance benefits.

As mentioned in section IV.A, the access to support of those jobseekers not entitled to any type of benefit is generally much more limited and fragmented. Moreover, most ALMP measures are discretionary also for the recipients of jobseekers' benefits, although the reasonability of allocation is subject to judicial review. An exception in both regards are programmes and initiatives in the spirit of the youth guarantee as envisaged by the 2020 Council Recommendation on 'A Bridge to Jobs',[12] which are generally designed as clear individual rights and independent of the applicant's entitlement to specific benefits.

ii. In-work Support

Empirical data[13] show that companies across countries are increasingly engaged in training their workforce, but unlikely to focus on those most in need of it with a view to concerns of employability. A pronounced culture of (ideally extensive, inclusive and high-quality) training of workers by their employers indisputably constitutes an invaluable asset for public labour market policies, as it provides a basis for regulation and/or financial incentives to steer such training activities to include those at risk of unemployment or labour market exclusion. The countries studied display sizable differences as regards the existence of a significant culture of in-work training, and the development of a dedicated life-long learning approach and the coordination between the training approaches of businesses and labour market authorities (with concerns raised notably relating to Italy). Across countries, though, such coordination has been strengthened in more recent ALMP approaches in various ways.

Among systems which mandate training by employers, duties of anticipatory re-skilling to avoid redundancies are particularly relevant. They may be stipulated

---

[12] Available at ec.europa.eu/social/BlobServlet?docId=23994&langId=en (last accessed 19 February 2023).
[13] See Eurostat data at circabc.europa.eu/ui/group/d14c857a-601d-438a-b878-4b4cebd0e10f/library/ac6f3889-ab25-4f75-9c7a-de997f65e2db?p=1&n=10&sort=modified_DESC (last accessed 19 February 2023).

indirectly via case law about the lawfulness of a dismissal or codified by law, as in the Netherlands and Sweden. In Sweden, the pertinent provision specifies that employers must contemplate up to six months of training for an employee if this would enable the latter to remain employed in the undertaking. Moreover, some country reports refer to a recently increased focus on measures to enable self-determined skills development for employees. Educational leave programmes installed by the Belgian regions allow employees to take up to 100 days of paid leave for an external training programme.

Non-mandatory, but highly institutionalised forms of in-work training exist, notably in the form of apprenticeship systems. These systems' key elements include notably the industry-led offer of training, which thus ensures the immediate relevance of the skills taught, combined with standardised, social partner-led requirements for certification, which ensure the inclusion of contents beyond the on-the-job needs of one employer, and the legal framework detailing the rights of apprentices (including initially low but incrementally increasing wage entitlements and special dismissal protection). Importantly, the most developed German system has traditionally functioned virtually without public subsidies. The significance of apprenticeship as a recruitment tool makes the majority of training companies train apprentices at a net cost, despite the prohibition of clauses which would oblige the apprentice to remain with the company after completion of the training period.

Within such established frameworks for mandatory and voluntary in-work training, ALMPs in the narrower sense can seek to foster the inclusion of those at risk of (long-term) unemployment and skills obsolescence in companies' VET activities. This includes the matching of supply and demand to the benefit of such vulnerable groups, and notably incentives and subsidies for the companies willing to train them. The social partners can play a key role not only in a consultive function for the determination of priorities of VET policies, but also for its organisation and immediate provision. Examples of this exist in all the countries studied.

C. Subsidised Placement

The PES in all of the countries studied have the option – under certain conditions – to facilitate the hiring of jobseekers who are particularly difficult to place. Such schemes are generally meant to overcome employers' hesitancy in regard of the target group of beneficiaries, and partly also to compensate for actual burdens which are difficult to quantify (for example, in relation to the expected productivity of disabled jobseekers and those with learning difficulties).

Wage subsidies are generally a controversial measure, not only due to deadweight losses that are difficult to estimate, but also due to their nature as a co-payment which enables employers to offer poorly paid employment to the target group – which may cause not only individual stigmatisation but also contribute to a low-wage culture on the labour market. Doubts about the motivation of the employing companies, concerns of abuse, and calls for targeting subsidies exclusively at individuals with pronounced barriers to hiring have been stressed notably in the Luxembourgish and Swedish context. Accordingly, the number of subsidised jobs has declined in Sweden in recent years. By contrast, Germany has significantly expanded the wage subsidy system for social assistance benefit recipients in the very recent past. The opposite is true for public works programmes, which have been substantially downsized in Germany due to concerns of displacing opportunities for 'real' employment, but actually assimilated to such real employment in Luxembourg, where the participants are entitled to receive the minimum wage. Finally, whereas none of the aforementioned concerns apply to start-up grant schemes for the self-employed (which equally exist in all countries in some form), the latter are subject to concerns (particularly in Sweden) about the long-term sustainability of the subsidised businesses and risks of incentivising bogus self-employment.

Despite these differences, there appears to be at least a certain degree of consensus among policy makers across countries that a well-targeted subsidy scheme can be vital for the labour market integration of the most marginalised groups, and ideally act as a stepping stone to future regular (non-subsidised) employment. This also corresponds to the designation of wage subsidies as a potentially effective instrument of ALMPs in the European Commission's Recommendation for Effective Active Support to Employment (EASE).[14] While the criteria for the grant of subsidies are highly complex in all countries, the main aspects considered are the duration of unemployment, age and disability.

V. Policies and Instruments Concerning Levels of Remuneration from Work

While at least certain core elements of ALMP and VET policies show strong similarities or comparable priorities across countries, the same cannot be said about policies concerning levels of remuneration, which are characterised by the most extraordinary degree of diversity. The by far most important legal instrument in this area is the stipulation of a minimum wage.

A. Scope of Minimum Wages

In all five countries with a statutory minimum wage (Belgium, Germany, Luxembourg, the Netherlands and Poland), coverage is basically comprehensive

---

[14] European Commission, 'Commission Recommendation for Effective Active Support to Employment (EASE)'. Available at ec.europa.eu/info/publications/commission-recommendation-effective-active-support-employment-ease_en (last accessed 19 February 2023).

for employees, albeit with exceptions that may particularly affect the VUP Groups – such as the exclusion of persons who have been employed in their current job for less than a month in Belgium and the formerly long-term unemployed (in their first six months of employment) in Germany. An extension to certain subgroups of self-employed workers has recently been introduced in the Netherlands and Poland, but doubts remain in both countries about the interpretation of the provisions at issue, as well as their implementation in practice.

A much more complex issue is the scope of collectively bargained minimum wages – which are often considered the preferable source of minimum wages,[15] as they ideally ensure employees a fair share while also taking the limits of employers' capacity for wage increases into account. Such coverage may be achieved via membership in the organisations concluding the agreements (the only option available in all countries studied); a declaration of universal (sector-wide) applicability; legally mandated application in specified cases; an erga omnes effect (among the entire workforce of a bound employer); case law; or voluntary application. The seven countries all use different combinations of these vehicles, with different effects for coverage outcomes.

The pure reliance on membership has allowed notably Sweden to keep up a system characterised by a comparatively very low degree of legislative intervention – which is essentially limited to mandating an erga omnes effect. Whereas this has so far proved sufficient to keep the large majority of workers covered by high and differentiated minimum wage standards negotiated by representative unions, attention may be required in relation to those excluded from coverage – among which vulnerable groups are naturally overrepresented. In comparison to the situation in Italy – the only other country of the sample without a statutory minimum wage – approaches of case law-based extension of collectively bargained standards to these workers are much less developed in Sweden and accordingly provide little legal certainty.

Other countries have at some point taken measures that ensure a high degree of collective bargaining coverage despite much lower unionisation rates – which, in addition to mandating an erga omnes effect, essentially consist in the case law-based extension in Italy mentioned above and the large-scale sectoral extension by governments in Belgium and the Netherlands. By contrast, Germany has given only a negligible role to either of these tools, and it has upheld the most uncompromising insistence on representativeness for collective bargaining coverage by not even mandating an erga omnes effect. Instead, a statutory minimum wage was introduced in Germany at a point where collective bargaining coverage had already declined to barely half of the workforce.

---

[15] See the European Commission's impact assessment accompanying the proposal for a directive on adequate minimum wages in the EU, SWD(2020) 245 final, 4. Available at ec.europa.eu/social/BlobSer vlet?docId=23093&langId=en (last accessed 19 February 2023).

The debate on the systems at issue very much reflects the dilemma that, in an era of falling unionisation rates, (near-)universal coverage can effectively be achieved only via mechanisms of sector-wide extension through governments or courts. This, however, gives rise to concerns of representativeness. The Dutch situation evidences that the social partners' awareness of the sector-wide relevance of bargaining outcomes significantly increases the motivation to participate on the employers' side but decreases it on the workers' side. The outcome is a highly unequal degree of representativeness of the bargaining partners. The Italian situation in turn bears evidence of the risk that non-representative unions may conclude agreements which seem fundamentally at odds with workers' actual interests.

All of this indicates a trend of increasing reliance on statutory minimum wages for the protection of the most vulnerable of workers – which is obviously most pronounced in Poland with its virtually non-existent sectoral-level bargaining practices and the practical non-application of (theoretically possible) sector-wide extension of collective standards.

B.　Amount of Minimum Wages

Despite the concerns regarding non-representative bargaining situations mentioned in the previous section, collective bargaining is basically subject to a presumption of relevance and adequacy, which has generally prevented legislative interference with the autonomy of the bargaining partners. By contrast, the determination of minimum wages is subject to criteria which are highly diverse in the five countries where they exist.

The main determinants are always either purchasing power, general wage developments or social partner consultation, or a combination thereof. Single-criteria systems leading to a straightforward determinability of the statutory minimum wage exist in Luxembourg (inflation-, and thus exclusively purchasing power-based) and the Netherlands (determination in line with the average growth of collectively bargained wages). In the other three countries, the social partners effectively have the last word, but are expected to take account of wage developments in Germany and purchasing power developments in Poland. The government ultimately decides the level in Poland if there is no agreement by the social partners, and in Belgium by means of intervention if there are concerns about the maintenance of cross-border competitiveness (a highly controversial option which seems unique in the European context).

Deviations are possible in most countries in the form of lower wage rates for certain groups of workers. Age-based differentiations (lower minima for young workers) exist in Belgium, Luxembourg and the Netherlands (where they are most pronounced); skills-based differentiations exist in Germany (lower minima for apprentices) and Luxembourg (higher rate dependent on accreditation by an official certificate).

Strikingly, empirical outcomes seem to be at odds with these criteria to a large degree. Notably, four of the countries studied (Luxembourg, Germany, the Netherlands and Belgium) occupy the four top positions among all European statutory minimum wages in terms of purchasing power.[16] At the same time, these very countries' minimum wages all amount to just somewhat above 40 per cent of the average wage in the respective country.[17] Such outcome could arguably be expected in Luxembourg with its inflation-based determination, but not for the other countries – particularly not for the Netherlands and Germany, which actually focus on keeping minimum wages in line with general wage developments. A 'poverty-proof' level of 60 per cent of the median wage[18] is not reached by any of the WorkYP countries' minimum wages, and the only country getting at least very close to this level is Sweden with its freely bargained wages.

This indicates that the method for determining adaptations may actually be less relevant than the 'original value' of the minimum wage, ie the level of purchasing power or share of sectoral wages which the minimum wage was originally designed to ensure. This underscores the importance of conscious one-off increases of this level outside the general adaptation mechanism – as has very recently happened both in Germany and the Netherlands, for the first time since the respective minimum wage systems were introduced.[19]

VI. Policies and Instruments Concerning Social Benefits

As opposed to regulation on wage levels – which, as shown in the last section, is generally based on few or even virtually no statutory rules – the social security component of workers' income levels is subject to extensive and complex legislative determination in all European countries. While almost all of social security effectively has a financial component and is of potential relevance for workers, four categories of benefits appear most immediately decisive for whether a working household's income is lifted above the poverty line, and/or influence a worker's potential to refuse poor wage offers from an employer: in-work benefits; jobseekers' benefits; temporary income replacement without job-search requirement; and universal structural income support.

---

[16] European Commission (n 14) 149.

[17] European Commission (n 14) 4.

[18] Based on the idea that if a workers' wage level reaches 60 per cent of the median wage it is at least rather likely that their equivalised household income reaches 60 per cent of the median income.

[19] See Federal Law of 28 June 2022 (BGBl. 2022 I S. 969) in Germany; Law of 3 October 2022 (Staatsblad 2022, 381) in the Netherlands. Moreover, on 7 February 2023, the Dutch Parliament adopted a law which introduces an hourly (rather than just monthly) minimum wage, resulting in increases of the minimum wage entitlements of workers with long weekly work hours.

A. In-work Benefits

In-work benefits are granted under the condition of being in employment – which may or may not be based on an express legislative intention to create an incentive for those out of work to join the labour force. They can be based on statutory law, collective agreements or employers' individual policies or initiatives. From an in-work poverty perspective, it may be noted that all of these policies are in fact likely to have regressive redistributive effects. Company welfare measures, as far as they are not obligatory, tend to be concentrated on larger companies where wage levels are higher on average – and thus rarely benefit those workers most at risk of poverty. Collective agreement coverage is found to be considerably lower among effectively all VUP Groups than among the general workforce in all of the countries studied. Statutory provisions may be most likely to benefit the working poor in the same way as other workers, but may still be less available for low-wage workers (if granted as a percentage of earnings) and – in the long term – for those with fragmented work biographies.

The opposite is the case if in-work benefits are either specifically designed to target low-wage workers or provide services of particular relevance for them. As far as benefits or their amount are expressly dependent on the wage level, the WorkYP country sample illustrates the tension between policy aims of supporting low-wage workers on the one hand and creating an incentive for extending labour market participation on the other. One Luxembourgish tax credit effectively aims to do both at the same time, by being granted on all incomes below €80,000, but designed to peak at an income of €10,000 and gradually decline with higher or lower earnings. A very similar concept underlies two German in-work benefits (child and housing support) which are dependent on having a labour market income within certain brackets and are meant, inter alia, to shield workers with low but not negligible income from having to apply for social assistance. Doubts about the effectiveness of these measures in their current form are raised in view of very high rates of non-take-up, though.

B. Jobseekers' Benefits

The second category includes jobseekers' benefits, ie all benefits granted to beneficiaries who are (expected to be) seeking employment or an improvement their employability, as their current job (if any) is insufficient to keep them and their family out of poverty. Those benefits may be relevant for the working poor in different ways. On the one hand, they frequently entail support for improving the labour market situation of the beneficiary; on the other, they usually contain elements which put beneficiaries under pressure to seek and retain employment so as to end their reliance on benefits – which may have an impact on the quality of the employment accepted by such beneficiaries, as well as its sustainability and the degree of protection it offers against in-work poverty.

None of the countries studied envisage any form of truly unconditional benefit in the sense of a universal basic income (UBI), so that the receipt of benefits for general subsistence is always coupled with a requirement to overcome a situation of dependency by labour market participation, for lack of specific reasons why this cannot be expected from the beneficiary. Consequently, in all countries, individuals whose income is not secured by own earnings or benefits as described below in this section are expected to register with employment offices or municipal authorities and commit to do whatever seems possible and necessary to improve their income situation by labour market activity.

Provided that a beneficiary shows the necessary commitment as described, they are, in any event, entitled to means-tested benefits as a last resort to avoid severe material deprivation. In most of the countries studied, such benefits have in some form existed for many decades. By contrast, Italy was among the last in Europe to introduce social assistance as an enforceable right, overcoming a system of piecemeal protection for specific categories of individuals and fragmented protection at municipal level. This was realised under a gradual and complex reform process starting in the late 1990s, until a system which entailed the two main elements of social assistance across countries – true universalism and conditionality upon labour market integration efforts – was finally introduced in 2017 (and superseded in 2019 by the currently applicable system as described in this section).

Beyond such last-resort entitlements, all countries operate at least one type of unemployment insurance scheme, which ensures wage-dependent and/or flat-rate benefits for those covered and fulfilling the conditions. While such first-tier benefits have long been conceptualised as jobseekers' benefits with a key focus on labour market reintegration, the emphasis on conditionality in combination with ALMPs in second-tier means-tested social assistance benefits has been strengthened more recently in several countries. This involved the introduction of new instruments, new administrative structures, partly also new benefit types. The German labour market policy reforms of the early 2000s are the most straightforward example of an approach of adamant pursuit of (re-)integration in employment. This makes it all the more noteworthy that the reform's reform in 2022 abolished both the unconditional priority for steering jobseekers into the first available job and the severe sanctions for violations of cooperation duties.[20]

The Dutch and Swedish systems, in particular, are characterised by the key role of employer-sponsored supplements to social security-based benefit entitlements. This includes statutory severance pay entitlements as well as benefits stipulated ad hoc in social plans, but also provisions in sectoral-level collective agreements. In the Netherlands, surveys found top-ups to benefits after dismissal to apply to 27 per cent of employees covered by such agreements. Such benefits, receipt of which is conditional on the beneficiary being out of work, come

---

[20] See Federal Law of 16 December 2022 (BGBl. 2022 I S. 2328).

in addition to severance pay entitlements, which employers must in principle provide at a predefined amount irrespective of their former employee's subsequent reintegration in paid employment. In Sweden, they complement the role of trade unions' income insurance policies, which effectively neutralise the effect of the upper threshold for unemployment insurance benefits as described in this section.

i. Scope

Issues of scope are highly complex in relation to a benefit architecture in which the risk of absent or insufficient income from work is covered by two or more benefit types in all countries. Since the reforms in Italy mentioned above, all countries have granted comprehensive coverage of the resident population by a safety net of social assistance benefits, which is designed as a jobseekers' benefit for those of working age who are able to work (and their households). In what follows, the emphasis will therefore be on questions of eligibility for higher-tier, non-means-tested benefits, while pointing out also and specifically whether the aspects mentioned may also affect the claimant's access to last-resort benefits. The factors determining this access are the scope of compulsory insurance and provisions delimiting benefit eligibility, as well as benefit conditionality and sanctions.

First-tier unemployment benefits are usually based on mandatory insurance, which covers all or most groups of dependent employees. By way of exemption, mini-jobbers in Germany and small-scale platform workers in Belgium are excluded from social insurance coverage and consequently also from insurance-based unemployment benefits.

An extension of the compulsory insurance system for employees under largely equivalent conditions to the self-employed in a broad sense exists only in Luxembourg, with very minor differences. However, the unemployment insurance system is extended to subgroups of the self-employed in Germany (with respect to home workers) and Italy (in relation to 'hetero-organised' workers). Italy additionally operates a separate benefit for dependent and solo self-employed workers. Importantly, also the scheme for the latter two groups is subject to essentially the same rules as that for employees – apart from the fact that contributions need to be paid by the self-employed workers themselves. A similar system of compulsory coverage of subgroups of the self-employed used to be applicable also in the Netherlands. However, since 2016, the categories concerned – home workers, musicians, artists, professional sportsmen, and 'other persons' who provide work personally for remuneration – have de facto obtained an opt-out possibility, so that their coverage can no longer be considered strictly mandatory. Belgium, by contrast, operates a separate 'bridging assistance', which differs from the unemployment insurance system for employees rather substantially, but is in turn comprehensive in its coverage of all groups of the self-employed.

Sweden stands out for, on the one hand, including the self-employed under essentially the same system as employees, but on the other hand not making insurance for income-related benefits mandatory for any worker. Although the Ghent system has long evolved so as to no longer require union membership as a precondition for membership in an unemployment insurance fund, membership developments are in practice still linked to unionisation and there are sector-specific differences. In this regard, concerns are raised with a view to the significant drop in membership (from 90 per cent to 70 per cent of the workforce), concentrated among lower-paid occupational groups, which followed increases in membership fees and tightened conditions for benefit eligibility. Despite more recent changes, which have halted the downward trend, membership rates in unemployment insurance funds have not rebounded to prior levels and still stood at barely above 70 per cent of the labour force in 2019. Only a further easing of access conditions in the context of the Covid-19 pandemic crisis led to a visible trend reversal, triggering discussions about making the changes permanent.

Apart from Sweden, voluntary unemployment insurance – as far as legally permitted – plays a negligible role in the countries studied. In Germany, the use of a voluntary insurance option for the self-employed expanded over a brief period after its introduction, when it was granted under very favourable conditions, about which starting employers were comprehensively informed when receiving a widely available start-up grant. Since then, that grant has been converted into a much more rarely awarded discretionary benefit, conditions for voluntary insurance have been tightened (including notably an increase of the fixed contribution basis from 25 per cent to 100 per cent of the current average wage) and access was restricted to former employees applying within three months of founding a self-employed business. Applications have receded accordingly, from over 100,000 to just 3,000 per year between 2010 and 2018.

Generally, persons included in the scope of an insurance system (and contributing to it) are also entitled to receive benefits in case of unemployment. An exception exists for managing directors and executives, and persons holding an establishment licence in Luxembourg, if they have incomes superior to a defined reference wage. More importantly, both Belgium and Luxembourg restrict benefit entitlements for smaller-scale part-time employees. Belgian unemployment benefits are denied to those having worked less than 12 hours per week; in Luxembourg, the threshold is even set at 16 hours. A similar outcome results from benefit calculation rules in Sweden, as the minimum threshold requires at least 50 hours of work in each month to be taken into account, and 80 hours on average. These restrictions constitute a striking contrast to the Dutch system, which ensures that even employees with less than 10 weekly working hours are entitled to partial unemployment benefits if they lose half of their previous working hours.

Notably for Luxembourg, the just described exclusion of small-scale part-time employment is highlighted as one of the key concerns regarding the benefit's scope. On the one hand, including those groups under the scope of insurance (and thus the obligation to pay contributions) avoids the concerns raised for example in relation to the German mini job rule, where the use and abuse of mini jobs by employers is incentivised by their exclusion from contribution obligations. On the other hand, systems just described in the last paragraph put an additional financial strain on a group of low-income employees, who have contributions deducted from their wages while in work, but can only fall back on means-tested benefits when out of work.

Apart from such general exclusion of groups of workers, eligibility is determined by factors relating to the applicant's age and capacity to work, to whether and for what reason they are considered unemployed, and to the duration of insurance affiliation.

All of the national systems studied make benefit receipt dependent on the recipient being willing to overcome a period of unemployment by taking up 'suitable work'. Statutory definitions of the concept of a suitable job tend to be specified by detailed guidelines in administrative regulation. Those (and partly statutory law itself) regularly envisage the standard to become stricter over the duration of benefit receipt. Dutch law even stipulates that all criteria of suitability apart from the basic reasonability assessment (see above) become inapplicable after six months of unemployment. The essence of every benefit based on a job-search obligation is a requirement for active job-seeking in cooperation with authorities – which obviously includes a duty to apply for vacancies to which the beneficiary is referred by authorities, in addition to independent search for suitable opportunities. To what degree this standard obligation is suspended for the duration of an ALMP measure (such as participation in vocational training or temporary placement) is regularly subject to an individual assessment of the merits by the institutions in charge. Violations of the beneficiary's duties of active search, acceptance of a suitable job, and cooperation with authorities are subject to sanctions which compromise their benefit entitlement in all countries.

Comparative statistics on coverage by unemployment benefits are rarely available and riddled by problems of the identification of meaningful concepts for comparison. The OECD's 'pseudo coverage rate' as calculated for 2018[21] relies on a highly formalistic classification of benefit types. For instance, German social assistance benefits, which are 'unemployment benefits' exclusively by name,[22] are included as 'unemployment assistance' and accordingly yield a coverage rate of 263 per cent of the unemployed. Social assistance benefits for any other of the WorkYP countries are not included, despite containing a job-search criterion just as the German benefit and thus not being distinguishable from it by any structural

---

[21] See OECD data at www.oecd.org/els/soc/SOCR_UBPseudoCoverageRates.xlsx (last accessed 19 February 2023).

[22] As they cover all members of households where at least one person is capable of working, irrespective of whether they are unemployed or working poor. The only condition is that the household income and assets are low enough to qualify under the strict means test as described in section VI.B.ii.

criterion. Even the Swedish second-tier benefit for non-members of unemploy-ment benefit funds is not included, although it is a non-means-tested flat-rate benefit based on a criterion of prior work – and thereby entirely comparable to the Polish first-tier benefit. While being mindful of these caveats, it is in any event clear based on available statistics that the regime applicable to the majority of jobseekers in most countries is not the insurance-based system, which tends to be the main or only focus in most debates regarding the design and adequacy of unemployment benefits, but the subsidiary one. As far as coverage rates are monitored, data refer to a clearly declining trend – which appears most striking in Sweden, where the rate fell from 80 per cent in 2006 to 40 per cent in 2013.

ii. Amount

Beyond the scope of different layers of benefit systems for jobseekers, the concrete benefit amounts are obviously decisive for the risk of poverty out of employment – and accordingly the beneficiary's likelihood of accepting poorly paid work in order to achieve a relative improvement of the household's income situation. Depending on the country and the type of jobseekers' benefit, the criteria determining the amount received by the beneficiary may relate to the beneficiary's previous wage level; the applicability of lump-sum entitlements, minima or maxima; the dura-tion of insurance and unemployment; previous working time; the beneficiary's age; their household or family situation; their participation in ALMP measures, and finally their income and assets.

With the exception of Poland, where even mandatory insurance-based benefits are subject to a flat-rate calculation, all studied countries' laws stipulate wage-related entitlements as the primary unemployment insurance benefit for employees. The Italian benefit system is the only one with a strongly progressive component. In 2021, it provided 75 per cent of previous income up to €1227.55 per month and 25 per cent of any amount exceeding this threshold. This focus on low-wage earners, in combination with a rather generous determination of the benefit's scope, give the system an overall pronouncedly redistributive character. To some degree, this may constitute a repercussion of the fact that, until recently (see reforms described in section VI.B.i), this entitlement was not complemented by a general subsidiary right to social assistance (which is per se the most redis-tributive benefit type, as it is financed by taxes and granted exclusively based on neediness).

The Italian system also represents the most systematic example of a decalage scheme, by which the benefit amount is gradually reduced with every month of receipt, thereby increasing the financial incentive (or pressure) to take up work. Other systems envisage a more radical drop in the level after specific durations of receipt. Yet, for beneficiaries who are originally covered by an insurance-based benefit entitlement, the probably most crucial aspect determining their poverty risks is the point at which this entitlement will be superseded by the subsidiary, usually means-tested entitlement. Such a point exists in all countries but Belgium.

With a view to the fact that minimum wages in the countries studied are generally below 60 per cent of the median income, it is clear that the replacement rates of first-tier unemployment benefits applicable in the countries studied over time (all somewhere between 40 per cent and 85 per cent of previous wages) are unlikely to secure a net income above the relative poverty line for a former minimum wage earner in any of them. While the unemployment benefit paid to these recipients will be at least close to the at-risk-of-poverty threshold of 60 per cent of the median income in the Netherlands, it will barely reach 40 per cent in countries such as Germany and Luxembourg. Nonetheless, depending on whether and how far the previous household income was above the poverty line, income-related benefits as described certainly reduce the risk of falling below it immediately in case of a job loss.

By contrast, social assistance benefits are essentially a tool to avoid severe material deprivation, based on an individual assessment of the applicant household's needs in all countries. Those needs are measured as the difference between the means available and a predefined amount meant to represent the recognised living costs of the household. Depending on the strictness of the means test, this amount is therefore reduced by the value of income and/or assets of which the household disposes or could dispose based on legal entitlements. The concrete benefit due in the national context consequently depends on the determination of those two components. Even if the criteria used are in principle suitable to keep households out of severe material deprivation, this aim may effectively not be reached in individual situations. This can be a consequence of imposed sanctions or requirements which the beneficiary household feels unable to fulfil (such as moving out of the current accommodation), but very often also partial or full non-take-up. The latter can be related to a lack of knowledge or resources, fear or frustration in the relationship with authorities, or stigmatisation. Generally, the more complex the conditions and elements of the means test, the more prominent many of those risks are becoming.

All in all, the development of the most recent decades indicates that, in most countries, both the scope and generosity of first-tier, insurance-based unemployment benefits have been on the decline, which underlines the importance of second-tier, usually means-tested benefits and the conditionality attached to them. As a result, VUP workers are effectively at a substantial risk of falling back on means-tested benefits far below the relative poverty line as soon as they are out of work – which, in combination with the strict criteria for a 'suitable job' – may put them under substantial pressure to accept and remain in poorly paid jobs.

This is obviously true to very different degrees for the countries studied. Notably, the Belgian system stands out for providing a single benefit of unlimited duration, which guarantees a non-means-tested minimum and even takes the household situation into account in this context. Means-testing may thus mainly be an issue for those not meeting the requirements to receive this benefit in the first place – which is obviously particularly relevant for VUP workers with either low-intensity, fragmented or (formally) self-employed work participation. At the other end of the scale, the first-tier benefit plays a particularly subordinate role in Poland, where VUP workers will regularly face poverty as soon as they lose their job.

Statistics on the incomes and poverty rates of the unemployed as compared to workers may serve as a rough indication of the adequacy of monetary benefits for jobseekers. According to Eurostat,[23] the median equivalised annual income of the unemployed in the EU in 2019 was somewhat above €10,500 (by purchasing power parity standards). This was less than half of the median income of employed persons in that year. This difference was smaller in Luxembourg and Poland (where the incomes of those who are unemployed reached about 60 per cent of workers' incomes), but particularly pronounced in Germany (where they were just over 40 per cent of those with a job). Considering that, as noted in section VI.B.i, wage-related benefits across countries (with the exception of Belgium and, possibly, the Netherlands) tend to reach only a minority of the unemployed, it may not be surprising that these shares are generally lower than the aforementioned wage replacement rates envisaged in unemployment insurance systems. Overall, the impact of the household context on the equivalised income can be assumed to be substantial – which may partly explain the counter-intuitive finding that the difference between workers and the unemployed appears comparatively small in Poland with its particularly low degree of benefit coverage and generosity.

The same is self-evidently true for poverty rates,[24] which stood at 49.2 per cent of the unemployed in the EU in 2019 – implying that the jobless were five times more likely to be poor than employed persons. The difference was even much more pronounced in Belgium and the Netherlands, where very low in-work poverty rates compare to 10 times higher rates for the unemployed. Overall, the German poverty rate of close to 74 per cent among the unemployed was the highest in the EU, followed with some distance by Sweden with its 62 per cent rate. Again, remarkably, the Polish value of just 38 per cent is among the lowest in the EU, indicating that the unemployed were 'only' four times more affected by poverty than employed persons.

All in all, these statistics leave no doubt about the substantial financial incentive for jobseekers to aim for labour market (re-)integration – particularly also in those countries which put less emphasis on punitive conditionality.

C. Temporary Benefits without Work or Job-search Requirement

The third category are temporary benefits which provide a certain level of wage replacement in periods of interruption or temporary reduction of work, for which

---

[23] See data at ec.europa.eu/eurostat/en/web/products-datasets/-/ILC_DI05 (last accessed 19 February 2023).

[24] See Eurostat data at ec.europa.eu/eurostat/databrowser/view/ilc_peps02/default/table?lang=en (last accessed 19 February 2023).

no ALMPs or job-search conditionality are deemed necessary. The most important benefit types relate to economic, family-related and health-related reasons for work suspension or working time reduction.

In the recent past, significant developments have taken place notably in relation to the first group, which includes short-term work (STW) and furlough schemes. In the context of the Covid-19 crisis, such schemes were partly introduced from scratch (Poland) or tested for the first time (Sweden), whereby all existing systems were modified so as to increase their protective effect. For VUP Groups, this could be particularly significant in several ways. First, measures which facilitated the use of STW benefitted notably those whose situation made them most likely to be dismissed by an employer without this option. Second, measures increasing the benefit level increased low-wage workers' likelihood of remaining above or at least close to the poverty line while drawing STW benefits. Finally, modifications expanding the target group (such as the inclusion of temporary agency workers in the scope of the German scheme for the first time in its long history) could at least reduce the share of VUP workers who were structurally excluded from STW schemes.

D. Benefits for Structural Income Support

The remaining category of benefits includes those offering structural support without a work or job-search requirement. In this respect, surveys in the Netherlands have indicated a lack of public support for unconditional benefits. Some country reports do refer to experiments with benefit types which at least reduce the strictness or comprehensiveness of conditionality of social assistance at municipal level (the Netherlands), or to ongoing independent research projects to test the implications of granting an UBI on individual behaviour and success (Germany). Apart from such minor deviations, all benefits which are granted structurally without work or job-search criteria are meant to compensate for specific expenses – notably for housing, children, healthcare and long-term care.

Overall, across the countries studied, the importance of benefits granted structurally without job-search requirements has been receding in past years. This is notably true for housing-related costs, support for which is in many countries granted to a very limited degree (or not at all, apart from regional or local initiatives), and thus to a large extent provided in the framework of social assistance benefits, which feature a job-search criterion. The trend is less clear with regard to family-related expenses, in relation to which universal systems have been strengthened in countries such as Italy.

VII. Concluding Remarks

The exact interaction of the described protective instruments among each other and with other aspects of the legal system seems very difficult to pinpoint. For instance, most of the countries studied have comparatively low or very low unemployment rates (including partly long-term unemployment rates).[25] This could be seen as a sign of success of labour market reintegration via supportive ALMPs (spending on which is above the EU average in all WorkYP countries[26]), or also the result of 'work first' approaches, which coerce jobseekers into potentially poor jobs. Not to mention the impact of the economic circle, which in open economies is determined by numerous variables beyond the reach of national-level policies, or the labour market effect of demographic developments.

Despite these restrictions, the results of the analytical comparison provide countless indications of the impact of various aspects of regulatory choices on the prevalence of in-work poverty. For instance, one important aspect of the systems in Belgium and the Netherlands – which stand out by comparatively very low in-work poverty rates – appears to be that insurance-based benefits are generally prevented from falling beneath a certain level, the determination of which takes the household situation into account. Thereby, they provide a high degree of protection against having to fall back on means-tested benefits, which in all of the countries studied are set far below the relative poverty line.

In the most recent past, a potentially highly important side effect of the introduction of measures to strengthen short-time work and equivalent or similar benefits in the context of the Covid-19 crisis in all countries was to showcase the very limited degree to which such situations used to be structurally addressed for various vulnerable groups of workers – such as most notably the self-employed but partly also temporary and low-hour part-time workers. Additionally, the introduction of benefits which were somewhat difficult to control as regards the legitimacy of a claim, and the absence of observations of widespread abuse, may have served as an inspiration for concepts of expanding the scope of or easing access to protective instruments.

One notable example of this is the German reform mentioned at section VI.B, which relaxed various aspects of the particularly strict conditionality of its means-tested benefit system for jobseekers, much of which was in line with the temporary relaxations during the Covid-19 crisis. Another one is the Netherlands, where an ongoing reform discussion focuses on companies' excessive use of self-employed and atypical work, which has been incentivised notably by cost advantages resulting from a lack of social protection for workers. This lack of protection became painfully clear during the pandemic, when the government felt forced to compensate the absence of social security funds for the workers in question by granting benefits from tax funds.

The current situation, in which unemployment across Europe is at a historic low point, and the job vacancy rate has surged after the pandemic to its

---

[25] See Eurostat data at ec.europa.eu/eurostat/databrowser/view/UNE_RT_M__custom_4884335/default/line?lang=en (last accessed 19 February 2023).

[26] See OECD data at www.oecd.org/employment/activation.htm (last accessed 19 February 2023).

historically highest value in 2022,[27] may to some degree have stolen the thunder of opinions which considered a large low-wage sector necessary in order to create opportunities for employment. This may arguably have helped to pave the way for improvements in statutory minimum wages, for example, as mentioned in section V.B.

All in all, the analysis of relevant rules of social security, labour law, collective bargaining and labour market policies, filtered by the degree to which they offer protections accessible for vulnerable and underrepresented groups, may have served to illustrate that policy approaches to combat poverty are by no means determined exclusively by the 'generosity' of certain protective measures. Instead, many of the most immediate challenges for a policy mix to comprehensively address poverty risks might be to ensure that protective measures are actually applicable to and accessible for those who would be most in need of them. All of the seven countries studied have turned out to represent 'best' and 'worst' practice in this regard in different areas of regulation, which underlines the potential of comparative research to arrive at solutions which combine the most promising aspects of existing approaches and develop them further.

---

[27] See Eurostat data at ec.europa.eu/eurostat/databrowser/view/JVS_Q_NACE2__custom_4884464/default/table?lang=en (last accessed 19 February 2023).

3

European Labour Law Harmonisation in Light of the Risk of In-work Poverty

MIJKE HOUWERZIJL

I. Introduction

Since the start of the European integration project in 1957, the European Union and its Member States have shared the social policy objective to improve and upwardly converge living and working conditions, 'so as to make possible their harmonisation while the improvement is being maintained'.[1] This includes adequate working conditions, proper social protection, dialogue between management and labour, lasting high employment, and the combating of social exclusion. Yet, in the course of the twenty-first century, European labour markets have developed in a direction sharply in contrast with the aspiration of upward social convergence. The increase in employment flexibility and use of short-term employment contracts in the aftermath of the 2008 economic crisis as well as the ongoing impact of globalisation and digitalisation trends, show a lasting divergence on the labour market and growing social inequality. Many EU Member States are facing an increasing share of low-paid occupations, and the erosion of traditional collective bargaining structures in some countries. The Covid-19 pandemic has accentuated the trends towards higher levels of financial insecurity, poverty and income inequality.[2] All these developments undermine the very promises of upward convergence and harmonisation enshrined in the EU Treaties.

The launch of the European Pillar of Social Rights (hereinafter 'EPSR' or 'Pillar') in 2017, signposted a renewed process of convergence towards better working and

---

[1] See Art 151 of the Treaty on the Functioning of the European Union (TFEU), which (in its current form) makes reference to fundamental social rights such as those set out in the European Social Charter signed at Turin on 18 October 1961 and in the 1989 Community Charter of the Fundamental Social Rights of Workers. The EU's constitutional commitment towards fostering social rights is also laid down in Arts 2 and 3 of the Treaty on European Union, Art 9 TFEU and in a number of social rights conveyed in the Charter of Fundamental Rights of the EU.
[2] EPSR Action plan (2021) 9, 11, 19.

living conditions across the EU. One of the promises the EPSR makes to EU workers is to address the challenges related to atypical forms of employment and the right to fair and good working conditions. Part of the right to secure and adaptable employment is that the transition towards open-ended forms of employment shall be fostered (Principle 5). Moreover, the Pillar brought new impetus to the debate on quality jobs, by including an explicit Principle 6 concerning the right to fair wages and the prevention of in-work poverty. In this respect, the importance of matters of social dialogue and collective bargaining are stressed as well (Principle 8).

Looking at the Vulnerable and Underrepresented Persons (VUP) Groups,[3] this chapter aims to flag possible issues with the current state of play of EU harmonisation of labour law in light of the risk of in-work poverty.[4] To this end, for each of the VUP groups identified, relevant EU labour law instruments and related EPSR principles are loosely explored regarding their contribution against in-work poverty. The chapter is structured as follows. For respectively low-paid standard workers (section II), flexibly employed workers (section III), and solo self-employed, casual and platform workers (section IV), parts of EU labour law harmonisation are addressed, testing how they contribute to combat risks of in-work poverty.[5] The last section summarises and concludes (section V).

II. EU Labour Law and In-work Poverty of Low-paid Standard Workers

Due to complex globalisation and Europeanisation processes combined with technological and organisational changes, the European economies now offer less protection against 'downward' working conditions for workers in the lower segments of the labour market, even if those workers are employed in an open-ended full-time job position. In sectors where enterprises typically offer low-skilled jobs,[6] both low wages and in-work poverty are quite common. Principle 6 of the EPSR refers to the right to fair wages and prevention of in-work poverty. However, the competence to regulate wage determination is fully in the

---

[3] The research project 'Working, Yet Poor' identified four groups of workers who are especially vulnerable to experience a higher risk of in-work poverty. These are low-skilled employees with standard employment contracts employed in poor sectors (VUP Group 1), solo and dependent self-employed persons and bogus self-employed (VUP Group 2), flexibly employed workers (VUP Group 3), and casual and platform workers (VUP Group 4). See especially chs 1 and 2, as well as L Ratti (ed), *In-Work Poverty in Europe. Vulnerable and Under-Represented Persons in a Comparative Perspective* (BCLR 111, Wolters Kluwer, 2022).

[4] Drawing on Deliverable 4.1 of the Working, Yet Poor project, by MS Houwerzijl and A Aranguiz (2021), available at workingyetpoor.eu/deliverables.

[5] For a more elaborate discussion on several of the topics dealt with in this chapter see especially chs 5, 6 and 7.

[6] It should be noted that people working in these jobs are often not unskilled or uneducated. This is particularly true for many migrant workers who are sometimes 'forced' to take any job that they can find.

domain of the Member States, including their national social partners. Hence, it is important to establish the role of EU labour law with regard to decent wage levels. Below in section II.A, this is further explored. Thereafter, this section turns to another aspect of the changed (macro-economic) context of work for these VUP Group 1 workers. In some sectors, there is a continuous changing of employer identities and/or strategies as a consequence of take-overs, mergers or (public) procurement processes. As part of these strategies, working conditions may be impacted by outsourcing, tendering and (sub)contracting processes. The EPSR affirms the transferability of workers' accrued training or social protection entitlements when they change employment status or employer (Principle 8). However, these workers might still suffer from (gradually) deteriorating working conditions, due to for instance expiring or new (decentralised) collective bargaining agreements. The (modest) role of EU labour law harmonisation in that regard is explored in section II.B. An interim conclusion is presented in section II.C.

A. The Right to Decent Wage Levels

Enjoying an adequate minimum wage level is a crucial ingredient of decent work, and for VUP Group 1 workers in a single-person household with no underlying conditions, the right to fair wages has the power to prevent workers becoming 'working poor'. EPSR Principle 6 links this right to Article 31(1) of the Charter of Fundamental Rights of the European Union (CFREU) as part of existing EU law in this field. However, there is no *explicit* mention of wage setting or even minimum wage requirements in the Charter.[7] According to the Court of Justice of the European Union (CJEU), working conditions also include 'pay'[8] although, when asked whether Article 31(1) CFREU on fair working conditions protected fair remuneration in the context of the austerity measures, the Court held that 'it had no jurisdiction' as the order for reference was not implementing EU law.[9]

There is, in fact, little EU law in the field of wages, and what exists covers mostly the right to equal pay. This scarcity is undoubtedly a consequence of the exclusion of 'pay' from EU competences under Article 153(5) of the Treaty on the Functioning of the European Union (TFEU). It must be noted, however,

---

[7] EU Charter of Fundamental Rights, 7 December 2000 [2000] OJ C 364/01. Critical of this omission: J Kenner, 'Economic and Social Rights in the EU Legal order: the Mirage of Indivisibility' in T Harvey and J Kenner, *Economic and Social Rights under the EU Charter of Fundamental Rights* (Oxford, Hart Publishing, 2003) 17.

[8] Case C-395/08 *Bruno and Others* EU:C:2010:329, [2010] ECR I-05119, paras 39–40; Case C-307/05 *Del Cerro Alonso* EU:C:2007:3, [2007] ECR I-07109, paras 39–46.

[9] In Case C-128/12 *Sindicatos dos Bancários do Norte ea* EU:C:2013:149, the CJEU was asked to clarify whether Article 31(1) of the Charter may be interpreted as meaning that employees have the right to fair remuneration which ensures that they and their families can enjoy a satisfactory standard of living? (question 4). A similar question was posed in Case C-264/12 *Sindicato Nacional dos Profissionais de Seguros e Afins* EU:C:2014:2036, para 19.

that the Court has upheld a restrictive interpretation of the exclusion of pay. Particularly, the Court has interpreted that Article 153(5) TFEU cannot hollow out the social competences of the EU as regards working conditions,[10] and it maintained that exclusion of pay applies only to 'the equivalence of all or some of the constituent parts of pay and/or the level of pay in the Member States, or the setting of a minimum guaranteed wage'.[11] Consequently, as long as measures do not directly regulate the level of pay, or some of its constituent parts, measures related to pay are not excluded from EU competence. In this vein, the proposal for the (recently adopted) Directive on adequate minimum wages was construed.[12]

The purpose of said Directive[13] is to establish a framework for promoting adequate levels of minimum wages and access of workers to minimum wage protection, in the form of wages set out by collective agreements or in the form of a statutory minimum wage where it exists (Recital 15 and Article 1). In accordance with the Court's interpretation of Article 153(5) TFEU, the Directive does not define a specific level of a minimum wage, but criteria for the adequacy of (statutory) minimum wages are mentioned (Article 5). Member States shall establish the necessary framework for setting and updating of statutory minimum wages. Such setting and updating shall be guided by criteria, based on national socio-economic conditions, to promote adequacy with the aim to achieve decent working and living conditions, social cohesion and upward convergence.

The adequacy of minimum wages should be assessed at least in relation to purchasing power, productivity developments, and gross wage levels, distribution and growth (Article 5(2)). The use of indicators commonly used at the international level, such as 60 per cent of gross median wage and 50 per cent of the gross average wage, can help guide the assessment of minimum wage adequacy in relation to gross level of wages (Article 5(3) and Recital 21). Hence, the Directive does not impose on the Member States hard obligations to ensure these standards, and thus the impact of the Directive remains to be seen, even though it confirms that these standards should be strived for. However, as EU Member States are also bound by the European Social Charter (ESC), there is reason to align the implementation of the Directive with their obligations pursuant to Article 4 ESC. This provision has repeatedly been interpreted by the ECSR as implying that any wage below 50 per cent of the median wage is unacceptable and to be considered 'unfair'. Also, the ECSR has held that in order to be considered decent, wages must at least reach 60 per cent of a national average equivalised wage. Moreover, to be

---

[10] Case C-307/05 *Del Cerro Alonso* EU:C:2007:3, [2007] ECR I-07109, paras 39–46.

[11] Case C-395/08 *Bruno and Others* EU:C:2010:329, [2010] ECR I-05119, paras 37–39; Case C-268/06 *Impact* EU:C:2008:223, [2008] ECR I-02483.

[12] COM(2020) 682 final. See for a detailed analysis: A Aranguiz and S Garben, 'Combating income inequality in the EU: A Legal Assessment of a Potential EU Minimum Wage Directive' (2021) 46 *European Law Review* 156.

[13] Directive 2022/2041 on adequate minimum wages in the European Union [2022] OJ L 275/33.

considered 'fair', the net value of the minimum wage provided by the statutory rule of collective agreement should be compared to the net average wage.[14]

B. Collective Labour Protection in Competitive Business Environments

Apart from statutory or collectively set minimum wage levels, sectoral collective bargaining by strong, representative trade unions is generally acknowledged as the most effective instrument to lift pay levels above the minimum as well as to establish other good working conditions, and more generally as a redistribution tool and a mechanism for 'workplace democracy'.[15] There is also historical proof for this broadly supported assumption. In the first four decades of post-war democratic Europe, in all democratic countries sectoral level collective bargaining had emerged (and became then firmly rooted) as the most important collective bargaining level. As a default, both skilled and unskilled workers on standard full-time contracts were employed under the supervision and authority of one (often large) liable and responsible employer, bound by a (generally applicable) sectoral collective labour agreement. This socio-economic model brought an unprecedented increase in living standards and purchasing power of 'the working class'.[16]

Since the 1980s, a period of economic stagnation and long-term unemployment paved the way for paradigmatic changes. Under the mixed influences of deregulation, privatisation,[17] technological developments and Europeanisation, business competition intensified in virtually all sectors of the EU labour markets. Labour-intensive services and manufacturing industries, in particular, went through a cost-driven process of transformation. Both in the private sector and in the (semi-)public sector, employers started to concentrate on their 'core activities'. Large employers, including public employers, changed their organisational structure by handing over work to external contractors, belonging (or sometimes pretending to belong) to other branches, such as specialised firms and (labour-only) subcontractors, with less attractive (collective) labour standards.[18]

---

[14] More elaborate: A Aranguiz, 'Bringing the EU up to speed in the protection of living standards through fundamental social rights: Drawing positive lessons from the experience of the Council of Europe' (2021) 28(5) *Maastricht Journal of European and Comparative Law* 618.

[15] G Davidov, 'Collective Bargaining Laws: Purpose and Scope' (2004) 20 *International Journal of Comparative Labour Law and Industrial Relations* 81.

[16] This changed in 1974, when for the first time an economic crisis showed the need for social policy at European level. See B Hepple, 'The Crisis in EEC Labour Law' (1987) 16 *International Law Journal* 77.

[17] D Grimshaw et al, 'Outsourcing of public services in Europe and segmentation effects: The influence of labour market factors' (2015) 21 *European Journal of Industrial Relations* 295.

[18] Also witnessed in other parts of the world. See eg D Weil, *The Fissured Workplace: How Work Became So Bad for So Many and What Can be Done to Improve It* (Cambridge MA, Harvard University Press 2014).

VUP Group 1 workers are often employed in cleaning, private security, logistics and public care sectors in which subcontracting and outsourcing are stimulated by (public) procurement. Although they are protected against worsening labour standards because of organisational changes and restructuring by an EU social acquis originally adopted in the 1970s,[19] their jobs often became lower paid, for instance due to decentralised collective bargaining or the expiration of sectoral collective agreements without renewal. This is evidenced by recent figures, showing that the share of workers in the EU services sectors covered by a collective agreement has dropped substantially since 2010 (from 72 per cent to 66 per cent overall).[20] But also in private sectors such as the retail and food processing sectors, with a significant concentration of low-wage workers, the intensification of business competition has had a profound negative impact on working conditions.

Under the influence of this highly competitive business climate, many collective bargaining systems have become more flexible: fewer *erga omnes* extensions, more opt-out and derogation clauses, and less continuation of collective agreements on expiry. While collective bargaining is a process that lies within the autonomy of social partners, national governments can and do shape the rules of the game. Several legislative changes at national level have weakened sectoral wage bargaining, such as the erosion of the 'favour principle' or the reversal of this principle when workplace agreements have gained priority over higher-level collective agreements. Another technique is the introduction or increased use of opening clauses. Also, some Member States that used to have mechanisms of automatic continuation of collective agreements on expiry, have revised these automatic prolongations. Many but not all of these changes were part of a response to the global economic and euro area crisis (2010–2015).[21] And while some disincentives for collective bargaining have been removed or repealed since, most are still there. Here, Principle 8 EPSR seems helpful for enhancing the position of VUP Group 1, since the Pillar aims to go beyond the current social dialogue acquis enshrined in Articles 152, 154 and155 TFEU and encourage the provision of support for increased capacity of social partners to promote social dialogue, while respecting their autonomy and the right to collective action. In a context of declining collective bargaining coverage, the Commission recently proposed a Council recommendation on strengthening social dialogue in the EU with the aim to support and complement Member States in implementing said goals.[22]

---

[19] In particular (what is now) Directive 2001/23/EC on the approximation of the laws of the Member States relating to the safeguarding of employees' rights in the event of transfers of undertakings, businesses or parts of undertakings or businesses [2001] OJ L 82/16.

[20] B Egan, L Nathan and W Zwysen, *Collective bargaining for European service workers in the 21st century* (Brussels, ETUI 2021), commissioned report for UniEuropa.

[21] Especially in Southern European Member States and in Ireland.

[22] COM(2023) 38 final, based on Art 292 TFEU in conjunction with Art 153(1)(f) TFEU, requiring unanimity voting.

Moreover, Directive 2022/2041 on adequate minimum wages acknowledges sectoral and cross-industry collective bargaining as essential to enhance workers' access to minimum wage protection (Recital 16). As Member States with a small percentage of low-paid workers have collective bargaining coverage rates of more than 80 per cent (Recital 25), the Directive obliges Member States that do not achieve this threshold to provide a framework of enabling conditions either by law after consultation of the social partners or by agreement with them. Next to that, an action plan to promote collective bargaining shall be established, including a clear timeline and concrete measures to progressively increase the rate of collective bargaining coverage (Article 4(2)).

C. Interim Conclusion

VUP Group 1 workers in the lower segments of the labour market often find themselves in persistent low pay levels and poor working conditions. Here, the Directive on adequate minimum wages could have a positive impact in some sectors. Organisational changes and restructuring, often happening in sectors employing VUP Group 1 workers are covered by an EU acquis originally adopted in the 1970s. Whereas the acquis certainly provides adequate protection in many situations, the remaining jobs often became lower-paid, for instance due to decentralised collective bargaining or the expiration of sectoral collective agreements without renewal. The problems identified relate with the trend to transfer away crucial social risks from the (former) large employer to small and medium-sized enterprises (SMEs). Hence, there is a need to boost social dialogue and sectoral collective bargaining, as set out in Principle 8 of the EPSR. Promising in this regard are the measures included in the Directive on adequate minimum wages to promote collective bargaining in order to enhance workers' access to minimum wage protection, as well as the proposed Council recommendation to help strengthening social dialogue and collective bargaining at national level.

III. EU Labour Law and In-work Poverty of Flexibly Employed Workers

It took a long time before what are nowadays 'traditional' forms of atypical employment were finally regulated at the EU level. It happened through three parallel Directives concerning part-time work, fixed-term work and temporary agency work (TAW) respectively.[23] Following the at that time rather new consultation and

---

[23] Covering the VUP Group 3 workers in the Working, Yet Poor project. For an analysis of the three instruments: N Countouris, *The changing law of the employment relationship. Comparative analyses in the European context* (Abingdon, Routledge, 2007) 246–66.

negotiation model, the European Social Partners concluded two cross-industry framework agreements on part-time and on fixed-term work, which were implemented through Directives.[24] Regarding temporary agency work, however, the social partners were unable to come to an agreement and in 2001 the legislative initiative went back to the European Commission, which finally managed to get a Directive adopted in 2008.[25] By then, the EU social policy was based on the so-called 'flexicurity approach'. In this context, atypical employment was explicitly encouraged as part of an agenda to modernise 'the organisation of work, including flexible working arrangements, with the aim of making undertakings productive and competitive and achieving the required balance between flexibility and security'.[26] Below, the adequacy of the three Directives in light of the risk of in-work poverty and Principle 5 EPSR on fostering secure and adaptable employment, is explored for VUP Group 3 workers, consisting of respectively part-time workers (section III.A), fixed-term workers (section III.B) and temporary agency workers (section III.C). This is followed by a short interim conclusion (section III.D).

A. Taking Stock of the Protection of Part-Time Workers

Although Clause 1(b) of the Framework Agreement annexed to Directive 97/81 clearly expresses the aim to 'facilitate the development of part-time work on a voluntary basis', it does not really provide effective tools to distinguish between voluntary or involuntary part-time work,[27] let alone to prevent involuntary part-time work abuses. Currently, more than 20 per cent of part-time work in the EU seems to be on an involuntary basis,[28] showing that a large amount of the working population is 'under-employed' with limited opportunity to make a decent living. From the perspective of avoiding and combating in-work poverty, this is worrying. A hard substantive right to the adjustment of the number of hours worked, is not (yet) constituted at EU level; the employer is only required to consider the requests of workers to switch from part-time to full-time work and vice versa (Clause 5(3)).

Part-time work can occur in a variety of forms. It may be constituted by a reduction in normal daily working hours (horizontal part-time), or by full-time working days carried out on alternate days (vertical part-time). Moreover, marginal work can be considered a specific form of part-time employment. However, in *Wippel*,[29]

---

[24] Council Directive 97/81/EC of 15 December 1997 concerning the framework agreement on part-time work [1998] OJ L 14/9; Council Directive 1999/70/EC of 28 June 1999 concerning the framework agreement on fixed-term work [1999] OJ L 175/43.

[25] Directive 2008/104/EC of 19 November 2008 on temporary agency work [2008] OJ L 327/9.

[26] Council Resolution of 15 December 1997 on the 1998 Employment Guidelines [1998] OJ C 30/1. See C Barnard, *EC Employment Law* (Oxford, Oxford University Press, 2006) 486.

[27] The former is at the request of the employee, and the latter is at the request of the employer, see Fagan et al, *Part-time work in European companies* (Dublin, Eurofound, 2008).

[28] Eurostat figures 2017: 20.9%.

[29] Case C-313/02 *Wippel* EU:C:2004:607, [2004] ECR I-09483, para 33.

the CJEU denied on-call workers the right to equal pay based on the Part-time Workers Directive. The Court clarified that on-call workers had the freedom to refuse work; other part-time (or full-time) workers did not have this freedom, and thus it was not possible to compare on-call workers to other part-time workers. In addition, Clause 2(2) of the Directive gives Member States the option of excluding casual workers from its scope[30] and allows access to particular conditions of employment to be made subject to a period of service, time worked or to certain earnings qualifications. According to the Directive, these requirements should be reviewed periodically having regard to the principle of non-discrimination.

According to Clause 4(1), 'Part-time workers shall not be treated in a less favourable manner than comparable full-time workers solely because they work part-time unless different treatment is justified on objective grounds'. Where appropriate for part-time work, the principle of *pro rata temporis* is applied. Different treatment is established by comparing the flexible worker with a comparable regular full-time worker, in the same establishment.[31] Whenever there is no such comparable worker, reference can be made to the applicable collective labour agreement, or where there is no collective agreement, to national law, collective agreements or practice. This clause provides ample freedom for Member States. Moreover, it has been heavily criticised for making an equality claim dependent on the identification of a comparable full-time worker. In light of the rapid emergence of flexible working practices in many sectors across Member States in the last 15 years, a worker will in several situations have no effective remedy against part-time work discrimination because there is no worker who actually works full-time or who is treated as full-time worker. Hence, the requirement of a 'comparable worker' may be considered to be a flaw in the Part-time Workers Directive. Arguably, a worker should be able to underpin a part-time work discrimination claim by making a hypothetical comparison with a full-time worker.

B. Taking Stock of the Protection of Fixed-term Workers

Whereas involuntary part-time work might be precarious from a (low) pay perspective, (full-time) fixed-term contracts are risky from the perspective of job insecurity. In fixed-term contracts, the end of the employment contract is determined by objective conditions such as reaching a specific date, completing a specific task, or the occurrence of a specific event. Or, perhaps more accurately: it seems to be implied that the fair reason for the end of the labour relation is given in the economic need to adjust the size of the workforce to the demands of the market. This assumption neglects the common practice amongst employers to

---

[30] For instance, in Germany, many so-called 'mini-jobs' exist. These are jobs not exceeding a specific income threshold. In return for not being required to pay any social security contributions, mini-jobbers are only marginally covered for (some) social security risks.

[31] Clause 3(2) of the Part-time Workers Directive.

utilise possibilities for fixed-term contracts to test the functioning of the worker and to rehire only the best performing individuals. Since accepting fixed-term work contracts implies abandoning the traditional starting point of a continuous labour contract and the requirement of a fair reason for dismissal, the European Trade Union Confederation (ETUC) was keen on limiting the use of all fixed-term contracts, whereas UNICE (now Business Europe) was only in favour of limiting the renewal of successive fixed-term contracts.[32] The compromise reached in the Fixed-term Workers Directive was that both contracting parties affirmed that 'employment contracts of indefinite duration will continue to be the general form of employment relationships'.[33]

An important strong point of the Fixed-term Workers Directive is its broad personal scope. In the CJEU's case law all possible limitations to the personal scope that are not explicitly provided for in the Directive have been rejected. Hence, the Fixed-term Workers Directive applies to all fixed-term contracts with the exception of initial vocational training relationships and apprenticeship schemes (Clause 2(2)(a)), as well as contracts concluded within the framework of specific public or publicly supported training, integration and vocational retraining programmes (Clause 2(2)(b)).

The framework agreements on part-time and fixed-term work have in common that they both seek to realise their goals by applying the principle of equal treatment. Discrimination with regard to employment conditions is forbidden, unless different treatment is objectively justified (Clause 4 of both Directives). Different treatment is established by comparing the fixed-term and/or part-time worker with a comparable regular worker, which poses the problem of finding a standard and/or full-time worker with comparable responsibilities and experience. This became very clear in a number of CJEU cases invoked by fixed-term workers in the public sector,[34] particularly in Member States that were heavily affected by budgetary constraints due to the financial economic crisis of 2008–2012, which forced them to reorganise their public administrations. This required, *inter alia*, a certain flexibility regarding new hires and employment policies. As such, many Member States moved from a traditional model of hiring civil servants on full-time indefinite contract basis to fixed-term contracts (ie involuntary transitions from VUP Group 1 to VUP Group 3). The cases brought before the Court showed the limitations of applying the principle of equality laid down in the Fixed-term Workers Directive. These limitations relate to the impossibility of comparing different categories of fixed-term workers, the absence of a full-time comparator,

---

[32] M Schlachter (ed), *EU Labour Law. A commentary* (Alphen aan den Rijn, Kluwer Law International, 2015), 226.

[33] Directive 1999/70, Preamble, recital 1; general considerations to the Framework Agreement, para 6.

[34] Case C-443/16 *Rodrigo Sanz* EU:C:2017:109; Case C-158/16 *Vega González* EU:C:2017:1014; Case C-596/14 *de Diego Porras I* EU:C:2016:683; Case C-677/17 *Montero Mateos* EU:C:2018:393; Case C-574/16 *Grupo Norte Facility* EU:C:2018:390; Case C-619/17 *de Diego Porras II* EU:C:2018:936; Case C-245/17 *Viejobueno Ibáñez* EU:C:2018:934.

and the broad possibilities for Member States to justify different treatment on the basis of public policy.[35]

In terms of combating abuse, part of the compromise between the European Social Partners was that the Fixed-term Workers Directive does not require an objective economical reason for the agreement of a (first) fixed-term contract. However, the Directive prohibits the abuse of successive fixed-term contracts and demands of the Member States to take legal measures to prevent abuse. More specifically, it requires the Member States to take measures on the following matters: to require objective justifications for renewal; to set a maximum duration of successive fixed-term employment contracts; or limit the number of renewals of such contracts or relationships. Further, the Directive requires Member States to define under what conditions fixed-term contracts can be defined as successive and clarify when they shall be deemed contracts of indefinite duration (Clause 5(2)).

Nevertheless, limiting the number of successive fixed-term contracts has little effect in low-wage sectors where workers can easily be replaced by other workers (jobs requiring low skills) and where the costs of recruiting and training new workers are low. This explains why the Court has in the past been confronted with the question of whether national authorities were doing enough to prevent abuse.[36] As the Court has reiterated several times, Member States have considerable discretion when preventing the abuse of successive fixed-term contracts and the Fixed-term Workers Directive neither requires employers to convert fixed-term contracts into contracts of indefinite duration nor compensate for the lack of such conversion.[37] With regard to renewal, the CJEU clarified that objective justifications can be found in the presence of specific factors relating in particular to the precise and concrete circumstances characterising a given activity. These circumstances may, according to the CJEU, lie in the specific nature of the tasks and the inherent characteristics of those tasks or from pursuit of a legitimate social-policy objective of a Member State. The CJEU clearly ruled in *Adeneler* that the mere fact that the use of fixed-term contracts is provided for in national law cannot constitute an objective reason for a succession of fixed-term contracts.[38] With regard to the question when fixed-term contracts can be considered to be successive and when not, the CJEU explained that the period between the contracts must be taken into account. Otherwise, in practice, the worker would be obliged to accept breaks in the course of a series of contracts with the employer, in order to avoid these being successive contracts. In any case, 20 days was deemed too short for such a period. Moreover, in this ruling the Court took into account the rationale of employment stability and job security behind the prohibition of

---

[35] See for an elaborate analysis: A van der Mei, 'Fixed-Term work: Recent developments in the case law of the Court of Justice of the European Union' (2020) 11 *European Labour Law Journal* 66.

[36] Case C-268/06 *Impact* ECLI: EU: C:2008:223, [2008] ECR I-02483, para 68.

[37] For example, Case C-494/16 *Santoro* ECLI: EU: C:2018:166, paras 26–28.

[38] Case C-212/04 *Adeneler and others* EU:C:2006:443, [2006] ECR I-06057.

misuse (namely that an employment contract for indefinite duration remains the standard).[39]

Whereas the Court had previously recognised that some sectors, because of their nature, may require fixed-term contracts to be used more frequently,[40] in *Sciotto*, it was not convinced by the arguments of the Italian government.[41] Italian legislation, by excluding an entire sector from this guarantee, was deemed to breach the Fixed-term Workers Directive.[42] In *Sánchez Ruiz*, the CJEU ruled that national practices that consider the succession of fixed-term contracts as justified when the employer (the public administration) uses these contracts for permanent and structural needs is contrary to Clause 5 of the Fixed-term Workers Directive.[43] In another case from Spain, the CJEU considered the use of specific temporary contracts to cover job positions in the Spanish public sector where the selection process (public competitions) for a permanent contract was not yet finalised. The CJEU found this to be in breach of the Fixed-term Workers Directive, as these contracts could be used for an indefinite (and unpredictable) period of time (in practice they were sometimes extended for decades). Moreover, the national scheme did not include any measure to prevent and/or sanction the abuse of these temporary contracts, such as conversion into permanent contracts, or compensation at the end of the contract.[44]

The abundant litigation on the Fixed-term Workers Directive shows mixed outcomes. Despite sometimes robust judgments of the Court, the Directive currently does not meet the promise enshrined in Principle 5 EPSR of fostering not only adaptable but also secure employment (which is crucial to reduce the risk of in-work poverty).

C. Taking Stock of the Protection of Temporary Agency Workers

What makes temporary agency work even more 'atypical' and controversial than part-time and fixed-term contracts, is that three instead of two parties are involved: the temporary work agency (TWA) is the formal employer while the agency worker is employed at the premises of a 'user company'. Similar to the Part-time and Fixed-term Workers Directives, in the TAW Directive national law is supposed to define the notions of 'contract of employment, employment relationship or worker'.[45] However, in the case *Ruhrlandklinik*, the CJEU rejected the

---

[39] ibid.
[40] Case C-238/14 *Commission v Luxembourg* EU:C:2015:128, para 51.
[41] Case C-331/17 *Sciotto* EU:C:2018:859, para 45.
[42] ibid paras 47–54.
[43] Joined cases C-103/18 and C-429/18 *Sánchez Ruiz* EU:C:2020:219, para 80.
[44] Case C-726/19 *Instituto Madrileño de Investigación y Desarrollo Rural, Agrario y Alimentario* EU:C:2021:439, para 88.
[45] See Arts 1(1) and 3(1)(a) of the TAW Directive.

limitation of the concept of 'worker' to persons falling within the scope of that concept under national law, and in particular, to those who have a contract of employment with the TWA, since such a restrictive approach would undermine the effectiveness of the Directive by 'inordinately and unjustifiably' limiting its scope of application.[46]

In contrast to the Part-time and Fixed-term Workers Directives, the principle of equal treatment (Article 5(1) of the TAW Directive) only applies to 'basic working and employment conditions',[47] laid down by legislation or collective agreements in force in the user undertaking. Clearly, this wording reveals a more limited application of the equal treatment principle than enshrined in the two framework agreement Directives on atypical work. On the other hand, the TAW Directive does not explicitly refer to possible justification of differences on 'objective grounds'. This implies a stricter requirement to guarantee this equal treatment obligation than in the Part-time and Fixed-term Workers Directives, since departure from the equality principle in the TAW Directive should only be possible if situations are not comparable. Moreover, the TAW Directive 'only' requires a hypothetical comparator. This means that regarding the provision on equal treatment one needs only to think about the conditions that 'would have applied' if the temporary agency worker would have been directly recruited by the undertaking. As compared to the other Directives, this facilitates the application of equal treatment.

As part of the difficult compromise to get the TAW Directive adopted, Article 5 provides several possibilities for Member States to deviate from the principle of equal treatment. Regarding one of the derogation options, the Court has recently clarified the obligation for social partners to respect the 'overall protection of temporary agency workers' when making use of it. According to the Court, a collective agreement which offers lower pay to agency workers compared to workers recruited directly by the user company must provide for countervailing benefits which compensate for the difference in treatment they suffer with comparable workers in the user undertaking, based on a concrete assessment for a given job.[48] As a consequence of this ruling, Member States that have made use of this derogation[49] must now examine how the 'overall protection' of temporary agency workers under Article 5(3) is ensured in their national systems, and either amend their legislation on this point, if necessary, or ensure that the social partners introduce the necessary provisions by means of an agreement subject to judicial review to determine whether the social partners have fulfilled their obligation to respect the overall protection of such workers.[50]

---

[46] Case C-216/15 *Betriebsrat der Ruhrlandklinik* EU:C:2016:883.

[47] Pursuant to Art 3(1)(f) this notion refers to working time, holidays and pay. The Court has favoured a broad interpretation. See Case C-681/18 *KG* EU:C:2020:823, para 54; Case C-426/20 *Luso Temp* EU:C:2022:373, para 40.

[48] Case C-311/21 *TimePartner Personalmanagement* EU:C:2022:983, paras 49–50.

[49] A decade ago, 10 Member States provided for this possibility in their national legislation, see COM(2014) 176 final, 7.

[50] Case C-311/21 *TimePartner Personalmanagement* EU:C:2022:983, paras 62, 67, 79.

Member States have different traditions in allowing or limiting the use of temporary agency work. In a number of Member States, some limitations on TAW have been lifted in recent years.[51] In others, limitations have been imposed by collective agreements, usually on sectoral level. This practice was contested in the *AKT* case.[52] However, the CJEU held that national authorities remain free to remove the prohibitions or restrictions that are not justified or to amend them in a way that they are compliant with the Directive. Hence, Article 4(1) of the TAW Directive ought to be understood as an obligation to review the legal framework on temporary agency work but does not require any specific legislation to be adopted.[53]

Despite its vague wording and notwithstanding the ambiguity in relation to the text of Article 4, in its Article 5(5) the TAW Directive clearly requires Member States to take measures against misuse in the application of Article 5, and in particular, to prevent successive assignments designed to circumvent the provisions of this Directive. In *KG*[54] the Court held that Article 5(5) does not preclude national legislation which does not limit the number of successive assignments that the same temporary agency worker may carry out in the same user undertaking and which does not make the lawfulness of the use of TAW subject to technical, production, organisational or replacement reasons justifying such use.[55] The Court confirmed the above discussed *AKT* case, where the CJEU held that the restriction and prohibitions on the use of temporary agency work does not entail an obligation for Member States to adopt a specific legislation, and this also applies regarding provisions to prevent abuse.

At the same time, the Court acknowledged the importance of the dual objective pursued by the Directive which is designed to reconcile the objective of flexibility sought by undertakings and the objective of security corresponding to the protection of workers.[56] Referring to recital 15 of the TAW Directive, which states that employment contracts for an indefinite term are the general form of employment, the Court elaborates that the twofold objective expresses the intention to bring the conditions of temporary agency work closer to 'normal' employment relationships. The TAW Directive therefore also aims to stimulate temporary agency workers' access to permanent employment at the user undertaking, an objective reflected in particular in Article 6(1) and (2) of the Directive, while the principle of equal treatment, as laid down in Article 5(1), contributes to that objective.[57]

---

[51] Cf A Sartori, 'Temporary Agency Work in Europe: Degree of Convergence following Directive 2008/104/EU' (2016) *European Labour Law Journal* 117.

[52] Case C-533/13 *AKT* EU:C:2015:173, para 14.

[53] ibid paras 29–31.

[54] Case C-681/18 *KG* EU: C: 2021: 823.

[55] ibid para 72.

[56] ibid para 50.

[57] ibid paras 51–52; confirmed and elaborated upon in Case C-426/20 *Luso Temp* EU:C:2022:373, para 43, 47.

Particularly, the CJEU held that Article 5(5) should be interpreted as an obligation for Member States to ensure that employment through a temporary employment agency with the same user undertaking does not become a permanent situation for the temporary worker.[58] Here, the Court emphasised that, based on the definitions provided in the TAW Directive 'the employment relationship with a user undertaking is, by its very nature, temporary'.[59] For the purposes of 'assisting' the referring court in its review of 'temporariness' the CJEU offered a number of points to take into consideration. First, whether or not the successive assignments result in a period of service that is longer than what can be reasonably regarded as 'temporary'.[60] Second, whether these successive contracts circumvent the very essence of the provisions of the TAW Directive and amount to misuse of that form of employment relationship, 'since they upset the balance struck by that directive between flexibility for employers and security for workers by undermining the latter'.[61] Lastly, the Court considered that where no objective explanation is given for the decision of the user undertaking concerned to have recourse to a series of successive temporary agency contracts, the national court will have to see if any provisions of the TAW Directive have been circumvented, especially where the series of contracts in question has assigned the same temporary agency worker to the user undertaking.[62]

However, in a follow-up case, the CJEU held that the word 'temporarily' is not intended to limit the application of temporary agency work to posts that would not exist on a long-term basis, because the notion of temporariness refers not to the job held at the user undertaking, but to the circumstances under which a worker is assigned to this undertaking.[63] This seems to confirm that temporary agency work can indeed be used to meet a permanent need of the user undertaking. Moreover, in absence of a sanction in national law of an employment relationship being presumed between the worker and the user company when the working relationship is no longer considered temporary, the Court ruled that no such individual right to an employment relationship with the user company can be derived from the TAW Directive.[64]

The ambiguous outcomes of case law on the TAW Directive reflect the vague and sometimes contradictory wording of its main provisions. It is positive that the Court recently reminded the Member States that derogations cannot undermine 'the overall protection' of temporary agency workers and that they have to act where (other) flexicurity promises are not met, such as when TAW fails to be a stepping stone to more secure employment in line with Principle 5 of the EPSR.

---

[58] ibid para 60.
[59] ibid para 61.
[60] ibid para 69.
[61] ibid.
[62] ibid para 70.
[63] Case C-232/20 *Daimler* EU:C:2022:196, paras 36–38.
[64] ibid para 100.

D. Interim Conclusion

The three Directives on atypical work recognise on the one hand the *status aparte* of flexibly employed workers in comparison with standard workers in relation to their rights on job protection and full-time work, and on the other hand, stress the importance of the application of the principle of equal treatment and the need for supplementary protection. However, in certain sectors and Member States flexible working practices have spread to such an extent that the VUP Group 3 workers run the risk of having no effective remedy against unequal treatment because there is no worker who actually works full-time or permanently.

In the case of the Fixed-term Workers Directive, and to a lesser extent also the TAW Directive, the EU acquis also contributes to fighting abuses in the use of said atypical contracts. Yet, there remain important obstacles. The provisions on fighting abuses of fixed-term and TAW contracts offer limited protection since Member States still enjoy considerable leeway not only on how, but also to what extent they choose to fight abuses. In addition, a number of provisions allow Member States or social partners to limit the scope of application by, for example, excluding casual workers, such as in the Part-time Workers Directive, thereby effectively limiting minimum protection for a considerable part of the workforce. Moreover, without distinguishing actual involuntary part-time from voluntary part-time work, this type of contract limits the opportunities for workers to make a decent living. The lack of an anti-abuse clause in the Part-time Workers Directive ignores the existence of involuntary part-time workers, who have no real alternative which would enable them to access a full-time position.

In its Principle 5, the EPSR emphasises the right to secure and adaptable employment, which requires support for transitions towards open-ended employment relationships. Moreover, the EPSR states that regardless of the type and duration of the employment relationship, workers have the right to fair and equal treatment regarding working conditions, access to social protection and training. In the last decades, as a result of the widespread of atypical employment contracts, this promise has been broken as there is an increasing in-work poverty trap amongst atypical workers due to the lack of transition chances. Hence, it is clear that the atypical work Directives are in need of improvement. For instance, a right to conversion into more secure contracts after a succession of fixed-term and temporary agency contracts could be created. In light of the difficult genesis of said Directives, this is however much easier said than done for the EU legislator.

IV. EU Labour Law and In-work Poverty of Self-employed, Casual and Platform Workers

One of the general aims of the EPSR was to respond to increasingly prominent labour trends such as those covered by (bogus) self-employment, casual and platform workers. This is why Principle 5 of the EPSR commits to extend the guarantee of equal treatment beyond the three forms of 'traditional' flexible employment relationships discussed in the previous section and to provide for equal treatment between workers irrespective of the type of employment relationship. Because the current regulatory framework relies heavily on a relatively strict dichotomy between the status of workers (employees) and the self-employed, the existing legislation does not always apply to those groups who do not qualify as workers, or fall somewhere in between this rigid dichotomy. However, those groups might be covered by a selected number of instruments but only insofar as the personal scope of these instruments is interpreted broadly by the relevant courts. For the existing rules to apply and thus grant these groups an adequate protection, it is therefore essential to not misclassify them. The following sections explore this issue respectively for VUP Group 2 workers (section IV.A) and VUP Group 4 workers (section IV.B). The section finishes with an interim conclusion in section IV.C.

A. Taking Stock of the Protection of (Dependent or Bogus) Solo Self-employed Persons

According to recent surveys, the proportion of solo self-employed workers as a share of all workers in the EU, has stabilised, but at the same time its composition has shifted. A decline of self-employment in agriculture has been compensated by increased proportions of self-employed workers in the services sector and public sector. Moreover, there has been a significant increase in workers registered as solo self-employed in about half of the Member States (eg Greece and the Netherlands), while the percentage significantly decreased in others (eg Poland, Portugal and Italy).[65] Moreover, many of the solo self-employed in lower segments of the labour market appear to be bogus or dependent self-employed.[66]

In *FNV Kunsten*, the Court was confronted with a situation of false self-employment in the context of competition law. The Court confirmed that the status of 'worker' within the meaning of EU law is not affected by the fact that the individual at stake has been hired as a self-employed under national law as long as the person acts under the direction of their employer with regard to: the freedom to choose the time, place and content of the work,[67] does not share the commercial risks,[68] and for the duration of that relationship, forms an integral part of that

---

[65] G Vermeylen et al, *Exploring self-employment in the European Union* (Eurofound 2017, updated in 2021).

[66] See C Schubert (ed), *Economically-dependent Workers as Part of a Decent Economy. International, European and Comparative Perspective. A Handbook* (Beck and Hart Publishing 2022).

[67] Case C-413/13 *FNV Kunsten* EU:C:2014:2411, para 36; Case C-256/01 *Allonby* EU:C:2004:18, [2004] ECR I-00873, para 72.

[68] Case C-3/87 *Agegate* EU:C:1989:650, [1989] ECR 04459, para 36.

employer's undertaking, so forming an economic unit with that undertaking.[69] Prior to this judgment, the CJEU had ruled that EU competition rules do not extend to collective agreements made in negotiations between the social partners when they serve the purpose of improving the employment conditions of workers.[70] In *FNV Kunsten* the Court took this a step further and ruled that just because someone is considered a self-employed person by national law, it does not preclude collective agreements concluded on their behalf for the purpose of improving their working conditions from falling within the competition law exception provided for in *Albany*.[71]

Applied to the exception on the application of competition rules, what the Court essentially did is to not deprive those service providers in a situation comparable to that of workers from the same protection that EU law offers to workers. This could in principle be extrapolated to other circumstances which would mean that, effectively, people in the VUP Group 2 could be protected by the same EU law rules as workers. In fact, the recent Directive on transparent and predictable working conditions[72] specifically excludes genuine self-employment from its application but dictates that bogus self-employment should be covered and that 'the determination of the existence of an employment relationship should be guided by the facts relating to the actual performance of the work and not by the parties' description of the relationship' (Recital 8). However, because most of the secondary legislation refers to the national definition of worker, it is ultimately up to the national courts to determine whether a person is a worker. In this vein, national courts have a duty to apply the objective criteria enshrined in the case law of the CJEU, which must not be interpreted narrowly.

B. Taking Stock of the Protection of Casual and Platform Workers

Regarding VUP Group 4, on-call, zero-hours (or other casual) employment manifests several of the quintessential characteristics of in-work poverty. First, the worker's annual income is often quite low, since the employer has no obligation to offer the individual any working hours *at all*. This kind of employment is, at best, irregular and unreliable; at worst, it is a sham. Currently, their household composition might shield zero-hour workers from poverty, but this means that they are not economically independent and therefore vulnerable to divorces or

---

[69] Case C-22/98 *BECU* EU:C:1999:419, [1999] ECR I-05665, para 26.

[70] Case C-413/13 *FNV Kunsten* EU:C:2014:2411, paras 27-30.

[71] For those assessed as 'genuine' self-employed, a positive development is the Communication of the European Commission, issuing: *Guidelines on the application of Union competition law to collective agreements regarding the working conditions of solo self-employed persons* (2022/C 374/02).

[72] Directive (EU) 2019/1152 on transparent and predictable working conditions in the European Union [2019] OJ L 186/105.

other personal life events which might undermine their economic 'safety'. Clearly, the lacking guarantee of a set number of hours of work makes it very difficult to achieve a stable and decent standard of living for a zero-hour worker who has an entire household to support. This is all the more so, since such casual workers are frequently low-paid and collective bargaining is particularly lacking in sectors where zero-hours contracts are most prevalent (eg personal services, such as retail, hospitality and health-care related branches). Lack of contact with other, similarly situated individuals (frequently due to the absence of a common workplace) further inhibits the enhancement of working conditions through unionisation.

At the moment of writing,[73] there are no specific EU labour law instruments addressing this segment of the workforce. However, a number of other instruments could in fact apply when casual workers are classified as workers. Much like in the case of the dependent or bogus solo self-employed (VUP Group 2), the lack of labour protection for this group is often a problem of misclassification that emanates from the national definition of worker. For example, the atypical employment Directives discussed in section III (part-time, fixed-term and TAW) refer to the national definition of worker and, accordingly, may exclude casual workers. However, where casual workers fit into the national definition of worker, they may be protected by such instruments. In contrast to VUP Group 2, however, those in VUP Group 4 often carry out micro-tasks and, as a consequence, their activity may be regarded ancillary or marginal.[74] And yet, the broad EU definition of worker has already generously factored in a number of characteristics that are innate to casual workers. The Court has confirmed, *inter alia*, that short duration[75] or discontinuity of work,[76] low-productivity[77] or limited hours[78] cannot prevent individuals from gaining the status of worker. In addition, the nature and type of employment do not affect the overall assessment of establishing the status of worker. Either way, supposing that casual workers are in fact considered workers and may thus fall under the scope of the existing employment regulations, there is an additional burden to be satisfied for the enjoyment of the atypical work Directives: the need of a comparator. As discussed in section III, both the Part-time and the Fixed-term Workers Directives require a comparable full-time and/or standard worker from the same establishment, which for many of the employment relationships in casual work may prove virtually impossible.[79] Thus,

---

[73] Exception made from the pending proposal for a Directive to improve the working conditions in platform work: COM(2021) 762 final.

[74] Case 53/81 *Levin* EU:C:1982:105, [1982] ECR 01035, para 17.

[75] Case C-413/01 *Ninni-Orasche* EU:C:2003:600, [2003] ECR I-13187, para 32.

[76] Case C-357/89 *Raulin* EU:C:1992:887, [1992] ECR I-01027, para 14.

[77] Case 344/87 *Bettray* EU:C:1989:226, [1989] ECR 01621, paras 15–16.

[78] Case C-46/12 *LN* EU:C:2013:97, para 41.

[79] Opinion of Advocate General Kokott in Case C-313/02 *Wippel* EU:C:2004:308, [2004] ECR I-09483, para 45; Case C-307/05 *Del Cerro Alonso* EU:C:2007:509, [2007] ECR I-07109; joined Cases C-378/07 to C-380/07 *Angelidaki and Others* EU:C:2009:250, [2009] ECR I-03071.

even if the Directives can apply, due to the lack of a comparator it would not be possible to determine when there is a violation of the prohibition of discrimination. In this vein, Bell argues in favour of introducing a hypothetical comparator to these Directives.[80]

Meanwhile, the EU institutions seem to have picked up on the problems arising from the misclassification of the workforce and its particular adverse effect on casual workers. In 2016 the Commission encouraged Member States to follow the EU concept of worker that emanates from the case law of the CJEU and see that those working on the collaborative economy are adequately classified and are entitled to the rights that emanate from that position. More importantly, recent legal initiatives in the EU have incorporated a hybrid definition of worker mixing the EU concept and the national definition of worker. An exemplary Directive is the Directive on transparent and predictable working conditions which applies to 'every worker in the Union who has an employment contract of employment relationship as defined by law, collective agreements with consideration to the case-law of the CJEU' (Article 1.2). This innovative hybrid notion of worker is new and has been included as well in the Work-Life Balance Directive[81] and the Directive on adequate minimum wages.[82] Because of the broad interpretation of worker in the case law of the CJEU, these Directives are less controversially going to grant ample room to the Court to expand this definition to more casual forms of work. In fact, Recital 8 of the Directive on transparent and predictable working conditions establishes that 'provided that they fulfil those criteria, domestic workers, on-demand workers, intermittent workers, voucher based-workers, platform workers, trainees and apprentices could fall within the scope of this Directive'. However, the Directive only applies where there is an 'employment relationship with predetermined and actual working hours that amount to an average of three hours per week' (Recital 11 and Article 1).

As for its material scope, the Directive on transparent and predictable working conditions grants workers the right to obtain more complete information about their employment relationship. Such information ought to be presented within a week (essential information) or a month (supplementary information) from the start of the employment relationship (Chapter II of the Directive). The Directive also imposes a limit on the length of probationary periods of six months unless a longer period can objectively be justified (Article 8). Moreover, the Directive protects workers' parallel employment outside the work schedule

---

[80] M Bell, 'Achieving the Objectives of the Part-Time Work Directive? Revisiting the Part-Time Workers Regulations' (2011) 40 *Industrial Law Journal* 254.

[81] Directive (EU) 2019/1158 on work-life balance for parents and carers [2019] OJ L 188/79. On the two 2019 Directives, which had to be implemented ultimately in August 2022, see B Bednarowicz, 'The tale of transparent and predictable working conditions intertwined with work-life balance: Assessing the impact of the new social policy directives on decent working conditions and social protection' (2020) 22(4) *European Journal of Social Security* 421.

[82] Directive 2022/2041 on adequate minimum wages has not been implemented yet.

established by the employer by prohibiting the use of exclusivity clauses and imposing a limit on the use of incompatibility clauses (Article 9). On top of this, the Directive establishes that outside the agreed working hours, workers retain the full right to refuse to be called in to work, enjoy protection against unfair treatment, and have a right to compensation when the employer cancels a work assignment after a specific deadline (Article 9). Worth noting in particular for the subject of this chapter is the specific clause on Article 11 that covers on-demand work. According to this, those working on-demand enjoy protection against abusive practices which is embodied in either a limitation in the use and duration of on-demand contracts and/or in a rebuttable presumption of an employment contract with a minimum number of paid hours that is based on an average calculated on the basis of a given period. Important for VUP Group 4 and VUP Group 3 workers alike, the Directive also encompasses the right to request a more stable form of employment and to receive a justified written reply, although there is no obligation for the employer to offer a stable contract.

C. Interim Conclusion

The protection offered by the EU acquis to VUP Groups 2 and 4 is very marginal. As regards VUP Group 2, (bogus or dependent) solo self-employed workers lack in principle any protection by EU labour law altogether, although the CJEU has addressed the issue of false self-employment by rejecting the limiting of the scope of protection based solely on a nominal reasoning. Instead, the Court focuses on the activities that are being carried out by the individual concerned. In the case of VUP Group 4, concerning casual and platform workers, some recent EU labour law instruments could in principle provide some protection, but this protection does not address category-specific problems and is, moreover, underpinned by a number of conditionals. The proposal for a Directive on platform work is, nevertheless, a promising path. In sum, the EU labour harmonisation acquis regarding VUP Groups 2 and 4 is still in its infancy. In particular, no EU instrument addresses directly (yet) the more and more frequent combination of self-employment with very short periods of (employed) work, and low remuneration, nor the consequences they have on the social security of these workers. As a result, it is mostly for national laws and courts to decide, in labour relation conflicts, whether the contracts involved are employment contracts submitted to labour law.

V. Summary of Findings and Concluding Remarks

The findings of the analysis in this chapter appear to be mixed. For low-wage standard workers (VUP Group 1) the risk of in-work poverty is lower than for the other groups and can be further diminished by recently adopted and proposed measures in line with the aims of Principles 6 and 8 of the EPSR. For flexibly employed workers (VUP Group 3), the guarantees offered by the atypical work Directives are too minimalistic to grant the necessary protection promised by Principle 5 of the EPSR, despite some relevant developments in case law. In the cases of dependent or bogus solo self-employed workers (VUP Group 2), casual and platform workers (VUP Group 4), little to no protection was found. Hence, harmonisation for these groups is still in its infancy and so far unable to cope with the increasingly dynamic world of work trends. Nonetheless, there is also reason to be positive, as some more recent developments aim at changing this reality.

To overcome the described shortcomings, it is submitted that a strategic intervention is necessary along two axes. On the one hand, the market-correcting characteristics of the EU harmonised labour law acquis should be strengthened, which inevitably means that the market-facilitating features of this social acquis will be (relatively) diminished, especially concerning vulnerable workers. Such approach is necessary to reinforce the protective power of EU labour law. The steps that are currently set in the framework of the EPSR go in the right direction. On the other hand, EU law in (core) economic policy domains sometimes negatively affect the chances of the four VUP Groups to access fair and just working conditions and stable employment perspectives. This asks for a consistent and genuine operationalisation of the so-called horizontal social clause in Article 9 TFEU,[83] requiring the EU legislature and policymakers to consider the objectives of social protection, social inclusion and of high levels of (good quality) employment into all its policy initiatives, instead of limiting this to the scope of its social policy only.[84]

---

[83] Exemplary in this regard, in Case C-620/18 *Hungary v Parliament and Council* EU:C:2020:1001, paras 26–48, the Court rules that Art 53(1) and Art 62 TFEU empowering the EU legislature to coordinate national rules which may, by reason of their heterogeneity, impede the freedom to provide services between Member States, cannot entail that that legislature need not also ensure due regard for, inter alia, the overarching objectives laid down in Art 9 TFEU.

[84] In essence, the twofold strategy boils down to a consistent and coherent exercising of labour and social rights in line with EU internal market law and the other way around. If there is a conflict between those rights, mutual optimisation of those rights will have to be achieved. See eg D Schieck et al, *EU Social and Labour Rights and EU Internal Market Law* (Brussels, European Parliament Policy Department A Study, 2015), 89; A Aranguiz, 'Social mainstreaming through the European pillar of social rights: Shielding "the social" from 'the economic' in EU policymaking' (2018) 20 *European Journal of Social Security* 341.

4

In-work Poverty and the Gender Paradox

MARTA CAPESCIOTTI AND ROBERTA PAOLETTI

I. Gendering the Approach to In-work Poverty

The possibility of being poor while working is now an undisputed fact: the grow-ing number of people at risk of falling below the poverty line despite having a job is alarming. This is a trend that has now attracted the attention of authoritative scholars and on which numerous analyses have now been conducted. Too often, though, this high-quality analysis still adopts a gender-neutral – or better said, gender-blind – approach to in-work poverty. This is despite the fact that labour market conditions, like poverty, are not at all gender-neutral: an awareness that has now been acquired and has made it possible to develop and adopt gender policies specifically combating these phenomena of discrimination.

Besides being an integral component of social relations based on perceived and regulated differences between men and women, gender represents an axis of power that translates into unequal access to opportunities and resources. The term 'gendering the workplace' refers, therefore, to a process of visualising how gender influences individuals' interaction within the workplace itself: the attribution of characteristics of masculinity or femininity has an impact on each individual's level of access to opportunities and resources, due to the structural privilege enjoyed by one of the two poles of the gender spectrum: the male.

In fact, gender and gender equality are crucial issues at stake in EU legislation and policies. Article 119 of the Treaty establishing the European Community (EEC Treaty),[1] now Article 157 of the Treaty on the Functioning of the European Union (TFEU),[2] addressing in particular equal opportunities and equal treatment of men and women in employment, already provided for the principle of equal pay for equal work or work of equal value. Furthermore, gender equality is fully enshrined as one of the EU's common values and inscribed in Articles 2 and 3(3) of the Treaty

---

[1] Treaty establishing the European Community (Consolidated version 2002) [2002] OJ C 325/33.
[2] Consolidated version of the Treaty on the Functioning of the European Union [2012] OJ C 326/47.

on European Union (TEU),[3] which stipulate that the EU should actively promote gender equality. It is also an integral part of the EU Charter of Fundamental Rights,[4] now a primary component of the EU treaties: Articles 21 and 23 prohibit discrimination on any ground, including gender, and require equality between men and women to be ensured in all areas, including work and pay, recognising the need for positive action to promote it. Several directives adopted by the EU between 2002 and 2019 set out the framework for gender equality in Europe, stipulating that EU Member States must make operational one or more bodies responsible for the promotion of gender equality and take appropriate measures to strengthen the dialogue between the social partners in order to promote equal treatment. The EU Member States also commit themselves to the production of comparable statistics disaggregated by gender, analysing them and making them available for a better understanding of the unequal treatment of men and women in employment and work-life balance.

Additionally, one remark concerning intersectionality must be put forward before continuing the analysis. To achieve a thorough perspective of in-work poverty through a gender-sensitive lens, the assumption that women are a homogenous group needs to be deconstructed. On the opposite, each woman copes with a specific form of discrimination on grounds of gender but, at the same time, she potentially faces other drivers of discrimination on grounds of, for instance, nationality, ethnic origin, age, sexual orientation, gender identity or disability. These are not separate components; rather, they intersect resulting in so-called 'multiple discrimination'.[5] The Gender Equality Strategy 2020–2025 explicitly recognises that the intersectionality of gender with other grounds of discrimination must be addressed across EU policies.[6] This is because '[wo]men are a heterogeneous group and may face intersectional discrimination based on several personal characteristics'.[7] For instance, a migrant woman with a disability may face discrimination on three or more grounds, because of her gender, because of her migration background, and because of her disability. As per the participation in the labour market, the European Commission's strategy acknowledges that, although women's employment rate in the EU is higher today than ever before, barriers remain for many women in terms of access to, and conditions of, employment. This structural underrepresentation is the result of the intersection of gender with additional conditions of vulnerability. In general terms, gender seems to intensify the disadvantages and discrimination associated with inequalities and social

---

[3] Consolidated version of the Treaty on European Union [2012] OJ C 326/13.

[4] Charter of Fundamental Rights of the European Union [2012] OJ C 326/391.

[5] The European Institute for Gender Equality (EIGE) defines multiple discriminations as any combination of forms of discrimination against persons on the grounds of sex, racial or ethnic origin, religion or belief, disability, age, sexual orientation, gender identity or other characteristics, and to discrimination suffered by those who have, or who are perceived to have, those characteristics.

[6] Communication from the Commission to the European Parliament, the Council, the European Economic and Social Committee and the Committee of the Regions, *A Union of Equality: Gender Equality Strategy 2020–2025*, COM/2020/152 final, eur-lex.europa.eu/legal-content/EN/TXT/?uri=CE LEX%3A52020DC0152.

[7] ibid 16.

identities that can also affect men. However, the multiplier effect of intersecting forms of discrimination is hard to capture and measure since statistical analysis on this issue is scarce and still marginal, compared with the analysis focusing on single-issue discrimination. The issue of intersectionality will not be dealt with in further detail in this chapter: however, it represents a pivotal driver of further research strands in the in-work poverty domain.

Most of the available literature on in-work poverty is focused on the impact of household composition on the working poor, considering income or consumption. However, the role of unpaid domestic and family care activities and the effective access of women to the household's financial resources are often overlooked and blurred in the overall household balance.[8] In view of this, the aim of this contribution is thus to broaden the reflection on the gender dimensions that affect the phenomenon of in-work poverty, starting from the observation of a basic bias that characterises the approach generally applied to this major issue. In fact, in-work poverty is analysed and measured by taking the household as the point of reference and adopting the minimum family income as the focal point. Such an approach not only risks failing to capture the specific challenges faced by working women and the consequent falling back into in-work poverty, but also assumes without actually having demonstrated it (and perhaps not even being able to demonstrate) that there is equal access assured to economic resources and material goods among the members of each household. Adopting a gender-sensitive approach to poverty and economic inequalities is crucial not only for reasons of general social justice, but also in order to gain a more comprehensive understanding of poverty, its causes and its consequences.[9]

This chapter will attempt to account for the fallacy of this assumption, starting with the analysis of other gender-disaggregated indicators that monitor the status of men and women in the labour market and in the management of family needs, first and foremost the distribution of care burden, and questioning the repercussions of the lack of an unambiguous definition of household at European level in terms of monitoring and assessing in-work poverty.

II. Gender and Labour Market: Which Working Conditions for Women and for Men?

Preliminarily, it is necessary to consider the position of women in the labour market in Europe. The differences between men and women in this area concern

---

[8] J Liu, 'What Does In-Work Poverty Mean for Women: Comparing the Gender Employment Segregation in Belgium and China' (2019) 11(20) *Sustainability* 5725, 5–7, www.mdpi.com/2071-1050/11/20/5725 (last accessed 23 February 2023).

[9] UN WOMEN, *Gender equality and poverty are intrinsically linked: A contribution to the continued monitoring of selected Sustainable Developments Goals*, 2018, p 1, www.unwomen.org/sites/default/files/Headquarters/Attachments/Sections/Library/Publications/2018/Discussion-paper-Gender-equality-and-poverty-are-intrinsically-linked-en.pdf (last accessed 23 February 2023).

both the extent of participation and the quality of the conditions of access to the labour market.

Regarding the first aspect, the EU average shows that the proportion of employed women in the workforce is not equal to the proportion of employed men; and when the quality of employment is taken into account, the quality of women's employment is more likely to be lower: fixed-term work, part-time work and lower-paid positions are more common among working women than among men.

The female employment rate during the fourth quarter of 2022 was 69.6 per cent, while male employment stood at 80.1 per cent.[10] In other words, there remains a gender employment gap of 10.8 percentage points (pp), which has decreased only slightly (−1.9 pp) over the past 10 years.[11] Women continue to face obstacles in gaining access to paid employment and, once employed, in remaining in the labour market or in gaining high-quality jobs and decision-making positions within key sectors.

Looking at forms of work, in 2021, 7.9 per cent of men in the 27 EU Member States were employed on part-time contracts, compared to 28.7 per cent of women.[12] Moreover, women and men end up working part-time for different reasons: for men, the main reason is the impossibility of finding a full-time job; a second reason is inadequate training. In contrast, for women, the main reason is care work for children and other dependent family members, followed by the lack of availability of full-time jobs. Working part-time is in most cases a voluntary choice for women, but not a free choice.[13] In addition to the persistence of gender stereotypes about care work, other more concrete constraints may influence the choice. Part-time work – whether voluntary or involuntary – is in any case a risk factor for in-work poverty as it often leads to marginalisation within the organisation and segmentation of part-time workers into specific underpaid tasks, less favourable working conditions and lower welfare benefits and/or coverage by social protection schemes.

In terms of wage inequality, women's wages are on average lower than men's – in 2020, women earned 13 per cent less than their male counterparts in equal

---

[10] Eurostat, *Employment and activity by sex and age*, 2022, ec.europa.eu/eurostat/databrowser/view/LFSI_EMP_Q__custom_5983758/default/table?lang=en.

[11] Eurostat, *Gender employment gap, by type of employment*, 2021, ec.europa.eu/eurostat/databrowser/view/sdg_05_30/default/table?lang=en (last accessed 23 February 2023).

[12] Eurostat, *Percentage of part-time employment of adults by sex, age groups, number of children and age of youngest child*, 2021, ec.europa.eu/eurostat/databrowser/view/LFST_HHPTECHI__custom_3724335/bookmark/table?lang=en&bookmarkId=787ada5b-3caa-4b86-8b88-452a9dbc1261 (last accessed 23 February 2023).

[13] PES Network, *43 million people across the EU are in part-time employment, this being 4.8 million more than ten years ago. Who, where and why?*, 2019, www.pesnetwork.eu/2019/11/05/lmb5-part-time-employment/#:~:text=Acrossper cent20theper cent20Europeanper cent20averageper cent20the,per cent25per cent20andper cent20womenper cent20atper cent2031.3per cent25 (last accessed 23 February 2023).

employment[14] – and in most cases women are second earners in the household. Women's income (and work) is therefore often considered secondary to that of their male partners: if there is a need to give up part of the household income for care – as was the case during the Covid-19 pandemic period – it is more likely that women's work will be sacrificed. In fact, we know that in the first quarter of 2020 (the quarter most affected by confinement measures adopted during the pandemic emergency) in all EU Member States (except Cyprus) more women than men were temporarily absent from work.[15] The same logic applies to women's choice to leave the labour market after the birth of a child: the opportunity cost to a woman of continuing to work when her salary is lower than the cost of formal childcare is likely to result in her leaving the labour market.

Finally, it is necessary to mention vertical and horizontal segregation of the labour market: these two variables are deeply intertwined since women in low-feminised sectors are often concentrated in specific occupations at the lower levels of the hierarchical ladder of work organisations. The combination of such variables results in an inefficient allocation of human resources in the labour market.

A. Horizontal Segregation

Horizontal segregation can be defined as the unequal presence of women across labour market sectors: statistics show that some sectors, such as care, education and public administration, are highly feminised, in contrast to other sectors, such as transport, construction and information and communication technology (ICT), where women constitute the minority of the employed workforce. In 2022, at EU level, 30 per cent of female workers were employed in education, health and social work, compared to 8 per cent of male workers.[16] Only 13 per cent of employed women in 2010 worked in male-dominated sectors (occupations in which more than 60 per cent of the employed were men), while 69 per cent of employed women worked in female-dominated sectors (occupations in which more than 60 per cent of employees were women). In contrast, men employed in typically female-dominated occupations were 26 per cent while 59 per cent of men worked in typically male-dominated occupations.[17]

---

[14] Eurostat, *The gender pay gap situation in the EU*, 2020, commission.europa.eu/strategy-and-policy/policies/justice-and-fundamental-rights/gender-equality/equal-pay/gender-pay-gap-situation-eu_en (last accessed 23 February 2023).

[15] Eurostat, *Temporary absence from work*, 2020, ec.europa.eu/eurostat/web/products-eurostat-news/-/ddn-20200708-2 (last accessed 23 February 2023).

[16] EIGE, *Gender Equality Index 2020: Digitalisation and the future of work*, 2020, eige.europa.eu/publications/gender-equality-index-2020-report/increases-womens-employment-have-not-challenged-gender-segregation (last accessed 23 February 2023).

[17] European Commission, Directorate-General for Justice and Consumers, V Hardy et al, *New method to understand occupational gender segregation in European labour markets*, Publications Office, 2015, data.europa.eu/doi/10.2838/748887 (last accessed 23 February 2023).

Some data dating back to 2018, but which – even in the wake of the Covid-19 pandemic – can still be considered valid, say that women make up 93 per cent of the childcare workforce, 86 per cent in health services and 95 per cent in domestic cleaning and hygiene. To make the picture even clearer, more than 50 per cent of the staff employed in health services make up the 30 per cent lowest paid workers in the EU labour market as a whole.[18]

In 2019, in the share of the population with tertiary education, women were least among the employed scientists and engineers (41.3 per cent). One area of the labour market in which women are significantly underrepresented is entrepreneurship in technology-oriented sectors. More specifically, a new indicator shows that women account for less than a quarter of self-employed professionals in the science and engineering (S&E) and ICT sectors.[19]

Gender stereotypes are one of the main causes of horizontal segregation. They influence, first and foremost, education choices: in 2022, women accounted for 27 per cent of those with tertiary education in the EU-27, compared to 26 per cent of men. However, they also represent 43 per cent of graduates in education, health and care, humanities and arts, compared to 21 per cent of their male counterparts.[20] Gender stereotypes also influence recruitment processes in that they reinforce the existing paradigm of what should be considered typically female and male also by employers: thus, in some sectors, such as transport or construction, which are considered typically male, there is a lack of job offers with effective work-life balance measures or flexible working hours, thus making the sectors themselves unattractive to women.[21]

A vicious circle exists whereby existing stereotypes reinforce negative attitudes and choices on both sides: on the side of potential employees and on the side of potential employers. Intervening in education and training to dismantle gender stereotypes is therefore a key measure. At the same time, the vicious circle can be broken by acting on the other factors that reinforce gender stereotypes. For example, EU policies have invested heavily in reducing the gender gap in technical and scientific disciplines, developing policies, programmes and projects to encourage women to pursue careers in these fields. The same effort, however, has not been made to encourage men to pursue careers in humanities, health or education.

---

[18] EIGE's estimate based on the EU LFS 2018 database.

[19] European Commission, Directorate-General for Research and Innovation, *She figures 2021: gender in research and innovation: statistics and indicators*, Publications Office, 2021, https://data.europa.eu/doi/10.2777/06090 (last accessed 23 February 2023).

[20] EIGE, *Gender Equality Index 2022. The COVID-19 pandemic and care*, 2022, 36–37, eige.europa.eu/publications/gender-equality-index-2022-covid-19-pandemic-and-care (last accessed 23 February 2023).

[21] S Sansonetti, *Women and transport*, European Parliament's Policy Department for Citizens' Rights and Constitutional Affairs, 2021, www.europarl.europa.eu/thinktank/en/document/IPOL_STU(2021)701004; Polis, *Women in transport, STEMing the gap*, 2022, www.polisnetwork.eu/news/women-in-transport-stem-ing-the-gap (both last accessed 23 February 2023).

B. Vertical Segregation

Vertical segregation can be defined as the unequal share of opportunities offered to men and women in career advancement and access to decision-making positions. A closely related concept is that of the 'glass ceiling': an invisible yet very effective barrier preventing women's access to top decision-making and managerial positions in organisations, whether public or private, in political representation as well as in private management, in any field.

According to the European Commission's 2021 Report on equality between women and men in the EU, the gender imbalance in the corporate leadership of most listed companies registered in the EU remains stark. Gender imbalance is also a persistent phenomenon in central banks, which are cornerstones of economic decision-making and shapers of social, political and economic realities.[22]

Data in this regard are eloquent. According to the European Institute for Gender Equality (EIGE), in 2022 in the EU, women represented 33.4 per cent of the members of national governments and 33 per cent of the members of parliaments. Furthermore, women represent 31.6 per cent of the members of the boards of directors of the largest listed companies, supervisory boards or boards of directors, as well as 26.4 per cent of the members of the boards of directors of central banks.[23] According to the Glass-Ceiling Index developed by *The Economist* in 2022, women are still underrepresented compared to their peers in senior corporate roles, representing on average only one-third of managers and just over one quarter of board seats in the Organisation for Economic Cooperation and Development (OECD).[24] The vertical segregation of women is also reflected in the task forces created to tackle the Covid-19 pandemic crisis. A 2020 study found that men far outnumbered women in the pandemic decision-making process. Of the 115 national task forces dedicated to Covid-19 in 87 countries, including 17 EU Member States, 85.2 per cent were mainly men, 11.4 per cent were mainly women and only 3.5 per cent had gender parity. Furthermore, 81.2 per cent of the task forces were headed by men. This is despite the fact that women make up the overwhelming majority of health workers in the EU.[25]

---

[22] European Commission, Directorate-General for Justice and Consumers, *2021 report on gender equality in the EU*, Publications Office, 2021, data.europa.eu/doi/10.2838/57887 (last accessed 23 February 2023).

[23] EIGE, *Gender Equality Index – Power*, 2022, eige.europa.eu/gender-equality-index/2022/domain/power (last accessed 23 February 2023).

[24] *The Economist*, Glass-Ceiling Index, 2022, www.economist.com/graphic-detail/glass-ceiling-index (last accessed 23 February 2023).

[25] EIGE, *Coronavirus puts women in the frontline*, 2020, eige.europa.eu/news/coronavirus-puts-women-frontline (last accessed 23 February 2023).

III. Finding a Balance between Work and Private Life to Tackle In-work Poverty

Addressing the conditions of women's work cannot avoid considering a further crucial element: the existence or non-existence of effective measures to allow an effective work-life balance, and mainly caring responsibilities. This is because women often experience a decrease in salary in conjunction with maternity and this penalty increases with the number of children. Moreover, this wage penalty seems to translate into a persistent wage inequality throughout women's working lives and careers. In contrast, male workers' earnings seem not to be negatively affected by paternity. In almost half of the EU Member States, women devote at least twice as much time to childcare as men, with a maximum of 50 hours per week in Austria and a minimum of 24 hours in Greece.[26]

All EU Member States respect the minimum parental leave of four months, which was already established by Directive 2010/18/EU, and is now enshrined in Directive (EU) 2019/1158 of the European Parliament and of the Council on the work-life balance for parents and caregivers. Yet, the overall duration of available leave varies considerably within the EU. Parental leave entitlements often have to be negotiated within workplaces, making public and private organisations key players in the practical implementation of reconciliation policies. EU Member States are divided between those where the total duration of parental leave available is less than 15 months (Belgium, Bulgaria, Croatia, Cyprus, Denmark, Finland, Ireland, Italy, Luxembourg, Malta, the Netherlands, Poland, Portugal and Slovenia); and those Member States where continuous leave is available for a maximum of three years or more (Czech Republic, Estonia, France, Germany, Hungary, Lithuania, Slovakia and Spain). Both types of leave (very short or very long duration) are associated with reduced female labour market participation.[27]

Work-life balance policies should contribute to the achievement of gender equality by promoting women's participation in the formal labour market, the equal sharing of care responsibilities between men and women and the reduction of the gender gap in terms of pay and pensions.

Measures to be taken to promote work-life balance and thus women's participation in the labour market include the following.

---

[26] Eurofound, *European Quality of Life Survey 2016*, 2016, www.eurofound.europa.eu/data/european-quality-of-life-survey (last accessed 23 February 2023) Note: Interviewees – employees and with depending children – reported the number of 'Hours spent caring for and/or educating your children'.

[27] Sweden falls between the two methods: paid leave is expressed in days (to emphasise that it can be taken very flexibly), and is equivalent to approximately 18 months if taken continuously, while each parent is entitled to take unpaid leave until the child is 18 months old; the same applies in Latvia. Greece is also an exception, with four months per parent in the private sector and 60 months per parent in the public sector.

Encourage fathers to apply for parental leave. EU Member States should set a standard level of pay or allowance in respect of the minimum period of paternity leave that is at least equivalent to the level of national sick pay. Granting paternity and maternity rights pursues the goal of creating a bond between parent and child, and EU Member States are encouraged to provide an allowance for paternity and maternity leave in order to fairly support fathers and mothers to take care of their children and to be responsible for care work.

Avoid penalising women who choose to have children. Explicit provision should be made to protect the employment rights of women on maternity leave and in particular their right to return to the same or an equivalent post, without prejudice to their working conditions, and to ensure that they benefit from any improvement in working conditions to which they would have been entitled during their absence. Women workers should also be able to adapt their working hours to their personal needs and preferences. They have the right to request flexible working arrangements in order to adapt their working patterns, including, where possible, the use of remote working arrangements, flexible working hours or reduced working hours.

An effective childcare system. Childcare services are not homogeneous across the EU and limited access prevents mothers from re-entering the labour market earlier and increases the opportunity cost of experiencing motherhood. Planning for childcare, old age or disability care is much more difficult if women cannot rely on care services, fixed shifts and a stable professional position. Moreover, if women work in professional sectors that offer lower wages and more precarious working conditions, it is very likely that the family income will depend on men's wages when in a heterosexual couple, thus making women's careers more open to variations and interruptions and less independent. The 'traditional' model of the full-time working male breadwinner is thus reaffirmed.

Encourage a cultural change towards a more equal distribution of care tasks between men and women. Working on policies and rights is certainly an essential step, but it is not enough if a cultural change is not encouraged, working on those stereotypes that at different levels influence the individual choices of men and women, and that inevitably have economic effects. This is also the reason why the European Commission puts the fight against gender stereotypes and sexism at the top of the Strategy for Gender Equality 2020–2025.[28]

Reducing the gender pension gap and offering long-term care services. From the age of 65 onwards, while the poverty rate for men remains more or less stable, the risk of poverty for women increases substantially and significantly (for women it is 17 per cent and for men 13.1 per cent).[29] This is also because women tend to

---

[28] European Commission, *A Union of Equality: Gender Equality Strategy 2020–2025*, 2020, eur-lex. europa.eu/legal-content/EN/TXT/?uri=CELEX%3A52020DC0152 (last accessed 23 February 2023).

[29] Eurostat, *At-risk-of-poverty rate by poverty threshold and most frequent activity in the previous year*, 2019, ec.europa.eu/eurostat/databrowser/view/ILC_LI04__custom_470517/bookmark/table (last accessed 23 February 2023).

live longer than men so that the influence of the family on their economic status is less visible in old age and their economic capacity as a unit becomes more apparent. Although the gender pension gap has decreased over time and is now almost five percentage points lower than in 2010 (34 per cent), in 2019 EU-27 women aged 65 and over received an average 29.4 per cent lower pension than men.[30] The gender pension gap can be interpreted as the result of women's intermittent presence in the labour market due to a prolonged engagement in unpaid care work. Voluntary part-time work, linked to the need to care for children, persons with disabilities and dependent elderly people, is also a factor affecting the gender pension gap. Moreover, involuntary part-time work is often encouraged by stereotypes perpetuating the idea that women's pay in heterosexual couples is second best, and that fulfilment for men is realised in a career and for women in a family (43 per cent and 44 per cent of Europeans respectively think this[31]). Lastly, the impact of gender stereotypes fuels the idea that women work better in certain sectors of the labour market, which respond to an assumed idea of women's natural inclination to care and nurturing, and which are just as often less remunerative, or with the highest percentage of low incomes and atypical contracts.

Promoting access to professional home care services. School closures during the Covid-19 pandemic and the reduction of childcare and elderly care services due to social distancing led to a further decline in the already low employment rates of women. This phenomenon particularly affected women between the ages of 25 and 49, who are more likely to be in a situation of care responsibility. Generally, the solution to the unpaid care work required by their families is for women to reduce working hours or even to give up paid work (even temporarily). Reducing working hours or temporarily giving up work to care for dependent family members we know from data that it can have long-term negative effects on women's labour market performance and work-life balance, and can also lead to wage penalties. During the pandemic, as reported by Eurofound's Covid-19 survey in April and May 2020, less than 4 per cent of women and men were able to obtain support from a service provider, institution or organisation if they needed help caring for their child/children, and one in four (25 per cent) were unable to receive support of any kind (EU-27).[32] The result of the survey found a general deterioration of the work-life balance among male and female workers in the EU during the first wave of the pandemic compared to the situation described in the 2015 European Working Conditions Survey of the same agency.

---

[30] Eurostat, *Gender pension gap by age group*, 2019, ec.europa.eu/eurostat/databrowser/view/ILC_PNP13__custom_470372/bookmark/table (last accessed 23 February 2023).

[31] European Commission, Directorate-General for Communication, *Special Eurobarometer 465: Gender Equality 2017*, 2017, data.europa.eu/88u/dataset/S2154_87_4_465_ENG (last accessed 23 February 2023).

[32] Eurofound, *Living, working and Covid-19*, 2020, www.eurofound.europa.eu/data/covid-19. (last accessed 23 February 2023).

Ensure respect for women's sexual and reproductive health and rights. Prolonged confinement increased women's exposure to domestic and sexual violence. The reduction of abortion services during the epidemic exposed women and girls to the danger of unplanned and unwanted pregnancies, including those resulting from sexual violence. Making sexual and reproductive services safe, accessible and available is not only a women's right to build their own existence and a responsibility towards those who are born, but also has the effect of responding to the needs of the labour market, which benefits from talent and needs them to be able to plan the moments of their existence to ensure continuity and avoid abrupt, unplanned and at-risk interruptions due to unwanted motherhood. According to a 2017 Council of Europe report,[33] obstacles to access to free and legal abortion in Europe are diverse. Some countries have introduced laws, policies and practices that limit women's autonomy and decision-making, particularly through regressive restrictions on access to contraception and abortion care. Financial, social and practical barriers still undermine women's ability to enjoy safe sexual and reproductive health, free from coercion. Recent events in the United States[34] and Europe[35] suggest that what had already been achieved in this regard is certainly not safe from regression. Reproductive decisions may also be influenced or limited by social, institutional and legal obstacles, such as the stigma against single-parent families; discrimination against children born to unmarried or non-heterosexual couples; the legality of abortion; and the availability of assisted reproductive technology. Moreover, poorer women have less access to sexual and reproductive health; are less able to exercise their reproductive rights; are more likely to be unemployed or underemployed; and likely to earn less than men. Free access to abortion and family planning, thus, is not only a matter of women's rights to decide about their own bodies, but also has an impact on women's access to education and opportunities for career progression.

According to the EU Commission, 7.7 million women will be out of work in 2022 due to unpaid care responsibilities. In 2019, only 27 per cent of children at risk of poverty and social exclusion were enrolled in early childhood education and care services compared to 35 per cent of the general child population. Moreover, about one-third of families including individuals with long-term care needs do not use home care services because they cannot afford them.[36] In light of these worrying figures, the Commission adopted a European Care Strategy on

[33] Council of Europe, *Women's sexual and reproductive health and rights*, 2017, www.coe.int/en/web/commissioner/women-s-sexual-and-reproductive-rights-in-europe (last accessed 23 February 2023).

[34] See interactive map on access to abortion in the US following the Supreme Court's June 2022 repeal of *Roe v Wade*, which had previously made abortion legal in the US since 1973: states.guttmacher.org/policies.

[35] For an overview of the situation in Europe on access to sexual and reproductive health services, see the European Parliamentary Forum 2021 map: www.epfweb.org/sites/default/files/2021-09/ABORTper cent20Atlas_ENper cent202021-v5.pdf.

[36] European Commission, *Factsheet – European Care Strategy for carers and care receivers*, 2022, ec.europa.eu/commission/presscorner/detail/en/fs_22_5363 (last accessed 23 February 2023).

7 September 2022,[37] accompanied by a proposal for a Council Recommendation on the revision of the 2002 Barcelona targets on early childhood education and care, and one on access to affordable high-quality long-term care. On 8 December 2022, the EU Council adopted the two Recommendations proposing to revise the 2002 Barcelona targets in order to encourage Member States to increase participation in early childhood education and care with a view to facilitating women's participation in the labour market and improving the social and cognitive development of all children and, in particular, of children in vulnerable situations or from disadvantaged backgrounds. It adds new dimensions to the original Barcelona targets, namely the need to close the participation gap between children at risk of poverty and the overall population and to pay attention to the time intensity of participation in early childhood education and care. It also calls on Member States to improve the quality, accessibility and affordability of early childhood education and care for all children.

Regarding long-term care, the European Strategy for Care proposes that Member States improve the adequacy of social protection for long-term care so that it is timely, comprehensive and affordable for those who need it; increase supply and close territorial gaps in access to long-term care; implement accessible digital solutions in the provision of care services and ensure that long-term care services and facilities are accessible to people living with disabilities; ensure a quality framework for long-term care services; addressing the challenges of vulnerable groups of domestic and care workers and people with migrant backgrounds, including through effective regulation and professionalisation of this work; addressing skills and labour shortages with education, training and legal migration pathways; supporting informal carers including through training, psychological and financial support; and improving fiscal sustainability by ensuring the cost-effectiveness of long-term care, for example through a coherent and integrated governance framework.

IV. In-work Poverty: Countering the Gender Paradox

From what has been said so far, it results that female workers are at greater risk of being employed in underpaid and under-skilled jobs, with non-standard and often poorly paid contracts. Despite this, looking at data from the Eurostat indicator that monitors in-work poverty, women do not appear to be at greater risk of in-work poverty than their male counterparts. In 2021, women at risk of in-work poverty were 12.5 per cent and men 13.1 per cent (EU average).[38]

---

[37] Communication from the Commission to the European Parliament, the Council, the European Economic and Social Committee and the Committee of the Regions on the European care strategy, Brussels, 7 September 2022, COM(2022) 440 final, ec.europa.eu/social/main.jsp?langId=en&catId=89 &furtherNews=yes&newsId=10382#navItem-relatedDocuments (last accessed 23 February 2023).

[38] Eurostat, *In-work at-risk-of-poverty rate by age and sex*, 2021, ec.europa.eu/eurostat/databrowser/ view/ILC_IW01__custom_4638283/default/table (last accessed 23 February 2023).

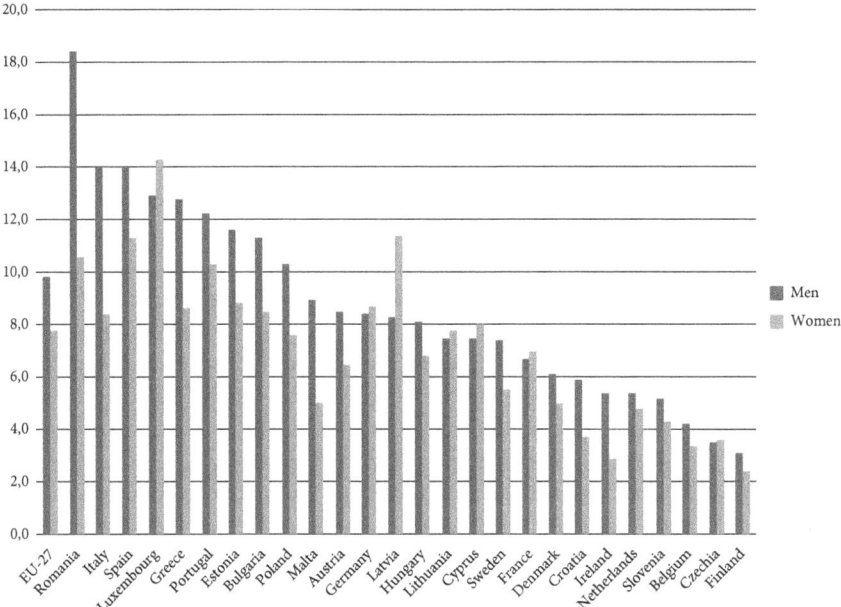

Source: Authors' elaboration on 2021 Eurostat data. Data from Slovakia is missing.

When we look at this data, it is important to be aware of what the In-Work Poverty Indicator adopted by the European Union defines as 'in-work poor' (IWP). According to the EU Indicator, an individual is considered IWP if he or she (this is a binary statistical survey that disaggregates data into men and women) declares to have been employed for seven months in the reference year, and if he or she lives in a household with an equivalised disposable income below the relative poverty line, which is 60 per cent of the national median income. The concept of IWP thus encompasses two dimensions: on the one hand, it is related to an individual, and implies the employment characteristics, such as salary, type of contract and working hours (part-time/full-time); on the other hand, there is the household dimension which concerns the composition, demographic and occupational characteristics of the household itself.[39]

Having clarified the two dimensions that define 'in-work poor' at the European level, it is easier to understand that the household dimension has a great impact on the outcome, as shown in the paragraphs above that have recounted the situation of men and women in terms of wealth, access to services, position and permanence in the labour market. It also helps us to comprehend the in-work poverty indicator results.

In addition, this definition excludes all those household members who work involuntarily for less than seven months during the year, who are probably among

---

[39] See further the contribution by García-Muñoz in this book (ch 1).

the most vulnerable. It also takes no account of the remuneration earned by individual household members in the labour market. This is why an in-work poor worker needs to be distinguished from a low-wage earner, which in the EU in 2018 was 18.2 per cent of female employees, compared with 12.5 per cent of male employees, highlighting again that women are more penalised compared to men.[40]

The basic assumption on which the indicator is built and which is considered to be the main cause of the bias is the contrast between the definition of the unit of analysis (the individual) and the identification of the available resources and hence the state of poverty (the household). This basic assumption presumes, without having the means to prove it, that the household's total income is divided equally among the household members. From a 'family' perspective, an individual, which can be properly defined as a low-wage earner, may not be in a poverty condition if he or she lives in a household with other income earners, while someone who receives a decent wage but is insufficient to meet the needs of a large household in which he or she is the only worker may be a working poor.[41]

This situation can be described as a paradox.[42] The criterion adopted to identify who is working, that is individuals who are employed for at least seven months during the relevant year, develop a result in the IWP indicator which could be significantly different when taking as reference the population aged 18–64, including those who worked at least one month in the year and excluding only the unemployed or inactive individuals in the relevant year or individuals who do not consider work to be their prevailing status.

By referring exclusively to household income to assess working poor status, the obvious paradox is that working women – who more often live in households with more than one income earner – are at lower risk of IWP than men, even though they run greater risks in the labour market in terms of employment and earnings opportunities. If the working situation of women is analysed at individual level – in terms of earned income and gender pay gap – the specific issues and challenges affecting female work are visible. In contrast, these disadvantages disappear when the household dimension is introduced: this phenomenon is precisely described as gender asymmetry between poverty in earned income and poverty risk.[43] If we stand by the definition of the IWP indicator, we face the risk of confusing the two individual/household dimensions, thus allowing it to prevent us from seeing the issues that cause in-work poverty and then intervening with appropriate policies to close the gap.

---

[40] Eurostat, *Low-wage earners as a proportion of all employees (excluding apprentices) by sex*, 2018, ec.europa.eu/eurostat/databrowser/view/earn_ses_pub1s/default/table (last accessed 23 February 2023).

[41] H Lohmann, 'The concept and measurement of in-work poverty' in H Lohmann and I Marx (eds), *Handbook on In-Work Poverty* (Edward Elgar Publishing, 2018) 7–25.

[42] P Barbieri and G Cutuli, 'Determinants and trends of in-work poverty risks in Italy. An analysis of the 2002–2012 years' in H Lohmann and I Marx (eds), *Handbook of Research on In-Work Poverty* (Edward Elgar Publishing, 2016), www.sisec.it/wp-content/uploads/2015/09/Ch_21_In-work-poverty-in-Italy.pdf.

[43] S Ponthieux, 'Assessing and analysing in-work poverty risk' in A Atkinson and E Marlier (eds), *Income and living conditions in Europe* (Luxembourg: Office for Official Publications of the European Communities, 2010) 307–28.

In fact, the only individual disadvantage that the indicator seems to reflect adequately is part-time work. In-work poverty is mainly a problem of the male household head in some Member States, such as Italy and, to a lesser extent, Portugal and France, while Germany stands out as having the highest in-work poverty rate among women.[44] The reason for this evidence is the high proportion of part-time work among women in this country, together with the high proportion of female-only households (women working part-time), which explains why Germany is the only country where most of the working poor are women. The indicator only shows unemployment or inactivity when this is not offset by overall household wealth; otherwise, the poverty situation remains hidden by the overall household situation. Moreover, it is more often the employment and low-income status of women that is hidden by this type of calculation, precisely because of the disadvantaged position that women experience in the labour market, which is well evidenced by other indicators.

In other words, exclusively considering the IWP indicator could lead to a misunderstanding of the importance of implementing gender policies in the labour market, or the direction of new policies to compensate for the gender gap in the labour market, since the disadvantages experienced by women do not have such a large impact on household income.

The assumptions underlying the IWP indicator are, however, very strong and dissonant with the reality of women's working and family life. Differences within the household in actual access to economic resources due to the gender division of labour within the household are neglected. It is also not possible to calculate the extent to which each individual contributes to the family income, nor the different roles each person plays within the family, where we have seen that women are still often seen as primarily responsible for care work, and the second income of the family, complementary to that of the male partner. Nor do the actual possibilities of utilising the resources available to the household emerge, just as there is a lack of information on income from household production of services for self-consumption and the amount of work involved in care work.

Before coming to preliminary conclusions, further attention must be paid to the definition of the household dimension. According to the Eurostat Glossary, a household is defined as a 'housekeeping unit or, operationally, as a social unit: having common arrangements; sharing household expenses or daily needs; in a shared common residence'. A household includes either one person living alone or a group of people, not necessarily related, living at the same address with common housekeeping, ie sharing at least one meal per day or sharing a living or sitting room.[45]

---

[44] S Ponthieux, 'Gender and in-work poverty' in H Lohmann and I Marx (eds), *Handbook on In-Work Poverty* (Edward Elgar Publishing, 2018) 70–88. Author calculation based on *EU-SILC 2013: Individuals in-work at-risk of poverty*, 80.

[45] Eurostat, *Glossary. Household*, ec.europa.eu/eurostat/statistics-explained/index.php?title=Glossary: Household_-_social_statistics (last accessed 23 February 2023).

The European Union, however, has not established a common definition of household, as the concept is primarily defined at the country level. It is worth noting that the definition of a household may vary slightly between different EU Member States depending on their specific national legislation or statistical practices. Statistical agencies in EU Member States may have their own specific definitions of household for the purpose of data collection and analysis. For example, in some countries, a household may be defined as a group of people who share the same address and have a common household head, while in others, it may be defined as a group of people who live together and pool their income and expenses.

In general, household statistics in EU Member States cover a wide range of information related to housing, living conditions, income and consumption patterns, among other topics. This information is used by policymakers, researchers and other stakeholders to better understand social and economic trends, inform policy decisions, and target interventions to address specific needs and challenges. The household dimension can be further broken down into various categories, such as the number of adults and children in the household, the age distribution of household members, and the relationship between household members (eg married couples, single parents, cohabiting partners, etc).

However, the core criteria of living together in the same dwelling and sharing meals or expenses is generally consistent across the EU. Here are a few examples. In Germany, a household is defined as a group of persons who live together in a common dwelling and have a shared budget.[46] This means that roommates who do not share expenses would not be considered part of the same household. In Italy, a household is defined as a group of people who live in the same dwelling and share common spaces for eating and sleeping. This includes both traditional families and unmarried couples or friends living together. However, there is no requirement that they share the same dwelling, so people who live in different apartments could be considered part of the same household.[47] In the Netherlands, a household is defined as a group of people who live together in a sustainable way and together provide for housing and/or other basic needs. This means that people who live in separate apartments would not be considered part of the same household.[48] In Belgium, the definition of a household in national statistics is based on the concept of 'private household' as defined by Eurostat.

---

[46] 'Haushalt: jede zusammen wohnende und eine wirtshaftliche Einheit bildende Personengemeinschaft sowie Personen, die allen wohnen und wirtschaften' (Staatlische Bundesamt 2003:16).

[47] Insieme di persone legate da vincoli di matrimonio, unione civile, parentela, affinità, adozione, tutela, o da vincoli affettivi, coabitanti e aventi dimora abituale nello stesso comune (anche se non sono ancora iscritte nell'anagrafe della popolazione residente del comune medesimo). Una famiglia può essere costituita anche da una sola persona. L'assente temporaneo non cessa di appartenere alla propria famiglia sia che si trovi presso altro alloggio (o convivenza) dello stesso comune, sia che si trovi in un altro comune italiano o all'estero.

[48] The term 'huishouden' is used to refer to a household. According to Statistics Netherlands (CBS), a household is defined as 'een persoon of een groep personen die duurzaam samenwoont en samen voorziet in huisvesting en/of in andere basisbehoeften' which translates to 'a person or a group of persons

A private household is defined as a group of persons who live together in the same private dwelling and who share at least one meal a day or who share economic resources for daily living expenses. According to the Belgian Statistical Office, a private household can consist of one or more persons, including families, single persons and non-family households (such as roommates). However, the following types of living arrangements are not considered households: institutions such as hospitals, nursing homes and prisons; collective living arrangements such as student dormitories and military barracks.[49] In Polish statistics on in-work poverty, a household is defined as a group of people who live together and live on a single source of income. According to the definition of the Polish Central Statistical Office (CSO) – *Centralnego Urzędu Statystycznego* (GUS) – a household includes people who live together and use one building or part of it, as well as people who live separately but share a common budget and financial management (eg married couples who live separately but share living expenses). In the case of children who live permanently in their parents' homes, they are usually considered part of their parents' household.[50] The Swedish Central Bureau of Statistics (SCB) uses the following definition of household size: the number of persons who live in a dwelling and who share household expenses, or would share expenses if they were not exempted from doing so.[51] This means that even if some individuals in a dwelling do not contribute to the household expenses, they are still counted as part of the household size. In addition to household size, Swedish statistics may also consider other dimensions of households, such as the number of children or the presence of older adults. In Luxembourg, the definition of a household is based on the European Union's Harmonised European Time Use Survey (HETUS) and the European Union's Labour Force Survey (LFS) recommendations. According to these recommendations, a household is defined as a group of persons who share the same living accommodation and who share meals together at least once a day or who have a personal interest in each other's welfare. This includes both traditional families and non-traditional arrangements such as cohabiting couples and friends living together.

It is worth noting that the definition of a household may vary depending on the purpose of the statistical analysis and the data source used. These differences in household definitions can have significant implications for statistics related to housing, poverty and social welfare.

---

who live together in a sustainable way and together provide for housing and/or other basic needs'. This definition includes people who live together in a family setting (such as a couple or a family with children) as well as non-family members who live together, such as roommates or cohabiting partners. The term 'duurzaam samenwoont' emphasises that the living arrangement is long-term and stable, rather than temporary or transient.

[49] StatBel Definitions are available at: statbel.fgov.be/en/themes/population/structure-population/households#documents (last accessed 23 February 2023).

[50] stat.gov.pl/metainformacje/slownik-pojec/pojecia-stosowane-w-statystyce-publicznej/103, pojecie.html (last accessed 23 February 2023).

[51] www.scb.se/hitta-statistik/sverige-i-siffror/manniskorna-i-sverige/hushall-i-sverige (last accessed 23 February 2023).

V. Conclusions and Ways Forward

The insufficient availability of gender-disaggregated data often makes gender issues disappear from the broader picture of the labour force presented as a homogeneous social group. Data on working conditions, poverty, access to services, care and decision-making should be systematically broken down not only by gender, but also by considering other discrimination factors, such as citizenship, migration background, age, disability, sexual orientation and gender identity, in order to provide a complete picture of the obstacles that potentially limit or prevent the successful and satisfactory integration of each individual into the labour market.

Furthermore, although the EU-SILC reports a higher risk of in-work poverty among male than female workers, this is mainly due to the inclusion of the household dimension in the indicator. The 'low-wage earners as a proportion of all employees (excluding apprentices) by sex'[52] shows in fact that women are in the position of earning lower wages than men. Further information is also provided by the indicator 'employees who could not find a permanent or full-time job, by sex and age',[53] where it is found that those who are at risk of not finding a permanent or full-time job are more likely to be women, rather than men. In this sense, a revision of the calculation criterion of the EU-SILC Indicator on in-work at-risk-of-poverty rate by age and sex needs to be developed, in order to receive results that are closer to the actual conditions of the phenomenon with respect to gender.

Adequate availability of gender-disaggregated data, which meets the gender bias test, would also make a gendered analysis of in-work poverty possible. By focusing not on the individual level but on the income level and risk factors of the household, the indicator reinforces the invisibility of the specific discrimination and challenges that working women face on a daily basis. The approach to in-work poverty should be transparent and accompanied by a solid analysis of how this problem impacts differently on family members and, more specifically, on working men and women.

Particular attention should also be paid to the different types of households in view of the increasing statistical incidence of single-parent families, which are among those most at risk of in-work poverty due to the availability of a single wage, or of non-heterosexual couples who suffer further discrimination on the basis of different national legislations (some of which, for example, deny the possibility of sharing parental leave), or of couples with a migrant background.

---

[52] Eurostat Data Browser, *Low-wage earners as a proportion of all employees (excluding apprentices) by sex*, Last Update 4 August 2021, ec.europa.eu/eurostat/databrowser/view/earn_ses_pub1s/default/table?lang=en (last accessed 23 February 2023).

[53] Eurostat Data Browser, *Employees who could not find a permanent or full-time job, by sex and age*, Last Update 15 February 2023, ec.europa.eu/eurostat/databrowser/view/lfsa_eetpgar/default/table (last accessed 23 February 2023).

The number of children and disparities between women's and men's income levels are also key factors to consider, helping to explain why the risk of in-work poverty might affect some households differently from others. The standard EU 'at-risk-of-poverty indicator' further hides the specific difficulties women face in entering and remaining in the labour market, as well as their efforts to reconcile work and career ambitions with care and nursing tasks, which – according to the stereotypical construction of gender roles – are still too often considered a female task.

The adoption of an individual and gender-sensitive approach to the analysis of in-work poverty could have a major impact on the development of new data more closely reflecting the real situations of men and women, and thus influence the development of more effective and necessary public policies, at all levels of governance, to address the problems and challenges of women workers. Female workers – due to the barriers hindering their full and successful participation in the labour market, and causing horizontal and vertical segregation – are particularly at risk of becoming parts of low or unskilled employees with standard employment contracts employed in poor sectors and flexibly employed workers, as defined in previous chapters of this volume.[54]

For this risk to be reduced, welfare and labour market policies must be tailored to consider the needs of female workers, in terms of, for instance, reducing stereotypes in education and career paths; making childcare services and sexual and reproductive health services affordable; increasing access to parental leave policies, including for fathers; making gender-based violence services available; reducing the gender pay gap; and investing in the implementation of positive actions on gender equality in the workplace, and thus contributing also to the households' wealth. These policies not only contribute to social justice in general but are also crucial to fuel the productivity of the general economic system, allowing everyone to invest and pursue their career ambitions.

---

[54] See in particular ch 1.

PART II

The Way Towards EU Social Citizenship

5

(De)constructing EU Social Citizenship

ANE ARANGUIZ

I. The EU's Social Purpose and the Threat of In-work Poverty

It is well-established that the origins of the EU did not conceive a social dimension for the then Community. Other than incorporating the idea that the task of the community was to promote 'an ever-increasing improvement in the standard of living' (Part 1, principles), the Treaty of Rome made no reference to any Community-wide social objective. The rather non-existent competences in the field of social policy,[1] matched this intention. It quickly became obvious, however, that at least a minimum level of social protection at the EU was necessary, if nothing else, to guarantee the economic development of the Union without promoting social dumping within the internal market and undermining the national social systems in place.

And so the social objective of the Union, and its competences, evolved gradually over the years. Taking some big steps in the history of social Europe, the Single European Act (1986) was determined to 'improve the economic and social situation'; the Treaty of Maastricht (1992) committed to promoting 'economic and social frontiers' and simultaneously established EU citizenship; and the Treaty of Amsterdam (1997) reiterated this idea while incorporating the Social Policy Protocol under the Social Policy Title in the foundational treaties. Today, the Lisbon Treaty establishes that the Union:

> shall establish an internal market. It shall work for the sustainable development of Europe based on balanced economic growth and price stability, a highly competitive social market economy, aiming at full employment and social progress, and a high level

---

[1] This is with the exception of Title III of the TEEC, which encouraged the close cooperation of Member States in several areas of social policy (Article 118 of the Treaty establishing the European Economic Community (TEEC)), established the right to equal pay between men and women (Article 119 TEEC) and the European Social Fund (Article 123 TEEC).

of protection and improvement of the quality of the environment [,] combat social exclusion and discrimination, and shall promote social justice and protection, equality between women and men, solidarity between generations and protection of the rights of the child [and] promote economic, social and territorial cohesion, and solidarity among Member States' (Article 3 of the Treaty on European Union (TEU))

Without any doubt, this represents an evolution in the EU's commitments to its social dimension. And yet, without exception, every single reference to the EU's social objective over the years has been tied to its economic purpose and to the deeply rooted idea that lifting the barriers of the internal market will lead to social prosperity. Accordingly, much of the social strategy of the EU – albeit with important differences over the years – and even the existence of EU citizenship itself is anchored on the promise of an internal market that is able to deliver social progress. The existence of in-work poverty and, in particular, the fact that it is a gradually growing phenomenon even in times of economic prosperity, challenges this promise. In-work poverty, with all its complexities,[2] is evidence that economic prosperity does not benefit EU citizens equally and that the prosperity generated by the internal market is failing even the parts of the population that actively participate in it. In the Working, Yet Poor project, focused on the increasing social trend of working people at risk or below the poverty line, four clusters of particularly Vulnerable and Underrepresented Persons (VUPs) were identified: respectively, low wage earners, the solo self-employed, workers with a flexible contract, and casual, zero hour or platform workers. These groups, alongside others vulnerable in our society, are put at a disadvantage, in this case because of their labour status, which impedes their full enjoyment of (EU) citizenship. These groups are the living proof that being an active part in the labour market is not enough to deliver quality of life.

In-work poverty hence signals the acute need to reconsider the social value of the EU and to re-evaluate the social contract between the EU and its citizens. This calls for reconceptualising the idea of EU social citizenship in a way that is capable to deliver a better quality of life, and work, to its citizens. This chapter aims precisely at this by fleshing out the idea of an EU social citizenship that is relevant for all and not only for movers and/or economically 'deserving' citizens. It questions whether a citizenship that does not benefit all citizens but only the few fits within the understanding of citizenship itself by analysing the literature on citizenship (section II). Based on this, the chapter then moves on to putting together the theoretical blocks that should build the edifice of EU citizenship (section III). It departs from the common underpinning of a value-based 'civitas' among Europeans and the rationale and mandates of the EU as a normative foundation to argue in favour of a more complete citizenship. It also elaborates on how this fits in a multitiered network of citizens, in which the EU plays primarily a complementary role (section IV). It then concludes (section V). The findings of this chapter also serve as the foundation for recommendations elaborated on in

[2] See also the contribution by García-Muñoz (ch 1).

the next chapters of this volume which, motivated by the dire need to combat in-work poverty, explore a number of different alleys to substantiate the container of EU social citizenship.

II. EU Citizenship versus Social Citizenship

In 1992, the Treaty of Maastricht introduced the idea of EU citizenship, which, in principle, all EU citizens acquire the minute that they obtain the nationality of a Member State. Nevertheless, in practice, the full enjoyment of citizenship seldom responds to this automatisation, and EU citizens only gain access to a full set of rights upon the fulfilment of certain economic conditions and/or when crossing the border of their Member State. This is particularly true for social rights. In spite of this, the European Pillar of Social Rights (EPSR),[3] conceived as the primary political compass for the revival of social Europe, gears its set of 20 rights to all EU citizens and even legally residing third-country nationals. Whereas this could be seen as a powerful political move, and there remain few who contest the relevance of the EPSR, the principles in it stay empty vessels if not implemented. This signals an important mismatch between the social aspirations of the EU for its citizens and the current use of it. What follows elaborates on what EU citizenship currently means in terms of social rights and what (social) citizenship should in theory entail.

A. EU Social Citizenship As Is

One of the accomplishments, if not the main one, of EU citizenship has been to open a set of rights originally reserved to economically active people to every national of a Member State regardless of their economic status, namely, the right to move and reside freely in the territory of the EU.

Today, EU citizenship is enshrined in Article 20 TEU which establishes that EU citizenship is not a stand-alone status but, rather, adds an additional layer to national citizenship. Whereas national citizenships are composed of a complete package of rights and duties, the EU layer, as an additional citizenship, offers a rather limited set of rights that is mostly accessible to those who exercise their right to free movement.[4] From the rights that EU citizenship grants to its members, only free movement has an adhered social dimension.[5] Hence, in

---

[3] European Commission, *Establishing the European Pillar of Social Rights*, COM(2017) 250 final.

[4] The discussion here focuses on social rights. Needless to say, EU citizenship also offers a number of civil and political rights, including the right to vote or stand as a candidate before the European Parliament.

[5] There is, of course, much more to the social dimension of the EU than that linked to EU citizenship, including a body of law, such EU antidiscrimination or labour law, that creates important social rights in the EU. But these are not linked to the notion of EU citizenship. Put otherwise, they are not

essence, only those crossing the internal borders of the EU can enjoy an 'additional layer of protection'. In this context, Magnette distinguishes 'sympolitical' citizenships, that is, those requiring vertical rights that stem from a common authority taking decisions for all community members, from 'isopolitical' citizenships that convey only horizontal rights.[6] The latter mostly confers upon individuals the right to become a member of another polity and enjoy the rights recognised by that given community while sympolitical citizenship grants citizens a whole body of rights. The vast majority of EU citizenship rights, especially those in the social dimension, are markedly isopolitical in that they entitle its holders to enter the citizenship of another space – and thus the rights and duties are mostly derivative of national citizenship – upon the condition that they exercise their right to free movement.[7] This means that a large majority of EU citizens[8] do not benefit from EU citizenship. After all, one of the main principles of citizenship lies in a common membership that grants members equal rights and duties. As it stands, EU citizenship mostly favours those economically and transnationally active, thus discriminating against those that do not check these boxes. This approach blurs the deep understanding of belonging to a community and who, and under which grounds, is deserving of solidarity. Even the isopolitical side of EU citizenship is not unproblematic regarding its social added value. For example, even with an originally progressive interpretation of the European Court of Justice (ECJ),[9] the doors of other Member States' welfare systems only open upon the fulfilment of certain conditions: being economically active; having sufficient resources; or having legally resided in the territory of the Member States for five years. These limitations have been heavily debated and criticised in the literature.[10] At times,

---

granted to individuals on the basis of their EU citizenship. M Houwerzijl and A Aranguiz, 'Labour Law Harmonization in EU Law and its (Limited) Protection of VUP Groups', Working, Yet Poor (2022), Deliverable 4.1, available at workingyetpoor.eu/deliverables.

[6] P Magnette, *Citizenship. The History of an Idea* (Colchester, ECPR Press, 2005).

[7] Undeniably, there are also limited traces of a sympolitical citizenship in those rights that have been harmonised (gender, equality and labour law), but those too require a national transposition in order to be implemented and, more importantly, are not conceived as rights linked to having an EU citizenship.

[8] Over 90 per cent of EU citizens. This is the estimated number of non-mobile citizens in the EU. It needs to be noted, moreover, that as mentioned above, even those who exercise the right to free movement may struggle to access citizenship-based rights. Eurostat 'Statistics explained: European Union citizenship statistics and cross-border mobilities' (2022).

[9] CJEU Cases: Case C-202/13 *McCarthy* EU:C:2011:277; Case C-356/11 *O and S* EU:C:2012:776; Case C-256/11 *Dereci* EU:C:2011:734; Case C-86/12 *Alokpa and Moudoulou* EU:C:2013:645. This approach has been constrained over the years, with the last strand of the case law either limiting access to social benefits for economically non-active mobile citizens or having to – questionably – rely on other legal tools than the ones prescribed for that purpose to grant citizens access to social benefits. See on this: H Verschueren, 'Het recht op sociale bijstand voor economisch niet-actieve migrerende Unieburgers: het Hof zet het evenredigheidsbeginsel opzij en laat het Handvest de scherpe kanten afvijlen (noot onder HvJ 15 juli 2021, C-709/20, CG)' (2022) *Tijdschrift voor Europees en economisch recht* 219; F Pennings, 'Does the EU Charter of Fundamental Rights have Added Value for Social Security?' (2022) 24(2) *European Journal of Social Security* 117; J Paju, 'The Charter and Social Security Rights: Time to Stand and Deliver?' (2022) 24(1) *European Journal of Social Security* 21.

[10] F Pennings and M Seeleib-Kaiser, *EU Citizenship and Social Rights: Entitlements and Impediments to Access Welfare* (Cheltenham, Elgar, 2018); C O'Brien, *Unity in Adversity: Union Citizenship, Social*

the benefits of EU citizenship will be limited even for mobile workers, which is particularly worth noting for the phenomenon of in-work poverty. Following the interpretations of the Court of Justice of the European Union (CJEU), in order to attain the status of worker, work has to be deemed 'genuine and effective' and not be of such small scale as to be considered 'marginal or ancillary'.[11] By requiring mobile citizens to surpass a certain threshold, either in cash or hours, to be considered workers under national legislation, even mobile workers might be deprived of the enjoyment of EU citizenship and refused access to the welfare system of other Member States. This is certainly the case for mobile citizens who are in low-paid and less secure employment, like zero-hour contracts or those engaged in activities that do not qualify as work, like *au pairs*. Likewise, continuous employment might be required for accessing certain rights, which can be an impediment for fixed-term workers.[12]

As it stands, only a limited number of EU citizens benefit from their status, which makes the 'added layer' of protection offered by the EU rather questionable, at least regarding social rights. Moreover, an EU social citizenship that is dependent on crossing borders and being economically 'deserving' somewhat conflicts with the constitutionalised spirit of the EU, which puts fundamental rights among its founding values (Article 2 TEU) and sets the objective of becoming a social market economy that combats discrimination and social exclusion (Article 3 TEU). This also contrasts with the CJEU's interpretations, even in its more restrictive cases, according to which EU citizenship is meant to be more than a mobility device 'destined to be the fundamental status of nationals of the Member States'.[13]

For EU citizenship to enjoy a fundamental status, and thus be enjoyed not only by the minority but by all citizens, it cannot remain primarily isopolitical. Neither inclusion in the labour market nor mobility (or even both combined) have so far conferred a full set of social rights, even for the 'ideal' EU citizen scenario. Relative poverty and social exclusion cut across those in and out of work as much as across those moving between countries and others staying in their Member State of nationality.[14] But what, if not mobility, should drive the development of

Justice and the Cautionary Tale of the UK (Oxford, Hart Publishing, 2017); H Verschueren, 'EU Migrants and Destitution: The Ambiguous EU Objectives' in F Pennings and G Vonk (eds), *Research Handbook on European Social Security Law* (Cheltenham, Elgar, 2015); D Kramer and A Heindlmaier, 'Administering the Union Citizen in Need: Between Welfare State Bureaucracy and Migration Control' (2021) 31(4) *Journal of European Social Policy* 380; S Mantu and P Minderhoud, 'EU Citizenship and Social Solidarity' (2017) 24(5) *Maastricht Journal of European and Comparative Law* 703; S Thym, 'The Elusive Limits of Solidarity. Residence Rights and Social Benefits for Economically Inactive Union Citizens' (2015) 52(1) *Common Market Law Review* 17.

[11] M Risak and T Dullonger, *The Concept of 'Worker' in EU Law Status Quo and Potential for Change* (ETUI, Report 140, 2018).

[12] F Rossi dal Pozzo, *Citizenship Rights and Freedom of Movement in the European Union*, (London, Kluwer Law International, 2013); B Anderson, S Walker and I Shutes, 'Citizenship and Work: case studies of differential exclusion/inclusion' (2016) bEUcitizen report.

[13] CJEU cases (n 9) and Case C-184/99 *Grzelczyk* EU:C:2001:458, para 10; Case C-333/13 *Dano* EU:C:2014:2358, para 58.

[14] B Anderson, S Walker and I Shutes, 'Mobility and Citizenship in Europe: From the Worker-Citizen to Inclusive European Union Citizenship' (2016) European Policy Brief.

EU citizenship? The next section briefly discusses the literature on what social citizenship should entail and then moves on to discuss how the container of EU citizenship can be substantiated in a way that no longer benefits only a minority.

B. Social Citizenship in Theory

Citizenship entails a full membership to a political and social community centred around the state, most commonly, but also possibly a city or as in the case of the EU, a region. While there is no universal principle on how this membership is acquired or what rights and obligations can be derived from it, it should be equal to every member of the community (citizens). Most of the literature agrees, moreover, that citizenship is composed of various dimensions that correspond, accordingly, to the rights and obligations, participation and legitimacy. The first dimension provides citizens the necessary rights for, on the one hand, individual freedom and, on the other, guarantee a minimum of economic wealth, social protections and a decent standard of living that considers the prevailing standards in a given society.[15] Accordingly, this dimension is composed of civil and political rights and socioeconomic rights. The second dimension, participation, provides individuals the political power to influence the relation between its citizens and the polity. Lastly, legitimacy establishes both the individual and collective relationship between members (citizens) and the community.[16]

   Key for the discussion on social citizenship is to understand that civil and political rights cannot be separated from socioeconomic rights. They are in fact necessary for a genuine enjoyment of citizenship.[17] Without them, citizens are not equally equipped to exercise civil and political rights, especially when considering their very different backgrounds and access to opportunities. Some have referred to this as the leap between nominal rights and the genuine possibility to use them.[18] For instance, in the EU, citizens have the right to move freely, but not everyone has a background (ie family or health situation) or the necessary requirements (ie linguistic skills, available funds) that allow them to exercise their right to move. Without a common social minimum, citizens cannot 'genuinely enjoy' the benefits of citizenship.

---

[15] TH Marshall, *Citizenship and Social Class and Other Essays* (Cambridge, Cambridge University Press, 1950).
   [16] D Leydet, 'Citizenship' in E Zalta (ed), *The Stanford Encyclopaedia of Philosophy*, (Stanford, Stanford University, 2017); Y Soysal, *Limits of Citizenship: Migrants and Postnational Citizenship in Europe* (Chicago, University of Chicago Press, 1994); A Amelina, 'Theorizing European Social Citizenship: Governance, Discourses and Experiences of Transnational Social Security' in A Amelina, E Carmel, A Runfors and E Scheibelhofer (eds), *Boundaries of European Social Citizenship EU Citizens' Transnational Social Security in Regulations, Discourses, and Experiences* (Abingdon, Routledge, 2019).
   [17] R Dahrendorf, *Law and Order* (London, Stevens, 1984) 94.
   [18] R Bauböck, *Transnational Citizenship: Membership and Rights in International Migration* (Cheltenham, Elgar, 1994).

In essence, social citizenship is about guaranteeing substantial equality to ensure that every citizen – poor and rich, active and non-active or mobile or not mobile – has a dignified participation in society:

> citizenship is a kind of basic human equality associated with the concept of full member-ship of a community ... The whole range from the right to the modicum of economic welfare and security to the right to share the social heritage and to live the life of a civilised being according to the standards prevailing in the society ... and the right to participate in the exercise of political power.[19]

This also means that the rights derived from citizenship need to be independent from the market and their personal income.[20] Only when social rights are granted 'on the basis of citizenship rather than performance, will they entail a decommodi-fication of the status of individuals vis-à-vis the market'.[21] This is the key to an active participation in democratic processes.[22]

This echoes the core of human rights theory, which emphasises that funda-mental rights are indivisible, inalienable and universal.[23] A similar reasoning has allowed the European Court of Human Rights (ECtHR) to interpret its civil and political bill or rights in an increasingly social way, allowing the Court to protect certain social rights in cases related to the right to life, privacy, health, housing or social security.[24]

Social citizenship finds a parallel in the idea of industrial citizenship, which was also included, albeit more marginally, in TH Marshall's work.[25] Industrial

---

[19] Marshall (n 15) 8

[20] R Plant, 'Citizenship, Rights and Welfare' in A Coote (ed), *The Welfare of Citizens. Developing new social rights*, (London, IPPR/Rivers Oram Press, 1992) 16.

[21] G Esping-Andersen, *The Three Worlds of Welfare Capitalism* (Princeton, Princeton University Press, 1947) 21; F Twine, *Citizenship and Social Rights* (London, Sage, 1994) 102 et seq.

[22] N Harris, 'The Welfare State, Social Security, and Social Citizenship Rights' in N Harris (ed), *Social Security Law in Context* (Oxford, Oxford University Press, 2000) 23–24; See for an overview: GS Katrougalos, 'The (Dim) Perspectives of the European Social Citizenship' (2007) Jean Monnet Working Paper 05/07.

[23] This suggests that human rights cannot be separated by their nature and that they should be inher-ent to every individual without discrimination and cannot be taken away, with the important caveat that for citizenship rights one condition ought to be fulfilled: that members have or maintain member-ship to the polity.

[24] L Lavrysen, 'Strengthening the Protection of Human Rights of Persons Living in Poverty under the ECHR' (2015) 33(3) *Netherlands Quarterly of Human Rights* 293; A Aranguiz, 'Bringing the EU Up to Speed in the Protection of Living Standards Through Fundamental Social Rights: Drawing Positive Lessons from the Experience of the Council of Europe' (2021) 28(5) *Maastricht Journal of European and Comparative Law* 601; K Kagiaros, 'Austerity Measures at the European Court of Human Rights: Can the Court Establish a Minimum of Welfare Provisions?' (2019) *EPL* 25, 535; F Tulkens, 'La Convention européenne des droits de l'homme et la crise économique. La question de la pauvreté' (2013) 1 *Journal européen des droits de l'homme* 1, 13; I Leijten, 'The Right to Minimum Subsistence and Property Protection under the ECHR: Never the Twain Shall Meet?' (2019) 21 *European Journal of Social Security* 307. For example see ECtHR, *Sali v Sweden*, Judgment of 10 October 2006, Application No 67070/01; ECtHR, *Goudswaard-Van Der Lans v the Netherlands*, Judgment of 22 September 2005, Application No 75255/01; ECtHR, *Koua v France*, ECtHR, *Hutten-Czapska v Poland*, Judgment of 19 June 2006, Application No 35014/97.

[25] This drew on a lecture given by Alfred Marshall to the Cambridge reform forum in which he reflected on the need to promote working-class citizenry to combat cultural blockage. Accordingly,

citizenship reflects on the culture, norms and values that emerge from the economic life. Some of these ideas are still relevant in fostering and enabling citizenship among the working class not only to make citizenship rights 'enabling' but also to ensure the collective participation and reflect on legitimacy rhetoric that consider not only the individual but also the collective dimension.[26] The latter has arguably received far less attention,[27] and emphasises the role of industrial citizenship in providing a moral framework that links individuals, in this case workers and employers, to a community.[28]

Although Marshall's theory of citizenship was based on national citizenship, it is clear that polities have now evolved well beyond the nation state, thus creating the need to clarify the bind between other polities, like the EU, and its citizens. The next two sections aim precisely at this by elaborating, on the one hand, upon the dimensions of EU social citizenship and, on the other, upon the relation between the EU and other citizenships.

III. Constructing EU Citizenship's Dimensions

What exactly the dimensions of citizenship, namely, legitimacy (the why), participation (the how) and the rights and obligations (the what), convey will depend on both the particularities of a given society and time to guarantee 'a continuous series of transactions between rulers and subjects'.[29] Accordingly, the social contract of each polity will adapt as the society evolves and the law should incorporate this social contract. In the recent history of the EU, the EPSR might be seen as a compass established by the 'rulers' to fulfil certain needs of the subjects, whereas in-work poverty could be understood as a red-flag in the former status quo which threatens the existing social contract.

The starting point of these dimensions should be the legitimacy, since this will establish the foundations that constitutes the community in which citizenry is based.

A. Legitimacy

Like any other polity, for the EU to have legitimacy, an interrelationship between solidarity and the community needs to be established. In other words, what

---

only enabling the working class (with fewer hours, better wages and other conditions) could they enjoy the fruits of civilisation and thus become full-fledged citizens. See more: T Strangleman, 'Rethinking Industrial Citizenship' (2015) 66 *The British Journal of Sociology* 673.

[26] For a complete discussion on trade unions and citizenship see: P Bagguley, 'Industrial Citizenship: A Re-conceptualisation and a Case Study of the UK' (2013) 33(5/6) *International Journal of Sociology and Social Policy* 265 and references therein.

[27] Strangleman (n 25).

[28] ibid.

[29] T Faist, 'The Transnational Social Question: Social Rights and Citizenship in a Global Context' (2009) 24(1) *International Sociology* 7.

gives EU citizens the right to claim membership of this community?[30] Unlike other polities, this question is levelled as it requires individuals' membership, but also, and perhaps even primarily, a collective identity between the different Member States.[31] Whereas, social rights may well be the 'last bastion of respectable nationalism',[32] in the erosion of sovereignty following Europeanisation and globalisation, there are important considerations that suggest at least some role for the EU social citizenship.

From a normative point of view, the departure point for any legitimacy of the EU –understood as a telic legitimacy[33] – lies in the constitutional promises embedded in primary law. There are two provisions on primary law that need to be explored for this purpose. On the one hand, Article 2 TEU, which enshrines the values upon which the EU is founded and, on the other, Article 3 TEU on the general objectives of the EU, which legitimate the EU to exercise its competences.

Article 2 TEU codifies the axiological heritage upon which the EU is built, as apparent from its preamble.[34] In fact, these values implicitly assist in defining what constitutes a European state when accessing the EU.[35] In principle, membership can only be acquired by respecting and promoting the values of the EU (Article 49 TEU) and Member States are bound by the Treaty to respect and promote such values. According to Article 2 TEU, the EU is founded on the values to respect the right to human dignity, freedom, democracy, equality, the rule of law and respect for human rights, which are *common* (emphasis added) to all Member States. These values are updated with every new Treaty, thus reflecting on the idea of (social) citizenship being 'a continuous series of transactions'[36] and how this changes over time. The Treaty of Lisbon, importantly, added 'solidarity' to the existing value catalogue.[37]

Whereas the exact substantive scope of what each value entails is unclear, the CJEU has often referred to values in its interpretation,[38] and has particularly emphasised that the protection of fundamental rights represents the milestone upon which the legitimacy of the whole Union is based.[39] This is a legacy of

[30] P Dwyer, *Welfare Rights and Responsibilities: Contesting Social Citizenship* (Bristol, Bristol Policy Press, 2000) 187.

[31] W Streeck, 'Neo-Voluntarism: A New European Social Regime?' in F Snyder (ed), *Constitutional Dimensions of European Economic Integration*, (London, Kluwer Law International, 1996) 232.

[32] G Davies, 'The Process and Side-Effects of Harmonisation of European Welfare States' (2006) Jean Monnet Working Paper 02/06, 34.

[33] A Sangiovanni, 'Debating the EU's Raison d'Être: On the Relation between Legitimacy and Justice' (2019) 57(1) *Journal of Common Market Studies* 13–27.

[34] Recital para 2 Preamble TEU.

[35] Article 49 TEU.

[36] Faist (n 29).

[37] S Nicolosi, 'The Contribution of the Court of Justice to the Codification of the Founding Values of the European Union' (2015) 51 *Revista de Derecho Comunitario Europeo* 613.

[38] For several examples on each value see: A Aranguiz, *Combating Poverty and Social Exclusion in European Union Law* (Abingdon, Routledge, 2022) 127–30.

[39] CJEU, Case C-402/05 P *Kadi and Al Barakaat International Foundation v Council and European Commission* EU:C:2008:461, para 285 reads: '[T]he obligations imposed by an international agreement cannot have the effect of prejudicing the constitutional principles of the EC Treaty, which include the

the failed Constitutional Treaty, in which human rights represented 'the very heart and soul of the document'.[40] This importance of fundamental rights in the Lisbon Treaty as something 'common' to Europeans can also be found in the Charter of Fundamental Rights (CFR), which structures its catalogue of rights under titles named after the values in Article 2 TEU. Similarly, Article 6 TEU establishes that fundamental rights as interpreted in the constitutional traditions common to the Member States (and by the ECtHR) constitute a general principle of EU law. In addition, the fact that social rights are enshrined in the solidarity chapter of the CFR, is unquestionable proof that there is a European common denominator. The more extensive and detailed catalogue in the EPSR only reinforces the idea that there is also a common social community, even if this is arguably aspirational.

The values enshrined in Article 2 TEU represent both the ethical essence upon which the EU is constructed and a constitutive legal norm.[41] Not only do these values represent a common ground between Member States and its peoples, thus representing a shared polity or – 'what makes men resemble each other and rally' ('Se rassembler et se ressembler')[42] – but also give legitimacy to the edifice of EU law.

This is closely tied to the objectives set in Article 3 TEU and the institutional framework set in Article 13(1) TEU, which establishes that it is the overall task of the institutional framework to enforce these values. Article 3 TEU promises a social market economy aiming at full social progress that fights social exclusion and discrimination and promotes social cohesion and solidarity among Member States. A Union that promises to fight social exclusion and discrimination reveals a broader understanding of the 'social' in the social market economy.[43] Here, much like in the concept of social citizenship, there is a departure from the market logic to pursue substantive equality in the EU population by targeting inequalities. The concept of social justice suggests some degree of distributional opportunities.[44] Article 3 TEU thus reinforced the idea of a common polity that aims, among others to achieve social progress. The idea of a 'social market economy', moreover, brings up a more traditional link between the EU and a social dimension, namely that a certain degree of social progress is necessary for the market to function.

principle that all Community acts must respect fundamental rights, that respect constituting a condition of their lawfulness which it is for the Court to review in the framework of the complete system of legal remedies established by the Treaty.'

[40] J Rifkin, *The European Dream: How Europe's Vision of the Future is Quietly Eclipsing the American Dream* (Cambridge, Polity Press, 2004).

[41] A von Bogdandy, 'Founding Principles of EU Law: A Theoretical and Doctrinal Sketch' (2010) 12 *Revus* 35.

[42] As cited by D Rousseau, 'Citizenship in Abeyance' (2005) 1 *European Constitutional Law Review* 44, 46.

[43] K Sommerman, 'Article 3 [The Objectives of the European Union] (ex-Article 2 TEU)' in H Blanke and S Mangiamely (eds), *The Treaty on the European Union (TEU): A Commentary* (Heidelberg, Springer, 2013) 175, para 39.

[44] J Rawls, *A Theory of Justice* (Cambridge, Harvard University Press, 1999) 6–9.

Without a certain quality of living that is common to all Member States, free movement is likely to ultimately lead to social dumping, brain drains and (the fear of) welfare tourism. This is problematic not only for the sustainability of a Union that is founded on the principle of free movement, but also key to ensure an equilibrium in the market and maintain the citizens' – especially the stayers' – political support in the long-term. In this sense, social rights can be conceived as provisions that enable conditions for the market to exist, whether this encompasses market-making or market-correcting arrangements.[45] Markets alone cannot fully realise the ideas of a social citizenship or social rights more generally, for which governments are indispensable. Claassen et al frame this inability in terms of inequality.[46]

Article 3 TEU is a recognition of the insufficiency of liberal markets to reach the objectives of the Union. A social market economy relies on the forces of a competitive economy, but it attributes a major role to the State in ensuring a 'fair play' in order to enable as many subjects as possible to participate in said economy.[47] In other words, it acknowledges that markets alone cannot fully realise the ideals of citizenship to the extent that they cannot guarantee equality among citizens. This ties closely to the 'social state' models implemented in many EU countries, which symbolises the constitutional obligation of the state to assume an interventionist function in the economic and social spheres.[48] Such a social state not only entails a series of social rights but also prescribes specific functions of the public powers, including the formulation of a system of values forming a constitutional 'ethos'. The adherence to this ethos, in turn, is what gives the state legitimacy and ensures that public actions are not merely a matter of the political discourse.[49]

The EPSR, more recently, offers a more up-to-date reflection on a social market economy, which ties social policy with economic progress, stating that '[s]ocial policy should also be conceived as a productive factor, which reduces inequality, maximises job creation and allows Europe's human capital to thrive'.[50] According to this, social policy is a productive factor that contributes to growth

---

[45] R Claassen et al, 'Four Models of Protecting Citizenship and Social Rights in Europe: Conclusions to the Special Issue 'Rethinking the European Social Market Economy' (2019) 57(1) *Journal of Common Market Studies* 159.

[46] Equal terms in this regard could convey both ideas of equal opportunities or equality of outcomes, depending on the political interpretation. Claassen et al (ibid).

[47] European Commission, *For a Highly Competitive Social Market Economy 50 Proposals for Improving Our Work, Business and Exchanges with One Another*, COM(2010) 608 final.

[48] Katrougalos emphasises here the difference between the 'welfare state' and the 'social state' in which the second forms a sub-category of the former. Accordingly, a welfare state represents a universal type of state emerging in the twentieth century as a response to the functional necessities of the capitalist economies. In this respect he puts the examples of Australia and the US as countries with a welfare state that have no constitutional foundation. Katrougalos (n 22).

[49] A Lyon-Caen, 'The Legal Efficacy and Significance of Fundamental Social Rights: Lessons from the European Experience' in B Hepple (ed), *Social and Labour Rights in a Global Context* (Cambridge, Cambridge University Press, 2002) 187.

[50] European Commission, *Launching a Consultation on a European Pillar of Social Rights*, COM(2016) 127, para. 2.1.

and competitiveness and, as it plays a specific role in the 'deepening' of the EU, it contributes to integration. Deakin calls these the two functions of social policy. On the one hand, the 'market reversing' (or market correcting) function refers to when social policy is used to reverse growing inequalities that result from economic integration, and on the other hand, the 'market constituent' (or market making) function implies that social policy is an input into growth and integration and not a consequence of it.[51]

The above confirms that, even from a legal point of view, legitimacy can be found for an EU social citizenship that transcends the current isopolitical model and establishes both a value-oriented normative core that builds a common 'we' and confirms the need for a socially aware market making policy for the survival of the more traditional economic ethos.

B. Participation

Once the existence of a common polity (legitimacy, the 'why') has been established, the discussion can then turn to how to build a relationship between rulers and members in a way that it provides individuals with the political power to influence this relation (bottom-up participation) and to enjoy the fruits of citizenship (top-down). Bottom-up participation of citizenship is necessary in order to have a continuous transaction between rulers and citizens and to formulate rights that are fit for purpose. In this vein, in-work poverty could be seen as a phenomenon flagging that rights are no longer (sufficiently) fitting. This participation entails that, as part of a community, citizens have the power to influence and participate in the development of such polity. In the case of social rights, there are two participatory models: political power and labour power, the latter amplifying the notion of industrial citizenship.

i. Individual Participation

In the EU, the most conventional form of participation is elections for the European Parliament. Without getting into the heavily criticised democratic deficit at the EU level,[52] something to consider when substantiating social citizenship, therefore, is to have the role of the European Parliament very present. In this sense, for citizenship to be as participatory as possible, it would be preferable

---

[51] S Deakin, 'What Follows Austerity? From Social Pillar to New Deal' in F Vandenbroucke, C Barnard and G De Baere (eds), *A European Social Union after the Crisis* (Cambridge, Cambridge University Press, 2017) 200–01.

[52] A Follesdal and S Hix, 'Why There is a Democratic Deficit in the EU: A Response to Majone and Moravcsik' (2006) 44 *Journal of Common Market Studies* 533–62; P Kratochvíl and Z Sychra, 'The End of Democracy in the EU? The Eurozone Crisis and the EU's Democratic Deficit' (2019) 41(2) *Journal of European Integration* 16985; Z Murdoch, S Connolly and H Kassim, 'Administrative Legitimacy and the Democratic Deficit of the European Union' (2018) 25(3) *Journal of European Public Policy* 389–408.

to adopt instruments according to the ordinary legislative procedure in which the European Parliament and the Council co-legislate. Unlike the extraordinary legislative procedure, this requires EU legislation to be adopted by – not merely consulted – the only directly democratically accountable EU institution.[53]

There are, in addition, other forms of political participation in the EU that emphasise the democratic value of EU citizenship. This is clearly the case of the European Citizens Initiative (ECI), which empowers citizens to launch their 'own' proposal.[54] This is a unique way of bringing the decision-making process closer to citizens that allows them to shape the EU by calling the Commission to propose new laws. Whereas there have been many social initiatives in the past,[55] the procedural requirements for the ECI are set at a rather high threshold, which remains very criticised and calls for the renegotiation of the rules of the game.[56]

There are also several interesting top-down resources available to citizens like SOLVIT or Your Europe Advice from which individuals can get targeted advice on their EU rights and thus facilitate their enjoyment of citizenship rights. These are key in avoiding unnecessary obstacles and raising awareness. Unlike Your Europe Advice, SOLVIT engages with different institutions and provides a solution to the citizen regarding a particular problem. However, the material scope of SOLVIT is limited to cross-border issues and it is thus not available for stayers, and so there is abundant room for improving participation.

ii. Collective Participation

Labour (collective) power is a 'secondary system of industrial citizenship parallel with and supplementary to the system of political citizenship'[57] which arises from collectivities based on class identities[58] and it essentially recognises the workers' participation in an otherwise purely economic freedom.[59] Trade Unions

---

[53] Elsewhere, we have discussed in detail the competences that can be used for this substantiation having in mind the three citizenship dimensions. A Aranguiz with M Houwerzijl, 'Reconceptualising EU Social Citizenship Towards the Social Citizenship That We Deserve', Working, Yet Poor Position Paper (2022), Deliverable 4.4, available at workingyetpoor.eu/deliverables.

[54] Note that this still requires at least seven citizens from seven different Member States to register the petition and launch a campaign to gather at least one million signatures.

[55] Available at: europa.eu/citizens-initiative/find-initiative/eci-lifecycle-statistics_en (last accessed 25 June 2023).

[56] E Longo, 'The European Citizens' Initiative: Too Much Democracy for EU Polity?' (2019) 20(2) German Law Journal 181–200; J Osun and S Schaub, 'Constructing Policy Narratives for Transnational Mobilization: Insights from European Citizens' Initiatives' (2021) 7 *European Policy Analysis* 344–64; M Geuens, 'Systemic Analysis of the European Right of Petition, the European Ombudsman and the European Citizens' Initiative: A New Approach?' in A Hoc, S Wattier and G Willems (eds), *Human Rights as a Basis for Reevaluating and Reconstructing the Law* (Brussels, Larcier, 2016).

[57] Marshall (n 15) 26.

[58] C Zhang and N Lillie, 'Industrial Citizenship, Cosmopolitanism and European Integration' (2015) 18(1) *European Journal of Social Theory* 93–111.

[59] H Sinzheimer, 'The Development of Labor Legislation in Germany', trans from D. Shumway, 'Social and Industrial Conditions in the Germany of Today' (1920) *The Annals of the American Academy of Political and Social Science* 9235–40, 38; R Dukes, *The Labour Constitution: The Enduring Idea of Labour Law* (Oxford, Oxford University Press, 2014).

and Works Councils[60] are the clearest participatory structures that attempt to put workers (representatives) on an equal footing with employers when deciding in the regulation of labour conditions, which should ensure a balance between the economic and social questions in the decision-making process. To a different extent, both structures are part of the EU's social acquis.[61]

EU law provides the constitutional foundations that protect labour power and aim to emphasise the collective side of labour standards by encouraging social partners' involvement. The Social Policy title in the Treaty on the Functioning of the European Union (TFEU) enshrines a general commitment to 'recognise' and 'promote' social partners (Article 152 TFEU) and mentions the principle of autonomy. This autonomy manifests, for example, in the fact that social partners are not bound to the Commission's consultation for a prospective proposal,[62] although this does not mean that the autonomy of social partners is limitless.[63] In addition, there is the possibility to entrust management and labour with the implementation of social policy (Article 153(3) TFEU), the obligation to consult the social partners before submitting a proposal (Article 154 TFEU) and the possibility for social partners to reach autonomous or semi-autonomous agreements (Article 155 TFEU).[64] The latter has successfully led to many agreements in the past.[65] The autonomy of social partners in this participatory model, however, has been criticised for not being completely autonomous, particularly in instances in which the Commission has interfered with their policy-making power.[66] These cases have been rather critically assessed in view of their 'chilling' effect for an already slow social dialogue at the European level.[67] A fully fledged social citizenship should

---

[60] N Vagdoutis, 'Hans Kelsen and Carl Schmitt in Weimar: A Riddle of Political Constitutionalism' (PhD thesis, University of Glasgow, 2018).

[61] The role of social partners is protected in EU primary law and the European Works Council directive is part of the EU's secondary legislation: Council Directive 2006/109/EC of 20 November 2006 adapting Directive 94/45/EC on the establishment of a European Works Council or a procedure in Community-scale undertakings and Community-scale groups of undertakings for the purposes of informing and consulting employees, by reason of the accession of Bulgaria and Romania [2006] OJ L 363/416.

[62] D Obradovic, 'The Impact of Social Dialogue Procedure on the Powers of the European Union Institutions' in H Compston and J Greenwood (eds), *Social Partnership in the European Union* (London, Palgrave Macmillan, 2001).

[63] CJEU cases: Case C-447/09 *Prigge and others* EU:C:2011:573, para 47; Case C-172/11 *Erny* EU:C:2012:399, para 50.

[64] European Commission, *Partnership for Change in an Enlarged Europe – Enhancing the Contribution of European Social Dialogue*, COM(2004) 557 final.

[65] Such as the Council Directive 97/81/EC of 15 December 1997 concerning the Framework Agreement on part-time work [1998] OJ L 14/9; Council Directive 1999/70/EC of 28 June 1999 concerning the framework agreement on fixed-term work [1999] OJ L 175/43; Council Directive 1999/63/EC of 21 June 1999 concerning the Agreement on the organisation of working time of seafarers [1999] OJ L 167/33; Council Directive 2000/79/EC of 27 November 2000 concerning the European Agreement on the Organisation of Working Time of Mobile Workers in Civil Aviation [2000] OJ L 302/57; or the Council Directive 2010/18/EU of 8 March 2010 implementing the revised Framework Agreement on parental leave [2010] OJ L 68/13, which is replaced by the Work-life Balance Directive.

[66] CJEU cases: Case T-135/69 *UEAPME v Council* EU:T:1998:128, para 85–89; Case T-310/18 *EPSU and Goudriaan v Commission* EU:T:2019:757; Case C-928/19 P *EPSU v Commission* EU:C:2021:656.

[67] A García-Muñoz Alhambra, 'An Uncertain Future for EU-Level Collective Bargaining: The New Rules of the Game After EPSU' (2022) 51(2) *Industrial Law Journal* 318; S Rainone, 'After the

reflect on the importance of the labour force in the development of social policy and bind the autonomy of the social partners in this process.

When substantiating the container of social citizenship, it is worth having in mind that only the Social Policy Title foresees and active and direct involvement of labour power – the employment, cohesion and European Social Fund title, instead, only give management and labour a consultatory role through the advisory role of the European Economic and Social Committee. This would suggest that if a social citizenship ought to promote labour power, at least under the current legislative framework, a significant part of the substantiation of the content of citizenship will have to be based on the social policy competences that are capable of accommodating an active role for the social partners.

From the above, it can be confirmed that there are many different ways in which the EU interacts with its citizens and vice-versa, also as far as social rights are concerned. Whereas this participatory model is far from ideal and leaves much room for improvement, it is still capable of accommodating participatory models that respond to both the political (individual) and labour (collective) powers.

C. (Social) Rights and Obligations

Now the fact that there is a community and links between individuals and collectives with it has been confirmed, we are confronted with the question of what is gained from this. Citizenship can be understood as the 'right to have rights',[68] and thus the rights and obligations can be considered the 'core' dimension of all citizenships, including EU (social) citizenship. For what concerns social citizenship, these should enable citizens to attain a decent standard of living and to exercise other (civil and political) rights. In this context, they provide the necessary tools to take the leap between being formally entitled to nominal rights and having a genuine possibility to enjoy their fruition.[69]

The very complexity of Europe's constitutional order creates opportunities for experiments and social policy inventions of this kind. Some have hinted at the importance of the CFR, as a human-rights approach to European citizenship.[70] The CFR could in principle act in a similar way to a national 'Bill of Rights' which often contain the 'rights' of individuals as members of a national collective. However, the current limits in the application of the CFR show that such an approach

---

"Hairdressing Agreement", the EPSU Case: Can the Commission Control the EU's Social Dialogue?' (2020) ETUI Policy Brief; EPSU, 'A Critical Evaluation of the General Court's Decision in EPSU vs the European Commission' (2020).

[68] S Benhabib, '"The Right to Have Rights": Hannah Arendt on the Contradictions of the Nation-state' in S Benhabib (ed), *The Rights of Others: Aliens, Residents, and Citizens* (Cambridge, Cambridge University Press, 2004).

[69] Bauböck (n 18).

[70] MP Granger, 'Revisiting the Foundation of European Union Citizenship: Making It Relevant to all European Union Citizens' (2016) bEUcitizen report.

would provide a rather 'thin' citizenship and not live up to Articles 2 and 3 TEU. Moreover, it would often remain dependent on a cross-border element. Others have advocated for the European Social Charter (ESC) instead.[71] Whereas this is a far more mature social instrument, it is not directly binding for the EU, and thus such an approach would raise issues of legitimacy. Originally, the notion of EU citizenship was developed by the ECJ, so one could argue that such 'substantiation' could be left to the EU judiciary. This not only raises issues of the legitimacy of the Court, but clearly also of the separation of powers and the principles of conferral. Thus, the way forward cannot come by the hand of the ECJ alone.

In contrast, the literature, including our own work,[72] has consistently found that the set of (social) rights provided by the EU is insufficient to live up to a citizenship promise. In her analysis, Börner tested four blocks of existing EU social policy instruments (harmonisation, coordination, funding and intergovernmental cooperation) against Marshall's theory to find, much like other authors, that the heart of social Europe lies with mobile citizens, which according to her suggests a 'misguided understanding of social rights' as they do not enable citizens to fully enjoy their citizenship. Whereas she finds this conclusion against an incomplete catalogue of what composes the social dimension of the EU – notoriously missing recent initiatives, much of the labour law and equality corpus and the charters – and the EU social policies examined miss important nuances,[73] we can agree with Börner and Thym that the current vision of social justice in the EU is incomplete.[74] Vandenbroucke et al develop this idea in terms of power resources.[75] Whereas based on this conceptual framework one can discern a greater wealth of resources that the EU offers to its citizens than often credited, it still shows a lack of justiciable social entitlements, in particular, for stayers.[76] Amelina too finds inequalities in the way some citizens enjoy their social rights,[77] which is inevitable in a mostly isopolitical citizenship.

On the basis of some general and concrete proposals, the next chapters of this volume elaborate on how the container of EU social citizenship, and in particular

---

[71] AM Świątkowski and M Wujczyk, 'The European Social Charter as a Basis for Defining Social Rights for EU Citizens' in Pennings and Seeleib-Kaiser (n 10).

[72] See all deliverables of Working, Yet Poor work package 4, available at workingyetpoor.eu/deliverables, as well as chs 3 and 6 in this book.

[73] She briefly examines harmonisation in the fields of occupational safety and gender, the European Social Fund, the coordination of national social security, and the Open Method of Coordination.

[74] S Börner, 'Marshall Revisited: EU Social Policy from a Social-rights Perspective' (2020) 30(4) *Journal of European Social Policy* 421; D Thym, 'The Failure of Union Citizenship beyond the Single Market' in R Bauböck (ed), *Debating European Citizenship* (Heidelberg, Springer, 2019).

[75] F Vandenbroucke et al, 'The Rationale for and the Nature and Content of European Social Rights' EuSocialCit (2020) deliverable, available at www.eusocialcit.eu/published-our-working-paper-on-the-nature-and-rationale-for-european-social-rights.

[76] A Aranguiz, 'The Potential and Limits for EU Social Policy in the Current Legal Framework', EuSocialCit (2022) deliverable, available at www.eusocialcit.eu/published-our-working-paper-on-the-potential-and-limits-for-social-policy-in-the-current-eu-framework.

[77] Amelina (n 16); while her analysis departs from a very different standpoint, her findings are not different from many other authors in that as a mostly transnational solidarity, EU citizenship does not live up to the expectations of a fully fledged social citizenship.

this third dimension on rights and obligations can be substantiated to make EU citizenship more equal, at least for the purpose of fighting in-work poverty. Before that, this chapter first offers some important considerations to bear in mind when developing a citizenship that acts not in isolation but instead as an added layer to national memberships.

IV. EU Citizenship in a Nested Civitas

Most citizenship theories, including Marshall's, are admittedly nation centred. However, over the last decades researchers have observed a de-nationalisation of citizenship, partly transferring the 'state' role to either the regional, transnational or even supranational level.[78] According to Börner, this diversification of the 'state' figure is evidence of the 'erosion of sovereignty and weakened social systems'. Consequently, there is an urgency to focus on defending (pluri)social citizenship and not the welfare state per se.[79] In our view, this does not entail a complete deconstruction of the nation-based welfare state, but rather to see this as one (arguably the main) piece of social citizenship, which is supported by local, regional and supranational actors. In a multi-level citizenship, something key is to determine how the different levels interact.

Faist's idea of 'nested citizenship' is quite helpful in understanding the interaction between national and European citizenship.[80] Accordingly, membership in the EU is embedded in a multi-tiered system composed by sub-state, state, inter-state and supra-state levels. Whereas this intricate web of governance gives room for enshrining a few new (social) rights and re-adapting existing ones at the supra-national level – in connection to and by no means independent from the domestic level – this does not create a federal welfare system. So understood, EU citizenship remains but one added layer to national citizenship, therefore going in line with Article 20 TFEU. This results in an 'extraordinarily intricate network' of social rights and complementary institutions at different levels, in which Member States remain playing a central role but no longer an exclusive one. The notion of 'nested' emphasises patterns of membership, which manifest in a variety of levels (EU and national, of course, but also regional and local levels). This understanding is able to accommodate the multiplicity of social memberships in current multi-level governance frameworks.[81]

Claassen et al, in contrast, pose two questions that should aid in determining the levels in which (social) citizenship rights are developed: who formulates the normative ideals for social protection and who provides for the social protection

---

[78] R Bauböck and V Guiraudon, 'Realignments of Citizenship: Reassessing Rights in the Age of Plural Memberships and Multilevel Governance' (2009) 13(5) *Citizenship Studies* 439.
[79] Börner (n 74).
[80] Faist (n 29).
[81] Amelina (n 16).

arrangements?[82] In answering these questions, they come up with a four-tiered spectrum of models of EU citizenship which they name 'passive spectator', 'patron of nations', 'guarantor of social rights' and 'protector of citizens', ranking from less to more EU involvement in social protection. The first and last models seem rather improbable. The 'passive spectator' model envisions no involvement for the EU whatsoever, which is already not the case. The latter, instead, suggests a comprehensive role for the EU regarding social rights as the direct provider of citizenship. Not only would this model not be possible from a competence point of view, but it would also not be desirable as proximity to citizens is necessary when regulating and providing (social) rights.[83] The second and third models, in contrast, already co-exist in the EU. In the 'patron of nations' model, nation states decide the level and form of social rights, but the EU can take an active role where market integration threatens the integrity of national protection systems. In this model, EU action is shaped to compensate for the negative side-effects of market integration. Much, if not most, of the legislative framework of the social dimension of the EU would fall under this model, most notably in the case of free movement and labour mobility instruments like social security regulations, posting of workers or the establishment of the European Labour Authority (ELA). As in the passive spectator model, this model only envisions a responsibility towards the Member States but not directly towards citizens. This is not the case in the third model, the 'guarantor of social rights', in which the EU determines a set of social rights but the operationalisation of these is left to the Member States. This is the case of the atypical work directives or occupational safe and health regulations.[84] This model goes along the lines of the European Social Union as proposed by Vandenbroucke, in which the EU supports national welfare states through social standards and objectives, 'leaving ways and means of social policy to the Member States'.[85]

Key in determining the level of EU intrusion are normative tools already existing in the EU constitution: the principles of conferral, subsidiarity and proportionality. In this vein, the EU has so-called 'functional competences': it only has powers to the extent that these are necessary to achieve pre-agreed upon objectives. In the idea of a nested citizenship, it is the EU's objectives and powers that will be decisive in determining whether certain social citizenship rights are to be developed at the supranational level.

In the case of social policy, broadly understood, the EU has shared and supporting competences which entitle the EU to various levels of intrusion in different fields. In order to interfere, however, having powers is not enough to

---

[82] Claassen (n 45).

[83] This goes in line both with the principle of subsidiarity as well as with the concept of cultural relativism of human rights, which encompasses the idea that while human rights are universal they still need to account for cultural particularities.

[84] This is not to say that this model excludes market ridden regulations. In fact, these two examples have a strong market rationale behind them. However, the way in which they embed this rationale is by creating a base of minimum standards that protect workers in the respective material scopes.

[85] F Vandenbroucke, 'The idea of a European Social Union: A Normative Introduction' in Vandenbroucke et al (n 51).

justify EU action. The EU will have to be better suited than the Member States to pursue such an objective through a particular measure, otherwise known as the principle of subsidiarity. Subsidiarity embodies the fundamental concern of federalism regarding the balance of powers between the Member States and the EU.[86] The last step is to establish the extent to which EU intervention is desirable, which is embodied in the principle of proportionality. Elsewhere the competences and potential role of EU law have extensively been studied, determining that, whereas limited in different fronts, there is still ample room for EU involvement.[87]

These three steps are key in defining the nested citizenship idea as they will determine when, how and to what extent should actions be taken at the EU level. This system presupposes that different levels – transnational, national and subnational – of social protection (broadly understood) coexist. For these to work, it requires that these levels interact and even promote some upward convergence.[88] In such nested[89] or multilevel systems[90] is it crucial that different levels are not self-contradicting so that a fully fledged and constantly progressing social citizenship can be guaranteed by regional, national and supranational institutions.[91]

V. Concluding Remarks

The growing phenomenon of in-work poverty signals that it is time for the EU to step out of its isopolitically-bound idea of citizenship and to mature towards a more all-encompassing form of citizenship that is able to deliver a decent standard of living for all its citizens. This chapter has briefly analysed the current status quo of EU citizenship and compared it to what a true citizenship should capture. On the basis of this, it then has moved on to argue that the necessary dimensions for a fully fledged citizenship already exist in the constitutional foundations of the EU: there is a common 'we' that legitimises the EU as a citizenship provider, different participatory models that allow for an interaction between rulers and members and there is a limited body of rights and obligations. Nevertheless, these,

---

[86] F Fabrini, 'The Principle of Subsidiarity' in R Schütze (ed), *Oxford Principles of European Union Law* (Oxford, Oxford University Press, 2018).

[87] Aranguiz (n 38) and specifically for in-work poverty Aranguiz with Houwerzijl (n 53).

[88] See C Barnard, 'Regulative Competitive Federalism in the European Union? The Case of EU Social Policy' in J Shaw (ed), *Social Law and Policy in an Evolving European Union* (Oxford, Hart Publishing, 2020).

[89] See Faist (n 29); O Golynker, 'Jobseekers Rights in the European Union: Challenges of Changing the Paradigm of Social Solidarity' (2005) 30(1) *European Law Review* 111; Streeck (n 31).

[90] G Marks, 'A Third Lens: Comparing European Integration and State Building' in J Klausen and LA Tilly (eds), *European Integration in Social and Historical Perspective: 1850 to the Present* (Lanham, Rowman & Littlefield, 2005) 35.

[91] M Weiss, 'Cumulative Objectives of Fundamental Rights' Protection in the European Union' in L Betten and D Mac Devitt (eds), *The Protection of Fundamental Social Rights in the European Union* (London, Kluwer Law International, 1996) 33–37; AK Kolb, 'European Social Rights Towards National Welfare States. Additional, Substitute, Illusory?' in J Bussemaker (ed), *Citizenship and Welfare State Reform in Europe* (Abingdon, Routledge, 1999) 171.

in particular the 'core' that makes citizenship, the rights and obligations, need to be further substantiated to live up to the idea of a social citizenship that enables all its members equally. Being the EU part of a complex network of (social) rights providers, the previous section has also elaborated on the workings of a multilevel citizenship. Here as well, the EU treaties already provide essential tools, namely, the principles of conferral subsidiarity and proportionality, to ensure that EU action is only conceived where the EU is in fact better placed.

The current treaties offer possibilities, and even give a mandate to, exploit the powers of the EU to target areas in which (a degree of) EU interference is necessary. In-work poverty is a blinking indicator that the current social contract is simply not working and simultaneously can be used to guide the substantiation of social rights. The next chapters elaborate on this theoretical framework and make a number of concrete suggestions to this end.

6

Adequate Wages Across the EU

GIULIA MARCHI

I. Adequate Minimum Wages: A Shield against In-work Poverty

The need to ensure adequate wages and decent standards of living is emphasised by the fact that 'for too many people, work no longer pays', as statistics on
in-work poverty (IWP) show.[1] This issue has become even more urgent due to
the impact of the Covid-19 pandemic and the consequent economic downturn,
which has had a significant impact particularly on those sectors, such as the
service sectors, small firms, and non-standard and precarious work, that have
felt a greater impact of the Covid-19 pandemic crisis, thus exacerbating an existing trend consisting of job polarisation and an increasing 'share of low-paid
and low-skilled occupations'. The situation is worsening and increasing wage
inequality in several EU Member States.[2]

To this respect, it must be noted that minimum wage policies and increasing
minimum wage levels cannot be considered as a panacea in fighting inequalities
and in coping with IWP. It is acknowledged that there is a weak connection between
low wages and poverty: on the one hand, although the risk of in-work poverty
is higher for low-paid workers, relatively few of them actually experience it. On
the other hand, in many countries in-work poverty is also linked to the intensity
of work within households and to the low quality of the employment.[3] Indeed,
while the notion of IWP is related to the household income – more precisely to
the family equivalised disposable income – the notion of low-wage worker refers
to a single person whose hourly earnings is less than two-thirds of median hourly
earnings. Therefore, the impact of low wages on an individual worker's risk of

---

[1] U Von der Leyen, State of the Union address of September 2020, in ec.europa.eu/commission/
presscorner/detail/en/SPEECH_20_1655.

[2] The need of action in this respect is highlighted also by L Visentini, 'Directive on adequate minimum wages: European institutions must respect the promise made to workers!' (2021) 4 *Italian Labour
Law e-Journal* 33.

[3] D Checchi and W Salverda, 'Labour-market institutions and the dispersion of wage earnings',
IZA Discussion Paper no 8220/2014 (2014).

IWP necessarily depends on the composition of that person's household and the institutional 'safety net' provided to both the individual worker and their family.[4] Thus, establishing an EU framework favouring an increase in minimum wages to a level allowing for a decent standard of living can only partially help to reduce this phenomenon.

Though insufficient alone to prevent IWP, adequate minimum wages are a necessary safeguard – a type of shield.[5] Furthermore, reasonable minimum wages may have a significant role in ensuring adequate social security benefits by having an impact on their amount, particularly where no minimum benefits are provided.

Wage dumping not only undermines the dignity of work, but also risks penalising those entrepreneurs who pay decent wages and distorting fair competition in the Single Market.

Thus, fair and adequate wages – even more than a minimum wage – pursue more than one objective: to 'make work pay', to prevent unfair competition, and, last but not least, as established by international laws, as a matter of human dignity: indeed, the 'respect for the dignity of the worker as a human being dictates that human labour should not be sold for less than a certain minimum'.[6]

In this chapter, the analysis of the notions of fair and adequate wages at national and international level (section II), as well as the study of the debate on the concept and the methods of calculation of living wage (section III), is the basis for a more in-depth reasoning on the criteria for the assessment of fairness and adequacy of minimum wages adopted at EU level in the Directive 2022/2041 (sections IV and V). The chapter concludes on a conceptualisation of what the fair and adequate wage should ideally be, ie a benchmark notion of fair and adequate wages against in-work poverty (section VI).

II. The Notion of Fair and Adequate Wages at National and International Level

Despite some differences – particularly with regard to the sources, the notions, the methods of enforcement, and the functions of minimum wages – crucial aspects derive from the notions of fair and adequate wage at national and international level.

---

[4] W Salverda, 'Low earnings and their drivers in relation to in-work poverty' in H Lohmann and I Marx (eds), *Handbook on In-work Poverty* (Cheltenham, Elgar, 2018); B Maitre, B Nolan and C T Whelan, 'Low pay, in-work poverty and economic vulnerability' in H Lohmann and I Marx (eds), *Handbook on In-work Poverty* (Cheltenham, Elgar, 2018); B Vanhercke, D Ghailani and S Sabato (eds), *Social Policy in the European Union: State of Play 2018* (Brussels, OSE-ETUI, 2018).

[5] A Horton and J Wills, 'Impacts of the living wage on in-work poverty' in H Lohmann and I Marx (eds), *Handbook on In-work Poverty* (Cheltenham, Elgar, 2018).

[6] G Davidov, *A Purposive Approach to Labour Law* (Oxford, Oxford University Press, 2016) 73 ff.

Reasoning on the role of wages in fighting against IWP, it is crucial to begin by focusing on the notion of fair and adequate wages and on the concept of a decent standard of living that a reasonable wage should ensure.

The importance of ensuring a fair and adequate wage as a means to protect human dignity is acknowledged. As an example, in Italy the notion of a fair and adequate wage expressly arises from Article 36 of the Constitution, which establishes two criteria for ensuring reasonable wage – the principle of proportionality and the principle of adequacy – that, at the same time, also identify the main functions of salary: it is due in return for the work or service provided and it should grant a decent standard of living.[7] While the principle of proportionality requires that wages match with the work performed by the employee, the 'social function of the wage' implies that the employer may sometimes be obliged to remunerate its employee even when the latter is not working, for instance when sick or pregnant.[8] According to the principle of adequacy, wages must be at least sufficient for a free and dignified existence. Thus, at least in theory, this principle aims to guarantee workers and their families not only the minimum income required for subsistence, but an income that also supports their social needs and enables a socially acceptable standard of living.[9]

The reference to human dignity is also relevant in other EU Member States, for instance with respect to the Belgian legal system. Article 23 of the Belgian Constitution states a more general right 'to lead a life worthy of human dignity', which implies fair working conditions, including the right to fair remuneration. Its content is intentionally left open. Even though there is no specific definition of the term 'fair remuneration' in the Constitutional provision, on the basis of the

---

[7] Pursuant to para 1 of Art 36 of the Constitution, 'workers have the right to a remuneration commensurate to the quantity and quality of their work and in any case such as to ensure them and their families a free and dignified existence'.

[8] L Zoppoli, *La corrispettività nel contratto di lavoro* (Napoli, ESI, 1991); P Ichino, 'La nozione di giusta retribuzione nell'articolo 36 della costituzione' (2010) 1 *Rivista italiana di diritto del lavoro* 719.

[9] However, according to the notion provided for by settled Italian case law – which is relevant since there is no statutory provision establishing a minimum wage – what constitutes fair remuneration is usually determined through reference to the 'basic wages' established in the national collective agreements signed by the most representative unions in that sector, even though – it must be said – such wage rates must be considered as non-binding parameters. Cf I Senatori, 'The Precarious Balance among Hierarchy, Coordination and Competition in the Italian System of Labour Law Sources' in T Gyulavári and E Menegatti (eds), *The Sources of Labour Law* (Kluwer Law International, 2019). More precisely, when an employee claims before a court that his or her wage does not satisfy the principle of fairness and adequacy provided in Art 36 of the Constitution, on the basis of their competence in accordance with Art 2099 of the Italian Civil Code, the courts determine the wage level, usually referring to the minimum wage rates set by national collective agreements for the sector. There are many issues concerning the effective functioning and enforcement of contractual minimum wages: for instance, the existence of a variety of agreements that might be applied by the employer regardless of the business conducted, that often results in severe reductions in terms of wages, and the increasing number of 'pirate' collective agreements signed by non-representative or poorly representative unions, which often negotiate downward as compared to the pay levels set in collective agreements signed by the most representative trade unions. Cf G Centamore, *Contrattazione collettiva e pluralità di categorie* (Bologna, BUP, 2020); E Menegatti, 'Wage-setting in Italy: The Central Role Played by Case Law' (2019) 12(2) *Italian Labour Law e-Journal* 61.

preparatory documents of the Parliament, remuneration must take into account the basic social, cultural and economic needs of the workers and their families, and also enable them to engage in education and social activities.[10]

The significance of minimum wage policies in ensuring the satisfaction of the needs of all workers and their families is emphasised also at international level,[11] for instance in ILO Recommendations and Conventions, that interestingly also include among the criteria to be taken into account in determining the level of minimum wages 'the needs of workers and their families' and the cost of living.[12] With regard to the assessment of the needs of workers and their families, Article 3 of ILO Minimum Wage Fixing Convention No 131 (1970) further specifies that 'the general level of wages in the country, the cost of living, social security benefits, and the relative living standards of other social groups' are relevant elements. Thus, even though the Convention uses the term minimum wage, it seems to refer to a wage level that ensures a steady income and livelihood security.

Also, Article 4 of the European Social Charter (ESC) recognises the 'right of workers to a remuneration such as will give them and their families a decent standard of living', importantly taking into account the relationship between the wage level and standard of living. According to the interpretation of this provision by the European Committee of Social Rights (ECSR), 'the concept of "decent standard of living" goes beyond merely material basic necessities such as food, clothing and housing, and includes resources necessary to participate in cultural, educational and social activities'.[13]

The ECSR has also developed a notion of fair remuneration, according to which 'the minimum wage paid in the labour market must not fall below 60% of the net average national wage'. According to ECSR's case law, if the lowest wage in a Member State does not satisfy the 60 per cent threshold, 'but does not fall very far below', meaning that it is between 50 per cent and 60 per cent, the State will be asked 'to provide detailed evidence that the lowest wage is sufficient to give the worker a decent living standard even if it is below the established threshold'. In particular, consideration will be given to certain costs, including health care, education, transport, and to some compensatory factors, such as taxes and substantial social benefits, including family and housing benefits. Only in

---

[10] To be more precise, the request of taking into account the needs of the family has been interpreted by some as giving a mandate more directed towards the design of social and fiscal policies. Cf A Barrio, E De Becker and M Wouters, 'National Report on in-work poverty in Belgium', Working, Yet Poor Project (2021).

[11] This is the case, for instance, in Art 23 of the Universal Declaration of Human Rights, Art 7 of the International Covenant for Economic, Social and Cultural Rights (ICESCR), the preamble to the International Labour Organization (ILO)'s Constitution of 1919, and ILO Declaration on Social Justice for a Fair Globalization of 2008.

[12] R Zimmer, 'Living wages in international and European law' (2019) 25(3) *Transfer* 285.

[13] Digest of the case law of the European committee of social rights, 2018, quoting Conclusions 2010, Statement of Interpretation on Article 4§1; Conclusions XIV-2 (1998), Statement of Interpretation on Article 4§1, rm.coe.int/digest-2018-appendix-en/1680939f7e.

'extreme cases', if the lowest wages are less than half the national average wage will the State be considered 'in breach of Charter independently of such evidence'. According to the ECSR,

> a wage does not meet the requirements of the Charter, irrespective of the percentage, if it does not ensure a decent living standard in real terms for a worker, i.e. it must be clearly above the poverty line for a given country.[14]

Nevertheless, in international provisions, the importance emerges of balancing this social function of wages, linked to workers' needs and their right to a dignified existence, with other factors, such as economic and labour market considerations and benefit system. For instance, for the purpose of determining the minimum wage levels, ILO Minimum Wage Fixing Recommendation, no 131 (1970) also refers to criteria, such as '(d) social security benefits; (e) the relative living standards of other social groups', and, lastly, '(f) economic factors, including the requirements of economic development, levels of productivity and the desirability of attaining and maintaining a high level of employment'. The significance of these factors is confirmed by the case law on Article 4 of ESC: according to the ECSR, the assessment of the fairness level is based on net amounts, after deducting social security contributions and taxes on earned income, excluding indirect taxes and social transfers or welfare benefits which are not directly linked to the wage, thus taking into account any 'redistributive effects of contributions and taxes'.[15] In this way, the Committee stresses the importance of taking into account other factors when assessing the fairness of the remuneration as a 'decency threshold for the lowest wage', for example taxes and an appropriate coordination with the welfare system.[16]

III. The Different Functions of Wages: Is there a Case for a Living Wage?

In the reasoning on fair and adequate minimum wages, different functions of wages must be taken into account, as well as the tensions between them, ie between the idea of 'wages as price', reflecting workers' productivity and/or on the employers' ability to pay, and the concept of 'wages as living', linked to the cost of living. These entail different perspectives in regard to what constitutes a fair wage.[17] As long as wages are the main source for supporting living standards, the latter seems

---

[14] ibid.
[15] ibid.
[16] Z Adams and S Deakin, 'Art. 4. The right to a fair remuneration' in N Bruun et al (eds), *The European Social Charter and the Employment Relation* (Oxford, Hart, 2017).
[17] J Rubery, M Johnson and D Grimshaw, 'Minimum wages and the multiple functions of wages' in I Dingeldey, D Grimshaw and T Schulten (eds), *Minimum Wage Regimes. Statutory Regulation, Collective Bargaining and Adequate Levels* (Abingdon, Routledge, 2021).

to be a convincing argument for establishing a minimum wage to protect against poverty.[18]

From this perspective, focusing on the social functions of minimum wages, the notion of living wage is of some interest: affirming that fair and adequate wages shall provide a decent standard of living to workers and their families entails that the notion of adequate wage is related to the idea of a living wage.[19]

Yet, minimum wage and living wage 'are not the same'. In setting minimum wages, two competing objectives must be taken into consideration: 'a desire to reduce poverty and provide for the needs of workers and their families through work' and a desire to stimulate – or not to undermine – employment and economic growth.[20] It has been emphasised that due to such 'cautious' fixing mechanism of minimum wage, 'it often falls short of providing recipients with a basic and decent standard of living'.[21] Conversely, a living wage can be defined as an income from work that allows an employee a modest but socially acceptable standard of living.[22] It is generally calculated on an estimation of costs for a basic acceptable living standard. Thus – as it is widely acknowledged – living wage is something independent from the notion of minimum wage: it belongs to the moral economy and is closely related to the subsistence and needs of individuals.[23]

A. The Notion of Living Wage and its Normative, Economic and Moral Justification

One of the first formulations of the living wage concept was elaborated by Adam Smith, who supported the idea that 'a man must always live by his work, and his wages must at least be sufficient to maintain him' and preferably 'something more, otherwise it would be impossible for him to bring up a family'. More importantly, Smith defined the sufficient wage by identifying the 'necessaries' that the wage is intended to cover, understanding with this term 'not only the commodities which

---

[18] L Ratti, 'The proposal for a Directive on adequate minimum wage in the EU' (2021) 3 *EU LAW LIVE*. Weekend edition, Special Issue 'In-work poverty in the EU', 7 ff.

[19] R Peña-Casas and D Ghailani, 'A European minimum wage framework: the solution to the ongoing increase in in-work poverty in Europe?' in B Vanhercke, S Spasova and B Fronteddu (eds), *Social policy in the European Union 2020* (Bruxelles, ETUI, 2021); Z Adams, 'The EU Minimum Wage Directive: A Missed Opportunity?' (2020) in uklabourlawblog.com/2020/11/12/the-eu-minimum-wage-directive-a-missed-opportunity-by-zoe-adams.

[20] R Anker and M Anker, Living Wages Around the World. Manual for Measurement (Cheltenham, Elgar, 2017).

[21] Eurofound, *Concept and practice of a living wage* (Luxembourg, Publications Office of the European Union, 2018).

[22] This is the definition provided by the United Kingdom Living Wage Commission. Cf P Kelly, A Ferro and S Jones, *In-work poverty in Europe: A growing problem* (Brussels, European Anti-Poverty Network, 2011).

[23] A Werner and M Lim, 'The Ethics of the Living Wage: A Review and Research Agenda' (2016) 137(3) *Journal of Business Ethics* 433. On the evolution of the notion of living wage in thinking, see also D Hirsch and L Valadez-Martinez, *The Living Wage* (Newcastle upon Tyne, Agenda Publishing, 2017).

are indispensably necessary for the support of life, but whatever the custom of the country renders it indecent for creditable people, even of the lowest order, to be without'. He comprehended not only the bare minimum, but also those commodities which 'the established rules of decency have rendered necessary to the lowest rank of people'.[24]

A similar notion was proposed by John Ryan, who restated the idea that the wage has to maintain decently all workers and provide a living standard that includes both basic needs, such as food, housing and clothes, as well as the possibility to participate in cultural and social life. He understood it as an absolute right, grounded in the human dignity of the person.[25]

The Webbs advocated for a national minimum wage, operating as 'ultimate' tool, while the standard rate must be settled by collective bargaining and set at a feasible subsistence level, on the basis of 'the cost of the food, clothing, and shelter physiologically necessary, according to national habit and custom, to prevent bodily and mental deteriorations'. In their opinion, it is an instrument 'to secure the community against the evil of industrial parasitism'. They harshly reprimanded those companies that did not pay living wages, as they de facto externalised the social costs of guaranteeing the workers' subsistence on to society.[26]

Considering the economic justification for the living wage concept, recently many academics have stressed the importance of introducing adequate minimum wages, as research has shown no – or minimal – adverse economic effects or negative impacts on employment levels of the increases in minimum wage, which, on the contrary may help in establishing a level playing field and boosting economic growth.[27] Minimum wages are also a means to regulate competition. Some argue that the only way to guarantee sustainable wages, allowing for a decent standard of living, is to make an adequate minimum wage – a living wage – a precondition for businesses to compete in the labour market.[28]

In addition, starting from the proposition that 'poverty and severe economic inequalities are unacceptable', it can be argued that a living wage 'is the most appropriate antidote' to these intertwined problems, even though not a panacea.[29] Therefore, in addressing the issues of the function of wages, the importance of wages that not only enable workers to sustain themselves, but also to reduce inequalities and 'to improve their abilities as workers and as members of society

---

[24] A Smith, An Inquiry into the Nature and Causes of the Wealth of Nations (Metalibri Digital library, 1789/2007).

[25] JA Ryan, Living Wage: Its Ethical and Economic Aspects (London, Macmillan, 1912).

[26] S Webb, 'The Economic Theory of a Legal Minimum Wage' (1912) 20 *Journal of Political Economy* 993. Cf also BE Kaufman, 'Sidney and Beatrice Webb's institutional theory of labor markets and wage determination' (2013) 52(3) *Industrial Relations* 765.

[27] M Mazzucato et al, 'Higher statutory minimum wages and stronger collective bargaining are good for the economy' (2021), available at www.etuc.org/sites/default/files/press-release/file/2021-05/Min%20wages%20op%20ed%20EN.pdf.

[28] Z Adams, 'Ancora sulla proposta di direttiva sui salari minimi adeguati nell'UE' (2021) 2 *Diritto delle relazioni industriali* 283.

[29] JL Waltman, *The Case for the Living Wage* (New York, Algora, 2004).

and to enhance those abilities in their children' must be considered.[30] This idea is linked to an interesting argument in favour of living wage policies: the capability approach. Guaranteeing a reasonable standard of living enhances citizens' freedom and autonomy and allows them to develop and effectively exercise their physical, intellectual, moral and spiritual faculties.[31] In this perspective, work contributes to participation in activities in the community and fosters political participation, in this way enhancing social cohesion and trust.[32] Furthermore, capability discourse is related to the idea of living wage as an absolute right, grounded in the human dignity of the person. The ability of workers to provide a decent living for themselves and their families strengthens their self-esteem and self-respect. It must be deemed also 'as part of our ability to live in dignity'.

B. Satisfaction of the Needs of Workers and their Families

The identification of an actual living wage level is closely related to the question of who is responsible for ensuring that every worker earns a sufficient minimum wage, the notion of the decent standard of living that the living wage is intended to guarantee, and the methods of calculation of the living wage.

It must be preliminarily said that the idea that minimum wages should be at least living wages is not universally accepted. According to the neoclassical economics perspective, employers pay workers only on the basis of their marginal individual productivity, thus only if it is economically sustainable. This is linked to the conception of wage as a 'market wage', as the price of a commodity. That perspective leads to a controversial issue concerning the question of who is responsible for ensuring that every worker earns a fair minimum wage. For neoclassical economics, it is the responsibility of the state to provide income support in order to guarantee workers with a minimum subsistence income level. From the opposite perspective based on the concept of living wage, it is the responsibility of the employer to provide an adequate wage level.[33]

This means that ensuring the satisfaction of the needs of workers and their families, guaranteeing a decent standard of living, may be considered as an obligation of the employer or of the welfare state on the basis of different economic theories.[34] This is not a trivial issue.

---

[30] DR Stabile, The Living Wage. Lessons from the History of Economic Thought (Northampton, Elgar, 2008).

[31] A Sen, *Development as a Freedom* (Oxford, Oxford University Press, 1999).

[32] Waltman (n 29); Werner and Lim (n 23).

[33] Z Adams, 'Understanding the Minimum Wage: Political Economy and Legal Form' (2019) 78(1) *Cambridge Law Journal* 42.

[34] I Dingeldey, T Schulten and D Grimshaw, 'Introduction. Minimum wage regimes in Europe and selected developing countries' in I Dingeldey, T Schulten and D Grimshaw (eds), *Minimum Wage Regimes. Statutory Regulation, Collective Bargaining and Adequate Levels* (Abingdon, Routledge, 2021). The relevance of this issue is also stressed by Davidov (n 6) 74 ff.

It also involves the choice of taking into account net or gross wages as a reference to assess the adequacy of minimum wages: this is closely related to the decision to assign the responsibility of ensuring fair minimum wages entirely to employers or to the state. Taxes and social security contributions can significantly reduce the take-home pay of workers. Opting for net minimum wages as reference means that the issue of ensuring fair and adequate take-home pay is the responsibility of the state, by reducing taxes and social contributions, thus 'externalizing the costs' of the business practice of paying unfair wages to society.[35] From the opposite perspective, considering the gross wage as a parameter means making it the responsibility of employers. Also, in the latter case, a cost for society stems from low wages, as they need to be supplemented by welfare payments to ensure a decent standard of living, which, according to some authors, substantially risks subsidising employers who pay unfair wages.[36] Once more, this varies on the basis of the commentators' different economic and political inclinations.

The matter of the responsibility for guaranteeing an adequate take-home pay entails the consideration of further social security and social assistance measures, such as benefits and the role of minimum income schemes. As it is a matter of balance between different policies and it is largely dependent on the welfare state features, it should be on the Member States to evaluate the interaction between them. In this view, 'the indirect costs of employment' should also be taken into account. For instance, Davidov argues that respect for human dignity implies that costs related to health and well-being of workers, such as those linked to workplace accidents and more in general to physical, psychological or social well-being, should also be taken into account when the worker is compensated. On the contrary, 'when compensation is below a certain minimum', the employer does not take into account the long-term costs associated with the work: in such cases, 'businesses in fact externalize the indirect costs that flow from their profit-making activities'.[37]

Another topic linked to the living wage discourse concerns the notion of a decent standard of living, whether it only includes basic material needs or something more, including those goods and services allowing for a truly free and dignified existence, ie 'the full development of the human person and the effective participation of all workers in the political, economic and social organisation of the country'.[38] Some scholars researching on living wages argue that the cost of a 'basic but decent life style', namely food, housing, and other essential expenses, must be considered, 'then adding a small margin for sustainability and emergencies'.[39] Certainly, it is an intricate debate.

---

[35] T Müller and T Schulten, 'The European minimum wage on the doorstep' (2020) ETUI Policy Brief no 1/2020.

[36] Ryan, *Living Wage* (n 25).

[37] Davidov (n 6) 74 ff.

[38] The quote is a section of art 3 of Italian Constitution. On the relevance of these elements with regard to living wage, cf B Fabo and SS Belli, '(Un)beliveable wages? An analysis of minimum wage policies in Europe from a living wage perspective' (2017) 4(6) *IZA Journal of Labor Policy* 1.

[39] Anker and Anker (n 20).

In addition, in literature, as well as in international legislation and charters, it is controversial whether the living wage is intended to cover the needs of the worker or also of the worker's family, and how to calculate such living wage as the number of dependants of a worker is very variable.[40] It is arguable that, looking at living or adequate minimum wage issue from an anti-poverty perspective, the household composition and the take-home pay necessary to maintain the family should be considered, as 'an in-work poor person is a working person who lives in a poor household'.[41] Therefore, an adequate wage policy or, in the worst case, a poverty-avoiding minimum wage policy should take this factor into consideration, at least in the calculation of an average basket of goods and services that ensure a decent living standard.

For the aforementioned reasons, it is difficult to identify a reasonable living wage level. As is well known, there is no universally accepted method of calculating a living wage, as it largely depends on the heterogeneity of wage-setting systems and welfare states, and the definition of the necessities of a decent life is also affected by cultural and geographical factors, thus differing from country to country. For this reason, the importance of setting the living wage by calculating the cost of the basket of essential goods and services at a national level or even locally is widely acknowledged.[42]

The case of the UK living wage, one of the most well-known and successful living wage campaigns, is interesting. It is promoted by the Living Wage Foundation with the aim of protecting the right of every worker to earn a sufficient wage to guarantee himself/herself and his/her family a decent living. The promoters had, in fact, noted that, despite having two or more minimum wage jobs, many workers still had income that was too low compared to family needs and did not have enough time for their families. This is not a statutory minimum rate, but a wage that any employer can voluntarily decide to apply. It is a system that relies on moral persuasion, based on the reputation of firms as responsible businesses and the Living Wage Foundation offers accreditation for employers paying a living wage.[43]

This living wage is calculated on the basis of the cost of living. It is more than a subsistence wage, as the calculation is based on a basket of goods and services, which draws on the Minimum Income Standard, which is estimated on the basis

---

[40] Werner and Lim (n 23); Stabile (n 30); J Rubery, M Johnson and D Grimshaw, 'Minimum wages and the multiple functions of wages' in I Dingeldey, T Grimshaw and D Schulten (eds), *Minimum Wage Regimes. Statutory Regulation, Collective Bargaining and Adequate Levels* (Abingdon, Routledge, 2021).

[41] L Ratti, A García-Muñoz and V Vergnat, 'The Challenge of Defining, Measuring, and Overcoming In-Work Poverty in Europe: An Introduction' in L Ratti (ed), *In-Work Poverty in Europe. Vulnerable and Under-Represented Persons in a Comparative Perspective* (Alphen aan den Rijn, Wolters Kluwer, 2022) 11; H Lohmann, 'The concept and measurement of in-work poverty' in H Lohmann and I Marx (eds), *Handbook on In-work Poverty* (Cheltenham, Elgar, 2018) 7 ff.

[42] Anker and Anker (n 20).

[43] In its implementation, also promoting a living wage through public procurement and requiring employers to promote the Living Wage among their suppliers have been crucial. Cf M Johnson, A Koukiadaki and D Grimshaw, 'The Living Wage in the UK: Testing the limits of soft regulation?' (2019) 25(3) *Transfer* 319.

of 'public consensus as to what constitutes an adequate standard of living'. Many household types are taken into account, therefore there are many baskets 'varying by family type to reflect their specific requirements'.[44] More in detail – as described in the briefing written by the Resolution Foundation involved in the calculation of the living wage on behalf of the Living Wage Foundation – it is

> calculated by taking a weighted average of the earnings required (accounting for tax and benefits) for a range of family types (with and without children) to earn enough to afford the items in that basket of goods and services, and therefore to meet that standard of living.[45]

Taxes and benefits systems are also considered, as they affect the households' take-home pay and their capacity to afford the items within the basket of goods and services.[46] In this way, the UK living wage considers the issue of the suitability of supporting an individual and also providing a worker with sufficient income to support their family.[47]

The case of UK living wage makes clear that, since it is necessarily also related to the welfare system, a cautious balance and a wide political agreement is necessary when determining the methods of calculation of an adequate minimum wage.

IV. A Coordinated Minimum Wage Policy at EU Level

In recent decades and, particularly, since the 2010s, the issue of fairness and adequacy of wages has also been topical in the political debate.

'Adequate wages are an essential component of the EU model of a social market economy'. This is one of the stated reasons for the proposal for a directive on adequate minimum wages in the European Union.[48] Guaranteeing adequate working and living conditions is one of the promises of the integration project, as stated in Article 3(1) of the Treaty on European Union (TEU): the European Union aims to promote peace, its values, and also 'the well-being of its peoples'. Furthermore, pursuant to para 3, the EU 'shall work for the sustainable development of Europe based on balanced economic growth and price stability, a highly competitive social market economy, aiming at full employment and social

---

[44] C D'Arcy and D Finch, 'The calculation of a living wage: the UK's experience' (2019) 25(3) *Transfer* 301 ff; A Davis et al, *A Minimum Income Standard for the United Kingdom in 2021* (Joseph Rowntree Foundation, 2021).

[45] N Cominetti, 'Calculating the Real Living Wage for London and the Rest of the UK: 2020–21' (Resolution Foundation, 2020) available at www.resolutionfoundation.org/publications/calculating-the-real-living-wage.

[46] On the role of the state and employers, cf D'Arcy and Finch (n 44) 301 ff.

[47] Cf EAPN task force on decent work, 'Background Note on Living Wages' (EAPN, 2015).

[48] Proposal for a Directive of the European Parliament and of the Council on adequate minimum wages in the European Union, Brussels, 28.10.2020, COM (2020) 682 final.

progress', 'it shall combat social exclusion and discrimination, and shall promote social justice and protection', and it shall 'promote economic, social and territorial cohesion, and solidarity among Member States'. These objectives are emphasised in Article 9 of the Treaty on the Functioning of the European Union (TFEU), according to which, in defining and implementing its policies and activities, the EU shall take into account requirements also linked to the guarantee of adequate social protection and the fight against social exclusion. Thus, an action of the EU on minimum wages is desirable – or this is supposed – since this is an issue that touches EU citizens deeply in their lives and 'convergence across Member States in this area contributes to the promise of shared prosperity in the Union'.[49]

For instance, Article 5 of the Community Charter of Fundamental Social Rights of Workers of 1989 states that 'all employment shall be fairly remunerated', meaning that 'workers shall be assured an equitable wage, i.e. a wage sufficient to enable them to have a decent standard of living'.

The 1993 Commission Opinion on an Equitable Wage has restated the importance of the right 'of all workers to be assured of an equitable wage, with particular attention being paid to the more vulnerable members of the labour force'. It also justifies the concept of 'equitable wage' with the fact that 'all workers should receive a reward for work done which in the context of the society in which they live and work is fair and sufficient to enable them to have a decent standard of living'. Furthermore, in the same Opinion, the Commission reaffirms that 'the pursuit of equitable wages is to be seen as part of the process of achieving the Community's basic objectives of greater economic and social cohesion and a more harmonious development within the framework of an increasingly integrated European economy'.[50]

Considering the most recent policy developments at EU level, the connection between wages and a decent standard of living – or, ever more, a dignified existence – described in the sections above can be found in Principle no 6 of European Pillar of Social Rights (EPSR), which also expressly links the right to fair and adequate wages to the prevention of in-work poverty. The introduction of the Social Scoreboard for monitoring the progress in the areas covered by the EPSR within the European Semester is also important, due to the social consequences of the decisions and policies in the context of the social governance.[51]

Based on this principle, the approval of the Directive 2022/2041 on adequate minimum wages in the European Union results of great political relevance: it has been considered a 'watershed'[52] – or a 'paradigm shift'[53] – in EU policies, as

[49] ibid.

[50] Commission opinion on an equitable wage (93/C 248/04), COM(93) 388 final.

[51] S Garben, 'The European Pillar of social rights: an assessment of its meaning and significance' (2019) 21 *Cambridge Yearbook of European Legal Studies* 101; B Hacker, 'A European Social Semester? The European Pillar of Social Rights in practice', ETUI working paper 2019.05 (2019).

[52] T Müller and T Schulten, 'Minimum-wage directive: yes, but … ', in Social Europe' (2020), available at socialeurope.eu/minimum-wage-directive-yes-but.

[53] Mazzucato et al (n 27).

it is a crucial step in ensuring the dignity of work across the EU.[54] Not long ago, austerity measures and country-specific recommendations required a moderate wage policy, consisting of reviewing wage-setting systems and wage indexation, aligning them with productivity developments.[55] With Directive 2022/2041, minimum wages are no longer exclusively viewed as an impediment to downward flexibility of wages and increasing competitiveness, as they were considered in the past.

This is clear also with respect to the stated goals of the Directive, which aims at improving living and working conditions and 'in particular the adequacy of minimum wages for workers in order to contribute to upward social convergence and reduce wage inequality'. To this purpose, it intends to achieve the adequacy of statutory minimum wages, to promote collective bargaining on wage-setting, and to enhance 'effective access of workers to rights to minimum wage protection where provided for in national law and/or collective agreements'.[56] Furthermore, it is doubtless that an upward convergence in the framework for minimum wages – and in general in social policy – is also relevant for the functioning of the single market, preventing significant discrepancies and competitive advantages between Member States, as well as in cross-border activities. For this reason, the Directive contributes to enabling fair competition based on innovation and productivity respecting adequate social standards.

From a political point of view, the importance of Directive 2022/2041 is undebatable.

Nevertheless, there are some inconsistencies. For instance, the scope of application is a critical issue. Pursuant to Article 2, the Directive applies to workers who have an employment contract or an employment relationship as defined by the law, collective agreements or practice in each Member State, with consideration of the case law of Court of Justice of the European Union.[57] Solo self-employed are therefore excluded, even though in many cases they experience financial or even personal dependence on a single client and their remuneration mainly or totally depends on the income generated from the business relationship with said client, often facing economic-social weakness.

Some provisions are arguably made in the light of ensuring a proper adequate wage that protects workers and their families from the risk of poverty and enables

---

[54] Directive (EU) 2022/2041 of the European Parliament and of the Council of 19 October 2022 on adequate minimum wages in the European Union [2022] OJ L 275/33.

[55] On EU economic governance during the 'austerity' period, cf L Bordogna and R Pedersini, 'What kind of europeanization? How EMU is changing national industrial relations in Europe' (2015) 3 *Giornale di diritto del lavoro e delle relazioni industriali* 183; T Schulten and T Müller, 'A new European interventionism? The impact of the new European economic governance on wages and collective bargaining' in D Natali and B Vanhercke (eds), *Social Developments in the European Union 2012* (Bruxelles, ETUI, 2012); D Grimshaw, *Minimum Wages, Pay Equity and Comparative Industrial Relations* (Abingdon, Routledge, 2013).

[56] Article 1, para 1, Directive 2022/2041.

[57] On the notion of 'worker' under EU law, cf N Countouris, 'The Concept of "Worker" in European Labour Law: Fragmentation, Autonomy and Scope' (2018) 47(2) *Industrial Law Journal* 192.

a dignified existence: the ones specifying criteria for setting adequate minimum wages are the most problematic.

V. The Criteria for Fairness and Adequacy Assessment of Minimum Wages in EU Directive 2022/2041

Directive 2022/2041 is based on the idea that adequate minimum wages shall be determined by law or through collective bargaining, in line with national practices, protecting the autonomy of the social partners. It is structured on two pillars, which are also its main objectives: adequacy and coverage. The first pillar, concerning adequacy, exclusively addresses Member States with statutory minimum wages; the second concerns the promotion of collective bargaining on wage-setting, on the basis of the inference that high collective bargaining coverage corresponds to wage adequacy, as stated in Recital 25. Indeed, according to recent studies, the countries with high collective bargaining coverage tend to present a lower share of low-wage workers and higher minimum wages relative to the median wage.[58]

On the one hand, Article 5 addresses the issue of adequacy with regard to national statutory minimum wages, listing some minimal principles and criteria for statutory minimum wage setting and updating. On the other hand, Article 4 aims at increasing the collective bargaining coverage and promoting the capacity of social partners to engage in collective bargaining on wage setting, requiring Member States to establish an action plan to promote collective bargaining, where collective bargaining coverage does not reach at least 80 per cent of the workers.

A. Procedure and Criteria for Setting Adequate Statutory Minimum Wages

The provisions concerning statutory minimum wages are enshrined in Chapter II of the Directive. This Chapter opens with Article 5, which notably identifies some elements aiming at ensuring statutory minimum wage adequacy. Thus, the criteria set for the adequacy assessment of wage levels seem to be applicable only to statutory minimum wages.

Article 5 provides that 'Member States with statutory minimum wages shall establish the necessary procedures for the setting and updating of statutory minimum wages' and lists some criteria to ensure the adequacy of wages, to achieve decent living conditions and upward convergence, as well as to eradicate the gender pay gap. Recital 28 specifies that the adequacy of statutory minimum

---

[58] Dingeldey, Schulten and Grimshaw, 'Introduction' (n 34).

wages is assessed in view of 'national socioeconomic conditions, including employment growth, competitiveness and regional and sectoral developments'. Interestingly, in the approved version, there is a specific reference also to the purpose of reducing in-work poverty, that must guide these setting and updating procedures. The list of elements that must 'at least' be taken into account in assessing the adequacy of wages includes criteria already enshrined in other international documents, namely '(a) the purchasing power of statutory minimum wages, taking into account the cost of living; (b) the general level of gross wages and their distribution; (c) the growth rate of gross wages; (d) long-term national productivity levels and developments'. Yet, such criteria seem to be 'too generic' to effectively guarantee the adequacy of minimum wages. For this reason, it is important to read them in the light of the above-mentioned directive's preambles and objectives.[59]

With a view to simplify the assessment, Article 5 requires MSs to use indicative reference values in relation to the general level of gross wages, inspired to the ones adopted at international level. The recommended threshold of 60 per cent of the gross median wage or 50 per cent of the gross average wage is ambitious: actually, in 2020 in all EU Member States minimum wages were lower than the percentage set by these indicators and too low to provide a decent living.[60]

Concerning the use of indicative reference values, Recital 28 states that 'minimum wages are considered to be adequate if they are fair in relation to the wage distribution in the relevant Member State and if they provide a decent standard of living for workers based on a full-time employment relationship'. This seems to suggest an equation between fairness in relation to the wage distribution and adequacy in providing a decent standard of living. A relative approach, such as the one identifying a threshold in relation to the gross median or average wage, is of course explanatory of the effect of minimum wages on wage inequality. Notwithstanding this, it has been argued that it is a 'rough indicator' for an adequate level of minimum wage that aims at providing a decent standard of living. Actually, in those countries where the majority of workers earn very low wages, the percentage of the median/average wage 'might be very high, but the absolute level still very low and often not sufficient to cover the costs of a decent living'.[61]

Commenting on the initial proposal for a directive on minimum wages in the EU, some authors suggested to adjust this relative indicator using the national criteria defining a sort of living wage, ie a reference income on the basis of a country-specific basket of goods and services or 'the wage that prevents workers

---

[59] Peña-Casas and Ghailani (n 19) 135 ff; Ratti (n 18) 7 ff.

[60] In 2020, not one EU Member State fulfilled the double decency threshold of 60% of the median and 50% of the average wage. Cf T Müller, K Vandaele and W Zwysen, 'Wages and collective bargaining: Is social Europe really back on the agenda?' in N Countouris, R Jagodzinski and S Theodoropoulou (eds), *Benchmarking Working Europe 2021. Unequal Europe* (Bruxelles, ETUI/ETUC, 2021), who elaborate data from the OECD earnings database 2021.

[61] T Schulten and T Müller, 'What's in a name? From minimum wages to living wages in Europe' (2019) 25(3) *Transfer* 267.

from relying on additional wage top-ups by the state in order to make a living'.[62] This option – closer to an 'absolute' or 'needs-based' approach – would consider the ability 'to make ends meet' that ensures a decent standard of living.

For this reason, it is significant that Recital 28 of the approved Directive proposes 'among other instruments', to adopt 'a basket of goods and services at real prices established at national level' to determine the cost of living 'with the aim of achieving a decent standard of living'. In addition, importantly, this basket 'could' take into account not only 'material necessities such as food, clothing and housing', but also 'the need to participate in cultural, educational and social activities'. This results to be in line with the idea of guaranteeing an adequate minimum wage that allows citizens to develop and effectively exercise their physical, intellectual, moral and spiritual faculties, and fosters participation in activities in the community, in this way making the concept of citizenship more effective.

B. Promotion of Collective Bargaining on Wage-setting: Benefits and Pitfalls

Taking a closer look on the part concerning the promotion of collective bargaining, further – and more serious – concerns arise with regard to Article 4, as amended after interinstitutional negotiations in the so-called 'trilogue'. First, the provision requires Member States to undertake action to increase the collective bargaining coverage and to strengthen the capacity of the social partners to engage in collective bargaining on wage setting at sector or cross-industry level, also guaranteeing that 'both parties have access to appropriate information in order to carry out their functions'. Article 4 also requires Member States to take measures to prevent all acts which undermine the right of workers and trade unions representatives to participate in collective bargaining on wage-setting discriminating them, and to protect social partners participating or wishing to participate in collective bargaining 'against any acts of interference'.

Moreover, with the aim of closing gaps in coverage of minimum wage protection for workers, where collective bargaining coverage is less than 80 per cent of workers, Article 4 requires Member States to 'provide for a framework of enabling conditions for collective bargaining' and, after consulting the social partners or by agreement with the social partners, 'establish an action plan to promote collective bargaining', that is public and notified to the Commission. In this way, the approved version of Article 4 has transformed a relatively generic obligation – such as the one contained in the original version of the proposed directive – into a potentially crucial instrument operating on a procedural level. Indeed, in full respect for the autonomy of the social partners and after consulting or by agreement with them, Member States shall set out, review and update if needed, an action plan providing

---

[62] ibid.

for a 'clear timeline and concrete measures to progressively increase the rate of collective bargaining coverage'.

However, it is arguable that a 'well-functioning' collective bargaining on wage setting – which is an important means to ensure that workers are protected by adequate minimum wages – should be considered as such only if it remains a prerogative of truly representative social partners, 'and it is not opened to other actors, obscure and non-representative associations or groups'.[63] This is a problematic issue in countries where the proliferation of a variety of competing sectoral collective agreements – particularly where they may be applied by employers regardless of the activity performed – lead to downwards negotiation and wage reductions.[64] Therefore, this 'equation' between adequacy and coverage on which the directive is structured is – at least – 'challenging'.[65]

In addition, in a directive promoting the adequacy of minimum wages, it is cause for concern that it does not illustrate what is the notion of adequacy, ie it does not indicate the criteria to assess whether the contractual minimum wages are fair and adequate, with regard to Member States where minimum wage protection is provided exclusively by collective bargaining.[66]

VI. Conclusion: A Benchmark Notion of Fair and Adequate Wages against In-Work Poverty

On the basis of the analysis in the previous sections and of the debate on the directive providing a framework for adequate minimum wages in the EU, as well as keeping in mind the important theories on and campaigns for living wage, a desirable notion of fair and adequate wage can be identified.

To this purpose, a reasonable balance is necessary, that takes into account the many aspects of setting adequate wage levels: sufficiency of the wages to make

---

[63] ETUC, Reply of the European Trade Union Confederation (ETUC) to the Second Phase Consultation of Social Partners under Article 154 TFEU on a possible action addressing the challenges related to fair minimum wages (2020), available at www.etuc.org/en/document/reply-etuc-2nd-phase-consultation-social-partners-fair-minimum-wages.

[64] This is the case of Italy, where the increasing number of 'pirate' collective agreements – signed by non-representative or poorly-representative unions – often result in severe reductions in terms of wages and working conditions. In addition, it must be noted that in Italy, sometimes also collective agreements signed by long-standing unions provide for an unfair wage level, determining a worrying downward competition. Since employers can apply a sectoral collective agreement regardless of the business conducted, they sometimes 'choose' the most convenient one, giving rise to competition between these collective agreements. See N De Luigi, G Marchi and E Villa, 'In-work poverty in Italy' in L Ratti (ed), *In-Work Poverty in Europe. Vulnerable and Under-Represented Persons in a Comparative Perspective* (Alphen aan den Rijn, Wolters Kluwer, 2022) 121 ff.

[65] Ratti (n 18) 7 ff.

[66] M V Ballestrero and G De Simone, 'Riallacciando il filo del discorso. Dalla riflessione di massimo Roccella al dibattito attuale sul salario minimo' WP CSDLE 'Massimo D'Antona'. IT 447/2021 (2021); O Razzolini, 'Salario minimo, dumping contrattuale e parità di trattamento: brevi riflessioni a margine della proposta di direttiva europea' (2021) *Lavoro Diritti Europa*.

ends meet, equality and contractual fairness of wages, as well as the interactions of minimum wage levels with social assistance policies, the welfare system and economic considerations. The multifaceted nature of this issue has consequences in identifying a benchmark notion of fair and adequate wages and measures and policies to ensure adequacy of minimum wages.

According to the notion arising from the interpretation of international charters and declarations, a fair and adequate wage is intended to ensure a decent standard of living for workers and their families, thereby guaranteeing the protection of human dignity. In understanding the relevance of these international instruments in our reasoning, it is remarkable that the EPSR mentions the fundamental social rights set out in the ESC as a reference for Member States in pursuing the promotion of employment and improved living and working conditions in line with Article 151 TFEU. The preambles of Directive 2022/2041 also refer to Article 4 of ESC and to ILO Convention 131, as standard and as a tool for teleological interpretation.

In the attempt to provide a benchmark notion of fair and adequate wages that may be helpful in the prevention and fight against IWP, it is a good starting point to consider the meaning of two essential concepts – adequacy and fairness, which describe different characteristics that minimum wages should have. Adequacy refers to 'the fact of being enough or satisfactory for a particular purpose'.[67] As stated by the ECSR, the purpose of adequate wages is to guarantee all the resources necessary to participate in cultural, educational and social activities in society, beyond material basic needs, and to prevent IWP. Therefore, reasonably, an adequate minimum wage should not be lower than the poverty threshold.[68] Fairness describes 'the quality of treating people equally or in a way that is right or reasonable'.[69] The importance of reducing inequality is widely acknowledged, not only because it is 'morally objectionable', but also because it negatively affects the fairness of political and economic institutions: it is a prerequisite to promoting the opportunity for all to take part in the cultural, social and economic organisation of a country.[70] More in detail, with regard to pay, fairness may have two different meanings: it can be interpreted as concerning the distribution of wealth, but also in relation to disparities of pay within organisations between employees, in particular between employees and the top management.[71] To this respect, the fairness of pay concerns – as Collins clearly explains – the associational principles of interpersonal justice, the principles of desert and of due recognition, that contain 'a strong egalitarian impulse'. Indeed, the first one

---

[67] Cambridge dictionary online.

[68] E Menegatti, 'Much ado about little: The Commission proposal for a Directive on adequate wages' (2021) 14 *Italian Labour Law e-Journal* 21.

[69] Cambridge dictionary online.

[70] TM Scanlon, *Why Does Inequality Matter?* (Oxford, Oxford University Press, 2018).

[71] H Collins, 'Fat cats, production networks, and the right to fair pay' (2022) 85(1) *The Modern Law Review* 7.

acknowledges that everyone should be rewarded in accordance with their contribution. The principle of due recognition insists that disparities in pay should not be so great as to imply that any member's contribution is worthless or of little significance with the consequence that they lose self-respect.

Therefore,

> the reason why the growing disparity in wages within organisations is morally wrong is that it appears to treat the contribution and abilities of some employees in a way that tends to undermine self-esteem and denies recognition to the low paid.[72]

On the basis of these notions, it is clear that 'fair and adequate' is not a hendiadys. Actually, these adjectives describe two different concepts: fairness concerns the relation to other wages, while adequacy addresses the sufficiency of the wages to make ends meet. Thus, 'fair and adequate wage' is a multidimensional concept.[73] On these premises, a 'combined' approach must be undertaken in order to identify what a fair and adequate wage should be.

Firstly, in order to ensure the fairness of a minimum wage, it seems important to take a relative – thus a 'distribution-oriented'[74] – and more 'pragmatic'[75] approach, such as the one adopted within the ECSR and proposed in the EU Directive. Member States should be required to use an indicative reference equal to 60 per cent of the national median wage or 50 per cent of the average wage. This threshold would boost minimum wages in the majority of the Member States, at least those with national statutory minimum wages, since in almost all Member States minimum wages do not meet these requirements.[76]

However, adequacy cannot be exclusively linked to a given percentage of median or average wages, as it may still not be enough to ensure a decent living standard, particularly in countries in which the entire wage structure is very low. Otherwise, it would 'make adequacy a function of the relationship between the lowest wage and the wages of others, rather than costs of living'.[77]

For this reason, in addition to the relative approach, it is necessary to use an absolute or needs-based approach, that takes into account the cost of living, based on country-specific baskets of goods and services. This option is preferable to setting a common basket of basic goods and services at EU level. The determination of a living wage depends on the country-specific features, and, not least, is more appropriate in accordance with EU competence and principles of subsidiarity and proportionality, as it respects well-established national traditions in minimum wage setting.

At EU level, an indicative list of goods and services to be considered can be suggested. It is intended to be a control mechanism – 'a real-life test' – of the

---

[72] Ibid 16.
[73] Eurofound (n 21).
[74] Dingeldey, Schulten and Grimshaw, 'Introduction' (n 34).
[75] Müller and Schulten (n 35).
[76] Müller, Vandaele and Zwysen (n 60).
[77] Adams (n 19).

60 per cent target. It is a way to assess 'whether a minimum wage of 60 per cent of the national median wage really amounts to a wage that ensures a decent living standard'.[78] In this way, the needs-based approach would also reduce the risks of cross-border unfair competition, stemming from an 'only relative' approach, based on a purely national application of the reference value.

This absolute approach would ensure the adequacy of minimum wages. In this sense, it is closer to a living wage concept, as it is intended to allow 'an employee a basic but socially acceptable standard of living'.[79] Therefore, an appropriate basket of goods and services must be identified, which ensures a basic living standard, that must include resources for effective participation in cultural, social and political activities, ie those means that make the concept of citizenship effective.[80]

Undeniably, the identification of goods and services to be included in the basket requires a significant political compromise, as well as specialist knowledge, in order to also assess the foreseeable impact of the proposed living wage on employment levels. For this reason, the full involvement of trade unions and employers' organisations is crucial, as well as that of civil-society stakeholders, academics and experts. The creation of a 'living wage commission' involving all these sides would fit this purpose.

In Member States where minimum wage protection is provided exclusively by collective bargaining, collectively-agreed minimum wages should also be subjected to this absolute approach.

Furthermore, as a 'well-functioning' collective bargaining on wage setting has proved to be an effective instrument to promote adequate minimum wages, it is important to set up an effective monitoring and data collection system. A national reporting procedure not only on the adequacy of statutory minimum wages and on the coverage of collective bargaining on wages, but also on wage levels set by collective agreements, and on how many and what sectors and workers do not have access to adequate minimum wage protection may also be beneficial. This may be a starting point to promote effective actions of Member States in ensuring effective collective bargaining on wages, and ensuring that this remains the prerogative of truly representative social partners.

While the relative approach has been conveniently included within the EU Directive on adequate minimum wages, inserting the absolute approach in hard law provisions may be more problematic, due to the difficulties in identifying cross-country comparable baskets of goods and services. For this reason, a soft

---

[78] Müller and Schulten (n 35).

[79] This is the notion of the living wage according to the UK Low Pay Commission.

[80] As it is acknowledged, if not adequately addressed, the phenomenon of people 'working, yet poor' risks emptying the substantive content of citizenship. Cf M Ferrera and M Jessoula, 'Poverty and Social Inclusion as Emerging Policy Arenas in the EU' in R Halvorsen and B Hvinden (eds), *Combating Poverty in Europe. Active Inclusion in a Multi-level and Multi-Actor Context* (Cheltenham, Elgar, 2016) 62; C Joerges, 'Europe's Economic Constitution in Crisis and the Emergence of a New Constitutional Constellation' (2014) 15(5) *German Law Journal* 15, 985 ff.

law instrument seems to be more suitable. Thus, for instance, the assessment of adequacy of wages through this absolute approach may be embedded in the European Semester, since country-specific recommendations have already been made on similar issues: these recommendations are one of the most appropriate instruments to consider countries specific characteristics. In addition, this seems less intrusive in national systems and social partners autonomy, compared to the imposition of this second approach by a Directive.

This may be the proper instrument for an overall assessment of the national systems of setting adequate and fair levels of minimum wages in order to ensure at least a decent standard of living of workers and their families. In this assessment, the role of the welfare state and the legal and institutional arrangements involved in the attempt to ensure workers a decent standard of living should and can also be properly assessed. To this respect, the commission should not only identify a feasible basket of goods and services for the absolute approach – in this way assessing the adequacy of wages – but also take into account the national institutional and regulatory framework and social security systems. In addition, this commission may also elaborate further policy proposals concerning those measures and characteristics, which can ensure households an adequate standard of living. As it is debated whether the living wage should be based on the needs of an individual or a family and by referring to what kind of households, the question concerning the relevance of welfare payments in determining a living wage rate is also problematic and requires broad political and social agreements, particularly since this issue involves the assessment of elements, such as the welfare state and its public infrastructure, that require a fair balance between the role of the state and the role of a minimum or living wage.

Finally, equally important appears to be transparent and publicly accessible information regarding minimum wage protection, collective agreements and wage provisions therein, as stated in Article 10, Directive 2022/2041. Pay transparency is crucial in ensuring a fair wage and in preventing discrimination. This would have a role also in supporting the principle of equal pay, as emphasised in the Directive to strengthen the application of the principle of gender equality.

In addition, in line with the promotion of contractual fairness of pay, transparency may play a role in contrasting wage disparity within organisations, discouraging excessive remunerations, through the disclosure of pay ratio of different wage groups inside companies, such as the ratio of median wages of employees and CEOs, and the determination of maximum wage ratio between highest and lowest paid workers.[81] As suggested in the literature, this may be implemented by requiring employers to engage in information and consultation procedures with works councils or company-level trade union representatives or, in order to make the right to fair pay even more effective, by providing a legal

---

[81] For example, it is the purpose of the 'Wagemark' international standard. Cf Collins (n 71) 20–21.

right – for the workers or the trade unions or both – to claim a pay rise and thus enforce this rationale.[82]

In conclusion, the introduction of a framework for a fair and adequate wage is not a remedy for in-work poverty, or at least not 'as a sole-standing policy'.[83] However, a policy promoting a fair and adequate wage is a step in the right direction: as argued by some leading economists in Europe, 'adequate minimum wages and strong collective bargaining are not only good for the people, they are clearly also good for the economy'.[84] For these reasons, this must be a policy priority and a 'social and economic necessity'.[85] Only by taking into account all the mentioned factors and dimensions, and reasonably balancing them, will the minimum wage be effectively adequate, fair and equitable.

---

[82] ibid 22 ff. Collins argues that not only single entities, but also 'closely integrated production networks' should be included in the disclosure and calculation of pay ratios; otherwise, 'business will be able to minimise pay differences in the core business whilst exporting all the low paid jobs to other contractors'.

[83] Ratti (n 18) 15; A Horton and J Willis, 'Impacts of the living wage on in-work poverty' in H Lohmann and I Marx (eds), *Handbook on In-work Poverty* (Cheltenham, Elgar, 2018).

[84] Mazzucato et al (n 27).

[85] Adams (n 19).

7

The Role of Social Security in the Combat of In-work Poverty

I. Introduction

The Working, Yet Poor project focuses on the rising trend of people working but not being able to afford a decent standard of living above the at-risk-of-poverty line. In 2019, almost one in ten workers in the European Union was considered at risk of poverty. Boosted by the economic crisis that proportion increased over the previous decade, from an average of 8.0 per cent in 2006 to 9.4 per cent in 2019.[1] The reasons for the problem of in-work poverty are manifold, such as individual and household factors (eg gender, skill level, household composition and household work intensity).[2] The applicable labour law, social security law and tax system in a given country can also have an important impact.[3] Another reason is the increase in non-standard work forms.[4] Even though the standard employment relationship (ie a worker with a full-time contract of indefinite duration) still serves as the most common work form, non-standard work has become increasingly

[1] See the discussion of L Ratti, A García-Muñoz and V Vergnat, 'The Challenge of Defining, Measuring and Overcoming In-Work Poverty in Europe: An Introduction' in L Ratti (ed), *In-Work Poverty in Europe. Vulnerable and Under-Represented Persons in a Comparative Perspective* (Alphen aan den Rijn, Kluwer Law International, 2022) 6–7 where the authors discuss the EU SILC data for the EU-27.
[2] See also R Peña-Casas et al, *In-Work Poverty in Europe: A Study of National Policies*, European Social Policy Network (Brussels, European Commission, 2019) 4 and Ratti, García-Muñoz and Vergnat (n 1) 3–7 and the references cited by Ratti, García-Muñoz and Vergnat.
[3] Eurofound, *In-Work Poverty in the EU* (Luxembourg, Publications Office of the European Union, 2017) 7.
[4] See also for the discussion of new forms of employment: Eurofound, *Overview of New Forms of Employment – 2018 Update* (Luxembourg, Publications Office of the European Union, 2018); and for a discussion on the precarity of new work forms: A Koukiadaki and I Katsaroumpas, *Temporary Contracts, Precarious Employment, Employees' Fundamental Rights and EU Employment Law*, Study for the Petition Committee (Brussels, European Commission, 2017) 19 as well as Ratti, García-Muñoz and Vergnat (n 1) 7.

diverse, eg part-time work, temporary employment and self-employment.[5] These work forms are not only becoming more common, they have also become more diverse, often occupying a grey zone between employment and self-employment. In the EU almost 40 per cent of employment consists of workers in non-standard work forms.[6]

The available data show the complexity of current labour markets in the EU Member States, which is further amplified by new digital evolutions and changed work patterns leading to less stable career patterns. The increasing trend in non-standard work, in combination with the Covid-19 pandemic, the climate crisis and the Ukrainian war, are important challenges for national social security systems that still use the standard employment relationship as their main framework. Several recent initiatives can be found at EU level to strengthen the social protection of non-standard workers, eg the right to adequate social protection for all workers and self-employed, as laid down in Article 12 of the European Pillar of Social Rights[7] (EPSR) and the Council Recommendation of 8 November 2019 on access to social protection for workers and self-employed ('the 2019 Recommendation').[8] The proposal for an EU Directive regulating platform work is another example.[9] Despite these initiatives, EU Member States struggle as to include non-standard work forms adequately in labour and social security law.

This contribution delves deeper into the problems that Vulnerable and Underrepresented Workers ('VUP Groups') face in receiving adequate social protection in seven EU countries (ie Belgium, Germany, Italy, Luxembourg, Poland, Sweden and the Netherlands). The four VUP Groups are the following, and are used throughout the Working, Yet Poor project:[10] ie (1) VUP Group 1 – low- or unskilled employees with standard employment contracts employed in poor sectors;[11] (2) VUP Group 2 – self-employed, particularly bogus self-employed

---

[5] High-level Group on the future of social protection and of the welfare state in the EU, *The Future of Social Protection and of the Welfare State in the EU* (Brussels, European Commission, 2023) 20.

[6] High-level Group (n 5) 46; European Commission, *Report from the Commission to the Council on the Implementation of the Council Recommendation on Access to Social Protection for Workers and for Self-employed*, COM (2023) 43 final.

[7] European Commission, *Communication to the Parliament, Council, the EESC and the Committee of the Regions establishing a European Pillar of Social Rights*, COM(2017) 250 final (EPSR).

[8] Council Recommendation of 8 November 2019 on access to social protection for workers and the self-employed [2019] OJ C 387/07.

[9] European Commission, *Proposal for a Directive of the European Parliament and of the Council on improving working conditions in platform work*, COM(2021) 762 final.

[10] The definitions used in footnotes 11–14 are developed in Ratti, García-Muñoz and Vergnat (n 1) and further explained in the contribution of García-Muñoz in this book (ch 1).

[11] For the purpose of VUP Group 1 employees are those persons who, under a contract of employment or as a party in an employment relationship, are obliged to perform work or services for another party in return for remuneration and subordination to this other party. Key for VUP Group 1 is to define which sectors are poor. Low-wage earners, in statistical terms, are those employees earning two-thirds or less of the national median gross hourly earnings. A sector is considered poor for the Working, Yet Poor project when 20 per cent or more of employees within the sector are low-wage earners.

and solo (economically dependent) self-employed;[12] (3) VUP Group 3 – flexible employed persons (ie temporary agency workers, part-time workers and workers with a fixed-term contract);[13] and (4) VUP Group 4 – casual and platform workers.[14] Three of the four VUP Groups can be considered non-standard workers; like other non-standard workers, those VUP Groups face significant problems in their access to social protection coverage. Analysing the social security coverage for the VUP Groups further in detail allows this contribution to map the problems faced by (some) non-standard work forms.

II. Mapping the Social Security Protection for the VUP Groups

In the section below, the social security protection in case of sickness and unemployment[15] for the four VUP Groups will be discussed further. Earlier research show that non-standard workers particularly face difficulties in accessing social protection coverage for (short-term) income replacement benefits.[16] In reviewing the social security protection of the four VUP Groups, this contribution will answer the following questions schematically: (1) *What are the challenges and impediments in design for the four VUP Groups in receiving social protection in case of sickness and unemployment, and what possible pathways to solve those challenges*

---

[12] For the purpose of VUP Group 2, self-employed persons are those persons who perform an activity under a contract that is not formally a contract of employment. Dependent self-employed are defined in VUP Group 2 as own-account workers who are completely or mainly engaged by a firm or principal and whose remuneration mainly or totally depends on the income generated from the business relationship with the said firm or principal. Bogus self-employed persons are those workers who, despite being formally defined as self-employed, perform the same tasks in the same way as the employees employed by the same firm or principal.

[13] Fixed-term workers included in VUP Group 3 are those persons having an employment contract where the end of the employment contract is determined by objective conditions such as reaching a specific date, completing a specific task or the occurrence of a specific event. Agency workers are those persons having an employment contract with a temporary-work agency with a view to being assigned to a user undertaking to work temporarily under its supervision and its direction. The group of involuntary part-time workers includes those employees whose normal hours of work are formally less than the normal hours of work of a comparable full-time worker, being in this situation against their will or due to family care needs.

[14] For the purpose of VUP Group 4, a casual worker is a person whose work is irregular or intermittent. This includes formally self-employed as well as employees. The concept of intermittent work refers to short-term contracts concluded to conduct a specific task, often related to an individual project or seasonally occurring jobs. The intermittent worker is required to fulfil a task or complete a specific number of working days. The category of casual work includes on-call that involves a contractual relationship in which the principal does not continuously provide work for the worker. VUP Group 4 also includes platform work. It concerns work by individuals using an app or a website to match themselves with customers, in order to perform specific tasks or to provide services in exchange for payment. This notion includes the following subcategories: crowdworkers and workers-on-demand via app.

[15] This contribution does not take into account the temporary support measures set up in the framework of the Covid-19 pandemic.

[16] High-level Group (n 5) 2.

and impediments can be found in the countries studied? and (2) *Do the four VUP Groups receive adequate access to social protection?* By answering those two questions, this contribution acquires a more in-depth view on whether the four VUP Groups are entitled to formal, effective and adequate access within the meaning of the 2019 Recommendation. This Recommendation aims at ensuring formal, effective, adequate and transparent access to social protection for *all* workers – regardless of whether they work in a standard or non-standard manner – as well as for *all* self-employed.

Belgium, Germany, Italy, Luxembourg, Poland, Sweden and the Netherlands are covered in the discussion below. That way, different types of social security systems are included, and this contribution can examine how they provide protection for non-standard workers. Besides the classical axis of Bismarckian systems (Belgium, Germany and Luxembourg) and Beveridgean systems (the Netherlands),[17] the Nordic/Scandinavian model (Sweden), the Southern/Mediterranean model (Italy) and the Post-Socialist model (Poland) are also taken into account in the discussion below. To this day, Bismarck-oriented systems in particular still depart to a large extent from the standard labour relationship and grant social insurance protection based on one's labour market status.[18] Professional status also remains an important criterion for receiving access to social protection in Mediterranean and Post-Socialist countries.[19] Beveridgean and Scandinavian systems traditionally focused rather on a uniform protection for all residents, yet the standard employment relationship also serves as a starting point for the risks connected to the performance of a professional activity, such as unemployment or sickness.[20]

A. The Protection for VUP Groups in the Case of Sickness and Unemployment

i. VUP Group 1

The first VUP Group in the Working, Yet Poor project are low and unskilled workers who work in poor sectors on the basis of a contract of indefinite duration

---

[17] In light of the extensive reforms of the Dutch social security system that were introduced in the previous decades, the Netherlands will serve as an example of a Beveridgean social security scheme. The Dutch social security system was traditionally designed as a continental system, but had already from the outset a more hybrid character, combining a continental approach with a more universal one.

[18] Although all countries will include elements of other social security models as well, see the discussion in J Berghman, 'Basic Concepts of Social Security' in D Pieters (ed), *Social Security in Europe* (Brussels, Bruylant, 1991) 16–17; B von Maydell et al. *Social Policy in the 21st Century* (Berlin, Springer, 2001) 19–20.

[19] See also for a discussion on the different social security models: von Maydell et al (n 18) 19–20, as well as the discussion in G Esping-Andersen, *The Three Worlds of Welfare Capitalism* (New Jersey, Princeton University Press, 1990).

[20] Berghman (n 18) 16–17.

on a full-time basis. It might sound illogical that the Working, Yet Poor project considers those workers as particularly vulnerable and underrepresented. Most social security systems are rooted in and based on this kind of employment (also called 'standard employment') and the (nowadays often) poor sectors. This also becomes clear when looking at their formal coverage in case of sickness and unemployment: in all the countries studied the workers in VUP Group 1 are formally included in the scheme for employees. Furthermore, the applicable rules on qualifying periods, the duration and the amount of sickness and unemployment benefits in the selected countries are often based on standard employment agreements, such as the workers in VUP Group 1. Nevertheless, the workers in VUP Group 1 face several obstacles in their social security coverage as well, which are discussed further in this section.

a. The Impact of Low Wages on Social Security Coverage

An important obstacle for the workers in VUP Group 1 are the low wages that are often paid to those workers and the impact of low wages on their social security coverage. Despite the fact that several of the selected countries have minimum wages in place, this appears to be insufficient to keep all employees out of poverty when they work.[21] Although earning a low wage does not necessarily imply that a person will end up in poverty, it might nevertheless increase their risk of in-work poverty.[22] Low wages will in most countries lead to even lower sickness and unemployment benefits; those benefits are often expressed as a percentage of one's previous earnings.[23] An important difference in approach can also be noted between sickness and unemployment benefits, as several countries grant higher benefits in case of sickness (Belgium, Germany, Italy (for white-collar workers), Luxembourg, Poland and Sweden;[24] see also the discussion in section II.B). An explanation can be that people who are sick are perceived more worthy of protection than unemployed.[25] Furthermore, not all selected countries grant minimum

---

[21] One of the reasons could be limited wage growth, as observed in the Netherlands. Taking into account that there has been barely any real wage growth, especially among low-skilled workers. In Belgium strong differences were also observed between countries resulting in difficulties in reaching an adequate minimum wage in certain sectors (eg accommodation or the textile care sector), see A Oostveen, *Thematic Report on In-Work Poverty in the Netherlands*, European Social Policy Network (Brussels, European Commission, 2017) 15 and E De Becker, A Dockx and P Schoukens, 'In-Work Poverty in Belgium' in L Ratti (ed), *In-Work Poverty in Europe. Vulnerable and Under-Represented Persons in a Comparative Perspective* (Alphen aan den Rijn, Kluwer Law International, 2022) 48–49.

[22] See also I Marx, J Vanhille and G Verbist, 'Combating In-Work Poverty in Continental Europe: An Investigation Using the Belgian Case' (2011) IZA DP no 6067, 7 (published in (2012) 41(1) *Journal of Social Policy* 19).

[23] Unemployment benefits in Poland are universal flat-rate benefits.

[24] Although the differences are not that notable for Sweden.

[25] D Pieters, *Navigating Social Security Options* (London, Palgrave Macmillan, 2019) 43–44 and 64–65.

benefits in case of sickness and unemployment (however, Belgium, Luxembourg and the Netherlands, for example, do grant minimum benefits). When the workers in VUP Group 1 do not have the necessary financial means, social assistance can act as a safety net. Strict income and activation conditions will, however, apply. The analysis below (section II.B) also shows that the workers in VUP Group 1 will often not receive any additional top-up on their sickness and unemployment benefit via social assistance, as those benefits will already exceed the income threshold applied in national social assistance schemes.

An example of how social security law can strengthen the position of workers with low wages can be found in the Netherlands in case of sickness: the Dutch legislation stipulates that in the first year of sickness of the employee, the employer needs to pay at least the minimum wage.[26] During the second year of sickness, in which the employer under Dutch legislation is still responsible for granting protection in case of sickness, this lower limit does not apply. However, the employee can rely on the top-up to the level of the minimum wage, as provided for in the Participation Act.[27] Supplementary forms of protection can also be found in other countries; however, they are not always well-adapted to workers in non-standard work forms or who receive a low wage. An example can be found in Sweden: those who are unemployed can receive additional forms of support, which consists of support for employees subject to redundancies at the workplace provided by trade union insurances. It is, however, only possible to benefit from such additional forms of support when 80 per cent of the previously earned wage exceeds the maximum wage cap for an unemployment benefit.[28] Hence, these benefits are only of importance for employees with higher earnings and are as such not very relevant for VUP Group 1 (or VUP Group 3 and 4).[29] Moreover, those who are self-employed, like VUP Group 2, will not have access to any additional form of support from trade unions.

b. The Impact of Activation Measures on Social Security Coverage

Another obstacle that can be discerned in the selected countries is the strong focus on activation measures, in particular for unemployment to increase the labour market participation. This is reflected (among other requirements) in the requirement to accept suitable work. In the Netherlands, for example, all work becomes suitable work after six months.[30] Hence, workers who already have a low-paid

---

[26] M Houwerzijl et al, 'National Report on the Netherlands', Working, Yet Poor (2021), Deliverable 3.2, 156, available at workingyetpoor.eu/deliverables.

[27] M Houwerzijl et al, 'In-Work Poverty in the Netherlands' in L Ratti (ed), *In-work poverty in Europe. Vulnerable and Under-represented Persons in a Comparative Perspective* (Alphen aan den Rijn, Kluwer Law International, 2022) 201–02.

[28] AC Hartzen, 'National Report on Sweden', Working, Yet Poor (2021), Deliverable 3.2, 32, available at workingyetpoor.eu/deliverables.

[29] Hartzen (n 28) 32.

[30] Houwerzijl et al (n 27) 202.

job can be pushed into a job with an even lower wage. It can also have the effect of low-paid jobs being taken up by people with higher skill levels, but who find themselves being pushed towards accepting lower-paid jobs (due to activation measures).[31] Some countries do set a minimum limit on the wage level of what constitutes suitable work, which means that a wage cannot fall below a certain level (eg 90 per cent of the unemployment benefit in Sweden[32]).

A strong focus on activation in the case of unemployment can also be found in Germany since the Hartz reforms in the 2000s.[33] Beneficiaries of unemployment benefits have been expected to accept offers of employment even where those do not match their skills level and/or significantly undercut their previous wage level. The Hartz reforms led to an important shift and now only about a third of the unemployed are entitled to insurance-based, wage-related benefits; furthermore, entitlements are short and limited to one year. An important spill-over effect of stringent activation measures can be that workers have fewer opportunities to collectively bargain over wages as their only 'exit' option is the receipt of means-tested benefits, as pointed out by Hiessl.[34] Stricter conditions for receiving insurance-based benefits can also be found in Sweden, which has led to a significant drop in the number of recipients of such benefits. Universal unemployment benefits serve as an important safety net but those benefits are granted at a much lower rate, leading to a higher risk of in-work poverty.[35] For Italy as well, Villa et al highlighted the problems for workers trying to find a suitable job offer when unemployed: an evaluation of the suitability of a job offer must take into account the experiences and skills of the unemployed person as well as geographical distance and commuting times, the duration of unemployment, and the wage level.[36] The wage must be 20 per cent higher than the unemployment benefit. However, the unemployment benefit in Italy decreases automatically from the sixth month,[37] even if the unemployed person has fulfilled the job-search requirements provided for.[38] Hence, Villa et al. argue that

---

[31] See C Hiessl, 'Working Yet Poor: A Comparative Appraisal' in L Ratti (ed), *In-Work Poverty in Europe. Vulnerable and Under-Represented Persons in a Comparative Perspective* (Alphen aan den Rijn, Kluwer Law International, 2022) 315.

[32] AC Hartzen, 'In-work Poverty in Sweden' in L Ratti (ed), *In-Work Poverty in Europe. Vulnerable and Under-Represented Persons in a Comparative Perspective* (Alphen aan den Rijn, Kluwer Law International, 2022) 289.

[33] C Hiessl, 'In-Work Poverty in Germany' in L Ratti (ed), *In-work Poverty in Europe. Vulnerable and Under-Represented Persons in a Comparative Perspective* (Alphen aan den Rijn, Kluwer Law International, 2022) 88–89 and 92.

[34] C Hiessl, 'National Report on Germany', Working, Yet Poor (2021), Deliverable 3.2, 57, available at workingyetpoor.eu/deliverables.

[35] Hartzen (n 32) 281.

[36] E Villa, G Marchi and N De Luigi, 'In-Work Poverty in Italy' in L Ratti (ed), *In-Work Poverty in Europe. Vulnerable and Under-Represented Persons in a Comparative Perspective* (Alphen aan den Rijn, Kluwer Law International, 2022) 132–33.

[37] The decrease of the benefit commences from the eighth month of unemployment when the unemployed person is over 55 years old.

[38] Workers who receive an unemployment benefit below a certain threshold can ask to be exempted.

the Italian unemployment benefit system risks forcing the unemployed to accept low-wage jobs.[39] It is also uncertain to what extent such low-wage jobs can serve as a stepping stone in finding employment with a higher wage.[40]

c. The Possibility to Combine Social Security Benefits and a Professional Income

Another element that can be observed in the countries studied is the rather rigid design in their social security schemes: the possibility to combine unemployment benefits with a professional income is quite limited. This can have a negative impact for workers combining different (part-time) activities, or for workers who cannot find full-time work. Although some initiatives can be found, countries fear that the possibility to take up part-time employment in combination with an unemployment benefit could lead to an inactivity trap. For that reason, countries impose several restrictions: part-time work cannot exceed certain income limits or the unemployed person will lose their unemployment benefit. Although such rules can stimulate the unemployed to take up new employment, a balance must be struck whereby workers are given the necessary incentives to find new employment. It most not lead to a situation where workers only work a limited number of hours over a longer period (even if they would want (and could) work more hours).

The Swedish legislation, for example, allows involuntary part-time workers to combine their unemployment benefit with their part-time salary, with a limit of 60 weeks.[41] After those weeks, the unemployed can only receive unemployment benefits if they become fully unemployed. This limit is intended to generate an incentive for part-time workers to find full-time work. The Dutch legislation, on the other hand, applies a rather flexible approach: since 2015 the Dutch legislation has made it easier to combine an unemployment benefit with a professional income.[42] This is possible as long as the income derived from the new employment does not exceed 87.5 per cent or more of the previously earned salary. As a result, the unemployment benefit no longer functions as an unemployment insurance scheme, but rather as a wage supplement scheme. The idea behind it is to stimulate people to take up new employment, so that the total income grows higher than the unemployment benefit alone. It is also possible to work as a self-employed person. However, Houwerzijl et al point out that the flipside of this reform might be that it potentially worsens the position of lower skilled workers.[43]

---

[39] Villa, Marchi and De Luigi (n 36) 133.

[40] High-level Group (n 5) 19; see also the discussion in M Filomena, and M Picchio, 'Are Temporary Jobs Stepping Stones or Dead Ends? A Meta-Analytical Review of the Literature' (2021) IZA DP No 14367.

[41] Hartzen (n 32) 281.

[42] Houwerzijl et al (n 26) 64; see also: Art 16(1) and Art 20(1)c Unemployment Act of 6 November 1986 (the Netherlands).

[43] Houwerzijl et al, (n 26) 65.

d. The Difference in Social Security Protection between Blue- and White-Collar Workers

Another obstacle for the workers in VUP Group 1 is the distinction still made in some countries between blue- and white-collar workers. Workers in VUP Group 1 will often be considered a blue-collar worker. In Belgium, less advantageous rules apply for blue-collar workers in the period of wage continuation paid by the employer.[44] The same rules for blue- and white-collar workers are applied once they receive a sickness benefit. A less advantageous regime of wage continuation is also in place for domestic workers who are bound by an employment agreement with the household for whom they deliver services. Domestic workers receive their full wage during the first seven days of incapacity and 60 per cent of their wage for the seven days afterwards.[45] Similarly, the Italian legislation also has different rules in place for blue- and white-collar workers: while the latter are entitled to full-pay throughout their sickness, blue-collar workers are guaranteed sick pay (at a lower rate),[46] unless a higher benefit is granted via the applicable collective agreement. However, almost all collective agreements provide further protection.[47]

ii. VUP Group 2

a. Divergent Social Security Protection for the Self-Employed Selected EU Member States

VUP Group 2 covers (economically) dependent and bogus self-employed persons. The protection offered varies among the countries studied. Some countries provide protection in case of sickness and unemployment, similar to employees, whilst other countries do not provide any protection or only in a limited form.[48] This limited protection can be explained due to the traditional idea that the self-employed can provide for their own (social) protection. Another problem with the

---

[44] Art 52 Act of 3 July 1978 on employment agreements (Belgium) and Arts 3–4 Collective Agreement no 12*bis* of 26 February 1979 concluded in the National Labour Council (Belgium), as discussed in De Becker, Dockx and Schoukens (n 21) 48–49.

[45] Furthermore, other less advantageous rules can be found for domestic workers as well; their employment contract cannot be suspended due to economic causes, different in the case of (some) white-collar and blue-collar employees: Arts 112–114 of Act of 3 July 1978 on employment agreements (Belgium), as discussed in De Becker, Dockx and Schoukens (n 21) 48–49.

[46] C Zoli et al, 'National Report on Italy', Working, Yet Poor (2021), Deliverable 3.2, 64, available at workingyetpoor.eu/deliverables, and Missoc Italy (2021). The Missoc tables for EU countries can be found online at www.missoc.org.

[47] Zoli et al (n 46) 64 and Missoc Italy (2021).

[48] See also the typologies applied in S Spasova et al, *Access to Social Protection for People Working on Non-Standard Contracts and as Self-Employed in Europe. A Study of National Policies* (Brussels, European Commission, 2017) 13 and P Schoukens and C Bruynseraede, *Access to Social Protection for Self-Employed and Non-Standard Workers: An Analysis Based upon the EU Recommendation on Access to Social Protection* (Leuven, Acco, 2021) 26–27.

members of VUP Group 2 is that – unlike VUP Group 1 – they do not fall under one clear-cut category within social security law. Solo and bogus self-employed will be considered self-employed and follow the general rules applicable to all self-employed. This can mean that they either fall under the general scheme of self-employment, or under a specific group for a specific sector or profession, or that there is no protection available. Those taking part in bogus self-employment should fall under the social security scheme for employees; however, unless a requalification occurs, they will continue to fall under the social security system for the self-employed.

A growing number of schemes at a global level can be seen to have been developed for economically dependent self-employed persons, providing social security coverage and in some countries labour law coverage as well.[49] Several policy options are applied by countries, eg by extending the protection of the general employee schemes to cover the economically dependent self-employed or by developing schemes in-between employment and self-employment for economically dependent self-employed persons that provide more protection than the schemes for other self-employed persons. This trend is less visible in the countries studied in the Working, Yet Poor project. Only Italy has developed several intermediate categories to grant a stronger protection for the economically dependent self-employed.

The Italian social security scheme traditionally does not grant protection for the self-employed in case of sickness and unemployment; the increase in solo self-employment and the uncertainty surrounding the notion of economic dependency, however, prompted the Italian legislator to review the protection for the solo self-employed.[50] Relevant for VUP Group 2 are the categories of heteronomous-organised collaborations and continuous and coordinate collaborations (co.co.co. work arrangements). Heteronomous-organised work is an activity that is continuous, performed mainly by the worker and organised by the employer in a heteronomous manner.[51] The social security legislation for employees applies to this group of workers.[52] Co.co.co. workers, on the other hand, are obliged to carry out their activity in accordance with the methods or organisation agreed upon in the contract, in order to integrate their work into the productive

---

[49] See the national examples cited in P Schoukens, *Expert Report for the European Commission. Improving Access to Social Protection for the Self-employed in the EU: State of Play and Possible Policy Reforms* (2022) 18–19 and C Schubert, 'Comparative Analysis' in C Schubert (ed), *Economically-Dependent Workers: Employment in a Decent Economy – International, European and Comparative Law Perspective. A Handbook* (Munich, Beck, 2022) 215–18.

[50] Villa, Marchi and De Luigi (n 36) 135–36 and the overview in M Del Conte and E Gramano, 'Italy' in C Schubert (ed), *Economically-Dependent Workers: Employment in a Decent Economy – International, European and Comparative Law Perspective. A Handbook* (Munich, Beck, 2022).

[51] Art 2 Legislative Decree no 81/2015; see also Italian Court of Cassation, 24 January 2020, no 1663/2020.

[52] Employment Ministry Circular no. 3/2016 and Italian Court of Cassation, 24 January 2020, no 1663/2020.

organisation of the client, but any power or interference by the client in their performance is excluded.[53] Co.co.co. work falls under the broader category of almost-subordinate-employment; such workers can receive protection in case of sickness and unemployment. The social security protection in case of sickness and unemployment for co.co.co. workers shows some resemblance to the protection offered for employees, although differences do exist (eg the duration and amount in case of unemployment).

Another example of a third category can be found in Poland, where civil law agreements are widely used. It concerns work performed based on civil law agreements regulated by the Civil Code (eg mandate contract[54] or a contract for a specific task).[55] Traditionally, the social security protection provided for such civil law agreements was lower than for standard workers. The steep increase in the use of civil law agreements led to some changes in the Polish legislation on the social security coverage provided.[56] Workers performing mandate contracts are situated in factual and legal terms between employees and self-employed. Voluntary protection in case of sickness and unemployment is open for workers under a mandate contract. However, often those workers do not pay the necessary social security contributions and, hence, do not receive any social protection in case of sickness and unemployment.[57] Sickness or unemployment protection for workers performing a contract for a specific task is not available.

When looking at the other selected countries, some provide self-employed (including VUP Group 2) protection in case of sickness and/or unemployment along the lines of the protection offered to employees: Belgium (only sickness), Luxembourg, Poland (on voluntary basis) and Sweden (voluntary for unemployment). Protection in Belgium is only provided in case of sickness; unemployment protection similar to that of employees is not open for the self-employed.[58] They can, however, make use of the bridging right scheme (but limited in time and only in case of a forced (temporary) cessation or a cessation due to economic difficulties).[59] The situation where a self-employed person is significantly economically dependent on one or more clients and needs temporary income

---

[53] See also the discussion in Del Conte and Gramano (n 50) 87.

[54] Such contracts are also called commission contracts.

[55] M Tomaszewska and A Peplinska, 'In-Work Poverty in Poland' in L Ratti (ed), *In-work Poverty in Europe. Vulnerable and Under-Represented Persons in a Comparative Perspective* (Alphen aan den Rijn, Kluwer Law International, 2022) 244.

[56] See also: 'With the support of the Recovery and Resilience Facility (RRF), at the end of 2021, Poland initiated a reform to extend mandatory insurance and improve coverage. It concerns in particular civil law contracts with provisions aimed at ensuring that they are covered by old-age/pension and accident insurance' as cited in European Commission (n 6) 14.

[57] See also the exception for workers under the age of 26 years, who are not covered as discussed in M Tomaszewska and A Peplinska, 'National Report on Poland', Working, Yet Poor (2021), Deliverable 3.2, 34, available at workingyetpoor.eu/deliverables.

[58] See the discussion in De Becker, Dockx and Schoukens (n 21) 55–58.

[59] In January 2023, this scheme was reformed to increase the take up of the bridging right: Art 188 and further Act of 26 December 2022 (Belgium).

support upon the loss of these client(s) does not seem to fall under any of the situations of the bridging right. Whereas such a situation could fall under the criterion 'forced cessation or interruption' or under the criterion 'economic difficulties', the solo (economically dependent) self-employed will not always have to (temporarily) forcefully cease their entire activity. In fact, the solo (economically dependent) self-employed will instead be confronted with a significant loss of turnover, where they continue to work while trying to find a new client. In that sense, the bridging right does not seem well-equipped to deal with VUP Group 2. As discussed above, sickness and unemployment protection in Italy is only open for a limited group of solo self-employed persons (including co.co.co. workers). The protection under both the Italian scheme and the Belgian bridging right scheme is less extensive than the protection provided for employees under the unemployment scheme.

Two additional comments can be made with regard to the existing schemes in the selected countries. Voluntary protection for the self-employed is not always taken up, due to the financial cost, in particular by the self-employed with a low income.[60] More flexible rules can help the self-employed to join the social security scheme. For example, Sweden gives the self-employed the possibility to choose their own waiting period in case of sickness. The longer the waiting period, the lower the social security contributions that the self-employed person has to pay.[61] Important to note as well is that coverage as a self-employed person in several countries is linked to a minimum work level that should be reached by the self-employed person (expressed in hours worked or income earned). Examples are Poland[62] and Sweden.[63] As will be discussed further for VUP Group 3, such thresholds can be difficult to reach for marginal work performed as a self-employed person. Furthermore, even though Poland applies the same eligibility criteria as for employees, the self-employed can only receive a benefit after 90 days of unemployment.[64] Similarly, Luxembourg does not grant the self-employed a benefit in the period of wage continuation for employees (77 days).[65]

While Germany and the Netherlands do not offer protection to all self-employed in case of sickness and unemployment, they do grant protection to certain subgroups of the self-employed. The Dutch scheme foresees the possibility for certain groups of employee-like persons to fall under the social security scheme for employees.[66] However, opt-out from this protection is possible.

---

[60] See also the comment made by Schoukens on the take up of voluntary protection: Schoukens (n 49) 31–32.

[61] Hartzen (n 28) 60–61.

[62] Tomaszewska and Peplinska (n 57) 68.

[63] See the discussion for VUP Group 3.

[64] Missoc Poland (2021).

[65] Missoc Luxembourg (2021).

[66] G Vonk, 'Extending Social Insurance Schemes to "Non-Employees" and Adapting Social Insurance Schemes to Hybrid Employment: The Dutch Example' in U Becker and O Chesalina (eds), *Social Law 4.0. New Approaches for Ensuring and Financing Social Security in the Digital Age* (Baden-Baden, Nomos, 2020) 153–54.

Germany, also, does not have a separate scheme in place for the self-employed, with the exception of certain professions. An example that could be of relevance for VUP Group 2 and 4 are home workers in Germany, ie persons who repeatedly and durably complete assignments for an organisation on which they depend economically at home or at a self-chosen workplace (alone or with family members).[67] The decisive factor is whether the majority of the worker's livelihood is obtained in this way. In practice, the notion may apply to activities such as product testing, text editing, translating, participation in surveys, etc. Hiessl argues that, the requirement of work based on assignments specified in advance prevents the category from being operationalised for broad groups of freelance teleworkers or platform workers.[68] Home workers are comprehensively covered by all branches of social insurance (including health care and unemployment).

The German legislation does allow the self-employed who previously fell under the employee scheme to continue to fall under this scheme on a voluntary basis. That way, they can still receive protection in case of sickness and unemployment. However, the self-employed will often face difficulties in reaching the thresholds of minimum insurance periods and minimum hours worked.[69] For example in the case of unemployment, the self-employed activity must be carried out for at least 15 hours a week. The self-employed must also apply for the voluntary insurance within three months after the start of the self-employed activity. As the conditions have been restricted in recent years, the number of self-employed who have continued their previous insurance have dropped significantly.[70] Notably, the lack of unemployment insurance may make the self-employed particularly likely to accept low levels of remuneration as their only 'exit option' is to file for social assistance.[71] Similar rules on voluntary insurance can be found in case of sickness.[72] Additional hurdles in the take up of voluntary insurance in Germany are the rather high social security contributions and low benefits for self-employed persons with a low skill level. The calculation of unemployment benefits are based on the qualifications required for the beneficiary's self-employed activity, although all pay the same level of contributions.[73] The higher the professional qualification, the higher the replacement income.

When no protection is provided in a country or the self-employed person does not fulfil the statutory conditions, they can still take up private insurance; however, the example of Germany shows that the self-employed with a low income

---

[67] Hiessl (n 34) 17–18.
[68] Hiessl (n 34) 18.
[69] Hiessl (n 34) 65.
[70] While there were almost 105,000 applications for insurance in 2010, this dropped to just over 23,000 in 2013, 19,000 of whom were admitted to unemployment insurance. In 2018, there were just around 3,000 new entries, as discussed in Hiessl (n 34) 66 and the references cited therein.
[71] P Schoukens and E Weber, 'Unemployment Insurance for the Self-Employed: A Way forward Post-Corona', IAB-Discussion Paper 32/2020, 21 and further.
[72] Art 9 Social Code Book V.
[73] Hiessl (n 34) 66.

are less inclined to take up such insurance.[74] In general take-up rates in voluntary opt-in schemes are low.[75] As discussed above for VUP Group 1, social assistance can also serve as a last safety net. However, this can be especially challenging for VUP Group 2 to access, as they have very often built up some form of savings over the years to compensate for the lack of social coverage, in particular in countries where no social coverage for self-employed is foreseen (eg Germany).[76]

b. The Difficulty in Mapping the Income of the Self-employed

An additional obstacle for countries in granting self-employed protection is the difficulty in measuring their income. The available at-risk-of poverty rates already make clear that mapping the income of self-employed is not an easy task: self-employed often face a high risk of in-work poverty, but have a lower risk of material deprivation. The reasons why it is more difficult to measure the income of a self-employed are manifold. One reason is the fact that their income is not periodically fixed, in contrast to standard workers. The income of a self-employed person will partly consist of the direct return on their professional activity and partly of the capital invested in their business. Another difficulty concerns the irregularity of the income of (some) self-employed persons. Periods of high earnings can be followed by financial difficulties and there might be serious fluctuations in income. Apart from that, the self-employed declare their own income, which can lead to an undervaluation of the earnings. Despite lack of official numbers, there is an assumption that the income declared by the self-employed is lower than what they earn in reality.[77]

The difficulty in determining the correct income for a self-employed person causes several problems for social security. For example: determining the correct income is necessary for (1) the payment of social security contributions and (2) the calculation of social security benefits, as benefits are often expressed as a percentage of the previously earned income. Due to the difficulties in mapping the income earned, Belgium works with universal flat-rate benefits for the self-employed (sickness and the bridging right). These are rather low benefits and can mean an important income drop for certain self-employed persons. Furthermore, such an approach also does not encourage the self-employed with higher incomes to pay more social security contributions, as they would not see an increase in the social security benefit received. The Belgian sickness scheme and bridging scheme does differentiate depending on the household composition of the self-employed: higher benefits are granted for those self-employed with dependants. Moreover, higher sickness benefits are also granted to self-employed people who had to stop their undertaking due to ill health.

---

[74] Hiessl (n 33) 101.
[75] See also European Commission (n 6) 11.
[76] Hiessl (n 31) 329.
[77] Schoukens and Bruynseraede (n 48) 77.

c. The Difficulty of Including Self-employed in Social Security Schemes

In general, social security schemes struggle to include the self-employed adequately in the scheme.[78] For example, in case of unemployment, the applicable legislation will often require a complete cessation of professional activities. Self-employed people who have to cease their activity completely may be less inclined to apply for an unemployment benefit if they face financial difficulties at some point or have to – due to circumstances outside their will, such as the end of a contract by their sole client – cease their professional activity. Moreover, when the self-employed can still take up certain administrative tasks to guarantee the continuation of their professional activities, it is difficult to draw a clear demarcation line between an activity for the continuation of their economic activity and a genuine economic activity. The Belgian scheme, for example, allows that the self-employed can still perform residual tasks when sick that allow the person concerned to earn a living taking into account the nature and scope of their professional activity. It is also possible to gradually take up work again, in combination with sickness benefits. In the first six months, sickness benefits are not reduced.[79] Another example is Sweden, where in a similar manner, some tasks for the continuation of the business activities can still be performed, without performing the actual work. However, if the self-employed reinitiates their work, they will need to liquidate their company completely in order to be able to be entitled to unemployment benefits again.[80] This means that self-employed persons who end up in recurrent periods of unemployment will face higher thresholds for accessing unemployment benefits than employees. In contrast to employees (see VUP Group 3), the self employed can not combine unemployment benefits with part-time work in Sweden.[81]

The problems set out above show that social security schemes should reflect on the social risk itself, and the protection they wish to grant: the underlying risk can and should even be defined differently for workers and (some group of) self-employed. For unemployment, the self-employed may be more interested in having a temporary reduction of work covered than a final closure of their business.[82] This will be different for standard employees, as the loss of work in such a case will more likely result in a cessation of one's professional activity. Similarly, for workers sickness benefits can address the loss of work capacity. For the self-employed, the work incapacity may be difficult to determine, especially in a first period of sickness,[83] as this does not automatically lead to a loss of income for a self-employed person. For that reason, Schoukens and Bruynseraede have

---

[78] See also European Commission (n 6) 2.
[79] Art 28*bis* § 3 Royal Decree of 20 July 1971 on the creation of a health care and maternity insurance for the self-employed and their helping spouses (Belgium).
[80] Art 35a Act of 29 May 1997 on Unemployment Insurance (Sweden) and Hartzen (n 32) 283.
[81] Hartzen (n 32) 283.
[82] Schoukens and Bruynseraede (n 48) 31.
[83] Schoukens and Bruynseraede (n 48) 51–52.

argued for a labour neutral and labour-specific approach to be applied: whereas protection should be granted in a neutral manner, different rules might be needed to cover the social risk adequately for different types of workers and the self-employed.

d. EU Competition Law and Minimum Wages for the Self-Employed

The self-employed are in principle not bound by minimum wage agreements or statutory minimum wages. As a result, the self-employed might be inclined to accept lower remuneration in order to gain or maintain a specific contract. In recent years, discussions have taken place at EU level and in EU Member States to what extent the self-employed can conclude price-fixing agreements. Such agreements and collective bargaining in general (with a group of the self-employed persons via trade unions, or organisations focusing on the self-employed)[84] can serve as an important tool to strengthen the position of (certain groups of) the self-employed and can ensure that they receive an adequate remuneration for the tasks performed.

Traditionally, in the EU concerns about violating competition law constituted a barrier to collective bargaining by the self-employed.[85] The recently adopted EU guidelines clarify that the solo self-employed[86] can under certain conditions conclude collective agreements, and agree on minimum wages, etc. This might prove important to achieve a more extensive protection for the solo self-employed in the coming years. Some of the countries studied already considered collective bargaining for the self-employed legal in principle (eg Italy) or at least so for dependent subgroups of the self-employed (Sweden and Germany).[87] In Poland the applicable legislation has also been extended in order to include solo self-employed persons (who find themselves in an economically dependent situation with a principal).[88] Before the adoption of the changed EU guidelines, Hiessl argued that the extensions in national law in terms of establishing protective standards via collective bargaining remained rather limited and typically concentrated

---

[84] The group of self-employed workers is not homogenous, but this group is rather diverse in the activities covered and the specific needs. Eurofound identified the following categories of organisations that represent the self-employed, ie trade unions, employer organisations, chambers of commerce or industry; for a more extensive discussion: Eurofound, *Exploring Self-Employment in the European Union* (Luxembourg, Publications Office of the European Union, 2017).

[85] For example, Hiessl (n 31) 327 and Schubert (n 49) 212–14.

[86] Following definition of a solo self-employed person is used in the Guidelines of the EU Commission, ie 'a person who does not have an employment contract or who is not in an employment relationship, and who relies primarily on his or her own personal labour for the provision of the services concerned', see: Art 1(2) Communication from the European Commission *Guidelines on the application of Union competition law to collective agreements regarding the working conditions of solo self-employed persons* [2022] OJ C 374/02.

[87] See also the discussion in Eurofound, *Regulation Minimum Wages and Other Forms of Pay for the Self-Employed* (Luxembourg, Publications Office of the European Union, 2022).

[88] Tomaszewska and Peplinska (n 53) 246–47.

in certain sectors.[89] It remains to be seen what the exact impact of the updated guidelines will be in the coming years.

In the countries studied only the Netherlands extended the scope of the minimum wage protection to include certain groups of self-employed persons (2018), unless they fiscally qualify as an undertaking ('entrepreneur'). Elements to distinguish between the different types of the self-employed are the number of clients, the business and debtor risk, and the presentation to the outside world. Yet, most self-employed persons will nonetheless register in the Netherlands as an undertaking, due to the tax advantages granted. Houwerzijl et al stated that it is still not clear how effective the extension in scope of the minimum wage act has been.[90] An overall extension of the statutory minimum wage to all self-employed persons was not introduced, due to administrative difficulties.[91]

iii. VUP Group 3

VUP Group 3 looks at temporary workers (ie fixed-term workers, temporary agency workers and involuntary part-time workers). This group of workers fall (in principle) under the social security scheme of employees. Moreover, a principle of equal treatment applies in labour law and social security law. Nevertheless, in-work poverty levels for this group of workers are remarkably higher than for standard workers.[92] Workers in VUP Group 3 also face several obstacles in their social protection. Some of these obstacles overlap with the obstacles for VUP Group 1 and are not repeated; other obstacles are discussed further below

a. Formal Access and Marginal Employment

In most cases, the workers in VUP Group 3 have formal access to social protection in case of sickness and unemployment. However there are some exceptions for marginal employment. A well-known example is the German mini-job scheme (ie employment with a monthly salary up to €520 or less than three months / 70 days per year[93]); other examples can be found in Belgium and Luxembourg where work of a limited nature is excluded from coverage in the case of unemployment, ie work performed for less than 12 hours (Belgium)[94] or 16 hours per week (Luxembourg)[95] in the case of unemployment. Similarly, the Luxembourgish legislation also stipulates that employees who are engaged only occasionally in

---

[89] Hiessl (n 31) 327.
[90] Houwerzijl et al (n 27) 211.
[91] Eurofound (n 87) 41.
[92] Ratti, García-Muñoz and Vergnat (n 1) 21.
[93] Missoc Germany (2021) and Section 18 Social Code Book IV.
[94] Art 33 Royal Decree of 25 November 1991 (Belgium).
[95] L Ratti and A García-Muñoz, 'National Report on Luxembourg', Working, Yet Poor (2021), Deliverable 3.2, 32, available at workingyetpoor.eu/deliverables.

a professional activity are not covered by the sickness benefit scheme, ie when the period of the activity does not exceed more than three months per calendar year.[96] Other examples can be found in the Netherlands and Sweden. The Dutch legislation excludes certain groups of employees from unemployment protection, eg the exclusion for persons who work fewer than four days a week in a private person's household, such as cleaners and home carers.[97] The Swedish legislation requires that a certain minimum level of income must be reached to qualify for a sickness benefit.[98] Two comments can be made with regard to the above. It is unclear to what extent the different forms of work mentioned are still marginal activities. Furthermore, such exceptions often find their root in administrative difficulties for countries in keeping track of marginal activities; however one could wonder if such rules are still necessary nowadays with more sophisticated IT tools available.[99] Moreover, earlier studies stressed the problematic nature of part-time work for women, eg in Germany where marginal part-time work was often the sole employment status available to women.[100]

b. The Difficulty for Flexible Workers to Receive
Effective Access to Benefits

In addition to the problems concerning formal access, workers in VUP Group 3 are often confronted with problems concerning effective access to social protection in case of sickness and unemployment: whilst they are formally included in the scope of application of the social security scheme for sickness and unemployment, they face more difficulties in fulfilling the statutory conditions than standard workers, eg waiting periods, etc. Countries often apply the same rules as for standard workers to other (more flexible) work forms, departing from the principle of equal treatment. However, the characteristics of other non-standard work forms will require countries to rethink the current social security rules, eg by formulating qualifying periods in a more flexible manner (eg the idea of labour neutrality and labour specificity, as discussed in section II.A.ii on VUP Group 2).

Stringent and long waiting periods not suitable for the workers in VUP Group 3 can be found in Poland and Germany (eg unemployment in Poland: 365 days in a period of 18 months for which at least the minimum wage was due;[101] unemployment in Germany: one year of work within the last 30 months[102]). Similarly, in the case of sickness, the Polish legislation applies a qualifying period

---

[96] Missoc Luxembourg (2021).
[97] Art 6(1)c Unemployment Act of 6 November 1986 (the Netherlands).
[98] Hartzen (n 32) and Missoc Sweden (2021).
[99] Schoukens and Bruynseraede (n 48) 71.
[100] Spasova et al. (n 48) 52.
[101] Missoc Poland (2021) and Tomaszewska and Peplinska (n 57) 66.
[102] Section 142 and 143 Social Code Book III (Germany).

of 30 consecutive days, which can be harder to fulfil for temporary employment agreements (except when the unemployed has paid compulsory contributions for 10 years).[103] In Italy, on the other hand, the qualifying period is formulated in a rather flexible manner and can be fulfilled by periods of work over a longer period of time (13 weeks in the four years preceding unemployment), giving more leeway to non-standard work forms to fulfil this requirement.[104] However, as the qualifying period is expressed in weeks, this may mean that part-time workers who work a limited number of hours a week will have to fulfil a longer qualifying period. For them, a working week will not correspond with an actual five-day work week.

When looking at the legislation in place, outspoken differences between countries can be observed. Some countries have more flexible systems in place to fulfil the applicable qualifying period (like Italy, as discussed in the previous paragraph). The Netherlands serves as another example, as the Dutch legisla-tion requires at least a certain period of work (ie no minimum requirement as to the hours worked and not consecutively and for one and the same employer).[105] Although this requirement is phrased in a flexible manner, it might put employees with short-term labour agreements and temporary agency workers at a disad-vantage as everyone needs to satisfy the week requirement, irrespective of the employment relationship (ie 26 weeks over a period of 36 weeks).

The qualifying period in the earnings-related unemployment in scheme in Sweden tries to provide coverage for non-standard work forms: it foresees differ-ent calculation methods expressed in hours.[106] Furthermore, an unemployed person who fulfilled the qualifying period for an unemployment benefit can take up temporary employment and will not have to fulfil the qualifying period again after the end of that unemployment. The qualifying period has been subject to criticism as it excludes a lot of persons from the coverage of the unemployment benefits. In 2017 the proportion of unemployed people receiving earnings-related unemployment benefit was 40.4 per cent, compared to 64 per cent in 2007.[107] Along with satisfying the qualifying period, an unemployed person also needs to have been a member of the unemployment benefit fund for at least 12 months. Hartzen stresses that there has been a high proportion of work-ers from the low-wage sectors leaving the unemployment benefits funds due to reforms concerning the fees for such funds, which were the highest in these sectors in Sweden.[108]

Similarly, Belgium also has rather flexible rules to calculate the qualifying period, making a difference on the basis of the age of the unemployed: the Belgian legislation looks at the days worked for standard employment agreements, for

---

[103] Missoc Poland (2021).
[104] Art 3, para 1 Act of 4 March 2015, no 22/2015 (Italy).
[105] Art 17 Unemployment Act of 6 November 1986 (the Netherlands).
[106] Hartzen (n 28) 76.
[107] Hartzen (n 28) 29.
[108] Hartzen (n 28) 78.

part-time workers half days are applied (irrespective of the hours worked on a weekly basis).[109] Although the rules in Belgium are formulated in a flexible way, Van Limberghen et al argue that the qualifying periods are too long for older employees, violating international social security standards.[110] Other elements also point towards a more flexible approach, eg certain periods of inactivity are equated with working days.[111] However, such rules also create concerns about the overall financial sustainability of the scheme, if no social security contributions were due.

c. Flexible Workers Challenge the Principles of Equivalence and Proportionality

As discussed above for VUP Group 1, most social security benefits for sickness and unemployment are awarded on the basis of the former wage earned. This may be the wage the person received before the loss of income. Some countries also look back several months and/or years and work with an average wage. A difference can be discerned between sickness and unemployment in the selected countries. In case of sickness, countries will often look back over a shorter period of time or at the work previously performed. This is different for unemployment. For example, the Italian legislation in case of unemployment uses as a wage the taxable salary over a period of four years to calculate the unemployment benefit.[112] The Italian sickness benefit, on the other hand, is based on the average daily wage of the month prior to the commencement of the sickness.[113] Similarly, the German legislation looks at the beneficiary's average monthly earnings over the preceding year unemployment;[114] the wage one earns at the moment of becoming sick is used to calculate the sickness benefit.[115] A different approach is applied in Poland: unemployment benefits are flat rate, and not related to the loss of earnings: benefits do vary depending on the employment seniority and the duration of unemployment.[116] In case of sickness, a link is made with the previous earnings, ie the salary earned during the 12 months preceding the cessation of work for which social security contributions were paid.[117]

An important challenge for the part-time workers in VUP Group 3 is the risk for low social security benefits. Benefits linked to the previously earned wage

---

[109] Art 33 Royal Decree of 25 November 1991 concerning the unemployment regulation (Belgium).

[110] G Van Limberghen et al, 'L'accès des travailleurs salariés et indépendants à la sécurité sociale en Belgique' (2020) report drafted for the FPS Social Security, 425.

[111] Art 42, § 2 Royal Decree of 25 November 1991 concerning the unemployment regulation (Belgium).

[112] Missoc Italy (2021).

[113] Missoc Italy (2021).

[114] Sections 149–54 Social Code Book III (Germany).

[115] Art 47 Social Code Book V (Germany).

[116] Missoc Poland (2021).

[117] Missoc Poland (2021).

are in principle calculated *pro rata* for part-time workers. The Belgian legislation applies this principle but not in full; it calculates unemployment benefits
for voluntary part-time employees on the basis of half working days, regardless of the exact hours worked. This constitutes a disadvantage for part-time
employees working in a regime of more than 50 per cent. This disadvantage is
not compensated for by the minimum amounts provided for under the unemployment benefit scheme, as this minimum amount is also halved for part-time
employees.[118]

Granting sickness and unemployment benefits pro rata in light of the hours
worked can be explained in light of the principle of equivalence and proportionality underlying social security schemes.[119] Although understandable in light of
the contributions paid, it can lead to lower protection for a precarious group of
workers. Minimum benefits are not in place in more than half of the countries
studied. Belgium does provide minimum benefits, but they are reduced in light
of the time worked (see however the discussion in the previous paragraph).[120]
An exception is foreseen in case of sickness: the same minimum benefits, irrespective of the hours worked, are granted in Belgium from the seventh month of
sickness. During the months before, minimum benefits are also granted (from
the first month, after the wage continuation by the employer as of 2024), but
they cannot exceed the previously earned wage.[121] Although this rule strengthens the protection of part-time workers, it also puts pressure on the financial
sustainability of the social security system and erodes the insurance principle
which originally served as one of the foundations of the Belgian social security
scheme. As discussed above regarding with VUP Group 1, Luxembourg and the
Netherlands also provide a top-up to ensure that social security benefits reach
the statutory minimum wage. Such a top-up cannot exceed the amount of their
previous salary;[122] hence, for part-time workers, this top-up is limited.

Strong differences between the countries studied can be observed in terms
of benefit duration. Again, differences can be noted between the two social risks
as well: the previous employment history plays a more important role in the
case of unemployment. Countries that link the duration of unemployment to

---

[118] S Remouchamps, 'La (non-)prise en compte du travail à temps partiel par la sécurité sociale: une
première vue transversale' in D Dumont (ed), *Questions transversale en matière du sécurité sociale*
(Brussels, Larcier, 2017) 143–44.

[119] See also the discussion in European Commission (n 6) 16 referring to the financial sustainability as
an explanation for such rules: 'For instance, in 2022, the qualifying period for unemployment benefits
stood at 1 year in 12 Member States and was as long as 2 years in two Member States'.

[120] See for unemployment: Art 115 Royal Decree of 25 November 1991 concerning the unemployment regulation (Belgium); see for sickness: Arts 213 and 213/1 Royal Decree of 3 July 1996 concerning
the sickness Act (Belgium).

[121] Art 213/1 Royal Decree of 3 July 1996 concerning the sickness Act (Belgium).

[122] For more information on this 'red line' in Luxembourg and the Netherlands: Missoc Luxembourg
(2021); Ratti and García-Muñoz (n 95) 26 (on the social minimum wage) and Houwerzijl et al (n 27)
201–02.

the period of insurance are Germany, Italy, Luxembourg and the Netherlands.[123] The same rules applies for all workers, even though temporary workers with different employment contracts will face more difficulties in meeting these conditions. The calculation method in Italy can also have a negative impact on part-time employees who work a limited number of hours a week: like the qualifying period, the duration of unemployment benefits is calculated on the basis of contribution weeks (see also the discussion on the difficulties to fulfil qualifying periods for VUP Group 3). Belgium is an exception amongst the countries studied, and grants unemployment benefits indefinitely over time. Sweden and Poland also do not look at the period worked, but consider individual circumstances (both countries)[124] and the unemployment rate in the region in question (Poland).[125] In contrast to unemployment, sickness in the countries studied does not depend on the former period worked, and the same period is applied to all groups of workers.

d. Wage Continuation for Flexible Workers?

For the protection in case of sickness, an important aspect is also the wage continuation by the employer. In the countries studied often a continued payment is provided by the employer in a first period of sickness. The same rules apply in principle for all workers, which can potentially lead to problems for non-standard workers. For example, when the employment contract ends (in case of temporary employment), the worker is no longer entitled to sickness benefits (eg Italy: benefits are also not granted for longer than the time spent working in the 12 months prior to sickness[126]). In Germany, the employment relationship must have existed for at least four weeks, but this period is waived in several collective agreements.[127] Whereas the continued payment from the employer works well for standard workers, this is not always the case for workers who frequently change employers and might find themselves in-between jobs. An example can be found in the Swedish legislation: all employees are in principle entitled to sick pay from the first day of employment, with the exception of workers with an employment agreement shorter than one month.[128] However, employees who are repeatedly employed on short-term contracts with the same employer can make use of previous periods of employment, under the condition that each new employment starts within

---

[123] See for Germany: Section 147 Social Code Book III (Germany); Luxembourg: Art L 521-11 Social Security Code Luxembourg with reference to Art L 521-6 Social Security Code Luxembourg (*condition de stage*) for the period of reference of 12 months (Luxembourg); and the Netherlands: Art 42 Unemployment Act of 6 November 1986 (The Netherlands).

[124] Art 22 Act of 29 May 1997 on Unemployment Insurance (Sweden) and Missoc Poland (2021).

[125] Missoc Poland (2021).

[126] Missoc Italy (2021).

[127] Hiessl (n 34) 45.

[128] Hartzen (n 28) 51 and Art. 3 Sick Pay Act of 3 June 1991 (Sweden).

14 calendar days after the last employment ended. Some countries provide that a person can then receive a (lower) unemployment benefit (eg Italy) or a sickness benefit from the national social security administration (eg Luxembourg, Sweden and the Netherlands).

The following two examples are discussed more in detail to show how the rules or practices in countries can have a detrimental effect for temporary workers. In the Netherlands, following practice was observed by Houwerzijl et al: a temporary agency contract ends automatically in case of sickness during the first 78 working weeks.[129] The effect of this clause is that the employment contract ends automatically if the temporary agency worker becomes ill. It is debatable whether such provision is legal, and a Dutch court has already ruled that such a practice is prohibited due to the prohibition to terminate an employment contract due to sickness.[130] The Dutch Supreme Court in March 2023 upheld this decision.[131]

In Belgium, short-term contracts (less than three months) for white-collar workers receive the same protection as blue-collar workers for the wage continuation. As discussed for VUP Group 1, this benefit is lower than the protection provided for white-collar workers. It leads to a lesser protection for white-collar workers with short-term contracts.[132] Furthermore, for contracts up until three months, the employer can end the employment agreement (without the need to pay a compensation) if the employee is sick for more than seven days.[133] For employments contracts longer than three months and a sickness of more than six months, the employer can also end the contract earlier, although in those cases an indemnity in lieu of notice has to be paid.[134] Such an indemnity is, however, limited to maximum a wage of three months. The employee will – after the end of their contract – still receive a sickness benefit, if the statutory conditions are fulfilled.

iv. VUP Group 4

VUP Group 4 covers casual and platform workers. Casual work in this contribution includes two work forms: intermittent work and on-call work.

---

[129] Houwerzijl et al (n 26) 143.

[130] As discussed in Houwerzijl et al, (n 26) 143; see for the case at hand: Appeal Court The Hague 17 March 2020, ECLI:NL:GHDHA:2020:460 (the Netherlands).

[131] Supreme Court 17 March 2023, ECLI:NL:HR:2023:426 (the Netherlands).

[132] Art 70 Act of 3 July 1978 on employment agreements (Belgium).

[133] Art 37/9 Act of 3 July 1978 on employment agreements (Belgium). The Belgian legislation does set certain limits as to when a contract of definite duration can be terminated: terminating the employment agreement without any payment is only possible when it is possible to terminate the contract of definite duration. Contracts of definite duration can be ended during the first period of the duration of the contract: Art 40 of the Act of 3 July 1978 on employment agreements (Belgium).

[134] Art. 37/10 Act of 3 July 1978 on employment agreements: already guaranteed wage can be deducted from the indemnity in lieu of notice (Belgium).

a. Casual Work

Intermittent work covers short-term contracts concluded to conduct a specific task, often related to an individual project or seasonally occurring jobs. The intermittent worker is required to fulfil a task or complete a specific number of working days.[135] In most of the countries studied intermittent work is not regulated by a specific legal regime; such activities are often performed under a fixed-term contract and hence follow the general labour law and social security law.[136] Some countries do have specific schemes in place regulating intermittent work in certain sectors, eg Belgium, Italy and Luxembourg.

The Belgian legislation allows for seasonal work limited to certain sectors, eg agriculture, and for a limited number of days.[137] Work under this scheme is subject to a more favourable social security regime, as social security contributions and benefits are calculated on the basis of a flat-rate wage. Italy allows intermittent work to be performed via voucher-based work. Originally, this scheme was intended for occasional work in specific sectors and for certain activities, but several extensions led to a wide-spread use.[138] The current voucher-based regime is a particular form of employment in which the employer pays workers for an occasional service with a voucher. There are different schemes in place, eg for domestic work. Several restrictions apply, eg a limit on the income earned on a yearly basis (€5,000) by the voucher-based worker. When those limits are breached, the employment relationship is converted into a full-time permanent employment agreement.[139] Voucher-based workers do not receive protection in the case of sickness and unemployment. In Luxembourg seasonal work is also limited to a limited number of sectors; moreover, seasonal work arrangements can foresee in a continuation over a longer period of time, but if an extension occurs for more than two seasons, the temporary contract will be transformed into a contract of indefinite duration.[140]

Another form of casual work discussed in this contribution is on-call work, ie an employment relationship between an employer and an employee in which the employer does not continuously provide work for the employee. Rather, the employer has the option of calling the employee in as and when needed. Some employment contracts indicate the minimum and maximum number of working hours; 'zero-hour contracts' do not specify a minimum number of working hours.[141] In most of the countries studied, on-call work follows the general rules

---

[135] See Ratti, García-Muñoz and Vergnat (n 1) 22 for the notion of intermittent work.
[136] See also Hiessl on the use of intermittent work in the countries studied: Hiessl (n 31) 348.
[137] Art 2/1, § 1 Act 27 June 1969 and Art 8*bis* Royal Decree 28 November 1969 (Belgium).
[138] Villa, Marchi and De Luigi (n 36) 149–50.
[139] Villa, Marchi and De Luigi (n 36) 149–50.
[140] L Ratti and A García-Muñoz, 'In-Work Poverty in Luxembourg' in L Ratti (ed), *In-Work Poverty in Europe. Vulnerable and Under-Represented Persons in a Comparative Perspective* (Alphen aan den Rijn, Kluwer Law International, 2022) 188.
[141] Ratti, García-Muñoz and Vergnat (n 1) 22 for the notion of on-call work.

under labour and social security law applicable to standard employees, although deviations apply.

The Swedish legislation does not have a specific regime in place for on-call contracts, but the requirements concerning fixed-term employment are formulated in a rather flexible way and can be used for intermittent and on-call work: neither temporary employment or substitute employment forms have requirements regarding the length of the contract, or on a minimum number of hours worked.[142] In some countries on-call work is performed, despite the lack of a separate legal basis, as the discussion of Ratti et al[143] and Tomaszewska et al[144] made clear for Luxembourg and Poland. Furthermore, in Poland on-call work will more often be performed on the basis of a civil law agreement (see also the discussion for VUP Group 2).[145]

Other countries have a specific regime in place for on-call work, eg the Netherlands. The Dutch legislation does not lay down a fixed number of working hours and the wage for the employee can vary every month. An employee will also perform on-call work when they do not have a right to a wage per time unit if they have not performed any labour.[146] Zero-hour contracts and the so-called mini-max. contracts are the most commonly used in the Netherlands, the latter stipulating both a minimum and a maximum number of hours per week that the worker is prepared to / may be requested to work.[147] In Germany, similar provisions can be found.[148] The use of on-call work is possible in Italy; although more restrictions apply than in Germany or the Netherlands. On-call work is limited to a specific number of days (ie 400 days over three years, although exceptions for certain sectors apply). If those time limits are exceeded, the contract for on-call work will be converted into a standard employment contract.[149] The Italian legislation differentiates between two types of on-call work. In the first, the employer can call the employee, who is not obliged to answer the call and who will not receive a wage or other benefits during the periods in-between work. When there is an obligation to answer in place, the employee has a right to an availability allowance.[150]

The flexi-job scheme in Belgium can also be considered a zero-hour-contract: flexi-job contracts are fixed-term employment contracts, and can only be used by a number of sectors, such as hotel and catering.[151] In December 2022 and

---

[142] Hartzen (n 32) 308.
[143] Ratti and García-Muñoz (n 95) 87.
[144] Tomaszewska and Peplinska (n 57) 149.
[145] Tomaszewska and Peplinska (n 57) 149.
[146] Houwerzijl et al (n 27) 229–30.
[147] Houwerzijl et al (n 27) 229–30.
[148] Hiessl (n 33) 115–16.
[149] Villa, Marchi and De Luigi (n 36) 150.
[150] Villa, Marchi and De Luigi (n 36) 150.
[151] Act of 16 November 2015 (Belgium); see for an in-depth discussion in English: E Dermine and A Mechelynck, 'Regulating Zero-Hour Contracts in Belgium: From a Defensive to a (too?) Supportive Approach' (2022) 13(3) *European Labour Law* 400–30.

in March 2023, the Belgian legislator has expanded the list of possible sectors that can make use of the flexi-job scheme again, due to the high labour shortages in certain sectors. This means that also, inter alia, the health sector can utilise flexi-job contracts, which has been strongly criticised by trade unions. An important difference with other zero-hour-contracts, is that the Belgian flexi-job scheme can only be used by workers who already enjoy social protection on the basis of an employment contract at a ratio of least 4/5th of a full-time equivalent.[152] That way, the worker performing a flexi-job activity receives social security protection via the worker's main activity. A wage lower than the minimum wage can be paid for flexi-work and only an employer contribution is due. Work performed under this scheme is taken into account for the build-up of social security rights, eg in the case of unemployment. However, an employee with a flexi-job cannot receive an unemployment benefit for the days that they do not work in the flexi-job or when their employment contract as a flexi-job has ended.

The national examples show the diversity between countries in the regulation of casual work; however, intermittent and on-call work will often be performed under a fixed-term or an open-ended contract. Hence, labour law and social security law for employees will apply in a similar manner to this group of workers. In that sense, casual workers are confronted with similar challenges and impediments in design as VUP Groups 1 and 3. However, the problems for workers with fluctuating work patterns or limited numbers of hours worked, as discussed for VUP Group 3, are more pronounced for workers in VUP Group 4. Despite the increased risk of precarity, casual workers do not receive additional attention in the countries studied; this creates difficulties, since social security law is not well-adapted to this group, as discussed above for VUP Group 3. The following example can illustrate this point: the Dutch sickness benefits were privatised in the 1990s, and employers have an obligation under labour law to continue payment of wages to employees who are too ill for work for two years. Employees with min-max contracts receive continuing payment for the minimum number of hours stated in their contract. On-call workers and workers with zero-hours contracts are entitled to continued payment only for the hours for which they are scheduled to work.[153] Hence, such workers will only receive limited protection.

b. Platform Work

The Working, Yet Poor project also looks at platform workers under VUP Group 4. The employment status of those workers has been an extensive topic of debate in

---

[152] However the legal provisions state that one needs to have a main activity as an employee three quarters ago: at the time one is employed as a flexi-jobber, this may be the only work performed as foreseen in Art 4, § 1 of 16 November 2015 (Belgium); see however the critique that this rule can be circumvented in practice: Dermine and Mechelynck (n 151) 417–18.

[153] See the discussion in Oostveen (n 21) 11.

EU Member States: divergent outcomes can also be found in the national court cases of the countries studied. This also led the EU Commission to intervene: a proposal for a directive regulating platform work was launched in December 2021. The proposal of the EU Commission introduces a rebuttable presumption: if a series of criteria are met, the platform worker should be considered an employee.[154]

Looking at examples in the current case law of the countries studied, some national courts, like in Italy and the Netherlands came to the conclusion that platform workers working as couriers are employees (eg Deliveroo or Foodora).[155] The Amsterdam Court of Appeal also held that platform workers performing cleaning activities on the Helping platform should be considered to be employed on the basis of a contract for temporary agency work.[156] In Belgium, on the other hand, the Brussels labour court decided that Deliveroo and Uber drivers operate as self-employed.[157] The Belgian legislator introduced as of January 2023 a (rebuttable) legal presumption of employment for platform workers.[158] This is partially based on the EU proposal for a Directive regulating platform work, but additional criteria were introduced as well. A legal presumption might provide more clarity and could lead to more formal access to social protection in case of sickness or unemployment. However, the problems in case of marginal employment will still apply (see the discussion for VUP Group 3 on formal and effective access). Moreover, a legal presumption of employment already applied for Deliveroo and Uber drivers, as the Belgian legislation has such a presumption as well for the transport sector. In both cases, the presumption was rebutted. Lastly, the European Commission also highlighted that a large number of platform workers are self-employed:[159] hence, the problems identified above for VUP Group 2 will apply to self-employed platform workers as well.

[154] European Commission (n 9) 202, 15 (Art 4).

[155] See eg: Court of Milan, 20 April 2022, no 1018/2022; See also Court of Palermo, 24 November 2020, no 3570/2020 (Italy) and Amsterdam Court of Appeal 16 February 2021, ECLI:NL:GHAMS:2021:392; and two cases of 21 December 2021 where the Court of Appeal Amsterdam applied a collective agreement to Deliveroo couriers: Court of Appeal Amsterdam 21 December 2021, ECLI:NL:GHAMS:2021:3978; Court of Appeal Amsterdam 21 December 2021, ECLI:NL:GHAMS:2021:3979 and Dutch Supreme Court 24 March 2023, ECLI:NL:HR:2023:443 (the Netherlands); see also the discussion in C Hiessl, 'The Legal Status of Platform Workers: Regulatory Approaches and Prospects of a European Solution' (2022) 15(1) *Italian Labour Law e-journal* 13.

[156] Amsterdam Court of Appeal, 21 September 2021, ECLI:NL:GHAMS:2021:2741, as discussed further in Houwerzijl et al (n 27) 231.

[157] Labour Court Brussels (French-speaking chamber) (25th chamber) 8 December 2021, AR 2021/014148, not published. The Commercial Court in Brussels came to a similar conclusion for Uber drivers in 2019: Chairman Commercial Court Brussels (French-speaking chamber) no A/18/02920, 16 January 2019, not published; at the end of December 2022 the Labour Court Brussels (French-speaking chamber) also reached the conclusion that Uber Drivers were self-employed in Labour Court Brussels (French-speaking chamber) (7th chamber), 21 December 2022, A/21/632, not published (Belgium).

[158] Art 15 Act of 3 October 2022 (Belgium). The Belgian legislation already has a rebuttable presumption in place for transportation services. However, in the Deliveroo and Uber cases the presumption was rebutted. It remains to be seen to what extent the change in legislation will have an impact.

[159] European Commission (n 9) 202, 2.

Belgium is the only country that has a specific scheme in place for platform work, ie as from 2016, a favourable tax regime applies if the income from platform work does not exceed a certain threshold (€7,170 in 2023).[160] Platform workers will not build up any social security rights for the work performed. This favourable tax regime is subject to several conditions, eg it is only open for natural persons and outside the context of a professional activity; only services can be provided; and the platform must have an official accreditation.[161] Social partners have taken a critical stance towards the specific scheme for platform workers, due to the lack of social protection for platform workers and the misuse of this scheme, eg by Deliveroo. In Sweden, platform work is often performed under the framework of umbrella companies.[162] The client and the worker will agree on the work and the remuneration. The umbrella company takes up the role of the employer, and deals with invoicing on behalf of the client, ensures that taxes and social security contributions are paid, and pays the platform worker. The platform worker is therefore most likely considered an employee in relation to income, taxes and social security. However, there is an ongoing discussion on whether these umbrella companies are actual employers.

An additional obstacle that came to the fore for the workers in VUP Group 4 is the uncertainty regarding the number of hours worked when performing casual or platform work. Periods in-between different jobs are not always taken into account and these workers therefore do not build up any social security rights. This makes it particularly difficult for them to meet the qualifying conditions for obtaining social security benefits. Furthermore, workers will not receive any continuing payment from the employer during a waiting period. In the Netherlands on-call workers have a right to continued payment of their salary by their employer if they get sick during or once the call was planned.[163] However if the employee becomes sick while waiting for the call, they are not entitled to the wage continuation by the employer, unless they become sick within four weeks after the last employment agreement had ended. As discussed above for temporary agency workers, a fall-back option applies and the on-call workers can receive a sickness benefit from the competent Dutch administration. To tackle the problem of on-call work and the lack of protection during waiting time, the Swedish legislation recently changed the applicable legislation to grant a stronger protection for workers with irregular work patterns.[164] It concerns workers on a casual employment contract where the person might not have working hours scheduled in a regular or structured manner. The new legislation foresees that intermittent employees shall be entitled

---

[160] Title 3. Chapter 2 Act of 1 July 2016 (Belgium).
[161] See the discussion in De Becker, Dockx and Schoukens (n 21) 80.
[162] Hartzen (n 32) 309; see also A Westregård, 'Looking for the (Fictitious) Employer – Umbrella Companies: The Swedish Example' in U Becker and O Chesalina (eds), *Social Law 4.0. New Approaches for Ensuring and Financing Social Security in the Digital Age* (Baden-Baden, Nomos, 2020).
[163] Houwerzijl et al (n 26) 156.
[164] Hartzen (n 32) 284.

to sickness allowance on the basis of income from work during the first 90 days of sickness if it is reasonable to assume that the worker would have worked unless having been sick.[165]

B. Do the VUP Groups Receive Adequate Protection in the Case of Sickness and Unemployment?

This section reviews to what extent the four VUP Groups have adequate access to social protection in case of sickness and unemployment. The 2019 Recommendation defines adequacy as the situation in which social security schemes provide an adequate level of protection to the socially insured in a timely manner and according to national circumstances. The level of protection is adequate if social security benefits guarantee beneficiaries a decent standard of living and keep them out of poverty. In reviewing whether the protection granted is adequate, the 2019 Recommendation stresses the need to look at the whole social protection system in the EU Member State at hand. However, one of the major drawbacks of the 2019 Recommendation is the lack of clarity surrounding adequacy of social protection. Despite some broad guidelines, the concept is not further elaborated in concrete terms.[166] To assess the adequacy of social security benefits, the monitoring framework includes indicators to measure the prevalence of poverty and of material and social deprivation.[167] In the absence of a clear-cut EU definition, this contribution applies a two-step approach, by look-ing at international social security standards (Step 1) and the at-risk-of-poverty level (AROP) at the EU (Step 2) to review the adequacy of sickness and unemployment benefits.

Before discussing the two steps more in detail, it should be underlined that there was not sufficient information available on the income earned for all VUP Groups. As hardly any data was available for VUP Group 4, this chapter only analyses the social security benefits in case of sickness and unemployment for the VUP Groups 1, 2 and 3 (part-time, work ratio of 50 per cent).[168] For the income

---

[165] Section 27 16 a) Social Security Code (Sweden) and Hartzen (n 32) 284.

[166] Recitals (17) and (19) 2019 Recommendation.

[167] See the monitoring framework of the 2019 Recommendation where this concern was also raised: Social Protection Committee and the European Commission, Monitoring framework on Access to Social Protection for Workers and the Self-Employed – Version 0 of the monitoring framework (Brussels, European Commission, 2020) 53–54 (on the indicators) and 56 (on the need to also reflect on other ways to measure adequacy) and Social Protection Committee and the European Commission, (Partial) Update of the Monitoring Framework – 2021 (Brussels, European Commission, 2021) 37–40 (where the same remarks are made as in the version 0 of the monitoring framework.

[168] The benefits for full-time employees with fixed-term contracts or employed full-time as temporary workers are similar to the benefits for VUP Group 1, although differences can exist between due to difficulties in fulfilling the history requirement.

for VUP Groups 1 and 3, the lowest average monthly income for a worker ('manual employee') in the poor sectors, as mentioned above, is used. The gross income earned in those poor sectors is available via the data from EUROSTAT (Structure of Earnings Survey 2018).[169] For VUP Group 2, this chapter uses the EU-SILC Data on the income of self-employed persons without employees (2019, income from 2018).[170] The monthly income used for the different VUP Groups is indexed by making use of the European Central Bank's Harmonised Index of Consumer Prices (HCIP)[171] (period June 2018 – June 2021).[172]

As a first step, this chapter reviews to what extent the social security systems studied allow the VUP groups to maintain their previous standard of living in case of sickness and unemployment.[173] International social security standards clearly spell out the different replacement rates that social security systems must reach in order to ensure a decent standard of living once the contingency covered has arisen.[174] Hence, these instruments provide a level that social security benefits should reach, but the national legislator can still determine at its own discretion how social security benefits should be calculated, provided that at least the prescribed level is achieved.[175]

Although international social security standards clearly spell out the replacement rate that must be achieved, such instruments have been subject to criticism; for example, that international social security standards are outdated and not adapted to the current society nor to the current labour market.[176] However, international social security standards do give expression to the principles of solidarity, proportionality and equivalence inherent in social security systems. The EPSR also underlines the importance of these international social security standards, and the rights of the EPSR should not be interpreted in such a way as to undermine the

---

[169] Eurostat, *Structure of Earnings Survey*, www.ec.europa.eu/eurostat/web/microdata/structure-of-earnings-survey (last accessed 11 May 2023).

[170] The idea was to make use of national data; however as such data was not available for all countries, use was made of the EU data available. An exception is Belgium, for which national data was used.

[171] In the euro area, the Harmonised Index of Consumer Prices (HICP) is used to measure consumer price inflation. That means the change over time in the prices of consumer goods and services purchased by euro area households, www.ecb.europa.eu/stats/macroeconomic_and_sectoral/hicp/html/index.en.html (last accessed 28 February 2023).

[172] A more detailed overview of the calculations of the different social security benefits in the countries studied can be found in the comparative report on social security drafted in the framework of the Working, Yet Poor project: E De Becker et al, 'Comparative Report on Social Security', Working, Yet Poor (2022), Deliverable 4.2 (on file with the author).

[173] See also the method applied by Van Limberghen et al (n 110).

[174] Explanatory report – ETS 139 – Social Security (Revised Code).

[175] P Schoukens, 'Instruments of the Council of Europe and Interpretation Problems' in F Pennings (ed), *International Social Security Standards. Current Views and Interpretation Matters* (Antwerp, Intersentia, 2007) 87.

[176] See eg D Pieters and P Schoukens, 'Social Security Law Instruments of the Next Generation: European Social Security Law as a Source of Inspiration' in G Vonk and F Pennings (eds), *Research Handbook on European Social Security Law* (Cheltenham, Edward Elgar Publishing, 2015); T Dijkhof, *International Social Security Standards in the European Union. The Cases of the Czech Republic and Estonia* (Antwerp, Intersentia, 2011) 7; Schoukens (n 175) 89 and the problems identified as of p 85 and further.

rights and principles recognised in international instruments.[177] To counter the critique set out above, this chapter uses the replacement rates set out in the revised European Code of Social Security (Code). This instrument was adopted in 1996, and although it has not yet entered into force, it does provide an update (including a higher level of protection) of the international social security standards adopted in the 1950s and 1960s, such as the ILO Convention no 102 and the European Code of Social Security.

As a second step, this chapter maps the adequacy of the income replacement benefits for sickness and unemployment in light of 60 per cent of the median equivalent income (AROP threshold). This will be done by calculating the net social security benefits in case of sickness and unemployment via a standard simulation model (microsimulation[178] – EUROMOD[179]) and review them in light of the AROP threshold.[180] It also allows us to gain on a preliminary basis more insight into the additional support by governments. Next to the income replacement benefits in the case of sickness and unemployment, EUROMOD takes into account the different support measures that can be granted to families, such as lower social security contributions or social assistance for families with a low income. For most workers and self-employed, the different measures available are difficult to map, and studies on the interlinkages between social security, tax law, social assistance and other measures remain scarce.

i. Step 1 – Revised European Code of Social Security

International social security standard instruments, like the Code, start from model beneficiaries and determine for those beneficiaries the replacement rates that the social risks mentioned in this instrument should reach.

For sickness and unemployment, the Code sets the replacement rate for a single person at 50 per cent of the former earned wage and at 65 per cent for a breadwinner with a partner and dependent children. To calculate the prescribed replacement rate by the Code for families with children, child benefits are also taken into account together with the income replacement benefit in case of sickness and unemployment. In addition to the household types set forth in the Code, this contribution goes a step further, as it also takes into account the situation of

---

[177] Recital 16 EPSR.

[178] The microsimulation model is also not entirely free from criticism either. Several scholars have argued that the hypothetical families are defined in rather general terms, because defining too specific characteristics would have an impact on the calculations and consequently the conclusions that can be drawn. Moreover, it is also argued that hypothetical households are not representative, see Van Limberghen et al (n 110) 536; see also B Cantillon, S Marchal and C Luigjes, 'Toward Adequate Minimum Incomes: Which Role for Europe?' in B Cantillon, T Goedemé and J Hills (eds), *Decent Incomes for all. Improving Policies in Europe* (Oxford, Oxford University Press, 2019) 275–76.

[179] See for more information on this method: I Burlacu, C O'Donoghue and DM Sologon, 'Hypothetical models' in C O'Donoghue, *Handbook of Microsimulation Modelling* (Bingley, Emerald Group Publishing, 2014).

[180] See Eurostat, Glossary: *At-risk-of-poverty rate*, ec.europa.eu/eurostat/statistics-explained/index.php?title=Glossary:At-risk-of-poverty_rate (last accessed 28 February 2023).

a single person with two children. This means that in the discussion below the income replacement benefit in case of sickness and unemployment (together with the child benefits for families with children) are reviewed in light of the replacement rates of the Code for the following three hypothetical families:

(1) a single person – replacement rate of 50 per cent;
(2) a single person with two children (two and four years old) – replacement rate of 65 per cent;
(3) a person with a dependent partner and two children (two and four years old) – replacement rate of 65 per cent.

The Code sets forward two approaches to calculate the replacement rates, either via the gross income and the gross social security benefits ('gross replacement rate') or the net income and the net social security benefits ('net replacement rate'). In this chapter, we calculate both.

On the basis of the available gross income for VUP Group 1, 2 and 3, the gross benefits in case of sickness and unemployment are calculated, as well as the child benefits awarded to families with children. This allows us to examine whether the gross income replacement benefits (together with child benefits for families with children) reach the gross replacement rates of the three hypothetical families. To calculate the replacement rates for VUP Groups 1, 2 and 3, we applied the following calculation for both social risks (sickness and unemployment): (Gross income replacement benefit and child benefits for families with children) / (Gross previously earned income and child benefits for families with children).

The quotient of that division, multiplied by 100, must be equal to or higher than the replacement rate for the social risk concerned as stated in the Code.[181]

The second approach put forward by the Code is a comparison of the net social security benefits with the net income to calculate the net replacement benefits. This chapter tries to shed light on the net replacement rates as well, by making use of the net benefits in case of sickness and unemployment as calculated via EUROMOD in Step 2. That way, this contribution also calculates in Step 1 the net replacement rates and reviews to what extent they comply with the replacement rates for the hypothetical families. The same formula as for the gross replacement rates is used to calculate the net replacement rates.

The gross and net replacement rates for the different VUP Groups in case of sickness and unemployment are summarised in Tables 7.1, 7.2 and 7.3. The period of wage continuation by the employer has not been taken into account: with year 0 in case of sickness, this contribution means the period as of which a statutory sickness benefit is granted. For the Netherlands sickness benefits granted by the employer are taken into account, as the sickness benefit scheme has been privatised.

---

[181] M Korda, *The Role of International Social Security Standards. An In-Depth Study through the Case of Greece* (Antwerp, Intersentia, 2013) 114–16; J Nickless, *Code européen de sécurité sociale: Vade-mecum* (Strasbourg, Council of Europe, 2002) 96.

Table 7.1 Replacement Rate VUP Group 1

		Replacement rate – VUP Group 1					
		BE	G	IT[182]	LUX	PL	SE[183]	NL
Sickness								
Y0	Single person	60% (G) – 67.72% (N)	61.15% (G) – 85.13% (N)	66.65% (G) – 62.87% (N)	100% (G) – 97.33% (N)	80% (G) – 92.40% (N)	80% (G) – 72.83% (N)	70% (G) – 73.18% (N)
	Single person + two children	67% (G) – 73.57% (N)	69% (G) – 83.89% (N)	72.06% (G) – 73.36% (N)	100% (G) – 98.08% (N)	86.98% (G) – 100.76% (N)	81.8% (G) – 75.97% (N)	72% (G) – 78.05% (N)
	Breadwinner + two children	67% (G) – 69.54% (N)	69% (G) – 84.79% (N)	72.06% (G) – 74.24% (N)	100% (G) – 98.55% (N)	85.76% (G) – 95.42% (N)	81.8% (G) – 75.97% (N)	87.27% (G) – 91.98% (N)
Unemployment								
Y0	Single person	65% (G) – 78.31% (N)	60% (G) – 82.94% (N)	60.26% (G) – 69.47% (N)	80% (G) – 83.03% (N)	42.22% (G) – 49.06% (N)	73.31 (G) – 67.32% (N)	75% (G) – 65.68% (N)
	Single person + two children	70% (G) – 77.44% (N)	73.37% (G) – 86.57% (N)	66.68% (G) – 74.86% (N)	87.27% (G) – 98.43% (N)	62.39% (G) – 77.09% (N)	75.78% (G) – 71.09% (N)	76.76% (G) – 69.58% (N)
	Breadwinner + two children	70% (G) – 73.83% (N)	73.37% (G) – 87.32% (N)	66.68% (G) – 72.50% (N)	87.27% (G) – 98.44% (N)	58.87% (G) – 86.84% (N)	75.78% (G) – 71.09% (N)	87.27% (G) – 79.58% (N)

182 Sickness benefits are calculated at a rate of 66.66 per cent of the average daily wage (blue-collar workers). Between day 4 and day 20 benefits are granted for blue-collar workers at a ratio of 50 per cent of the average daily wage.
183 Earnings-related unemployment benefits.

Table 7.2 Replacement Rate VUP Group 2

		BE	G	IT	LUX	PL	SE	NL
				Replacement rate – VUP Group 2				
				Sickness				
Y0	Single person	69.64% (G) – 72.86% (N)	No benefits are granted.	Not enough data on the income of co.co.co. workers	100%[184] (G) – 100.7% (N)	80% (G) – 106.37% (N)	80% (G) – 97.37% (N)	No benefits are granted
	Single person + two children	77.48% (G) – 86.8% (N)			100%[185] (G) – 100.55% (N)	86.62% (G) – 103.85% (N)	84.4% (G) – 100% (N)	
	Breadwinner + two children	77.48% (G) – 90.89% (N)			100%[186] (G) – 100.98% (N)	85.44% (G) – 103.25% (N)	84.4% (G) – 100% (N)	
				Unemployment				
Y0	Single person	69.64% (G) – 80.34% (N)	No benefits are granted.	Not enough data on the income of co.co.co. workers	80% (G) – 95.91% (N)	42.22% (G) – 49.06% (N)	80% (G) – 97.37% (N)	No benefits are granted
	Single person + two children	77% (G) – 90.82% (N)			86.44% (G) – 100.01% (N)	62.39% (G) – 77.09% (N)	84.4% (G) – 100% (N)	
	Breadwinner + two children	77% (G) – 90.54% (N)			86.44% (G) – 104.84% (N)	58.87% (G) – 86.84% (N)	84.4% (G) – 100% (N)	

[184] In the case of voluntary contributions to the social security scheme by the self-employed.
[185] In the case of voluntary contributions to the social security scheme by the self-employed.
[186] In the case of voluntary contributions to the social security scheme by the self-employed.

Table 7.3 Replacement Rate VUP Group 3

		BE	G	IT[187]	LUX	PL	SE	NL
				Replacement rate – VUP Group 3				
				Sickness				
Y0	Single person	60% (G) – 94.08%(N)	61.15% (G) – 72.11% (N)	66.66% (G) – 68.87% (N)	100% (G) – 96.71% (N)	80% (G) – 89.89% (N)	80% (G) – 72.89% (N)	100% (G and N)
	Single person + two children	71.7% (G) – 98.64% (N)	74.01% (G) – 78.68% (N)	75.94% – 73.33% (N)	100% (G) – 98.03% (N)	90.35% (G) – 97.76% (N)	83.37% (G) – 78.16% (N)	100% (G and N)
	Breadwinner + two children	71.7% (G) – 107.67% (N)	74.01% (G) – 84.93% (N)	75.94% (G) – 78.72% (N)	100% (G) – 98.41% (N)	88.94% (G) – 100% (N)	83.37% (G) – 81.29% (N)	100% (G) – 99.34% (N)
				Unemployment				
Y0	Single person	65% (G) – % 94.08(N)	60% (G) – 70.26% (N)	60.26% (G) – 63.36% (N)	80% (G) – 97.71% (N)	No unemployment benefit	73.31% (G) – 67.02% (N)	100% (G and N)
	Single person + two children	75% (G) – 98.64% (N)	73.37% (G) – 91.54% (N)	71.31% (G) – 83.26% (N)	88.95% (G) – 98.96% (N)	No unemployment benefit	77.82% (G) – 73.43% (N)	100% (G) – 96.31% (N)
	Breadwinner + two children	75% (G) – 107.61% (N)	73.37% (G) – 84.93% (N)	71.31% (G) – 78.72% (N)	88.95% (G) – 99.12% (N)	No unemployment benefit	77.82% (G) – 81.29% (N)	100% (G) – 99.34% (N)

[187] Sickness benefits are calculated at a rate of 66.66 per cent of the average daily wage (blue-collar workers). Between day 4 and day 20 benefits are granted for blue-collar workers at a ratio of 50 per cent of the average daily wage.

Overall, for the countries studied, different replacement rates are reached for the VUP Groups 1, 2 and 3. The fact that the replacement rates are reached makes clear that for most VUP Groups social security schemes do what they have been designed to do, at least in terms of the underlying objectives of equivalence and proportionality. Some exceptions apply for countries that do not grant protection for the self-employed (Germany and the Netherlands). In Poland, the income earned from part-time work (on the basis of the Eurostat data) does not reach the income threshold for unemployment; which means that no unemployment benefits are granted, despite the social security contributions paid.[188]

Strong differences can be noted between the gross and net replacement rates. In the countries studied, net replacement rates are higher (all benefits in the following countries: Belgium, Germany, Poland; sickness benefits for VUP Group 1 in Italy and the Netherlands; unemployment benefits for VUP Group 3 and sickness benefits for VUP Group 2 in Sweden). This can be explained due to the lower taxes and/or social security contributions that are due and/or the protection offered via social assistance. Lower net replacement rates were to be found in Italy (unemployment – VUP Group 1), Luxembourg (unemployment) and Sweden (VUP Groups 1 and 3).

ii. Step 2 – AROP Threshold

As a second step, this chapter maps the adequacy of net income replacement benefits in case of sickness and unemployment in light of 60 per cent of the median equivalised income (AROP – threshold).[189] The net income and net social security benefits in case of sickness and unemployment are calculated by means of a standard simulation model (microsimulation – EUROMOD) using the three hypothetical families in Step 1 (single person, single parent with two children of two and four years old and a breadwinner with partner and two children of two and four years old). When applying this method,[190] the net disposable

---

[188] As a rule, the right to unemployment benefit depends in Poland, inter alia, on: (1) the payment of contributions to a separate earmarked fund – Labour Fund and (2) the rate of the income earned which cannot be lower than the minimum wage for work in a given calendar year. Hence, this could lead to the situation *in casu* where a part-time worker is not entitled to unemployment benefits. This case applies to a situation where the received income is lower than the minimum remuneration. The condition of the minimum remuneration applies to every employee, regardless of the number of hours of work.

[189] See Eurostat, Glossary: *At-risk-of-poverty rate*, ec.europa.eu/eurostat/statistics-explained/index.php?title=Glossary:At-risk-of-poverty_rate (last accessed 28 February 2023).

[190] See for more information on this method: I Burlacu, C O'Donoghue and DM Sologon, 'Hypothetical models' in C O'Donoghue, *Handbook of Microsimulation modelling* (Bingley, Emerald Group Publishing, 2014).

income is calculated for the three hypothetical families on the basis of the gross income replacement benefits (as calculated in Step 1) in case of sickness and unemployment, which can then be compared with the AROP threshold of each of the selected countries.[191]

The AROP threshold is based on the median equivalent income, which is defined as the total disposable income of the household divided by its equivalent size, to take into account the size and composition of the household. This contribution uses the OECD-modified equivalence scale for this purpose.[192] This scale assigns a value of 1 to the head of the household, 0.5 to each additional member aged 14 or over, and 0.3 to each member younger than 14. The OECD-modified equivalence scale for the three hypothetical families can be summarised as follows:

(1) single person: 1;
(2) single person with two children (two and four years old): 1.6; and
(3) a breadwinner with partner and two children: 2.1.

For the median equivalent income of the countries studied in this contribution, the information published by EUROSTAT based on the EU-SILC data is used. The data of 2019 (income year 2018) is applied, which has been multiplied by the HCIP Index for the selected country (period July 2018 – July 2021) in order to compare the social security benefits of 2021 with the median equivalent income.

To calculate the net income in case of sickness and unemployment for the three hypothetical families via EUROMOD, several characteristics had to be given to them, as explained in Table 7.4. The three hypothetical households were given similar characteristics. Those characteristics will have an impact on the net income, as slight differences can lead to important differences in the benefits granted (eg social assistance or social security contributions). This is of course an important point of attention for future research. Nevertheless, the idea of this chapter was to map the protection provided for the VUP Groups on a preliminary basis. Future research is needed to explore this further.

---

[191] The microsimulation model is also not entirely free from criticism either. Several scholars have argued that the hypothetical families are defined in rather general terms, because defining too specific characteristics would have an impact on the calculations and consequently the conclusions that can be drawn. Moreover, it is also argued that hypothetical households are not representative, see Van Limberghen et al (n 110) 536; see also B Cantillon, S Marchal and C Luigjes, 'Towards Adequate Minimum Incomes: What Role for Europe' in B Cantillon, T Goedemé and J Hills (eds), *Decent Incomes for all. Improving Policies in Europe* (Oxford, Oxford University Press, 2019) 275–76.

[192] OECD, 'What are equivalence scales?', available at www.oecd.org/els/soc/OECD-Note-Equivalence Scales.pdf (last accessed 28 February 2023).

Table 7.4 Characteristics of the Different Hypothetical Households

Type of hypothetical households	Characteristics
Single person	40-year-old male, lower education, own property (housing cost: 0 EUR) and with a work experience of 200 months.
	Professional status: see VUP Group. This contribution assumes that the person in question has been working throughout their entire career under this legal regime.
Breadwinner with partner with two children (two and four years old)	40-year-old male, with spouse (female, 40 years old) and two children, two and four years old, own property (housing costs: €0). The breadwinner and the partner both have a lower education. The breadwinner has a work experience of 200 months. The spouse does not have an income out of work.
	Professional status: see VUP Group. This contribution assumes that the person in question has been working throughout their entire career under this legal regime.
Single parent with two children (two and four years old)	40-year-old male (single) and two children, two and four years old, own property (housing cost: €0) and with a work experience of 200 months.
	Professional status: see VUP Group. This contribution assumes that the person in question has been working throughout their entire career under this legal regime.

As stated above, we start in Step 2 from the gross social security income replacement benefits in case of sickness and unemployment. Via EUROMOD, the net social security benefits granted in case of sickness and unemployment for the three hypothetical families can be calculated, taking into account the additional social security benefits (eg child benefits and social assistance as a top-up) that persons could receive and the taxes and social security contributions that are due. The net social security benefits in case of sickness and unemployment are calculated under the assumption that a person is entitled to social security benefits during the entire year; personal income tax is calculated on an annual basis. Tables 7.5, 7.6 and 7.7 summarise whether the net benefits awarded in case of sickness and unemployment reach the AROP threshold for VUP Groups 1, 2 and 3. If, according to the EUROMOD simulation, benefits in addition to the income replacement benefit in case of sickness and unemployment and the child benefits for the hypothetical families with children are granted, this is mentioned in a footnote.

Table 7.5 AROP Threshold – VUP Group 1

		AROP threshold – VUP Group 1					
		BE	G	IT[193]	LUX	PL	SE	NL
		Sickness						
Y0	Single person	94.56%	91.66%	99.97%	123.73%	129.09%	115.10%	97.88%[194]
	Single person + two children	85.26%	86.74%[195]	92.28%	110.30%[196]	138.10%	84.83%	94.01%[197]
	Breadwinner + two children	67.06%	70.73%[198]	73.48%	97.07%[199]	105.22%	64.63%	68.63%[200]
		Unemployment						
Y0	Single person	109.35 %	89.30%	110.43%	105.56%	68.54%	106.39%	87.85%[201]
	Single person + two children	89.73%	89.51%[202]	94.19%	110.68%[203]	105.66%	79.39%	83.81%[204]
	Breadwinner + two children	71.20%	72.85%[205]	71.76%	96.96%[206]	95.76%[207]	60.48%	59.37%[208]

193 Sickness benefits are calculated at a rate of 66.66 per cent of the average daily wage (blue-collar workers). Between day 4 and day 20 benefits are granted for blue-collar workers at a ratio of 50 per cent of the average daily wage.

194 Care allowance.
195 Child supplement scheme.
196 Social assistance.
197 Care allowance and child-related allowance.
198 Child supplement scheme.
199 Social assistance.
200 Care allowance and child-related allowance.
201 Care allowance.
202 Child supplement scheme.
203 Social assistance.
204 Care allowance and child-related allowance.
205 Child supplement scheme.
206 Social assistance.
207 Social assistance.
208 Care allowance and child-related allowance.

Table 7.6 AROP Threshold – VUP Group 2

		AROP threshold – VUP Group 2						
		BE[209]	G	IT	LUX	PL	SE	NL
Sickness								
Y0	Single person	94.94%	No benefits are granted	Not enough data on the income of co.co.co. workers	165.94%	123.68%	45.36%	No benefits are granted
	Single person + two children	96.50%			126.95%	134.72%	43.73%[210]	
	Breadwinner + two children	79.67%			103.59%	102.64%	43.44%[211]	
Unemployment								
Y0	Single person	104.69%	No benefits are granted	Not enough data on the income of co.co.co. workers	158.04%	68.54%	45.36%	No benefits are granted
	Single person + two children	100.97%			126.28%	105.66%	43.73%[212]	
	Breadwinner + two children	79.67%			107.56%[213]	95.76%[214]	43.44%[215]	

[209] Self-employed are not entitled to an unemployment benefit, but can receive a bridging right.
[210] Social assistance.
[211] Social assistance.
[212] Social assistance.
[213] Social assistance.
[214] Social assistance.
[215] Social assistance.

Table 7.7 AROP Threshold – VUP Group 3

		BE	G	IT[2-6]	LUX	PL	SE	NL
				AROP threshold – VUP Group 3				
				Sickness				
Y0	Single person	78.29%[217]	45.83%	66.42%[218]	93.10%[219]	66.0%	62.30%	80.91%[220]
	Single person + two children	89.16%[221]	62.11%[222]	60.0%[223]	104.75%[224]	104.4%[225]	51.83%	82.51%[226]
	Breadwinner + two children	67.85%[227]	57.44%[228]	49.0ε%[229]	91.89%[230]	95.76%[231]	43.44%[232]	67.99%[233]

(continued)

216 Sickness benefits are calculated at a rate of 66.66 per cent of the average daily wage (blue-collar workers).Between day 4 and day 20 benefits are granted for blue-collar workers at a ratio of 50 per cent of the average daily wage.
217 Social assistance.
218 Social assistance.
219 Social assistance.
220 Care allowance and social assistance.
221 Social assistance.
222 Child supplement and social assistance benefit.
223 Social assistance.
224 Social assistance.
225 Social assistance.
226 Care and child allowance and social assistance.
227 Social assistance.
228 Child supplement and social assistance benefit.
229 Social assistance.
230 Social assistance.
231 Social assistance.
232 Social assistance.
233 Care and child allowance and social assistance.

Table 7.7 (*Continued*)

Y0	Unemployment				No unemployment benefits are granted	
Single person	78.29%[234]	44.65%	61.11%[235]	94.06%[236]	57.28%	80.91%[237]
Single person + two children	89,16%[238]	72.26%[239]	68.13%[240]	105.74%[241]	48.69%[242]	79.47%[243]
Breadwinner + two children	67.85%[244]	57.44%[245]	49.08%[246]	92.56%[247]	43.44%[248]	67.54%[249]

234 Social assistance.
235 Social assistance.
236 Social assistance.
237 Care allowance and social assistance.
238 Social assistance.
239 Child supplement.
240 Social assistance.
241 Social assistance.
242 Social assistance.
243 Care and child allowance and social assistance.
244 Social assistance.
245 Child supplement and social assistance benefit.
246 Social assistance.
247 Social assistance.
248 Social assistance.
249 Care and child allowance and social assistance.

Whilst replacement rates were reached for in most countries for VUP Groups 1, 2 and 3, a more diverse picture emerges for the AROP threshold.

However, some common trends can be discerned. First, families where only one partner works face more difficulties in reaching the AROP threshold. Single persons, particularly in VUP Group 1, will be more likely to receive an income in case of sickness or unemployment that reaches the AROP threshold. This will become more difficult for families with one dependent partner and two children, and in most countries the AROP threshold is not reached. A similar picture emerges for VUP Group 2; again, families where only one partner works will face difficulties in reaching the AROP threshold for the benefits they receive.

The AROP threshold is not reached in most countries studied for all three hypothetical households for part-time workers (VUP Group 3), even though such workers often also receive social assistance. In particular for those workers the importance of different benefits (child benefits, unemployment or sickness benefits and/or social assistance) needs to be stressed. Sickness or unemployment benefits taken alone would not give a sufficient clear picture.

A remarkable picture emerges: whereas benefits for the VUP Groups 1, 2 and 3 will for most countries studied respect the principles of the European Code, such benefits are not high enough to grant adequate protection in case of poverty. Hence, both objectives of the 2019 Recommendation are not reached, namely adequate protection taking into account the principles of equivalence, proportionality and solidarity on the one hand and poverty reduction on the other hand.

III. Concluding Remarks

The aim of this chapter was to delve deeper into the problems of the four VUP Groups in receiving adequate social protection in the following EU Member States: Belgium, Germany, Italy, Luxembourg, Poland, Sweden and the Netherlands. This section summarises the problems identified higher and looks at the role of the EU in strengthening the protection of the four VUP Groups via the 2019 Recommendation.

Workers who perform work in a standard employment relationship, like VUP Group 1, still receive the broadest protection in case of sickness and unemployment in the countries studied. The analysis made clear that those with non-standard work forms, like the VUP Groups 2, 3 and 4, face more problems in their access to adequate social protection. Despite the call of the 2019 Recommendation to extend the social protection to non-standard work forms and ensure that they receive adequate social protection, several obstacles remain in place. For example, problems in formal access can be found for VUP Group 2, but also for marginal work forms. Several of the countries studied have a minimum work requirement in place, which will hinder the build-up of social security rights for those with marginal work forms. The report from the EU Commission on the implementation of the 2019 Recommendation also highlights the different gaps in formal coverage that remain in place, in particular in case of unemployment (eg for the self-employed, domestic workers and platform workers). According to the EU Commission roughly 5.6 million non-standard workers are without access to unemployment benefits, while 366,000 have no access to sickness benefits.[250] Several initiatives can be noted in countries, but extending coverage remains a difficulty as Member States fear the financial repercussions.

Another problem that could be discerned is the lack of effective access for certain groups. Whilst eligibility criteria translate the principles underlying social security schemes, such as proportionality and equivalence, and ensure the financial sustainability of the social security scheme, they are in some countries still tailored to the needs of standard workers, which can negatively affect both the access to a benefit and the composition of a benefit for non-standard workers.[251] This became evident from the analysis of VUP Groups 3 and 4; often no specific rules are adopted in the countries studied to provide effective and adequate access to social protection. Similarly, some countries also apply the same protection to the self-employed, although those rules cannot always be easily extended. On the other hand, other countries highlighted that the differences between the self-employed and 'standard employment relationships' justify the lack of protection or limited protection provided for the self-employed.[252] In order to include non-standard work forms more adequately in national social security schemes, eligibility criteria should be worded in a neutral manner, so that they do not exclude from the outset one or the other professional group. Overall, it requires EU Member States to rethink current exclusions in place, and the protection they want to offer in the occurrence of a social risk: once it is clear what kind of protection countries want to offer, they can start to reflect on how the eligibility criteria should be designed to include different groups (eg formulating the qualifying period in short time units). Specifically for VUP Group 2, one could wonder whether the social protection for employees should be extended to (economically) dependent self-employed. Although they may not formally stand in a legally subordinate relationship to an employer, their way of working strongly resembles that of employees.

The analysis in section II.B on the adequacy of sickness and unemployment benefits shows that the benefits granted in the countries studied respect the principles set out in the revised European Code of Social Security. The replacement rates were reached, irrespective of the household composition, for almost all VUP Groups studied (VUP Group 1, 2 and 3 – part-time workers at a ratio of 50 per cent). A different picture emerged in light of the AROP threshold: even for the standard workers in VUP Group 1, the sickness and unemployment benefits were not high enough when the worker had a dependent partner and two children.

---

[250] See also European Commission (n 6) 11.
[251] Schoukens and Bruynseraede (n 48) 62–63.
[252] See also European Commission (n 6) 14.

This trend was even more clear for VUP Group 3 where in most of the countries the benefits, irrespective of the household composition, did not reach the AROP threshold. The strong differences in outcome also shows the need for a diversified approach in measuring the adequacy of social protection schemes in light of the 2019 Recommendation.

In general, more clarity is needed on what the EU understands regarding adequacy: the 2019 Recommendation spells out the need to provide adequate social protection, but contains no clear criteria to define this notion further.[253] In the absence of a clear-cut EU framework on adequacy and given the difficulty of developing indicators for social security benefits, the two-step approach applied in this contribution can be further developed. Such an approach should allow the EU to map whether or not national social security schemes achieve the two goals set out in the 2019 Recommendation, ie (1) to protect the previous standard of living of workers and self-employed, and (2) to ensure that those persons do not fall into poverty.

Furthermore, in measuring adequacy a broader view on social security should also be applied at EU level. Currently, the 2019 Recommendation only takes into account the traditional labour-related insurance schemes, ie unemployment benefits, sickness and health care benefits, maternity and equivalent paternity benefits, invalidity benefits, old-age benefits, and benefits in respect of accidents at work and occupational diseases.[254] Child benefits, social assistance including minimum income schemes, and private insurance arrangements are not included in the material scope. While these exclusions may be due to the 2019 Recommendation's focus on labour-related schemes, the analysis higher shows the importance of other benefits (eg childcare benefits and social assistance) in providing adequate social protection.

Even for VUP Group 1 (who can be called 'standard employees') child benefits played an important role in providing adequate social protection. Moreover, the overall protection provided for families should not be ignored: a large degree of flexibility and uncertainty in the number of hours worked, may put greater demands on parents (eg in accessing childcare) and the necessary protection should be available to cover those needs as well.[255] Social security branches in most social security systems are not isolated but closely interrelated. If social assistance, child benefits and other benefits are not taken into account, the 2019 Recommendation ignores the reality that non-standard workers and the self-employed face. After all, they are often obliged to resort to these schemes when their formal, effective or adequate access to social security schemes is not ensured. The 2019 Recommendation is aware of the importance of other protection measures, in addition to the social risks explicitly mentioned in the

---

[253] See also the discussion above on adequacy.
[254] Art 3 2019 Recommendation.
[255] See also on the role of in-work poverty and child benefits: Marx, Vanhille and Verbist (n 22).

Recommendation: it stresses the need, when addressing adequacy, to take into account the whole social protection system of an EU Member State.[256]

An important accompanying instrument to the 2019 Recommendation is the 2023 Recommendation covering minimum income. Explicitly mentioned in the Action Plan on the European Pillar of Social Rights, a proposal for a Council Recommendation was launched in September 2022 and adopted in January 2023. The 2019 Recommendation and the 2023 Recommendation can play an important role in strengthening the protection of precarious workers who receive or are in need of social assistance, in addition to social security benefits or when no social security benefits are granted because the employee does not fulfil the statutory conditions. In the EU monitoring process the two recommendations will need to be closely linked to get a clear overview of the protection granted for workers and the self-employed. However, it remains to be seen how other benefits are taken into account in the monitoring framework, such as child benefits. The 2019 Recommendation also does not consider the composition of the household in which the worker or the self-employed person find themselves; it merely addresses social protection from an individual perspective. Yet child benefits, social assistance and socio-fiscal benefits depend largely on the family composition of the worker or the self-employed person (ie number of dependent family members, number of professionally active persons, income generated by each family member, etc.). Moreover, although difficult to map, the diversity in work patterns must also be taken into account, as combining different activities at the same time or over a longer period of time can lead to the loss of social security rights.

Furthermore, in terms of benefit adequacy, the (traditional) social security benefits, such as sickness and unemployment benefits, meet their limits when applied to some VUP Groups, in particular workers with a low or marginal income. The 2019 Recommendation requires that persons should receive an income replacement benefit of a decent level. On the other hand, workers and the self-employed should also sufficiently contribute to social protection schemes so as to make adequate protection happen. A balance must be found between solidarity, proportionality and equivalence. Non-standard work, in particular marginal work, challenges the underlying foundations of social security schemes. If states and/or the EU want to address poverty (for non-standard workers) other strategies/policies are required that complement social insurances, such as social assistance schemes providing supplementary income support, social tax welfare schemes (granting additional benefits and/or protection through the tax scheme), and/or by universalising protection. However these complementary protection tools should in their design not undermine social insurances. Complementary protection may consolidate or even enhance low wages/low payments, grey work,

---

[256] European Commission, *Communication from the European Commission to the European Parliament, the Council, the European Economic and Social Committee and the Committee of the Regions, The European Pillar of Social Rights Action Plan*, COM(2021) 102 final.

or even the development of a split labour market. Incentives should be built in to promote decent work and strategies of alternative financing where the beneficiaries of low-paid (non-standard) work are addressed to contribute for the complementary social protection granted to vulnerable workers.[257]

Lastly, an essential part of strengthening the protection of (standard and non-standard) workers and the self-employed at EU level will be the follow up of the 2019 and 2023 Recommendations. The 2019 Recommendation stipulates that the EU Commission had to review the progress made in the implementation (Article 22) by 15 November 2022. The report was adopted in January 2023) and shows that there is a considerable variation in the level of the ambition of the EU Member States in introducing changes to their social security schemes in line with the 2019 Recommendation. How the Recommendation will be further implemented at EU level and anchored in the broader socio-economic policies at EU and national levels remains unclear. In the previous couple of years, it was already unclear what exact role the 2019 Recommendation played in the EU Semester and the Recovery and Resilience Facility (RRF).

A recent study has shown that in the years after the adoption of the EPSR some socialisation did take place in the EU Semester, in particular in the first set of country-specific recommendations under the von der Leyen Commission.[258] However, in mapping the impact of the EU on social protection schemes via monitoring close attention also needs to be paid to the RRF,[259] which was adopted as a response to the Covid-19 pandemic. The RRF is a temporary recovery instrument to support EU Member States in implementing reforms and investments in line with EU priorities.[260] The RRF finances reforms and investments in the EU Member States through loans and grants (period February 2020 – December 2026).[261] The legislative framework of the RRF underlines the importance of the EPSR,[262] eg the measures implemented by EU Member States must be in line with the rights under the EPSR and the initiatives flowing from it. However, there was

---

[257] The High-level Group on the future of social protection and of the welfare state in the EU also strongly focused on the financing of social security schemes, and how it can be made more robust for the future: see High-level Group (n 5) 61 and further.

[258] See for a discussion: S Rainone, *An Overview of the 2020–2021 Country Specific Recommendations (CSR's) in the Social Field: The Impact of COVID-19* (Brussels, ETUI, 2020).

[259] See also S Rainone, *The 2022 Country Specific Recommendations in the Social Field: Quo Vadis, EU Recovery?* (Brussels, ETUI, 2022).

[260] Art 4 Regulation 2021/241 of the European Parliament and the Council of 12 February 2021 establishing the Recovery and Resilience Facility [2021] OJ L 57/17.

[261] Art 24 Regulation 2021/241 of the European Parliament and the Council of 12 February 2021 establishing the Recovery and Resilience Facility [2021] OJ L 57/17.

[262] Recital (39), Art 4 and Art. 19(3)(c) Regulation 2021/241 of the European Parliament and the Council of 12 February 2021 establishing the Recovery and Resilience Facility [2021] OJ L 57/17; see also Recital (3) Commission Delegated Regulation (EU) 2021/2105 of 28 September 2021 supplementing Regulation (EU) 2021/241 of the European Parliament and of the Council establishing the Recovery and Resilience Facility by defining a methodology for reporting social expenditure [2021] OJ L 429/79.

no clear obligation imposed to respect the EPSR and/or the 2019 Recommendation or a clear translation of the principles in those two instruments into binding legislation.[263]

Despite the uncertainty surrounding the follow up of the 2019 Recommendation, this instrument, along with the newly adopted 2023 Recommendation and the EPSR, shapes more clearly what the EU social model stands for. However, the non-binding nature of the 2019 Recommendation entails a potential risk that the Recommendation's salient principles may fall into oblivion. The moderate interest shown by Member States in reforming their social security systems in line with the 2019 Recommendation shows that this risk is real. For that reason, a reflection on what can be done to strengthen the 2019 Recommendation is much-needed and to ensure a coherent application through the different EU policy domains. Moreover, a more in-depth reflection on how to deal with non-standard work forms and the protection that EU Member States wish to grant them is much-needed as well. It will be necessary to go back to the basics and to rethink not only the underlying foundations of national social security systems but also what the role of the EU should be in a changed world of work.

---

[263] For other policy domains such obligations were adopted, such as the obligation for Member States to spend at least 37 per cent or 20 per cent of their expenditure on the climate target and digital target: Art 16(2)(b)(i) Regulation 2021/241 of the European Parliament and the Council of 12 February 2021 establishing the Recovery and Resilience Facility [2021] OJ L 57/17; see also S Rainone and A Aloisi, 'Time to Deliver? Assessing the Action Plan on the European Pillar of Social Rights', *ETUI Policy Brief 2021.08*, 7–8.

PART III

Addressing In-work Poverty

8

Policy Proposals at EU level to Better Address In-work Poverty while Implementing the European Pillar of Social Rights

RAMÓN PEÑA-CASAS, DALILA GHAILANI
AND KORINA KOMINOU

I. Introduction

This chapter aims to make general policy recommendations for the European Union to tackle in-work poverty (IWP), building on the main findings of the Working, Yet Poor (WorkYP) project, and considering the European Pillar of Social Rights (EPSR) principles, which point to key issues in the enhancement of EU social citizenship.

The reality of IWP is in flagrant contradiction to the main objective of full employment underpinning the socio-economic model prevailing in the EU and its Member States. The findings of the WorkYP project confirm that IWP is also a significant and persistent challenge for European societies. Unfortunately, IWP can be expected to become even more prominent, as a consequence of the major external shocks that European economies and societies have experienced in recent years – the Covid-19 health crisis, the subsequent surge in energy prices and an unprecedented escalation of inflation. This will further exacerbate the risk of IWP for some vulnerable groups who were already particularly exposed to it but may also encourage a slide into IWP for a substantial share of individuals and households who were previously not threatened by it.[1]

The in-work poor represent a substantial share of people at work. In 2017, 9.4 per cent of employed people in the EU were at risk of poverty: this figure has

---

[1] Eurofound, 'The Cost-of-living Crisis and Energy Poverty in the EU: Social Impact and Policy Responses – Background Paper' (Dublin, Eurofound, 2022).

remained stable in recent years, similarly to the at-risk-of-poverty rate for the whole population. In 2017, nearly 20.5 million European workers lived in households at risk of poverty. This is similar to the quantified target for the number of persons that the Europe 2020 Strategy aims to lift out of poverty and social exclusion; this underlines at the outset that IWP is far from being a negligible issue in the EU.[2]

The EPSR refers to IWP explicitly in its 6th Principle, stating that 'adequate minimum wages shall be ensured, in a way that provides for the satisfaction of the needs of the worker and his/her family in the light of national economic and social conditions, while safeguarding access to employment and incentives to seek work. In-work poverty shall be prevented' (EPSR, Chapter II, para 6(b).[3] Preventing and tackling IWP requires a complex and multidimensional approach that encompasses a wide range of policies. Effective implementation of the rights and principles enunciated in the EPSR could be equally important to tackle IWP, notably by improving the job quality and well-being of European citizens. Nearly all the principles included in the three chapters of the EPSR (equal opportunities and access to the labour market, fair working conditions, social protection and inclusion) are relevant to tackling IWP.

The chapter is structured around five lines of action: improve the assessment of IWP in the EU social indicators framework; mainstream IWP as a cross-sectional concern into all EU socio-economic policies and purposes; ensure access of low-skilled workers and non-standard workers to learning and training; improve the access to social protection for vulnerable workers; and revive and stimulate a participatory social dialogue on IWP in the EU.

II. Improve the Assessment of In-work Poverty in the EU Social Indicators Framework

EU agreed indicators play a central role in the benchmarking of Member States, not only scientifically but also politically, in the context of the 'soft' governance processes of national structural reforms implemented at European level (the European Semester, Employment and Social OMCs (Open Method of Coordination)). Agreed by the EU and its Member States, they are used to assess the situation in order to formulate recommendations to EU countries and monitor their application in national structural reforms, but also to set quantified objectives at European level and to evaluate the progress made in achieving these objectives. When used in monitoring scoreboards, these indicators serve as warning signals

---

[2] For a detailed overview of the extent of in-work poverty in Europe, see the contribution by García-Muñoz in this book (ch 1).

[3] European Commission, Secretariat-General, *European Pillar of Social Rights* (Luxembourg, Publications Office of the European Union, 2018).

to draw attention to particular problems or developments, whether positive or negative, general or related to vulnerable groups.

Already at the turn of this millennium, in the framework of the Lisbon Strategy, an EU key indicator was adopted to measure IWP, accompanied by a portfolio of secondary indicators embedded in a comprehensive multidimensional scoreboard making it possible to embrace IWP in its complexity.[4] But this set of EU indicators dates from 2003 and needs to be improved 20 years later in the light of current EU social policy making, notably the implementation of the rights-based approach of the EPSR. The EU IWP indicators should be given more prominence in the assessment frameworks used to monitor the employment and social policies of the Member States, and particularly the 'Revised Social Scoreboard' used to monitor the implementation of the EPSR (see section III.A.i).

A. Refinement of the EU Portfolio of IWP Indicators

The EU portfolio of IWP indicators should be enhanced to provide a more in-depth assessment of IWP related to its multiple facets. From this perspective, more attention should be paid to the dynamics of IWP and notably persistence in IWP situations.

– Following the example of the persistent at-risk-of-poverty indicator[5] used in European social scoreboards, an indicator of persistent IWP could usefully be added to the EU set of IWP indicators. An additional indicator on persistent IWP would identify a core group of long term In-work poor who would need more detailed attention as a particularly vulnerable group in order to design effective preventive policies.

– Similarly, it would be desirable to include more indicators related to upward transitions; this would bring a more dynamic perspective to the monitoring of EPSR implementation. These could be, of course, the transitions of people exiting IWP, but also the upwards transitions related to the labour market situations of the in-work poor (from unemployment to part-time or temporary work) and to their contractual situations (from temporary work to a permanent contract; from part-time to full-time jobs). There could be a specific indicator on upwards transitions out of IWP. In the same vein, an indicator on persistent IWP could be used to warn of a problematic increase in this particularly vulnerable group.

---

[4] Eurostat, *In-work Poverty in the EU* (Luxembourg, Publications Office of the European Union, 2010).

[5] The persistent at-risk-of-poverty rate (Eurostat indicator ilc_li21) is defined as the share of people who are currently poor and were also poor for two out of the three previous years. See Eurostat website at ec.europa.eu/eurostat/statistics-explained/index.php?title=Glossary:At-risk-of-poverty_rate (last accessed 18 February 2023).

Particular attention should be paid to the specific gender paradox inherent to the measurement of IWP and alternative measures should be explored.[6] This gender paradox of IWP can be summarised as follows: while women on average are highly overrepresented in the less favourable labour market positions and at the bottom of the earnings distribution, they do not face a disproportionate risk of IWP. The breakdown by gender of the IWP indicator does not show a particular gender model, as the incidence of IWP appears slightly higher for men than women.[7] This apparent gender neutrality of IWP is highly counter-intuitive, as abundant literature has shown that women suffer from multiple disadvantages in the labour market compared to men.[8] IWP is a statistical construction which combines being at work, an individual status assessed at the individual level, and being poor, a status assessed on the basis of measurements of income variables at the household level, with the questionable underlying assumption that all incomes are pooled and shared equally within households, so that the well-being of all the household members is similar. This gender bias may also convey the mistaken idea that gender inequality in the labour market is not a significant problem, since women's disadvantages in terms of employment characteristics and subsequent earnings do not disproportionately put them at risk of poverty. Concern about the gender-biased picture of in-work poverty has motivated a number of researchers to propose alternative measures of IWP at the individual level. A common practice to provide a more encompassing picture is to counterfactually decompose and individualise income components.[9]

An alternative gender-sensitive and individualised approach to IWP should be developed, to shed light on the above-mentioned gender paradox and the real issues and challenges faced by female workers in relation to IWP. In this respect:

–   This individualised approach should be integrated into the assessment of (in-work) poverty, in order to consider the individual's employment-related characteristics in the context of their individual situation in terms of disposable income and work intensity. This complementary view should be promoted

---

[6] See also the contribution by Capesciotti and Paoletti (ch 4) in this book.

[7] In 2021 in the EU-27, the IWP rate of men was 9.8 per cent, compared with 7.8 per cent for women (Eurostat, EU-SILC indicator ILC-IW01).

[8] B De Micheli et al, 'Gender Policy and Indicators Report', Working, Yet Poor project (2021), Deliverable 2.2, FGB, available at workingyetpoor.eu/deliverables; European Institute for Gender Equality (EIGE), *Poverty, Gender and Intersecting Inequalities in the EU – Review of the Implementation of Area A: Women and Poverty of the Beijing Platform for Action* (Luxembourg, Publications Office of the European Union, 2016).

[9] S Ponthieux, 'Gender and In-Work Poverty' in H Lohmann and I Marx (eds), *Handbook on In-Work Poverty* (Cheltenham, Edward Elgar Publishing, 2018); R Peña-Casas and D Ghailani, 'Towards Individualizing Gender In-Work Poverty Risk' in N Frazer, R Guttierez and R Peña-Casas (eds), *Working Poverty in Europe: A Comparative Approach* (London, Palgrave Macmillan, 2011); D Meulders and S O'Dorchai, 'Revisiting Poverty Measures towards Individualization', ULB-Dulbea Working Paper no 10.03 (Brussels, 2010).

by the Commission and the European institutions in their approach to and assessment of poverty and exclusion, notably in the social scoreboards used in the employment and social OMCs in the European Semester process and for implementation of the EPSR. Such an individualised approach to income is also consistent with the promotion of an individualisation of rights. It is particularly useful for the gender paradox but could also be applied to other vulnerable groups (eg migrants).

– The calculation method used for the EU-SILC Indicator on IWP rate by sex needs to be revised, based on individual income rather than household income. This alternative assessment of IWP could be used as an additional measurement in European social statistics on (in-work) poverty, enabling a sounder and more transparent analysis of the gender dimension of IWP.[10]

B. Enhancement of Some Key Measurements of Precarious Work in EU Data Sources

The availability and quality of data sources has improved greatly over the last decade. But literature on employment and poverty measurement rightly points out deficiencies in data sources which also apply to the measurement of IWP. Further work is needed to better assess in the main EU data sources certain aspects of IWP, as well as specific features of employment that are important to understanding IWP, notably among particular vulnerable groups of workers and citizens. The Commission and the European bodies could usefully continue to develop certain features related to understanding and measurement of non-standard employment and particularly of precarious employment and the so-called new forms of employment. The WorkYP project, by structuring its approach around certain groups of workers particularly at risk of IWP, highlights a number of issues on which the European data sources should be deepened or developed.

– Flexibility through atypical work should be a voluntary choice of the worker. This is why it is important to deepen the understanding and measurement in the European data sources of the reasons motivating atypical work, in order to better distinguish between a choice by the worker and a situation constrained by the circumstances of the job offer (no alternative, low job quality) and/or individual obligations (care and childcare, for instance) not supported by an adequate supply of affordable quality services. Notably, the reasons for (bogus/false) self-employment should also be better assessed in this perspective.

---

[10] For a discussion and a comparative analysis of EU countries using this individualised measurement of disposable income, see for instance Ponthieux (n 9). The results clearly highlight the greater vulnerability of women to IWP.

- The WorkYP findings also highlight the need to address the weaknesses or gaps in the European data sources concerning the assessment of certain forms of non-standard work: casual work; zero hours contracts; on-call work; (very short) part-time work; and self-employment, particularly bogus self-employment.

- The focus in WorkYP on certain groups of citizens and workers who are particularly vulnerable to IWP but relatively invisible in the statistics highlights the need to improve the representativeness of these groups in European surveys and data sources. This should be done not only to improve knowledge of specific groups with specific challenges, but also to better understand the consequences of the intersectionality of these diverse layers of vulnerability to (in-work) poverty and exclusion of European citizens and workers.

Various channels at EU level could be used to enhance information on the above-mentioned matters:

- The European Commission should continue to foster these needed improvements, through specific European bodies (Eurostat, indicators sub-groups of the Employment Committee and the Social Protection Committee) but also through joint work between European agencies and also the Member States.

- Full use should be made of the opportunities offered by several European regulations to enhance the data in the European surveys, by enabling the Member States to add administrative data on income and labour market situation.

- Scientific research on precariousness of work and intersectionality of disadvantages should be further encouraged through the funding of dedicated EU research projects.

III. Mainstream IWP as a Cross-sectional Concern into all EU Socio-economic Policies and Purposes

A. Enhance the Consideration of IWP in the EPSR

The EPSR, adopted in 2017, sets out 20 key principles and rights essential for fair and well-functioning labour markets and social protection systems. It explicitly recognises the need for policies and measures to tackle IWP and inequality. On 4 March 2021, the European Commission presented its Action Plan to fully implement the EPSR, turning the principles into concrete actions to benefit EU citizens, while also supporting the recovery from the impact of Covid-19. It proposes a new target for the EU: to reduce the number of people at risk of poverty or social exclusion by at least 15 million by 2030. The implementation of the EPSR principles in EU Member States' structural policies is assessed through a scoreboard of indicators, called the Revised Social Scoreboard (RSS). The RSS indicators are used to track trends and performances across EU countries in three areas related to the principles of the EPSR (equal opportunities, fair working conditions, social protection and inclusion).[11] These indicators act as warning signals to draw attention to particular problems or developments in Member States, whether positive or negative, general or related to vulnerable groups.

i. *Enhance the Revised Social Scoreboard*

The EPSR Action Plan included a proposal to revise the EPSR Social Scoreboard, through updating the existing set of indicators so as to make it possible to track progress in the implementation of the Pillar in a more comprehensive manner. This included proposals for the addition of some new headline indicators for the scoreboard as well as a range of additional secondary indicators. The Social Protection Committee (SPC) and the Employment Committee (EMCO) have reviewed the proposal for revising the existing Social Scoreboard. They support the objective of improving monitoring and assessment of the employment and social situation across the Union in an integrated and more visible way and have agreed on including the proposed new headline indicators together with the existing ones in the Social Scoreboard. These new headline indicators extend the scoreboard to include coverage of the dimensions of child poverty, adult participation in learning, housing cost overburden, and the employment gap for persons with disabilities.[12] Currently, the RSS feeds into the European Semester of economic policy coordination and serves to assess progress towards a social 'triple A' for the EU as a whole.

The findings of the WorkYP project confirm that IWP remains a central challenge in many Member States for the application of European employment and social policies and the vesting of social rights of European workers and citizens, especially those belonging to specific vulnerable groups. From this perspective, the RSS should be enhanced to better highlight the multifaceted complexity of IWP.

- The IWP rate should be placed among the headline indicators of the RSS, and not as a secondary indicator in the 'Fair working conditions' section.

- The secondary indicators of the RSS already include an indicator on the proportion of involuntary fixed-term work. It would be desirable to add an indicator on the share of involuntary part-time work.

- At present, the RSS only includes a secondary indicator on transitions from temporary to permanent contracts. There could be a specific indicator on

---

[11] European Commission, *Communication from the Commission to the European Parliament, the Council, the European Economic and Social Committee and the Committee of the Regions – the European Pillar of Social Rights Action Plan*, COM(2021) 102 final.

[12] Social Protection Committee, *2021 SPC Annual Review of the Social Protection Performance Monitor (SPPM) and Developments in Social Protection Policies. Report on Key Social Challenges and Key Messages* (Luxembourg, Publications Office of the European Union, 2021).

upwards transitions out of IWP. In the same vein, an indicator on persistent IWP could be used to warn of a problematic increase in this particularly vulnerable group.

ii. *Enhance the Content of the EPSR*

Tackling IWP should be a key cross-cutting concern mainstreamed into the EPSR and into core structural employment and social policy reforms in the European Union and its Member States. The EPSR and its Action Plan are useful instruments for effectively monitoring the acquisition of a wide range of social rights that are key to avoiding IWP.

– IWP should be more prominent, as a key cross-cutting challenge, in the other principles of the EPSR, when relevant, and not referred to solely with regard to the issue of fair wages in Principle 6. Almost all the principles of the EPSR[13] relate directly or indirectly to the various facets of job quality.[14] The analysis carried out in WorkYP and the focus on particular Vulnerable and Underrepresented Persons (VUP) groups in the project highlight the intricate relationship existing between the multi-layered realities of IWP and the multi-faceted features of poor-quality jobs (low income; low employment intensity of individuals and households; precarious and atypical work; poor working conditions; limited access to social protection; limited workers' rights, etc). This complex interaction underpins the necessity to mainstream the issue of IWP into European policy. Mainstreaming IWP implies that when designing, implementing and monitoring policies at national and European levels, their impact on IWP would be taken into consideration; this would allow them to be adjusted where necessary in order to mitigate negative outcomes or to increase their positive impact on reducing IWP. Such an approach would help to strike a 'virtuous balance' between various policy strategies (economic, fiscal, environmental, employment and social matters; equality and non-discrimination), to ensure that economic growth and increased employment do not result in a worsening of IWP and a deterioration of the rights of the in-work poor. Well-designed fiscal and budgetary policies must not only ensure a balanced budget, but also allow for adequate social investment in education, health, care and the provision of quality, affordable and accessible public services for all.

---

[13] Chapter I – Equal opportunities and access to the labour market (education; training and life-long learning; gender equality; equal opportunities; active support to employment); Chapter II – Fair working conditions (secure and adaptable employment; wages; information on employment conditions and protection in case of dismissals; social dialogue and involvement of workers; work-life balance; healthy, safe and well-adapted work environment and data protection); and Chapter III – Social protection and inclusion (social protection; unemployment benefits; minimum income; health care; disability; access to essential services).

[14] European Commission and Council, *Proposal for a Joint Employment Report from the Commission and the Council*, COM(2021) 743 final.

B. Enhance the Consideration of IWP in the EU Semester Governance Process Through the EPSR

Designed to monitor macroeconomic policies, the European Semester provides a general framework for policy coordination, including soft and hard law instruments, and allows for regular monitoring of the different instruments as well as a continuous dialogue with stakeholders, Member States and civil society. As various policy areas, including social policy, are monitored simultaneously, the Semester could also serve to mainstream social objectives across policy domains.[15]

In implementing the EPSR, synergies on tackling IWP should be fostered with the existing EU social policy instruments and governance processes, such as the European Semester (including the Social OMC and the European Employment Strategy). Country-specific recommendations could be issued to Member States, not only if a country had a high overall incidence of IWP or a recurrent upward trend, but also when a worsening of IWP is observed for particular groups, such as atypical workers, or as a consequence of structural reforms in other areas of the National Reform Programmes (IWP-proofing). There should be regular peer reviews on the issue of IWP in its multiple dimensions, in order to encourage exchange between countries on strategies and policies implemented to counteract IWP and some of its aspects.

C. Adopt a Holistic Approach in all Other Soft Social Governance Tools

The Social OMC is a voluntary process of cooperation between Member States at EU level; its objective is based on policy exchange and the establishment of commonly agreed indicators and benchmarks for upward convergence. It has kept social policy on the EU agenda (particularly in the second half of the Lisbon Strategy) but has been widely criticised for its lack of progress, transparency and democratic legitimacy[16]).

– Given the multifaceted, complex nature of IWP, a holistic approach is necessary to grasp the issue from a policy perspective and in all its complexity at European and national levels. IWP is at the crossroads of several policy domains with complex interactions. Hence, it is necessary to promote at European level and among the Member States a holistic approach to the policies, which could help to eradicate IWP through integrated and coordinated strategies or

---

[15] A Aranguiz, 'Social Mainstreaming Through the European Pillar of Social Rights: Shielding "the Social" from "the Economic" in EU Policymaking' (2018) 4 *European Journal of Social Security* 20, 341–63.

[16] M Dawson and B De Witte, 'Welfare Policy and Social Inclusion' in A Arnull and D Chalmers (eds), *The Oxford Handbook of European Law* (Oxford, Oxford University Press, 2015).

programmes. The European Commission and other EU stakeholders could help to design this approach carefully through dedicated means.

–   This holistic perspective should be combined with targeted approaches to specific groups of citizens and workers who are more vulnerable to IWP, such as those considered in the VUP groups of the WorkYP project but also, for instance, single-parent households, migrants, the poorly educated and the low-skilled, or homeless persons. As an individual and/or member of a poor household, the working poor may belong to several of these vulnerable groups at the same time. A female part-time worker may also be a low-skilled single mother, for example. This intersectionality of individual characteristics leads to an intersectionality of policies and measures targeted at these vulnerable groups. This dual intersectionality needs to be taken into account in a well-designed holistic approach to IWP in European and national policies.

–   The in-work poor should also be added to the list of vulnerable groups eligible for actions supported by EU funding, from structural funds such as the European Social Fund Plus or the European Regional Development Fund, the Multiannual Financial Framework 2021–2027 and the Social Investment Package, as well as from temporary measures funded by the Recovery and Resilience Facility and included in the NextGenerationEU package.

–   The European Social Dialogue at cross-industry and sectoral levels should include the multifaceted nature of IWP and its intricate relationship with poor job quality patterns among the issues to be debated between European social partners, in order to establish common positions expressed in framework agreements or resolutions. In the sectoral social dialogue, a bargaining process should be launched in sectors characterised by low quality jobs and high risks of IWP. Shared achievements at European level could help to foster awareness and bargaining at national level.

IV. Ensuring Access of Low-skilled Workers and Non-standard Workers to Learning and Training

In 2000, the Lisbon Strategy set out its ambition to make the EU and its Member States the most competitive knowledge-based economies in the globalised context. Since then, the issues of skills acquisition and upskilling have been at the heart of the European employment and social policy agenda. To increase labour market participation, active labour market policies (ALMPs) and their focus on improving employability have gradually been extended from unemployed jobseekers to various categories of social benefit claimants, provided they are able to work.

The first principle of the EPSR stipulates that 'everyone has the right to quality and inclusive education, training and life-long learning (LLL) in order to maintain and acquire skills that enable them to participate fully in society and manage successfully transitions in the labour market' (EPSR – Principle 1). The effective implementation of this EPSR principle is grounded in the 'European Skills Agenda' launched in July 2020, which includes no less than 12 flagship actions[17] and four EU quantified objectives to be achieved by 2025.[18] This is accompanied by an extension of potential funding from the European structural funds (ESF+) or temporary funds (NextGenerationEU and the Recovery and Resilience Facility) to support the skilling and upskilling of all EU citizens and workers. Moreover, the EPSR Action Plan set a new EU target of 60 per cent of adults participating annually in training by 2030. The Commission also published a proposal for a decision for a European Year of Skills 2023, indicating the high priority given to EU actions addressing the significant challenge of low-skilled working-age adults. These skills correspond to skills for life: those supporting lifelong pathways but also, most relevant to this analysis, skills for jobs.[19]

Inclusive and accessible lifelong learning (LLL) and vocational education and training (VET) policies could significantly contribute to reducing IWP. They are a prerequisite for improving the skills of the in-work poor and their access to fairly and decently paid jobs. However, for many in-work poor considered in the VUP groups of the WorkYP project, access to and provision of LLL and VET is scarce and fragmentary. The low participation of in-work poor in training activities also reinforces the skills mismatch problem and structural unemployment in the labour market. Temporary agency workers, part-time and fixed-term employees, self-employed people, casual workers, and employees on zero-hour contracts have few or no options to acquire, certify new skills or reskill, allowing them to exit IWP. Therefore, access to and availability of LLL and VET for non-standard workers should be considered as a cross-cutting challenge in all strategies related to the acquisition and development of skills by vulnerable groups.

– The inclusion of non-standard workers in LLL and VET opportunities should be added as a cross-cutting concern to the European Skills Agenda and its flagship initiatives, notably the Pact for Skills initiative but also in the support of national skills strategies and the Skills for Life initiative. The connection of

---

[17] European Commission, *European Skills Agenda for Sustainable Competitiveness, Social Fairness and Resilience*, COM(2020) 274. To name but a few points of particular interest to the in-work poor: the Pact for Skills (EU support for strategic national upskilling strategies, future-proof vocational education and training); the Skills for life action; the Initiative on individual learning accounts; and the European approach to micro-credentials.

[18] These quantified targets include the participation in learning of all adults aged 25–64 (50 per cent), but also of low-skilled adults (30 per cent) and the unemployed (20 per cent).

[19] European Commission, *Proposal for a Decision of the European Parliament and of the Council on a European Year of Skills 2023*, COM(2022) 526 final.

the Agenda with the European Green Deal[20]) and its need for new green and digital skills can also build the right momentum for synergies that can benefit vulnerable workers. Moreover, the individual learning accounts initiative and the European approach to micro-credentials should allow non-standard workers to improve the portability of acquired skills when they move from one situation to the next in their work-life course. Also, through this credit system, the observed focusing of learning and training provisions on already highly educated individuals can be better tackled.

– The scarce or non-existent access of non-standard workers to LLL and VET should also be taken up as a cross-cutting concern in the structural reforms undertaken by Member States as part of the European Semester process. Specific Country-specific Recommendations could be issued on improving participation in training and learning activities for all vulnerable groups of workers, including through a range of new institutional arrangements.

– The peer review processes used in the social and employment OMCs should include the issue of problematic access to LLL and VET of various types of non-standard workers as one of the themes for exchange of experiences and good practices between Member States. Furthermore, the Education and Training Monitor, which contributes to evidence-based policy making in this area, can enhance the analysis with dedicated data and relevant information, notably on the access and availability of learning and training opportunities for atypical vulnerable workers across the EU.

– 2023 is the European Year of Skills. It is an opportunity to communicate, debate and undertake targeted actions at the European and national levels on the issue of skills and sustainable learning. The European Commission and social stakeholders more broadly should seize this opportunity to shed light on the difficulties faced by certain vulnerable groups in accessing learning and vocational training, thus enabling them to progress in their professional and personal lives. The various types of non-standard workers mentioned in this project could usefully be highlighted as one of these groups.

– EU social partners at interprofessional and sectoral levels should begin debating a resolution or a framework agreement concerning the problematic access to LLL and VET of various types of non-standard workers, including those in 'new forms of employment', to encourage their national members to act on this issue. It is also important to discuss and implement social responsibility initiatives to address inequality of access between low-skilled and more skilled workers to formal and informal training in enterprises, and particularly in small and medium enterprises.

---

[20] European Commission, *Communication from the Commission The European Green Deal*, COM(2019) 640 final.

V. Improve the Access to Social Protection
for Vulnerable Workers

In the EPSR, the right to access social protection is mentioned several times: in terms of non-discrimination in Principle 3[21] of workers' right to safe employment in Principle 5[22] and of employees' and self-employed workers' right to social protection in Principle 12.[23] There are also dedicated principles on specific social protection schemes: unemployment benefits (Principle 13[24]); minimum income (Principle 14[25]); maternity and care benefits (Principle 9[26]); pensions (Principle 15[27]); and disability benefits (Principle 17[28]). Even though the endorsement of the EPSR Action Plan provides strong political legitimacy to act on this extensive headline target,[29] the widespread phenomena of non-typical work and low-work intensity households are challenging the delivery of fair social results. Turning the rights to social protection enshrined in the EPSR into reality requires transnational cooperation and consent by all involved parties, to adopt a consistent and intra-life course perspective.[30]

Even though the right to social protection broadly covers standard workers, it does not cover some atypical workers, including the self-employed, or certain

---

[21] *Principle 3 – Equal opportunities*: 'Regardless of gender, racial or ethnic origin, religion or belief, disability, age or sexual orientation, everyone has the right to equal treatment and opportunities regarding employment, social protection … Equal opportunities of under-represented groups shall be fostered.'

[22] *Principle 5 – Secure and adaptable employment*: 'Regardless of the type and duration of the employment relationship, workers have the right to fair and equal treatment regarding working conditions, access to social protection and training …'.

[23] *Principle 12 – Social protection*: 'Regardless of the type and duration of their employment relationship, workers, and, under comparable conditions, the self-employed, have the right to adequate social protection.'

[24] *Principle 13 – Unemployment benefits*: 'The unemployed have the right to adequate activation support from public employment services to (re)integrate in the labour market and adequate unemployment benefits of reasonable duration, in line with their contributions and national eligibility rules. Such benefits shall not constitute a disincentive for a quick return to employment.'

[25] *Principle 14 – Minimum income*: 'Everyone lacking sufficient resources has the right to adequate minimum income benefits ensuring a life in dignity at all stages of life, and effective access to enabling goods and services …'.

[26] *Principle 9 – Work-life balance*: 'Parents and people with caring responsibilities have the right to suitable leave, flexible working arrangements and access to care services. Women and men shall have equal access to special leaves of absence in order to fulfil their caring responsibilities …'.

[27] *Principle 15 – Old age income and pensions*: Workers and the self-employed in retirement have the right to a pension commensurate to their contributions and ensuring an adequate income. Women and men shall have equal opportunities to acquire pension rights …'.

[28] *Principle 17 – Inclusion of people with disabilities*: 'People with disabilities have the right to income support that ensures living in dignity, services that enable them to participate in the labour market and in society, and a work environment adapted to their needs.'

[29] B Vanhercke and S Spasova, 'Conclusions. Dealing with the Pandemic; Re-emerging Social Ambitions as the EU Recovers' in B Vanhercke and S Spasova (eds), *Social policy in the European Union; State of Play 2021* (Brussels, ETUI and European Social Observatory, 2022).

[30] European Commission, *The Future of Social Protection and of the Welfare State in the EU*, High-Level Group on the Future of Social Protection and of the Welfare State in the EU (2023).

categories of standard workers who are considered in the project as being particularly vulnerable to IWP. The employment status of these vulnerable workers places them on a scale of access to social protection schemes ranging from equivalent social protection to that of standard low-qualified workers in poor sectors (VUP group 1), to almost no social protection for workers occupied in casual employment and the platform economy (VUP group 4), but also for the self-employed and particularly the bogus self-employed (VUP group 2), as well as for workers in the particular atypical jobs discussed in VUP group 3 (notably temporary agency work). Social protection gaps for non-standard and self-employed workers have been identified in the countries screened in the WorkYP project regarding access to sickness and unemployment benefits, protection against accidents at work and occupational diseases, as well as maternity benefits.[31]

Various EU initiatives have been taken in the course of implementing the EPSR to extend the right to social protection to non-standard workers and the self-employed. Although these acts are welcome, the harmonisation of social protection of atypical workers remains a complex issue that is still in its infancy.[32] The non-binding 'Council Recommendation on access to social protection for atypical workers and the self-employed' adopted in 2018 encourages Member States to bridge formal coverage gaps for both atypical employees and the self-employed and to promote adequate effective coverage by taking measures to ensure access to benefits.[33] However, the Recommendation remains vague when defining the employment status of self-employed workers, neglecting the possibility that they are bogus self-employed. This shortcoming is remedied in the 2021 'Proposal for a Directive on improving working conditions in platform work',[34] which includes measures to properly assess the employment status of people working through digital work platforms and new rights for workers and the self-employed in algorithmic management. In particular, it establishes a test for determining whether a base is a de facto employer. If it meets at least two of the five proposed criteria, the platform is considered to be an employer and people working for the platform are automatically reclassified as having employee status, which gives them access to the same rights as standard workers. Directive 2019/1152 on Transparent and Predictable Working Conditions[35] ensures that workers' rights are effectively respected and protected for people in all forms of work, including those in the most flexible non-standard and new forms of work such as zero-hour contracts, casual work, domestic work, voucher-based work or platform work. Currently,

---

[31] C Hießl, 'Comparative VUP Groups Report' Working, Yet Poor project, Deliverable 3.4 (Frankfurt, Goethe University, 2022), available at https://workingyetpoor.eu/deliverables.

[32] P Schoukens and others, 'Comparative Report on Social Security' Working, Yet Poor project, Deliverable 4.2, (Leuven, KU Leuven, 2022), available at workingyetpoor.eu/deliverables.

[33] Council Recommendation of 8 November 2019 on access to social protection for workers and the self-employed [2019] OJ C 387/1.

[34] European Commission, *Proposal for a Directive of the European Parliament and of the Council on Improving Working Conditions in Platform Work*, COM(2021) 762 final.

[35] Directive (EU) 2019/1152 of the European Parliament and of the Council of 20 June 2019 on transparent and predictable working conditions in the European Union [2019] OJ L 186/105.

platform work status is receiving a lot of attention from stakeholders and policy-makers. Awareness is being raised at EU level, including awareness of the need for improved social security coverage that fits the specific design needs of national social security systems.

The setting and support of common minimum standards is a powerful tool to harmonise social protection across the EU. Although indirectly related to social protection, a good example is the adoption of Directive 2022/2041[36] as a valuable and binding tool to boost statutory minimum wages through the enhancement of adequacy and coverage of the schemes, by strengthening social dialogue and collective bargaining on the issue. It could also be seen as a landmark moment in social policy making in the EU.[37] Nonetheless, the effective transposition of the Directive into national law should be ensured at EU level. In this respect, strong national social dialogue mechanisms and extended collective agreement coverage to secure fair minimum wages for all vulnerable workers should be closely monitored and supported with appropriate resources at the EU level. Needless to say, the same approach to improving the coverage and adequacy of various social protection schemes may be a way forward.

- As part of implementing the EPSR, in 2020 the European Commission announced in its initial work programme the intention to introduce a European Unemployment Reinsurance Scheme (EURS). The EURS was conceived of as a solidarity instrument to support those in work and protect those who have lost their jobs because of external shocks, notably by supporting their reskilling.[38] The EURS could also act as a shock absorber and economic stabiliser across the EU.[39] With the advent of the Covid-19 crisis and in the presence of diverging views between Member States, this proposal remained on the shelf and was not submitted to public and institutional consultation. Instead, the Commission introduced a temporary financial instrument (SURE) to lend money to Member States; this money would be used to finance the short-time working schemes introduced to cushion the impact of the Covid-19 crisis and allow workers and companies to stay afloat during the crisis.[40]

- By way of effective implementation of the EPSR, it would be advisable to put the EURS back on the table and to launch consultations for its approval; this

---

[36] Directive (EU) 2022/2041 of the European Parliament and of the Council of 19 October 2022 on adequate minimum wages in the European Union [2022] OJ L 275/33.

[37] T Müller and T Schulten, 'Minimum-wages Directive – History in the Making' (2022) Social Europe website, available at www.socialeurope.eu/minimum-wages-directive-history-in-the-making (last accessed 25 February 2023).

[38] European Commission, *Commission Work Programme 2020 – A Union that strives for more, Communication from the Commission to the European Parliament, the Council, the European Economic and Social Committee and the Committee of the Regions*, COM(2020) 37 final.

[39] M Beblavy, G Marconi and I Maselli, *A European Unemployment Benefit Scheme, The Rationale and the Challenges Ahead* (Luxembourg, Publications Office of the European Union, 2017).

[40] European Commission, *Proposal for a Council Regulation on the Establishment of a European Instrument for Temporary Support to Mitigate Unemployment Risks in an Emergency (SURE) Following the COVID-19 Outbreak*, COM/2020/139 final.

would provide a European solidarity-based financial instrument enabling Member States to allocate unemployment benefits of an amount and duration that allow for a decent life.

– Minimum income guarantee schemes have an important role to play in countering IWP, by contributing to the income support of the most vulnerable workers with limited or no access to other social protection schemes. They can also be used, subject to means-testing, to supplement low in-work income, enabling the worker to avoid poverty. In this spirit and following on from EPSR Principle 14 on minimum income and the Recommendation on adequate minimum income ensuring active inclusion,[41] it would also be desirable to introduce a European solidarity-based financial instrument to help Member States improve their guaranteed minimum income schemes and progressively raise the amount allocated, to the level of a national poverty threshold equivalent to 60 per cent of median disposable income.

VI. Revive and Stimulate a Participatory Social Dialogue on In-work Poverty in the EU

EU and national implementation of the EPSR principles should be a participatory process involving all stakeholders, including social partners and civil society organisations. In a broader sense, the (r)evolution of social protection but also the world of work should be part of a more general perspective encompassing the green and digital transitions. These debates must take place gradually and be anchored in a multilateral dialogue involving all social actors and organisations (public authorities, trade unions and employers, civil society and citizens, academics, politicians) on the needs of citizens (eg professional and social security throughout the life course; actual acquisition of labour and social rights), the challenges to be met (eg segmentation and precariousness of atypical employment, poverty and IWP; balanced sustainable financing) and the issues at stake (eg a harmonious balance between professional and social life, and between chosen flexibility and security for workers and employers). This would encourage a convergence towards 'social pacts' built on a comprehensive, consensual and legitimate foundation.[42] The issues of poverty and IWP cut clearly across the strands of these debates.

– At European level, the European Economic and Social Committee (EESC) should be a place where social actors can meet to have this dialogue at European

---

[41] European Commission, *Proposal for a Council Recommendation on adequate minimum income ensuring active inclusion*, COM(2022) 490 final.

[42] 'Social pacts – that is, peak-level agreements between governments, trade unions, employers' organizations, and sometimes other civil society organizations (the latter generally with an ancillary role) – are effective tools to reconcile the objectives of economic growth, social cohesion, and equitable distribution': L Baccaro and M Galindo, *Are Social Pacts Still Viable in Today's World of Work?* (Geneva, Governance and Tripartism Department, International Labour Office, 2017).

level and exchange views on national practices. The EU should also be encouraged to converge towards a model of socio-economic growth that is sustainable in the medium and long term, based on sound budgetary and fiscal policies that allow for adequate and sustainable financing of the social investment that the EU and the European countries must make to improve and guarantee the quality of life of their citizens. In this perspective, effective implementation of the social rights enshrined in the EPSR should be plainly included as a cross-cutting issue in the internal organisation and work of the EESC.

– The national Economic and Social Committees (or their functional counterparts) should also be fora for this sort of societal dialogue in the Member States. The resources existing at European level should be used to support and feed into this broad national dialogue, notably in terms of communication, organisation of meetings/seminars, research funding or support to participants, but also through current tools such as the peer review processes enshrined in the various OMCs at European level. These European and national strategic dialogues could be used as input to the guidelines issued in the Annual Sustainable Growth Survey and the European Semester.

– The European social dialogue, through non-binding acts such as joint resolutions, can help to encourage and consolidate the participation of the social partners in national debates. Collective bargaining between social partners has a key role to play in this enlarged dialogue. The social partners can define common or unilateral positions, helping to develop points of convergence and alliances with other participants in the wider dialogue on social investment and the future of work and social protection.

9

The Role of Social Partners in Addressing In-work Poverty

ANN-CHRISTINE HARTZÉN AND VINCENZO
PIETROGIOVANNI

I. Introduction

Social partners play a distinct role in the realm of both their collective autonomy – which is usually translated into self-regulatory tools, such as collective agreements – and in their activism in society at large, from social mobilisation to more political-economic campaigns. Social partners, indeed, can play a role that goes beyond their traditional regulatory agency in the labour market; in particular, if they so decide, they can take responsibility in identifying policy priorities and in monitoring the social situation in Member States; in implementing the European Pillar of Social Rights and social policies; and in influencing national governments in respecting and guaranteeing social rights.

Framed in this context, this chapter aims to provide a better understanding of the current role of the social partners in addressing in-work poverty, along with some proposals for future actions and policy ideas. This contribution will identify some core differences and similarities in the countries covered by the Working, Yet Poor project,[1] and suggest consequent actions. Proposals for the social partners and policy makers will be based on a minimum scope of action in relation to what are identified as necessary steps for addressing in-work poverty or (in some countries where social partners and policy makers are evidently lagging behind) getting started.

As for the structure of this chapter, section II provides an overview of the current situation along with the challenges and opportunities identified at the time being. Section III elaborates on the need for increasing awareness of the problems related to in-work poverty amongst social partners and also policy makers in the specific

---

[1] The countries of study in the project are: Belgium, Germany, Italy, Luxembourg, the Netherlands, Poland and Sweden.

context of employment conditions and collective bargaining structures. Section IV discusses issues related to identified needs and/or ambitions of strengthening social partners and collective bargaining structures. Section V provides a concluding analysis.

II. Challenges and Opportunities

The seven different countries covered in our analysis are fairly heterogenous, showing different characteristics both in relation to in-work poverty as such, and in relation to industrial relations systems. Such differences involve the extent to which social partners already direct interest and actions towards the issue of in-work poverty as well as the type of challenges and opportunities they may face in future actions.

In-work poverty is a multifaceted and complex concept.[2] As a consequence, there are also difficulties and challenges for social partners in formulating strategies for addressing the problem. Only few social partners have run campaigns and activities directed specifically to in-work poverty. While almost all investigated countries report activities and, in general, strategies to counteract unfair wage levels or precarious employment, the inclusion of in-work poverty in such campaigns is very limited. As such there is a varying lack of awareness. In order to provide a better understanding thereof, examples from different countries will be presented.

In some contexts, the idea of poverty being closely connected to unemployment and conceived almost exclusively in terms of severe material deprivation, seems dominant. The risk of poverty, however, is underestimated or not considered particularly central for social partners' activities and strategies. In Sweden[3] and in Italy,[4] trade unions have been committed to addressing issues that are linked to the problem of in-work poverty and the need for poverty prevention and protection for vulnerable workers, especially due to the impact of the Covid-19

---

[2] The complexity of the concept was identified as 'definitional chaos' in E Crettaz and G Bonoli, 'Why are Some Workers Poor? The Mechanisms that Produce Working Poverty in a Comparative Perspective', REC-WP Working Papers on the Reconciliation of Work and Welfare in Europe No 12-2010, available at papers.ssrn.com/sol3/papers.cfm?abstract_id=1691662 and has been further discussed since then, see eg: B Jansson and L Broström. 'Who is counted as in-work poor? Testing five different definitions when measuring in-work poverty in Sweden 1987–2017' (2021) 48(3) *International Journal of Social Economics* 477, 491.

[3] See inter alia K Nelson and J Fritzell, *ESPN Thematic Report on In-work Poverty Sweden*, European Commission, Directorate-General for Employment, Social Affairs and Inclusion (2019); and P Hällberg and C Kjellström, *Collective Agreements and Minimum Wages* (Swedish National Mediation Office, 2020). Also S Carlén, 'Vilka löner och arbetstider kan man försörja sig på? En studie av löner, löneinkomster och arbetstider i detaljhandeln', Handels rapporter 2019:5.

[4] M Carrieri, 'Il sindacato dei poveri, una formula impegnativa' (2021) *Il diario del lavoro*, 5 February 2021, www.ildiariodellavoro.it/il-sindacato-dei-poveri-una-formula-impegnativa (last visited 3 March 2022).

pandemic, but the working poor have not been addressed or mentioned as an overall phenomenon. Thus, even though some social partners have addressed the issue of poverty in general,[5] the problem of in-work poverty seems not to be explicitly a priority in their agenda.

In the Netherlands,[6] trade unions have run initiatives on income insecurity, risks of social exclusion and practices of circumventing labour law protection for certain categories of workers, notably temporary agency workers in terms of income insecurity, and platform workers in terms of circumvention of labour law protection.[7] These trade unions have also directed campaigns for improved and increased wage revisions to better align them with price increases, especially for low and middle-income earners.[8] Nevertheless, even in the Netherlands the main idea seems still to be that poverty is linked to unemployment, which is also indicated by statistics that show how poverty risks exist mainly for persons in self-employment or different forms of flexible employment.[9] On a similar note of activities not explicitly linked to in-work poverty, there have been actions and initiatives by trade unions in Poland, where the flexibilisation of the labour market with the relatively extensive use of self-employment or other non-employment contracts for work has led the main trade unions to focus their attention on influencing legislative changes.[10] More recently, awareness raising activities, such as

[5] For example, through the work conducted by 'Alleanza contro la povertà', an association bringing together social partners and stakeholders in order to contribute to the debate and policy development to counteract absolute poverty.

[6] For example, the campaign and collective bargaining commitment from the large trade union FNV on general price compensation in wage revisions and increases of minimum wages as reported on in media and press releases from FNV. See eg www.ad.nl/werk/fnv-lonen-stijgen-door-maar-inflatie-spook-blijft-probleem~a3e5d878 (last visited 3 March 2022) or FNV press release from 15 December 2021, available at www.fnv.nl/nieuwsbericht/algemeen-nieuws/2022/01/lonen-moeten-automatisch-meestijgen-met-de-prijzen (last visited 27 June 2023).

[7] On the problems facing temporary agency workers the trade union CNV conducted research in 2019 that showed vast problems for these workers to make ends meet, which has been picked up by the media (see 'Uitzendkracht komt amper rond', *De Telegraaf* (22 October 2019)) and political parties (through questions asked by the Labour Party in the Parliament, with the Minister of Social Affairs responding, see Parliamentary Documents 14 November 2019, no 732). In relation to platform workers, ie workers who find work through the use of digital platforms, the trade union FNV has initiated court cases in order to get these workers classified as employees and as such fall under the application of collective agreements.

[8] In addition to the examples on price compensation in wage revisions FNV has also campaigned for tax relief for certain groups of people with very low incomes, see www.fnv.nl/nieuwsbericht/sectornieuws/uitkeringsgerechtigden/2021/10/fnv-presenteert-plan-voor-lokale-armoedebestrijdin (last visited 27 June 2023).

[9] As discussed in relation to the different VUP Groups in M Houwerzijl et al, 'National Report: The Netherlands', Working, Yet Poor (2021), available at workingyetpoor.eu/deliverables.

[10] For the extension of the scope of application of the minimum wage rate see: Polish Journal of Laws of 2016, item 1265. A trade union has been created for the self-employed, with the website: www.prawo.pl/kadry/jest-pierwszy-zwiazek-zawodowy-samozatrudnionych,510673.html. The positive potential, but somewhat limited impact, of the activities, is discussed more in detail in: M Tomaszewska, 'National report: Poland', Working, Yet Poor (2021), available at workingyetpoor.eu/deliverables.

trainings and workshops concerning the working poor, have been organised by one of the main Polish trade unions.[11]

In Germany both awareness and interest in addressing the issue of poverty is fairly developed amongst social partners, especially trade unions. In addition to setting up specific departments dedicated to dealing with different policy areas,[12] German trade unions also run campaigns against what they coin as 'poverty wages' in connection to collective bargaining rounds.[13] However, poverty is in general understood as tantamount to 'receipt of social assistance benefits' and connected to severe material deprivation rather than relative poverty.[14]

Explicit reference to the problem of in-work poverty seems to be less common, but there are examples, such as Luxembourg where the Workers' Chamber (Chambre des Salariés, 'CSL') has included a section on in-work poverty in its annual publication since 2018,[15] although mainly focusing on the issue of raising the minimum wage. The largest trade union has demanded a net increase of the minimum wage, but this campaign seems not to have been actively linked to the issue of in-work poverty.[16] Trade union activities and engagement in policy and law-making debates have an impact, but the low degree of awareness and/or interest directed towards in-work poverty may be connected to the fact that poverty problems are mainly affecting foreigners and non-voters, causing weak incentives for political parties to engage.[17]

In Belgium, examples of explicit reference to in-work poverty can be found on the websites of the major social partners (especially trade unions), which have also shown interest in poverty,[18] and on minimum wages as a means to combat in-work

---

[11] Initiatives aiming at raising awareness of the consequences of precarious employment were initiated by the trade union NSZZ Solidarność; information about this can be found at www.solidarnoscfiat.pl/biedny-jak-pracownik.html (last visited 3 March 2022).

[12] The German Trade Union Confederation DGB has policy departments directed towards: labour market policy; education and training; digital work environments; fundamental questions and social policy; international and European trade union policy; legal issues; social security; structural, industrial and service policy; and economic, financial and tax policy. Larger trade unions also have such departments, see eg the case of ver.di at www.verdi.de/wegweiser/++co++d4f7c526-62bb-11e1-725e-0019b9e321cd (last visited 3 March 2022).

[13] For an example in relation to recent such activities see: www.dgb.de/aktuelle-nachrichten/tarifver-handlungen-tarifrunden-tarifrunde-streiks-warnstreiks (last visited 3 March 2022).

[14] In spite of the large low-wage sector in Germany and discussions on low wages and wage equality being important issues for social partners, the implications for relative income poverty are rarely referred to. For further discussions relating to the large German low-wage sector see eg: B Waas and C Hiessl, 'National Report: Germany', Working, Yet Poor (2021), especially 67 ff, 88, 95, 105 ff and 111 ff, available at workingyetpoor.eu/deliverables.

[15] See CSL, *Panorama Social 2018*, pp 107–10, with reference to the proposal of increasing the minimum wage at 26; CSL *Panorama Social 2019*, 117,120; *Panorama Social 2020*, 120, 123 and *Panorama Social 2021*, 98, 101.

[16] R Urbé, *In-work poverty in Luxembourg* (European Social Policy Network, 2019) 15, 16.

[17] ibid 15 and footnote 56.

[18] As found in the research project IPSWICH and explained in M Goos, G Van Gyes and S Vandekerckhove, *IPSWICH Policy Note II – Minimum Wages and In-Work Poverty*. Belspo (2018), available at hiva.kuleuven.be/nl/onderzoek/thema/arbeidenor/p/Docs/ipswichdocs/ipswich_pn2 (last visited 3 March 2022).

poverty.[19] The situation in Belgium appears very unusual in comparison with the other countries.

Thus, when the problem is addressed, it is usually done only on a specific issue, for example low minimum wages, but most often in-work poverty is only implicit within the campaigns. Explicitly targeting in-work poverty is rare, and a holistic approach where the issues of low wages, part-time work, fixed-term contracts and precarious forms of employment, and consequences for social security schemes are linked to each other in relation to the problem of in-work poverty, is lacking.

Worth noting is that the activities accounted for are in general activities driven by trade unions. Employers' organisations seem to be generally silent on this issue.[20] This cautious position can be problematic because a joint effort from both sides of the labour market would most likely render the fight against in-work poverty more effective.

Awareness of in-work poverty is a preliminary condition of social partners' ability to address the issue. However, there are challenges mainly relating to two problems for social partners: membership levels, especially for trade unions, and the structures of collective bargaining in some countries.

A. Opportunities for Addressing In-work Poverty

We have identified some developments that can be considered as opportunities for the social partners to gain momentum, legitimacy and new arenas for activities and strategies aiming at combating in-work poverty risks. Two broader spheres of such opportunities can be explained as tendencies for increasing awareness of the risks associated with precarious employment conditions and a current increasingly active EU policy maker in the realms of social and employment policy.

In more recent years, the risks associated with precarious employment have gained attention in the public debate, but during the Covid-19 pandemic precarious work was clearly linked to broader societal risks.[21] For example, the poor employment and working conditions for employees within Swedish health and care services were a contributing factor for the many deaths amongst elderly

---

[19] In this regard the campaign for a minimum wage of €14 is notable (see O Flohimont, ' "Fight for 14". The campaign for a decent minimum wage of €14 per hour in Belgium' (2019) 25(3) *Transfer* 381.) and with the views of trade unions discussed in Goos, Van Gyes and Vandekerckhove (n 18).

[20] A clear example of this is the contribution by a representative of the German employers' organisation BDA in the coming German publication from the Working, Yet Poor project: B Baykal, 'Gesellschaftliche Erfolge wahrnehmen – Chancen anerkennen – Brücken nutzen' in C Hiessl and B Waas (eds), *Sozialer Fortschritt – Sonderausgabe: Armut trotz Arbeit in Deutschland, Sozialer Fortschritt*, (2023), Vol 72, Issue 2, 171.

[21] A more detailed discussion with useful references to several studies can be found in D Purkayastha et al, 'Work, Health and Covid-19: A Literature Review', Report 2021.03, ETUI, especially section 4.2.

persons in Swedish elderly care during the pandemic.[22] The focus on precariat generates a momentum to further address the issue of in-work poverty in a holistic way.

After almost a decade in which the EU institutions undertook initiatives to support austerity measures and structural reforms concerning mostly the decentralisation of collective bargaining structures and wage stagnation or deflation, especially in relation to the countries that were hit the hardest by the crisis,[23] during the pandemic crisis the direction of EU measures turned in a completely different direction. Focus was directed towards securing the existence of jobs and enterprises. EU Member States were given room to support companies.[24] The social consequences of crises are now of higher importance, and it is now considered necessary to invest in order to limit social risks rather than simply focus on cutting costs and assuring economic savings in a short-term perspective. This changed direction in the development of EU policy is reflected by the most recent initiatives that are relevant to the issue of in-work poverty and the four Vulnerable and Underrepresented Persons (VUP) groups, namely the Directive on adequate minimum wages in the EU, the package of initiatives involving a proposal for a Directive concerning improvement of working conditions in platform work[25] and a proposal for guidelines on the application of collective agreements for solo self-employed in light of EU competition law.[26] These initiatives highlight the need to address poor working and employment conditions as well as the importance of collective bargaining structures for a well-functioning regulation of labour markets in the EU.

III. Articulating of In-work Poverty as a Problem

Understanding the driving factors behind in-work poverty shows possibilities for a shift towards a discussion of what risk factors contribute to the problem

---

[22] The recommendation on this with adjacent motivations can be found in the Government White Paper presenting the first conclusions of the Corona commission concerning Swedish elderly care specifically. See SOU 2020:80 *Äldreomsorgen under pandemin*, section 10.2.2.

[23] Discussed in depth from different angles, but importantly in relation to the financial and economic crisis in 2008–2009, in: N Bruun, K Lörcher and I Schömann (eds), *The Economic and Financial Crisis and Collective Labour Law in Europe* (Oxford, Hart Publishing 2014).

[24] This change in the focus of the EU is briefly discussed in relation to the concept of solidarity in A Hartzén, A Iossa and E Karageorgiou, 'Introduction to *Law, Solidarity and the Limits of Social Europe*' in A Hartzén, A Iossa and E Karageorgiou (eds), *Law, Solidarity and the Limits of Social Europe: Constitutional Tensions for EU Integration* (Edward Elgar Publishing, 2022). For an insight into the different measures and approaches taken in specific countries see Special Issue: Covid-19 and Labour Law – A Global Review (2020) 13(1S) *Italian Labour Law e-Journal*.

[25] European Commission, Proposal for a Directive of the European Parliament and of the Council on improving working conditions in platform work, Brussels, COM(2021) 762 final.

[26] European Commission. Annex to the Communication from the Commission – Approval of the content of a draft for a Communication from the Commission. Guidelines on the application of EU competition law to collective agreements regarding the working conditions of solo self-employed, Brussels, C(2021) 8838 final.

and how they can be addressed. Such a shift in focus would most likely be more conducive for providing solutions, than focusing the discussion on whether or not in-work poverty is a problem, because of the multifaceted character of the concept.

The lack of explicit articulation of the problem of in-work poverty in a holistic manner relates both to the social partners and to the attitude of national policy makers. Under these circumstances, the visibility of in-work poverty in the public debate will most likely be very low, but if social partners were more active in setting the issue on the agenda for the public debate, the general understanding of the problem would also increase. As such, there are reasons to reflect on both how social partners and national policy makers could deal with the potential for social partners to address or be given the possibility for addressing in-work poverty in a more constructive manner. Below, we will start by discussing potential for future increased articulation of the problem of in-work poverty amongst the social partners as a way forward in their role of addressing this problem.

A. Social Partners' Possible Strategies

As has been discussed above, it is not exactly the case that social partners are completely unaware of the problem of in-work poverty. However, in several cases there seems to be a reluctance to address the issue explicitly and a preference for formulating campaigns and activities mostly aiming at decent working conditions in general, or higher wages in particular. The issue of poverty seems more often discussed in terms of severe material deprivation in circumstances of unemployment or in relation to low minimum wages, than in connection to the problem of in-work poverty with its complex and multifaceted causes. With the rather important role that collective bargaining and collective agreements still play for the labour markets in many of the countries investigated, there are opportunities for the social partners to actually address the issue of in-work poverty if they wish to do so.

i. Trade Unions

Trade unions face the difficult task of balancing claims based on arguments relating to poverty reduction and holding a strong negotiating position in relation to the employers' side in collective bargaining. There is a clear risk that antipoverty campaigns might sound like arguments asking for charity from the employers in the first case, whereas arguments based on workers' fair share of the gains they participate in creating for the employer is definitely more into the skills of trade unionists.[27]

---

[27] We are grateful to Christina Hiessl for highlighting this issue in the German version of the national analyses complementing previous deliverables in the preparation of this report.

In addition, only a few of the Member States hold structures of collective bargaining where trade unions are currently in a position of securing, in collective agreements, claims that would explicitly address and contribute to a reduction of in-work poverty.[28] As such, the main channel for trade unions to strengthen their role in addressing in-work poverty is likely to be lobbying and participation in the general debate. Trade unions do promote issues of relevance for the problem of in-work poverty and several of these issues could possibly render increased visibility and public support if placed in a framework of driving factors for in-work poverty. By connecting arguments relating to problems caused by precarious employments with the problem of in-work poverty, it is not unlikely that trade unions would secure both an increased public support for such arguments, and also gain visibility and credibility as unions striving to promote the interests of workers by improving conditions on the labour market.[29] This would most likely require increased knowledge and a potential change of strategy among trade unions. A first step for trade unions would thus be to include the problem of in-work poverty in activities promoting learning and strategy formation amongst their staff, representatives and members. Initiating training programs, workshops and activities through which knowledge could be shared and action plans could be formed, potentially also in cooperation with in-work poverty researchers, would thus be a useful start.[30] From there, initiatives seeking to assure that campaigns go through an internal check in relation to their relevance for factors affecting in-work poverty and assuring that such a connection is clear in all relevant campaigns could be the next step.

There are also possibilities for trade unions to develop strategies for addressing in-work poverty from the perspective of so-called 'free runner' companies that stay in business mainly due to exploitative practices. There is an example within the restaurant sector in the city of Malmö in Sweden, where trade unions in cooperation with local civil society organisations have joined forces in creating awareness of and protests against businesses run with exploitative practices. In this case, a local trade union organisation and a neighbourhood civil society organisation

---

[28] Even though there are examples of clauses relevant to the situation of some of the VUP groups in collective agreements in different Member States, the impact on in-work poverty is questionable in most cases. For a discussion relating to the countries covered in the Working, Yet Poor project see: C Zoli et al, 'Social partners and industrial relations system report', Working, Yet Poor (2021), especially chapter 5.

[29] The importance of focusing on improving the conditions for the more vulnerable workers on the labour market as a factor underlying the formation of trade union strategies that also become successful in improving conditions on the labour market in relation to international trade union cooperation is discussed in: A Hartzén, 'The European Social Dialogue in Perspective: its future potential as an autopoietic system and lessons from the global maritime system of industrial relations' (Dissertation, Lund University, 2017), eg at 323 ff.

[30] The fact that initiatives for awareness raising on the dangers of precarious employment have been taken in the form of training and workshops in Poland (information about this can be found at www.solidarnoscfiat.pl/biedny-jak-pracownik.html last visited 3 March 022) is a strong argument in favour of trade unions in other countries with stronger trade union structures to also be able to do so.

cooperated and started boycotts against restaurants run by employers who were deemed to apply indecent working conditions at their workplace. Information about the boycott and the restaurants concerned was spread by both the trade union and the neighbourhood organisation using social media and posters in the neighbourhood. The action led to several restaurants being put out of business due to lack of customers.[31]

This example shows how cooperation between trade unions and local civil society organisations can make an impact in terms of eroding the market for business run through the use of exploitative practices and, as such, improving the competitive situation for decent employers. This, in turn, can contribute to decreasing the pressure on employers to make use of employment practices that contribute to in-work poverty risks. Such forms of cooperation do of course require a certain organisational capacity within the trade union as well as the presence of civil society organisations with suitable local connections and organisational resources to handle the initiative. As such this might not be an alternative readily available everywhere, but it is certainly a form of strategy to be used as best practice and included as part of training activities and workshops for strategy formation, when such initiatives are launched.

ii. Employers' Organisations

As has been mentioned above, employers' organisations have been less active or at least less visible than trade unions in relation to the issue of in-work poverty. When these organisations do engage, the stance taken seems more likely to be in the form of redirecting the discussion away from the problem of in-work poverty and instead focusing on the possibilities for labour market entry generated through some of the jobs with higher in-work poverty risks.[32] This situation might rise concern and, also to some extent, may represent a missed opportunity for employers' organisations in managing responsible businesses. The example given above, on the restaurant sector in the Swedish city Malmö, shows the potential of raising awareness amongst customers concerning working conditions and employment practices.

Another example, showing the potential that employers and their representative organisations may have in relation to decent working conditions and assuring better competitive practices on the market for responsible businesses is the temporary agency work sector in Sweden. This is a sector where initial fears of a growing

---

[31] The whole situation and events were covered in a series of articles in local press, see the article series with the theme "Krogbojkotten på Möllan" (the boycott of restaurants in the quartiers of Möllan) in Sydsvenskan, available at www.sydsvenskan.se/story/6220ebdb-5fcc-4790-b81d-ea4ef7300dac (last visited 24 March 2022).

[32] This is for example the case in the contribution by a representative of the German employers' organisation BDA in the coming German publication of the Working, Yet Poor project; see Baykal (n 20).

market for poor employment conditions have been addressed in sectoral collective agreements, in a manner that both assures decent wages and limits the use of
precarious forms of employment contracts. Such clauses in collective agreements
were not only demands from trade unions; instead, the employers' organisation
also saw a need for assuring decent standards in order to legitimise the sector and
increase the market potential. In line with this, the employers' organisation for the
sector also required the application of sectoral collective agreements in order for
temporary work agencies to become members and be registered as certified agencies in the sector.[33] This has generated a situation where risks of in-work poverty
seem lower for temporary agency workers than other flexible forms of employment in Sweden today.[34] Thus, running business responsibly, in a manner that
limits risks of in-work poverty amongst employees, can be a market advantage if
clients are well-informed and aware of the problem of in-work poverty.

In this sense employers and employers' organisations have an interest in join-
ing trade unions in activities that aim to increase awareness concerning in-work
poverty. For employers' organisations and their members, in-work poverty could
be an issue worth reflecting upon in development of sectoral practices, certificates
or other forms of documentation that could be useful in order to highlight and
spread information about decent employment practices in a specific sector or a
specific geographical area. In addition to potential marketing advantages for businesses participating in such initiatives, there could also be results in the form of
pressure on less responsible employers to improve working conditions in order to
maintain their position on the market. Inspiration for this could be found in developments of corporate social sustainability practices at international level, where
increasing attention towards workers' situation within the company's supply chain
and methods for controlling and assuring decent conditions have been adopted in
various forms.[35]

Adapting such forms of strategies to a 'local level social sustainability strategy'[36]
could thus be a useful strategy for employers and their representative organisations to contribute to raising awareness and addressing in-work poverty. How such
initiatives would be best formed are likely to vary between sectors and possibly
also countries, but initiating discussions and developments of relevant activities
through training programmes and workshops, possibly also in cooperation with

---

[33] For a discussion on the temporary agency work sector and its regulation in Sweden see: A Berg,
*Bemanningsarbete, flexibilitet och likabehandling: En studie av svensk rätt och kollektivavtalsreglering
med komparativa inslag*, Juristförlaget i Lund (2008).

[34] For further discussion on the situation of in-work poverty for temporary agency workers in Sweden
see: A-C Hartzén, 'National Report: Sweden', Working, Yet Poor (2021), especially 127 ff, available at
workingyetpoor.eu/deliverables.

[35] For a highly interesting study on corporate social sustainability practices through global collective
agreements, see F Avelar Pereira, 'Global Collective Agreements: A Response to Urgent Global Labour
Concerns' (Dissertation, Lund University, 2021).

[36] The term 'local level' here is intended to indicate the entities and activities of the company taking
place at the market where the company interacts with its customers. For example, stores or warehouses
located in Europe for retail companies selling their products to consumers in Europe.

trade unions, would be a first important step. Moreover, in this direction, such activities and strategies will definitely benefit from cooperation with organisations active in consumers' consciousness, at national as well as local level. The past experience has shown that alliances of social partners with societal organisations and communities are beneficial in achieving the goals. Since in-work poverty is a complex phenomenon and tackling it requires several actors acting at several levels, such alliances would pave the way for more effective campaigns and initiatives.

B. Policy Makers

At EU level the issue of in-work poverty has been put in the spotlight, not least through the fairly strong focus on this issue in the European Commission documents related to the proposal for a Directive on adequate minimum wages.[37] As has been discussed above, the issue is gaining importance with EU policy making institutions and this will most likely affect policy makers at national level.[38] Even though the situation concerning in-work poverty differs between Member States, there are some issues which all Member State policy makers could actually consider, and develop an approach bringing stronger awareness of the issue of in-work poverty. Broadly defined these issues can be divided into a field encompassing the link between employment conditions and in-work poverty on the one hand, and the relevance of collective bargaining structures for assuring protection against in-work poverty risks on the other hand. However, the initial step would in several countries actually be to raise awareness and increase knowledge about the problem as such amongst the policy makers themselves. An initial step with training sessions and knowledge formation would thus be desirable in most countries.

In relation to the issue of collective bargaining structures, their relevance for addressing in-work poverty and the role of national policy makers in raising awareness, we have in principle identified one form of suggestion possible for all national policy makers. However, the suggestion as such could be developed to varying degrees depending on circumstances and specific national contexts. The suggestion is already indicated above in terms of the suggestion that policy makers could serve from participation in training activities in cooperation with social partners. In other words, we propose that policy makers should initiate various forms of training and knowledge generating activities in order to assure possibilities for creating a dialogue with social partners on potential actions for addressing

---

[37] As discussed above. European Commission, Proposal for a Directive of the European Parliament and of the Council on improving working conditions in platform work, Brussels, COM(2021) 762 final.

[38] This chapter does not attempt to provide concrete policy proposals in relation to eg social security structures, since this aspect will be developed in other parts of this volume. Instead, this chapter discusses the role of social partners in addressing in-work poverty and how policy makers can contribute.

in-work poverty. Depending on national conditions, such dialogue could be developed into discussions and evaluations of social partner involvement and actions concerning future policy proposals and their consequences for in-work poverty. In countries where social partners are less equipped to take concrete actions or responsibility for policy development or implementation it could instead be useful for the national policy maker to explicitly include the issue of in-work poverty as a problem to be assessed when social partners are invited to express opinions or statements[39] in relation to debate and developments of national policies.

IV. Strengthening Social Partners

Amongst the challenges for social partners to address in-work poverty, we have identified the issue of weakening of collective bargaining structures as recurrent, for example in the problems with declining trade union density and various forms of destabilisation of collective bargaining structures. In order for the social partners to be able to constructively and legitimately contribute to the regulation of labour market and, as such, pave the way for them to more efficiently address the problem of in-work poverty, there is a need for strengthening the social partners. Thus, the social partners themselves have a role to play, but national policy makers can definitely make a difference. The ambition in this section is to provide suggestions for the different actors in the strive to strengthen social partners, with specific focus on increasing their legitimacy for addressing in-work poverty.

A. Increasing Membership Incentives

As has been discussed above, national systems of collective bargaining are being challenged in various manners, not least in terms of decreasing membership levels for trade unions and to varying degrees from decentralisation tendencies and increasing tensions between employers in various sectors and/or at different levels. These developments call for a need to increase the incentives for membership and participation in collective interest formation both for trade unions and employers' organisations. Action is needed from both sides of industry in order to counteract the tendencies of erosion of collective bargaining systems. Such actions need to be understood in relation to the ongoing developments involving increasing labour market flexibilisation and movement. The following sections will provide some

---

[39] Regardless of the actual strength of national collective bargaining structures it seems as if social partners, in all countries included in the Working, Yet Poor project, to some degree have a voice in relation to development of national policy and/or legislation relating to the labour market. The national analyses on which this chapter relies all indicate some form of voice for social partners in policy creation at the national level.

suggestions in relation to the need for adaptation due to increasing labour market movements, both for trade unions and employers' organisations.

i. Increasing Labour Market Movements Require Adaptation

With increasing shares of unstable employments on the labour market,[40] there is likely to be an increased form of movement on the labour market. Since younger workers tend to be over-represented in temporary and precarious employments,[41] they are also likely to be part of labour market movement in terms of moving between employment statuses and between jobs, potentially also between sectors. Under such circumstances, the role (and the benefits to be part) of a trade union might not be evident to these categories of workers, either because the workplaces they work in are less unionised or because their experience at a workplace usually lasts too short time for them to be able to build the sense of solidarity that generally would be an incentive for union membership.

Young people do not show stronger anti-union sentiments than older workers; instead, their low degree of membership is connected to a lack of awareness of the role and importance of trade unions.[42] Therefore, the movement of young people on the labour market mentioned above means that workplace information and communication may not be the most efficient manner of seeking to spread awareness of the role and importance of trade unions to young people. There is a need for adaptation in terms of the societal conversation about collective bargaining, workplace representation and the role of trade unions in the workplace as well as a need to increase visibility for these discussions and assure better chances of, for example, reaching young people in order to deal with their lack of awareness. It might be that the labour market parties and policy makers need to further consider the role of the educational system in providing knowledge about labour market structures and the role and function of trade unions in order to bridge the awareness gap. Lobbying for increased coverage of labour market structures in school curricula may thus be an important way forward, but there are also other forms of adaptation needed and, even though trade unions themselves are key actors in this context, employer organisations can also play an important role.

---

[40] Even though the share of fixed-term work may indicate a fairly stable level, the form of fixed-term contracts used seem to undergo some changes towards shorter contracts or contracts with less predictable working patterns. For a study discussing this and the consequences for workers, not least young workers, in Sweden see: J Alfonsson, *Alienation och arbete: Unga behovsanställdas villkor i den flexibla kapitalismen* (Arkiv, 2020).

[41] The national reports from the Working, Yet Poor project show that younger workers are over-represented amongst fixed-term workers and involuntary part-time workers in practically all the countries included in the project.

[42] The question of lack of awareness and absence of membership traditions in workplaces, rather than anti-union sentiments, are highlighted as more important explanations for non-membership amongst young workers in: K Vandaele, *Bleak prospects: mapping trade union membership in Europe since 2000* (ETUI, 2019), eg at 29 ff.

In order to uphold and/or strengthen systems of industrial relations and their role in addressing in-work poverty (along with other problematic issues on the labour market), both trade unions and employers' organisations need to take responsibility and act consequently.

In the following sections we will discuss possibilities for social partners in seeking to increase incentives for membership through, for example, increased knowledge about the positive aspects of well-functioning collective bargaining structures on the labour market. We will first provide some suggestions for trade unions and, then, for employers' organisations on issues relating to the need to increase incentives for both membership and participation in collective bargaining structures.

ii. Trade Unions

Trade unions are, as mentioned above, facing challenges of declining trade union membership in combination with increasing age amongst their members.[43] As such, trade unions need to adapt their strategies not only to assure that they reach and are heard by younger workers, but also to assure that trade union membership appears attractive to young workers and other workers that tend to be under-represented by trade unions. This is especially the case in relation to workers in precarious forms of employment among whom it seems trade unions have more difficulties in building awareness. In our opinion, this indicates that trade unions need not only to reconsider their communication channels and activities for reaching potential new members, but they also need to reconsider and reassess their membership strategies and services. It would be extremely beneficial for trade unions to assure that what their membership offers is attractive enough to workers moving between employment statuses, workplaces, and potentially also sectors of the labour market; ultimately, non-unionised workers should see easily the substantial gains of becoming a trade union member.

When declining membership levels are one of the most important challenges facing trade unions – and this challenge is particularly pertinent in relation to workers who potentially find themselves amongst those with higher rates of movement on the labour market – then trade unions need to consider whether existing loyalty strategies are still adequate and relevant. It seems to be fairly common that trade unions apply different forms of embargo periods for new members in relation to certain services.[44] However, these practices can constitute obstacles or forms

---

[43] Vandaele (n 42).

[44] In Germany, IG Metall requires prior membership of three months before granting its members any support in legal disputes or industrial conflicts and also applies differentiated amounts of strike pay depending on length of membership (sections 23, 24 and 27 of the IG Metall bylaws). The Dutch FNV does not provide legal assistance for cases that have arisen before a person became a member and they also require newer members to remain as a member for two years in order to provide legal assistance other than mere information or advice (Articles 3.4, 3.6 and 4.1.2 in FNV General Terms and

of disincentives for atypical workers in the short run. After all, low paid workers would find it difficult to pay a membership fee to an organisation from whom they may not be offered support if needed during the first period of membership, especially if this happens in the framework of an uncertain employment situation. These issues may be particularly acute in countries where trade unions are structured according to professions and the next employment move for a person would also generate a need to change their trade union membership. It may simply be that it is time for trade unions to drastically reconsider their practices for achieving loyalty amongst their members. Trade unions need to direct more focus on how to become more relevant and interesting for all workers, not mainly those in stable employment who are already members of the trade union or working in a workplace where trade union membership is considered natural.

In order to achieve such increased relevance, trade unions thus need to increase the visibility of the work they do and activities carried out for protecting interests of workers. In sum, it has to become evident to non-members why trade unions are relevant and what added value trade union membership has. Adopting and framing campaigns and activities through the in-work poverty lens may contribute to this, by sharpening the tone of communications and showing clearly that trade union activities are relevant for workers in precarious employments. As has been discussed above, such reframing of communication would require trade unions to gain more knowledge and insight into the issue of in-work poverty and its driving forces.[45] Many of the issues trade unions actually do promote are of relevance from an in-work poverty perspective, but nevertheless the problem is not highlighted in their campaigns, except for some examples related to minimum wage levels. Framing campaigns and communication towards the aim of combating in-work poverty could in our view also contribute to increased visibility.

iii. Employers' Organisations

As discussed above, employers' organisations have been less active than trade unions and also to some extent have sought to redirect the debate on in-work poverty towards other issues such as flexible employments as stepping stones for labour market establishment in relation to persons facing challenges to enter the labour market.[46] This does not indicate that they are incapable or unwilling to address in-work poverty or some of the factors causing in-work poverty.

Conditions for Individual Legal Assistance). Also Swedish trade unions apply different forms of clauses to foster loyalty such as requirements of a certain seniority of membership in order to receive strike pay (Article 8.2 in the bylaws of If Metall) or restrictions on legal advice and services for newer members (Article 5.4 in the bylaws of Kommunal or Article 2.2.3 in the bylaws of Unionen).

[45] As discussed above in section II.A, even though trade unions are aware, to some extent, of the phenomenon of in-work poverty, it seems to be a problem that they mainly address within campaigns concerning minimum wages, and the holistic understanding of the problem of in-work poverty may not be fully understood or assessed.

[46] See section II.A above for this discussion.

Instead, employers' organisations have proven themselves apt of finding methods for assuring decent conditions amongst their members, not least when problems within the sector concerned cause difficulties due to bad reputation of the sector or unfair competition based on low standards.[47] With current developments in proposals for due diligence meeting support from industry,[48] it seems there could be an opportunity for developing further initiatives amongst employers and their organisations addressing problems of unfair competition based on employers applying employment practices that contribute more or less directly to in-work poverty. Adopting authorisation or certification processes for companies that comply with set criteria for counteracting in-work poverty could be one way for employers' organisations to take a more active role in addressing in-work poverty in the future. Such authorisation/certification could be combined with the establishment of principles for selecting suppliers and/or cooperation partners only amongst other in-work poverty certified companies in order to further enhance market opportunities and competitive advantages for companies that fulfil the authorisation/certification requirements. The existence of certifications involving quality and regulatory compliances show that such procedures can have impact[49] and including criteria related to in-work poverty causes in existing processes or setting up new structures for such criteria could thus be a possible way forward.

B. Potential Support of Collective Bargaining from Policy Makers

As discussed in the previous section, with stronger social partners and collective bargaining structures there is also a higher probability that the social partners will address problems such as in-work poverty though protective mechanisms in collective agreements or other forms of collectively bargained protections. Policy makers could provide support, for example, to collectively agreed insurance schemes that complement social security, specifically for workers at risk of in-work poverty, in a manner that relieves costs for employers. If suitable conditions for such schemes could be identified, then those schemes could also fill a dual function. They could both provide incentives for unionisation of workers at risk of in-work poverty, since they in many cases are less likely to be unionised, and support and encourage the strengthening of collective bargaining structures.

---

[47] In this regard it serves to once again highlight the example of the Swedish temporary agency work sector with the employers' organisation setting up authorisation requirements and actively participating in assuring decent wage regulations for workers in order to improve the image of the sector and increase market possibilities for temporary work agencies.

[48] See, eg European Commission, Directorate-General for Justice and Consumers, et al, 'Study on due diligence requirements through the supply chain: final report' (Publications Office, 2020).

[49] In relation to this it is worth mentioning eg ISO certification.

Other forms of initiatives by policy makers may include setting up funds and initiatives to allow for reductions of normal working time without lowering the total pay. Specifically directed financial support for sectors where collective agreements reduce the normal working hours without pay decreases could have a high impact on the possibilities for social partners to address the problem of in-work poverty. This is due to the strong link between in-work poverty and part-time work, where issues such as health problems or high demands of the job in certain sectors also cause difficulties for workers to retain a full-time job throughout their working life. Specific financial support for reduction of the normal working hours through collective agreements in sectors where these problems with part-time work are more pertinent would not only address the issue of in-work poverty, but could also have an impact on work-life balance. At present there seem to be fairly low degrees of activities relating to shortened working weeks,[50] but the strong link between part-time work and in-work poverty, with high shares of involuntary part-time workers actually working part-time for health reasons, highlight the need to take the issue of reduced working hours more seriously. As such, national policy makers would need to step in and provide the right incentives for putting the issue back on the agenda.

V. Concluding Remarks

Throughout this investigation, it has been evident that the role of social partners in addressing in-work poverty is relevant, however it is quite limited due to a variety of structural problems. In recent decades, waves of flexibilisation of the labour market along with profound changes in the workforce have resulted (among other things) in weakening the traditional labour laws' employment protection as well as decreasing the social strengths of trade unions in supporting decent conditions of employment. So, we can say that the legal framework, especially following the structural reforms that several Members States have been undertaking in the aftermath of the financial crisis, has played a decisive role in letting working poverty spread without due legal support. Indeed, if one of the major problems that lead to in-work poverty is short or unpredictable working time arrangements (no matter what employment contract specifically considered), then a change in the law in impeding at least the worst casual forms of employment practices would be useful.

At this point, a revision of existing EU provisions on working time would be appropriate. This is definitely one area on which trade unions and, in general, social partners would be well placed to immediately start a serious discussion.

---

[50] The national analyses prepared within the Working, Yet Poor consortium for this chapter indicated that, at best, there were some examples of workplaces where reduced weekly working hours were implemented for a while, but the issue remains more or less dormant within most trade unions in the countries concerned.

Fortunately, after two decades of austerity, there seem to be consensus in Europe on the importance of effective and protected social rights,[51] thus at least at policy level the new context is very welcome. Any considerations on the actual impact of the many initiatives that are currently discussed or have been recently adopted (in primis, the Directive on adequate minimum wages) would definitely sound premature and, to some extent, reckless. However, the context is promising and opens room for more effective initiatives from all stakeholders, including social partners at all levels and national policy makers.

This chapter has also shown a problem with actors being not completely aware of the complexity of the phenomena behind the label of working poor (mainly for the trade union side) or almost indifferent to it (mainly for employers' associations). Further investigations and alliances between researchers with social partners can actually foster the circulation of knowledge among labour market actors. But when it comes to concrete actions and initiatives, it seems that the multifaceted dimension of in-work poverty asks social partners to seek alliances and cooperation outside the labour market. It would be useful for them to engage with civil society entities and movements that can bring into the strategy the considerations and the capabilities of consumers or local and community activists, as the inspiring experience on the Swedish city of Malmö clearly showed.

To this extent, it is evident that social partners should be put in the position to express their potential, and not only in the traditional realm of industrial relations, with measures aiming to increase trade union membership and employers' association density, or to re-centralise the collective bargaining structure. Social partners should also be able to participate fully in the economic and political debate about concrete and effective measures to fight in-work poverty through policy and regulatory tools that the Member States and the EU institutions are equipped with.

---

[51] As discussed for example in T Schulten and T Müller, 'A paradigm shift towards Social Europe? The proposed Directive on Adequate minimum wages in the European Union' (2021) 1(14) *Italian Labour Law e-Journal*.

PART IV

Identifying New Pathways
for Further Research

10

Socio-fiscal Welfare: Unveiling the Hidden Welfare State

PAUL SCHOUKENS, ALEXANDER DOCKX
AND ELENI DE BECKER

I. Introduction

Socio-fiscal welfare is traditionally understood as a form of welfare where no actual money is transferred to the beneficiary in any way. Rather, tax expenditures are usually regarded as the bedrock of benefit distribution. These are special provisions in the tax code that deviate from standard taxation rules on income, usually to benefit specific activities or groups of taxpayers. The result is that the beneficiary is released from having to pay the full, standard amount of tax (hereafter: 'benchmark tax') by being offered 'tax expenditures'. In practice, individuals entitled to a tax expenditure indicate so in their tax file. The amount of the granted expenditure is intended to lower the person's tax burden by the same value as direct social transfer would have had. The intended consequence is, of course, citizens being able to spend the income they are not owed in taxes on private social schemes instead. The end result is that this alleviates the need for the state to create social services to distribute benefits, as the private market fulfils this role.[1]

---

[1] S Barrios et al, 'The Fiscal and Equity Impact of Tax Expenditures in the European Union', JRC Working Papers on Taxation and Structural Reforms No 1/2016, 2; P Macdaniel and S Surrey, *Tax Expenditures* (Cambridge, Massachusetts, Harvard University Press, 1985) 3; N Morel, C Touzet and M Zemmour, 'Fiscal Welfare in Europe: A State of the Art', LIEPP Working Paper no 45 (2016) 4; N Morel, C Touzet and M Zemmour, 'Fiscal Welfare in Europe: Why Should We Care and What Do We Know so Far?' (2018) 28(5) *Journal of European Social Policy* 551, 556; J Owens, 'Tax Expenditures and Direct Expenditures as Instruments of Social Policy' in C Sijbren (ed), *Comparative Tax Studies* (Amsterdam, North Holland Publishing Company, 1983) 171–80; A Sinfield, 'Social Security Through Taxation' in J Berghman et al (eds), *Social Security, Taxation and Europe* (Antwerpen, Maklu, 1993) 21–25; A Stebbing and B Spies-Butcher, 'Universal Welfare by "Other Means"? Social Tax Expenditures and the Australian Dual Welfare State' (2010) 39(4) *Journal of Social Policy* 585, 585–86; C Touzet, 'The Politics of Negative Expansion – The Left's Turn to Fiscal Welfare for Low-income Groups in Britain and France in the 2000's' (DPhil, Oxford, University of Oxford, 2019) 69.

In more recent years, some socio-fiscal welfare schemes have evolved towards direct benefit payments, as tax agencies started to pay out benefits directly to individuals and/or families; this can be the result of a policy where negative income tax is concretely paid out (as there is nothing left to deduct from, and the deduction turns into a direct cash transfer in benefit form). It can go one step further when the tax agency starts to pay out benefits directly to the individual (even when no tax is due). In other words, socio-fiscal welfare started to embrace direct money transfers as well (benefit payments), as we can see happening, eg in the Netherlands (see section IV.D).

The Working, Yet Poor project offers a vast array of analyses on the effects certain policy choices have on poverty among working people. A large part of the effort invested went towards mapping out the various measures through which the partner countries tackle in-work poverty, as well as the results of those measures. While this approach has allowed for a comprehensive overview of the *status quo* of in-work poverty, it has sometimes proven difficult to confirm which action or measures provides which part in the eventual protection. This became clear from the comparative analysis of the impact of social security protection conducted by the KU Leuven,[2] in which for some defined household situations of the Vulnerable and Underrepresented Persons (VUP) groups identified by the Working, Yet Poor project, simulations were carried out on the income replacement rates for unemployment and sickness schemes. Overall, we noted that for the selected households, the income replacement benefits were shown to be proportional and equivalent in relation to the previous professional income earned within the household, yet were not always sufficiently high to keep the household from poverty. Even though the poverty thresholds were not always reached, the available data also showed the importance of social assistance and other income support arrangements, such as family benefits and other targeted social measures, in particular for part-time workers. The example of the Netherlands clearly showed the importance of additional measures, alongside unemployment and sickness benefits which guaranteed that income of at least the poverty threshold of 60 per cent of the median equivalent income was achieved for single persons and single parents with two young children.[3]

In other words, there was a gap between the Working, Yet Poor macro-data on poverty and the micro-analyses of the comparative study which could not be explained. To what extent this additional protection is provided by which component of income support is also difficult to explain. In relation to the VUP groups, we can conclude that income support measures, such as social assistance, family benefits, housing benefits, income tax and/or targeted tax deductions do have an impact on keeping families out of poverty, but we do not always know to which extent each of these components has a concrete impact on the family income.

---

[2] The findings of this research are summarised in the contribution by De Becker in this book (ch 7).
[3] See for an in-depth discussion the contribution by De Becker in this book (ch 7).

This is definitely the case for more indirect support measures that are not (always) expressed in terms of defined benefits yet are granted by reductions to what one normally has to pay (eg to the tax systems). Tax deductions ('less tax paid') can also lead to income support, the amount of which will depend largely on the level of declared income and the personal situation of the tax payer (family composition, ownership of goods, mortgage, etc).

A large amount of these 'indirect support' mechanisms go unrecognised as belonging to the overall social welfare regime, but turn out to be important in combating poverty among the working poor. In some situations these mechanisms remain altogether unnoticed as even being related to social welfare, as they belong to other domains such as taxation or occupational (labour) protection. Hence these benefits are brought together under the term 'hidden welfare state'.[4] These hidden structures are hidden in both a horizontal and a vertical sense. They are 'horizontally hidden' in the sense that there is uncertainty about which structures should be considered a part of the social security system (to what extent can tax be considered social security?) Various structures contribute to the social security system without being regarded as a part of it, which leads to them being hidden in a vertical sense as well, due to the fact that it is uncertain how deep that structure is entangled within social security law.[5] Because they are not apparent, hidden welfare measures are easily overlooked when creating an overview of national welfare measures. The sum of the logged national measures does not necessarily equal the statistical results on in-work poverty. As such, hidden welfare measures constitute the blanks in this equation.

To fill in part of those blanks, this contribution will focus on describing part of this 'hidden welfare state' by analysing 'socio-fiscal welfare' measures (for an extensive description, see below) and the role these measures may have in reducing in-work poverty. On the one hand, there is lack of insight into which policies constitute socio-fiscal welfare, hiding it horizontally. On the other hand, a painful lack of data – nationally and European-wide – makes it difficult to assess the impact and size of these various socio-fiscal welfare structures, and thus hides it vertically. So far, socio-fiscal welfare has not received much attention in a European context; legal literature on the topic has been even more scarce (as the publications referred to in this chapter show). The topic, in fact, has mainly been addressed in economic studies and in a largely US-centred approach. For this reason it is important to delineate the concept and develop a typology of socio-welfare arrangements.

By functionally defining socio-welfare arrangements (section II), and by having them further categorised in a typology (section III), we hope to contribute to a further unravelling of the hidden character of these welfare arrangements.

---

[4] See on this: J Berghman, 'The Invisible Social Security' in K Boos, H Peeters and W Van Oorschot (eds), *Invisible Social Security Revisited – Essays in Honour of Jos Berghman* (Leuven, Lannoo Campus, 2014) 34.

[5] Berghman (n 4).

Inevitably this brings us to the relation socio-fiscal welfare has with (the extensively researched area of) tax expenditures as well (for an extensive description, see section IV below). While the two concepts are related, they should not be regarded as synonymous to one another. In academic literature, however, the two concepts have in fact been intertwined, to the point of being seemingly inseparable from each other. However, socio-fiscal welfare needs to be understood as a much broader concept, which includes but is not limited to social tax expenditures. In section IV, attention will be given to how to differentiate between both tax benefits and what this differentiation means for the typology of socio-welfare tax arrangements. In section V, we will focus on the European Union. More precisely, we will indicate how a functional definition and typology of socio-fiscal welfare arrangements may help the EU institutions to a more effective monitoring of national policies in relation to combating poverty and social support of working poor (families).

II. Towards a Definition of Socio-Fiscal Welfare

A. From the American Hidden Welfare State to Socio-Fiscal Welfare in the European Context

The hidden welfare state is often described as a typically American phenomenon, with the majority of academic literature on the subject being written from that perspective.[6] Tax expenditures lie at the core of the hidden welfare state and were first introduced in the American legal system by Assistant Secretary for Tax Policy Stanley Surrey. It was not until the 1974 US Congressional Budget Act that tax expenditures would first be granted a definition enshrined in law, as 'revenue losses attributable to provisions of the Federal tax laws which allow a special exclusion, exemption, or deduction from gross income or which provide a special credit, a preferential rate of tax, or a deferral of tax liability'. American legal scholar Richard Titmuss coined the term 'socio-fiscal welfare' in the 1950s to refer to a collection of tax expenditures with a social policy goal (or social tax expenditures).[7]

Since then, despite its American origins, European states have implemented a myriad of systems that also generate(d) 'hidden' welfare distribution. Naturally,

---

[6] See eg T Callaghan and A Olson, 'Unearthing the Hidden Welfare State: Race, Political Attitudes, and Unforeseen Consequences' (2017) 2 *Journal of Race, Ethnicity and Politics*; J Hacker, 'Privatizing Risk without Privatizing the Welfare State: The Hidden Politics of Social Policy Retrenchment in the United States' (2004) 2 *American Political Science Review* 98; C Howard, 'The Hidden Side of the American Welfare State' (1993) 3 *Political Science Quarterly* 108; M Prasad, 'Tax "Expenditures" and Welfare States: A Critique' (2011) 2 *The Journal of Policy History* 23.

[7] R Titmuss, *Essays on the Welfare State* (London, Allen & Unwin, 1958) and published in a re-issue in 2018: R Titmuss, 'The Social Division of Welfare' in R Titmuss, *Essays on the Welfare State (re-issue)* (Bristol, Bristol University Press, 2018) 23.

there is extensive diversity between them – although among European Organisation for Economic Co-operation and Development (OECD) countries, socio-fiscal welfare primarily appears in the context of pensions and healthcare.[8] This diversity has led to broadened and adapted definitions across Europe.[9] This brings with it difficulties on comparative inter-state reporting, as different countries use different data and calculations. As a result, a detailed numerical analysis of the implications of socio-fiscal welfare has been rather problematic.[10] In the European context, this diversity has also led to a nebulous understanding of what defines socio-fiscal welfare.[11] Additionally, several measures are often labelled as socio-fiscal welfare while they would in practice not always qualify as such. Systems (in Europe) may use their own definition of 'tax expenditures'; hence one has to settle for a broad definition able to cover the various European applications of socio-fiscal welfare in a comparative manner (see also below).[12] Socio-fiscal welfare is then mainly described as 'a collection of social tax expenditures', which shows the relevance of defining social tax expenditures well (see infra). Consequently, the description of socio-fiscal welfare relies completely on the definition of social tax expenditures. As will be discussed later in more detail, this approach is too narrow, as socio-fiscal welfare may go beyond the taxation system and thus the use of social tax expenditures. Before addressing this need for a broad(er) definition, we first highlight the relevance of tax expenditures for the welfare regimes and social policy more in general.

B. The Diverse Role of the Hidden Welfare State: From Reducing In-Work Poverty to Supporting Middle and High Incomes

In mapping out the distributive dimension of socio-fiscal welfare and its effect on the working poor, tax-based methods have often gone unnoticed. The direct

---

[8] N Morel, C Touzet and M Zemmour, 'A Bismarckian Type of Fiscal Welfare? Insights on the Use of Social Tax Expenditures in French Social and Employment Policy', LIEPP Working Paper no 65 (2016) 1–2; Morel, Touzet and Zemmour, 'Fiscal Welfare in Europe: A State of the Art' (n 1) 1–2; Morel, Touzet and Zemmour, 'Fiscal Welfare in Europe: Why Should We Care and What Do We Know So Far' (n 1) 549–53.

[9] See R Ervik, The Hidden Welfare State in Comparative Perspective – Tax Expenditures and Social Policy in Different Welfare Models (London, VDM, 2009).

[10] D Pieters, P Schoukens and B Zaglmayer, 'Cooperation in the Financing of Social Security and the Payment of Benefits' IBM Center for the Business of Government Collaboration Series (2005) 1–13; Morel, Touzet and Zemmour, 'Fiscal Welfare in Europe: Why Should We Care and What Do We Know So Far' (n 1) 549–53; based on A Sinfield, 'Tax Benefits and their Impact on the Social Division of Welfare', Paper presented at the Fiscal Welfare in Europe workshop, Paris, 2016; Touzet (n 1) 1–59.

[11] Morel, Touzet and Zemmour, 'Fiscal Welfare in Europe: Why Should We Care and What Do We Know So Far' (n 1) 549–53; based on A Sinfield, 'Tax Benefits and their Impact on the Social Division of Welfare', Paper presented at the Fiscal Welfare in Europe workshop, Paris, 2016; Touzet (n 1) 1–59.

[12] Pieters, Schoukens and Zaglmayer (n 10) 1.

provision of social security benefits and services to the public have taken centre stage. In his analysis of the social division of welfare, Titmuss claimed that this trend was problematic. It supported the false narrative that social welfare regimes only support the poor, while ignoring the benefits middle- and high-income households enjoy through other, hidden means of governmental intervention. This could eventually – according to Titmuss – result in political division on whether or not to support the concept of a welfare state itself, based on misconceptions. If the intent is to provide a clear and complete picture, research and analysis has to recognise the full range of techniques that are used to generate social welfare systems. This inevitably includes welfare through fiscal systems.[13]

In contrast to direct social transfers, socio-fiscal welfare measures are not primarily used as an instrument for redistributing wealth. In the first place, socio-fiscal welfare is used by the government to steer societal behaviour by offering financial incentives, for example by incentivising individuals to switch to *merit goods*, which are private goods and services deemed preferable for the citizen's needs by the government. In the context of social security, this pertains eg to various (supplementary) insurances and healthcare needs.[14] Incentives are not exclusively economical in nature, as they may also be used to steer labour market participation or even influence the way citizens organise their private lives, eg by offering tax advantages for married couples or households with children. Through these objectives, socio-fiscal welfare is used to steer 'deservingness of welfare' in targeted benefit schemes.[15]

Socio-fiscal welfare does not inherently benefit the working poor compared to social policies executed through direct spending means. Titmuss even labelled socio-fiscal welfare as social policy for middle- and higher-income groups.[16] Furthermore, the term 'tax expenditures' was first used to mark US fiscal measures that disproportionally benefited those higher-income groups. Hacker argues that social tax expenditures are often used as tools in efforts to diminish the welfare state, serving as replacements to traditional direct spending measures through a cover platform of reform to later be retrenched.[17] Whatever the reason for their

---

[13] See also the discussion in Morel, Touzet and Zemmour, 'Fiscal Welfare in Europe: Why Should We Care and What Do We Know So Far' (n 1) 550.

[14] Barrios et al (n 1) 1–5; M Bouwmeester, B Brink and G Vonk, 'De toegevoegde waarde van de inkomensafhankelijke toeslagen in het stelsel van fiscaliteit en sociale zekerheid' (2020) *Maandblad Belasting Beschouwingen* 311, 311–13; Morel, Touzet and Zemmour, 'Fiscal Welfare in Europe: Why Should We Care and What Do We Know So Far' (n 1) 556–57.

[15] Bouwmeester, Brink and Vonk (n 14) 311–13; D Clegg, 'The Demise of Tax Credits' (2015) 4 *The Political Quarterly* 86; Morel, Touzet and Zemmour, 'Fiscal Welfare in Europe: Why Should We Care and What Do We Know So Far' (n 1) 556–57.

[16] Titmuss (n 7) 28.

[17] Hacker (n 6) 243–44; Touzet (n 1) 114.

implementation, socio-fiscal welfare measures may have the paradoxical effect that an increase in tax expenditures and thus a decrease in the state's total collected taxes, is regarded as an increase in the state's involvement in social policy.[18] It is tailor-made for situations where it is no longer economically – and politically – viable to increase budgetary spending. Due to the fact that the measures are not just intended to support the working poor but often serve as labour incentives, it has been politically viable for political players on every side of the spectrum to support socio-fiscal welfare. After all, introducing those measures can be framed as limiting public spending and boosting privatisation for right-wing governments and employers' organisations or as expanding welfare infrastructure by left-wing governments.[19]

C. Tax Expenditures and Socio-Fiscal Welfare as an Alternative to Direct Spending

Traditionally, social security benefits are paid out directly by governmental agencies, funded by both tax revenue and social security contributions paid by employees, their employers, as well as the self-employed.[20] Generally speaking, those governmental agencies that pay out social security benefits will not be the tax agencies that are responsible for collecting taxes. Rather, the relevant social security fund will be responsible for delivering the benefit to its beneficiary. With this method of distribution, income support measures are made available through direct spending, meaning that the benefit in question is paid out directly by transferring an amount of money to the beneficiary's bank account. However, an alternative method of distributing benefits is also possible: income support can be offered through the indirect payment of benefits eg through tax advantages,[21] which does involve the tax agencies directly in the allocation of social security benefits.[22] When first describing this method of distributing benefits, scholars referred to it with terms such as *socio-fiscal welfare* or simply *fiscal welfare*. Through its alternative method of distributing benefits, it offers new ways of implementing social security policy in general (see section III).

---

[18] Morel, Touzet and Zemmour, 'Fiscal Welfare in Europe: Why Should We Care and What Do We Know So Far' (n 1) 554.

[19] ibid 556–57.

[20] Pieters, Schoukens and Zaglmayer (n 10) 9.

[21] Bouwmeester, Brink and Vonk (n 14) 313; Pieters, Schoukens and Zaglmayer (n 10) 9, 13; see also C Howard and E Howard, *The Hidden Welfare State: Tax Expenditures and Social Policy in the United States* (New Jersey, Princeton University Press, 1997); Titmuss (n 7).

[22] Pieters, Schoukens and Zaglmayer (n 10) 13.

III. Typology of Socio-Fiscal Welfare Based on Existing Literature

In European literature on socio-fiscal welfare, Touzet, Morel and Zemmour extensively described various national examples of socio-fiscal welfare arrangements[23] and analysed their possible effect on the (related) social security system. Their analysis can be synthesised as illustrated in Figure 10.1.

Figure 10.1 A representation of socio-fiscal welfare in a European context as currently understood by jurisprudence

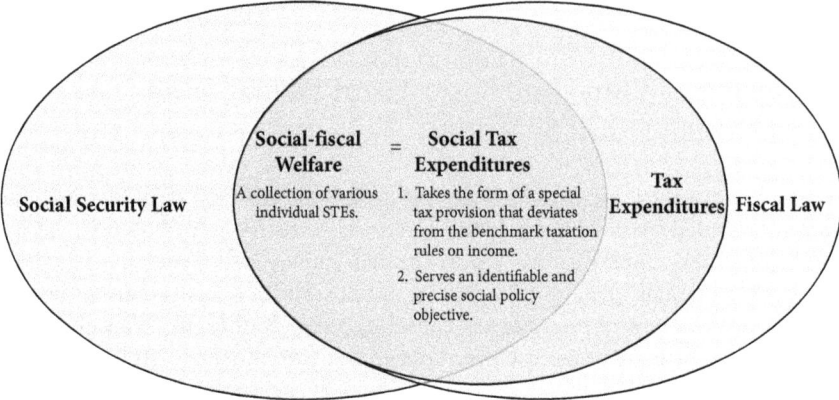

A. Tax Provisions with an Identifiable and Precise Social Policy Objective

So far, we have delineated socio-fiscal welfare as 'tax expenditures *sensu lato*'. By doing so we mainly focused on the technique or the form in which the fiscal welfare is materialised and omitted the underlying objective of the tax expenditures. Not all of these expenditures have been developed with a social objective. At the core of socio-fiscal welfare lie not simply tax expenditures in general, but

---

[23] See Morel, Touzet and Zemmour, 'Fiscal Welfare in Europe: A State of the Art' (n 1); Morel, Touzet and Zemmour, 'A Bismarckian Type of Fiscal Welfare?' (n 8); Morel, Touzet and Zemmour, 'Fiscal Welfare in Europe: Why Should We Care and What Do We Know So Far' (n 1) 549–60; C Touzet, 'Fiscal Welfare for the Poor: What is the Logic? Insights on the Political Economy of In-Work Tax Benefits in the United States, the United Kingdom and France', Paper presented at the CES Conference, Philadelphia, 2016; Touzet (n 1); M Zemmour, 'Les dépenses socio-fiscales ayant trait à la protection sociale: état des lieux', LIEPP Policy Paper (2013), hal-sciencespo.archives-ouvertes.fr/hal-01064750/document (last accessed 8 May 2023).

more specifically 'social tax expenditures', often abbreviated to 'STEs'. STEs are fundamentally tied to our current understanding of socio-fiscal welfare. The limited European jurisprudence that set out to describe socio-fiscal welfare, has defined it as a collection of various individual STEs.[24] Howard even went so far as to consider STEs being the cornerstone not only of socio-fiscal welfare, but also the concept of the hidden welfare state in general.[25]

In their analysis, Morel, Touzet and Zemmour differentiate between four types of STEs:[26]

(1) Tax breaks on resources designated for social protection purposes, such as social security contributions.
(2) Tax breaks for social purposes equivalent to cash benefits, meaning they are reliant on the beneficiary's personal circumstances, such as being affected by social risks or being part of a low-income group.
(3) Tax breaks for social purposes conditional on participation in private social protection schemes, such as insurances or care services.
(4) Reduced tax rates or exemptions from social benefits.

Regardless of which of these four types the STE manifests itself as, the existing legal literature establishes that it *always* takes the form of a tax provision. As a tax expenditure, that tax provision fundamentally provides a deviation from the benchmark taxation rules on income. The specific form the expenditures can take include, among others: tax exemptions,[27] deductions,[28] exclusions,[29] deferrals,[30] rebates,[31] credits[32] and preferential tax rates. However, this requirement regarding what form an STE may take (that of a tax provision that deviates from the benchmark taxation rules on income), does not differentiate STEs from tax expenditures in general.

This tax provision also needs to serve an identifiable and precise social policy objective. This characteristic is what differentiates social tax expenditures from tax expenditures in general, as well as other tax instruments that seek to achieve more widely-defined policy objectives, such as redistribution of wealth or the implementation of progressive taxation. However, in practice the differentiation

---

[24] Touzet (n 1) 68.

[25] Note however, that C Howard applied this link between STEs and the hidden welfare state to the context of the United States of America, see Howard and Howard (n 21) 3.

[26] Morel, Touzet and Zemmour, 'A Bismarckian Type of Fiscal Welfare?' (n 8) 6; see also Zemmour (n 23).

[27] A *tax exemption* is the general right for (a part of) income to be excluded from taxation.

[28] A *tax deduction* refers to the portion of the taxable income being excluded from taxation.

[29] A *tax exclusion* refers to income that is not included in the gross income on which taxes are calculated.

[30] A *tax deferral* is a provision allowing a taxpayer to delay paying taxes to some point in the future.

[31] A *tax rebate* is an amount paid back to the taxpayer when the taxes paid exceeded the taxes owed.

[32] A *tax credit* is an amount that the taxpayer can subtract directly from the total amount of taxes owed. Note that tax credits differ from tax deductions, in that the former directly reduces the owed tax while the latter reduces the income on which the tax is calculated.

between general tax exemptions and those with precise social policy objectives is not a clearly drawn line. For example, with regards to the issue of in-work poverty, a social security system could feature tax deductions for lower incomes. Such an expenditure could constitute a measure with the clear and identifiable goal of supporting the working poor. However, it could very well be regarded as a standard feature of progressive taxation as well.[33] (See Table 10.1.)

Table 10.1 Schematic Overview – Part I

Tax expenditure	Special provision in the tax code that deviates from benchmark taxation rules on income.
Social tax expenditures	(1) Takes the form of a special tax provision that deviates from the benchmark taxation rules on income. (2) Serves an identifiable and precise social policy objective.
Socio-fiscal welfare	A collection of various individual social tax expenditures.

B. STEs Affecting the Working Poor

When STEs are specifically implemented to support certain low-income groups, they can be differentiated from one another based on their respective beneficiaries. For example, there are STEs specifically for low-income pensioners, disabled individuals or, for the purposes of the comparative report, the working poor.[34] Within the STEs, one could even further differentiate and single out STEs for the working poor as different to the other social tax expenditures. This is done by reference to an additional set of characteristics relating to the objective of the expenditure, being that it either targets low-income groups specifically or is more generous for low-income groups.[35]

Low-income groups are specifically targeted by STEs when accessibility to a certain social security scheme is dependent on either a household's income falling below a set income limit, or when the beneficiaries of the social security scheme are part of a group associated with low incomes. When it comes to STEs that are more generous for low-income groups, universal tax expenditures – benefiting everyone – could also be considered STEs, on the condition that they are progressive and become more beneficial as income decreases. For example, the Dutch general tax credit on income tax had a flat rate before 2014. This means lower-income groups did not enjoy a more generous taxation scheme than higher-income groups, so the

---

[33] Pieters, Schoukens and Zaglmayer (n 10) 14; Touzet (n 1) 68–70.
[34] Touzet (n 1) 2.
[35] Macdaniel and Surrey (n 1) 3; Morel, Touzet and Zemmour, 'Fiscal Welfare in Europe: Why Should We Care and What Do We Know So Far' (n 1) 551; Owens (n 1) 171–80; Stebbing and Spies-Butcher (n 1) 586; Touzet (n 1) 69.

tax credit could not be considered an STE. The flat rate tax credit became progressive in 2014, however, and as such it *did* constitute an STE from then on, as it was more generous for low-income groups.[36] (See Table 10.2.)

Table 10.2 Schematic Overview – Part II

Social tax expenditures …	(1)	Takes the form of a tax provision that deviates from the standard taxation rules on income.
	(2)	Serves an identifiable and precise social policy objective.
… specifically targeting low-income workers	(1)	Low-income groups are specifically targeted: (a) income falls below set income limit; (b) beneficiary is part of a group associated with low incomes.
	or (2)	The STE is more generous to low-income groups.

IV. Socio-Fiscal Welfare Across Europe: Going Beyond Mere Social Tax Expenditures

A. Concrete European Socio-Fiscal Welfare Measures Clash with Current Understanding of Socio-Fiscal Welfare

Concrete socio-fiscal welfare measures do not always fit well with the standard demarcation criteria as to what is and what is not an STE, as we can see with eg the employment bonuses in Belgium, Sweden, Luxembourg and France.

The French *prime pour l'emploi* was originally designed as a measure that benefited the working poor through annual refundable tax credits. Beneficiaries needed to both have an individual income that was below a set ceiling, as well as an entire tax unit's income – the household's income – that could not surpass a predetermined total income. When these two requirements were met, a refundable credit was granted individually, calculated as a percentage on the income earned.[37] The *prime pour l'emploi* was conceived as an alternative strategy to improve low-wage incomes instead of raising the minimum wage. Though presented as a policy with the objective to boost income for low-wage employees, a redistributive effect also took place due to the wide scope of beneficiaries provided for by the employment bonus.[38]

---

[36] Article 8.10 Dutch Wet Inkomstenbelasting 2001, 11 July 2000; Touzet (n 1) 72.

[37] Touzet (n 1) 110.

[38] Morel, Touzet and Zemmour, 'A Bismarckian Type of Fiscal Welfare?' (n 8) 18; based on Touzet (n 22).

The Belgian employment bonus – *bonus à l'emploi* or *werkbonus* – is a reduction on social-security contributions for employees with low wages, allowing them to be left with a higher net wage. The reduction is a fixed amount, but this will be lower or higher depending on the wage bracket of the employee. While the employment bonus enlarges the employee's taxable income, it is accompanied by a tax reduction intended to alleviate this effect. In practice, the provisional tax levy by the company for employees entitled to the employment bonus is diminished by about 1/3. By compensating the extra amount in taxes which would normally be owed due to receiving a higher income, the employment bonus gives an actual benefit to employees with low wages.

The Belgian and French employment bonuses can be put in contrast with the Swedish *jobbskatteavdraget*, which literally can be translated as employment tax deduction, but should more accurately be described as an earned income tax credit. In 2007, the income tax on labour was reduced in Sweden after promises to make work more profitable. This was done through the *jobbskatteavdraget*. While earned income tax credits are present in other legal systems – eg the employment bonus in Belgium but also in more faraway systems such as the US – the Swedish *jobbskatteavdraget* differentiates itself from the Belgian employment bonus by being universal and thus applicable to the entire working population instead of specific groups of taxpayers, such as employees. A tax deduction – proportional to the municipality where an individual lives – is applied at lower income levels and lowered at higher income levels, which affects the marginal tax rate for the beneficiaries of the deduction.[39] As the deduction is based on the amount of earned income from labour, it serves as an incentive to seek employment.[40] The objective was the labour activation of the population. This was done by offering tax expenditures on income from work, instead of direct monetary transfers conditional on employment and based on income.[41] As such, the Swedish *jobbskatteavdraget* contains the elements to constitute an STE as described above (see section III.A). It is a tax provision that, fundamentally, allows for a deviation from the benchmark rules on taxation, introduced with an identifiable and precise social policy objective.

In a similar fashion as the Swedish case, the Luxembourg employment bonus can be considered to be a tax credit. In 2019, the *credit d'impôt salaire social minimum* (hereafter: CISSM) was introduced in Luxembourg to support low-income wage earners. The CISSM was introduced alongside an increase (of 2.01 per cent) of the social minimum wage (*salaire social minimum: SSM*). Both measures have

---

[39] K Edmark et al, 'The Swedish Earned Income Tax Credit: Did It Increase Employment?' (2016) 72(4) *Public Finance Analysis* 479; M Wikander, 'The Swedish EITC and its Effect on the Employment Rate – Master Essay II' (Unpublished, *Lund University School of Economics and Management*, 2014) 2, 6, 9.

[40] Edmark et al, (n 39) 475–76; M Wikander (n 39) 2, 6, 9.

[41] Ch 67, para 5–8 Sweden's Inkomstkattelag 1999:1229; Touzet (n 1) 2.

as objective the revalorisation of the minimum wage. Whereas the SSM focused on a linear increase of the (minimum) wage, the CISSM has been designed as an incremental revalorisation of the lowest wages by means of a tax expenditure. The amount varies depending on the monthly gross wage that one effectively receives as wage earner. The amount can thus be different across the workers, but it can also be different (for the same worker) on a monthly basis, if the amount of the wage changes. For the first tier (wage between €1500 and €2000), the CISSM is a fixed amount (ie €70 euro) and it becomes degressive for the second tier (between €2500 and €3000). The tax credit is paid both for full-time and part-time workers; in the latter case the amount is calculated on the basis of a fictitious wage that the worker would have received if they worked full-time that month, and then reduced in a proportional manner reflecting the effective hours of work. Contrary to the other described systems, the amount of the CISSM is paid directly by the employer as they are responsible for the direct withholding of provisional income tax from the wage for tax purposes. If there is no such employer present (eg during maternity or parental leave of the worker), the social security administration (and not the tax system) takes care of the eventual payment of the amount. Although the calculation of the tax credit is based upon taxable income, the eventual payment is (contrary to the previous systems in France, Belgium and Sweden), left to the employer (as tax agent) or to the social security administration.

While the French *prime pour l'emploi* has been absorbed into a broader activity bonus for low-income workers, the Belgian employment bonus and Swedish *jobb-skatteavdrag* are still active. All these schemes, at a cursory glance, seem to serve as prime examples of STEs. They are tax provisions that deviate from the standard taxation rules on income, with an identifiable and precise social policy objective. Throughout the (scant) literature on socio-fiscal welfare, these two requirements (tax provisions that deviate from standard tax rules, having a precise social objective) are now accepted as constituting elements for tax exemption to be considered as a socio-fiscal welfare measure. However, several European systems that are often associated with or labelled as socio-fiscal welfare can, after review, not be accepted as such, as one of the elements is missing.

B. The Difficulty with Reductions of Social Security Contributions

A caveat comes up when discussing the Belgian employment bonus, which comes with a reduction of social security contributions that at first glance seems to fit the qualification of a social tax expenditure.

Belgium has a wide range of targeted reductions for employer social security contributions, such as the employment bonus discussed above. By and large, these can be classified as reductions for vulnerable groups and reductions for vulnerable situations due to company circumstances. In the first case, reductions are, among others, offered per employee of at least (approximately – it depends on the region) 55 years old, per employee under 26 years old, and per employee who was recruited after a period of long-term unemployment. The latter reductions are granted when the long-term unemployed employee is hired through professional transition programmes or when the company has an explicit social aim[42] (the latter fitting in nicely with the second requirement of the identifiable and precise social policy objective). In the second case, namely reductions offered due to company circumstances, the situations include new companies hiring their first employees, hiring employees above 45 years old who lost employment due to restructuring elsewhere, or companies experimenting with a four-day working week.[43]

French STEs mainly support employment policy, totalling around 40 per cent of the tax revenue that goes to socio-fiscal welfare. Comparatively, the three largest sectors where STEs are applied (family, health and income support) amount to 45 per cent combined. This is a defining characteristic of French socio-fiscal welfare, as other European countries tend to lean towards pensions being the biggest share of tax revenue spent on welfare. Additionally, the French welfare state relies on strong funding through traditional social security contributions.[44] Morel, Touzet and Zemmour note that one of the defining characteristics of French socio-fiscal welfare is that many of its measures are exemptions or reductions of social security contributions. Over the past decades, French employment policy has come to rely heavily on the systematic reduction of the rate of social security contributions that employers pay on low wages (hereafter: *general exemption of social contributions on low wages*). Principal contribution rates that apply to all workers are still in force and the targeted low-wage workers are still entitled to their contributions, but the reduced amount is compensated for by state contributions to the social security fund. This measure has been through several expansions. By 2016, more than 50 per cent of the private sector benefited from it, with the French state providing €22 billion to the social security fund yearly.[45]

Morel, Touzet and Zemmour argue that a general exemption on social security contributions constitutes an STE.[46] They argue that this is due to:

– the officially statutory rate common to all workers remaining in force;

– the state being legally committed to refund the entire revenue foregone for each concerned worker to the social security fund;

– contributory entitlements of concerned workers not being affected by the exemptions.

---

[42] See Belgian Programmawet (I)/Loi-programme (I), 24 December 2002; Belgian National Office of Social Security, *Administrative Instructions for Employers*.

[43] Belgian National Office of Social Security, Administrative Instructions for Employers.

[44] Morel, Touzet and Zemmour, 'A Bismarckian Type of Fiscal Welfare?' (n 8) 12–13.

[45] Morel, Touzet and Zemmour, 'A Bismarckian Type of Fiscal Welfare?' (n 8) 8–9.

[46] Morel, Touzet and Zemmour, 'A Bismarckian Type of Fiscal Welfare?' (n 8) 15.

However, in another – more recent – publication, Touzet concluded that a fundamental characteristic of STEs was that they take the form of tax provisions that offer deviations from standard taxation.[47] Accepting that an exemption on social security contributions is an STE stretches the definition of an STE to its boundaries. Can we consider a social security contribution as a tax, taking into account the fact that they are considered to be affected levies, the revenues of which go directly to the social security budget, and not to the overall (tax) budget? Social security contributions are traditionally considered to be of a parafiscal nature. Moreover, the publication states that STEs fundamentally have to manifest themselves as tax provisions deviating from the benchmark rules on taxation. According to OECD definitions, taxes are 'compulsory, unrequited payments to general government. They are unrequited in the sense that benefits provided by government to taxpayers are not normally in proportion to their payments'. Social security contributions, in contrast, are defined as 'compulsory payments paid to general government that confer entitlement to receive a (contingent) future social benefit'. By equating social security contributions with taxes, the unrequitable character of the latter comes into conflict with the former's conferment of entitlement to receive a (contingent) future social benefit.[48] The definition used refers to the benchmark rules on taxation being deviated from, not social security contributions. As a result, it is difficult to accept that the general exemption of social contributions on low wages is an STE and thus part of the socio-fiscal welfare measures in Belgium or France. Strictly speaking, reductions of any kind on social security contributions are not tax provisions (in the strict sense), even if they could be argued to have social policy objectives.

C. Socio-Fiscal Welfare Entrenched in Family Policies (through 'Quotient Familial' and 'Quotient Conjugal')

While the general exemption on social security contributions is an archetypal example of how reductions on social security contributions are not STEs, there is another interesting aspect of the Belgian and French welfare system that is worth analysing in the context of socio-fiscal welfare. The French system in particular is strongly characterised by 'familialism' (referring to a welfare system wherein it is presumed that families will take prior responsibility for the care of their members, rather than leaving that responsibility to the government); it combines a high level of social expenditures with a generally high level of STEs.[49] In 2014, French

---

[47] Touzet (n 1) 68–70.

[48] OECD, Social security contributions, *OECD Library*, www.oecd-ilibrary.org/taxation/socialsecurity-contributions/indicator/english_3ebfe901-en (last accessed 8 May 2023).

[49] W Ademi, P Fron and M Ladaique, 'How Much Do OECD Countries Spend on Social Protection and How Redistributive Are their Tax/Benefit Systems?' (2014) 1 *International Social Security Review* 67; Morel, Touzet and Zemmour, 'A Bismarckian Type of Fiscal Welfare?' (n 8) 3. See also Morel, Touzet and Zemmour, 'Fiscal Welfare in Europe: A State of the Art' (n 1).

socio-fiscal welfare and familialism overlapped to the amount of €19.65 billion worth of tax expenditures in the field of family policy. The most prolific post-war French family policies in the field of social security are the *quotient familial* and the *quotient conjugal*, both present in Belgium as well and typical for both countries.[50]

The *quotient familial* and the *quotient conjugal* are both adjustments to the amount of personal income tax that is owed by spreading the household amount across everyone in the household, including those who do not have an individual income. Due to progressive taxation schemes that are then applied, the non-obligatory *quotient* familial offers a preferential tax rate based on the composition of a household. The net taxable income is divided by a number of 'household shares'. The amount of shares is determined by the number of adults and children, with more or less being allocated based on the family members' ability to contribute financially. The result is the *quotient familial*, on which the progressive taxation rates are applied before being multiplied by the amount of household shares.[51]

Both the *quotient familial* and the *quotient conjugal* have been qualified as STEs in legal literature.[52] They certainly adhere to the first prerequisite of the proposed definition of STEs, being tax provisions that create a deviation from the standard taxation rules on income. However, since these tax provisions are firmly entrenched as policies that seek to incentivise societal organisation into a family unit, it is debatable if they serve an identifiable and precise social policy objective, the second necessary requirement. As stated above, the line between what does and what does not constitute a social policy objective is not always clear (see section III.A).

D. Allowances to Deal with the Cost of Living

i. *The Dutch System of Income-Related Allowances*

The Dutch system of income-related allowances is traditionally considered as an example of socio-fiscal welfare. More specifically, it belongs to the more

---

[50] In 2014, the amount of tax revenue foregone by the state by the application of the *quotient famil-ial* amounted to €8.5 billion; Ministry of Economy, Finance and Industrial and Digital Sovereignty of France, Quotient familial et impôt sur le revenu: comment ça marche?, www.economie.gouv.fr/particuliers/quotient-familial (last accessed 8 May 2023); Morel, Touzet and Zemmour, 'A Bismarckian Type of Fiscal Welfare?' (n 8) 11.

[51] Arts 193–199 French Code Général des Impôts, 6 April 1950; Morel, Touzet and Zemmour, 'Fiscal Welfare in Europe: Why Should We Care and What Do We Know So Far' (n 1) 554. For the *quotient conjugal* this was €5.2 billion (2014); Morel, Touzet and Zemmour, 'A Bismarckian Type of Fiscal Welfare?' (n 8) 3. The measure replaces individual taxation for a joint taxation of couples who are married or in a public union; G Allegre, H Perivier and M Pucci, 'Imposition des couples et statut marital – Simulation de trois réformes du quotient conjugal en France' (2021) 526 *Economie et Statistique* 5.

[52] Morel, Touzet and Zemmour, 'A Bismarckian Type of Fiscal Welfare?' (n 8) 9–12.

recent group of allowances that are granted as a benefit (by the tax authorities). However, it is questionable whether it fully fits the definition of an STE. The system uses both the definitions and calculation methods found in the Dutch fiscal system, and as such is an extension of the principles originating from there. The household income is used as reference to calculate the allowances, rather than individual incomes, with the aim of curbing both excessive government spending and unnecessary aid for households not in need of it.[53] The allowances differentiate themselves from other monetary support based on income, like tax reductions, which are based on the individual rather than the household income.

There are four different income-related allowances:

(1) Support towards rental costs (*rent allowance*).
(2) Support towards health insurance costs (*healthcare allowance*).
(3) Support towards the costs of childcare (minors) in general (*childcare allowance*).
(4) Support towards the costs of day-care for children (*day-care allowance*).

The Dutch system of allowances functions much the same way as the UK's Working Tax Credit. It is calculated based on an estimation of the recipient's income and is then deposited in the form of a provisional advance, so the sum actually serves as a support on top of the income of that year. Note that no income tax is owed on the allowance. Afterwards, at the end of the fiscal year, the income is finally determined and the allowance is definitively awarded. If a surplus was deposited, the recipient is obligated to reimburse the state.[54]

It is important to highlight that the income related allowances are not awarded in the form of a reduction on income tax, even though they are calculated based on it. While the functioning of the allowance does depend on mechanisms inherent to the fiscal system, the allowance in and of itself should not be described as a tax instrument. A more fitting classification would be as a social payment with fiscal tools being used to determine the means of the beneficiary and the amount of the allowance.[55]

It should be noted that income redistribution was never explicitly an intended consequence of the allowance system.[56] More so than the redistribution of wealth, the income-related allowances were meant to supplement income, to compensate for shortcomings in fulfilling basic living necessities – like housing and

---

[53] Ministry of Finance of the Netherlands, *IBO Toeslagen Deelonderzoek 2 – Eenvoud of Maatwerk: Alternatieven voor het bestaande toeslagenstelsel* (2020), www.kences.nl/wp-content/uploads/2020/07/20200110-FIN-Rapport-IBO-Toeslagen-deel-2.pdf (last accessed 8 May 2023)., 9, 29; S Marchal, I Marx and G Verbist, 'Income Support Policies for the Working Poor' in H Lohmann and I Marx, *In-Work Poverty* (Cheltenham, Edward Elgar Publishing, 2018) 11.

[54] Art 8-42a Dutch Algemene Wet Inkomensafhankelijke Regelingen, 23 June 2005.

[55] Bouwmeester, Brink and Vonk (n 14) 314–15.

[56] Bouwmeester, Brink and Vonk (n 14) 314; C Caminada et al, *Verschillen in niveau en ontwikkeling van de inkomensongelijkheid, -herverdeling en -armoede in Nederland en België sinds 1995* (Leiden, University of Leiden, 2018) 17.

childcare – for lower-income households. These are services that in principle are to be purchased on a private market on the basis of market tariffs. Instead of socially correcting those markets by public interventions it has been opted to grant benefits to low-income families, empowering them to buy at market price.[57] In other words, the government does not interfere as a direct provider of public services, but rather as an intermediary that ensures that citizens will be able to purchase those services on the private market. This stimulation of privatisation is characteristic for socio-fiscal welfare.[58] In practice, though, since lower incomes receive higher allowances and these beneficiaries are given support at the expense of public funds, a redistributive effect has taken place.[59] Due to the substantial number of recipients of the allowances, they have become powerful instruments to steer purchasing power upwards and as a result are a key tool when designing the national economic policy.[60]

ii. An Effective Measure for the Working Poor

The income-related allowances seem to play in reality an important role in supporting the diminishing income of the working poor, even though they do not differentiate between those who work and those who do not.[61] On average, the allowances account for 21 per cent of the disposable income of low-income households in the Netherlands, which includes the category of the working poor. Five million households (60 per cent of the country's total) benefit from the allowance system, due to the wide income margins implemented by the system to determine its beneficiaries.[62] Taking this widespread use of the income-related allowances into consideration, Bouwmeester, Brink and Vonk argue that they should not be regarded as measures merely intended to guarantee a minimum living subsistence, since the system has become crucial for many households, including those who are capable of supporting themselves.[63]

Social security in the Netherlands does not have any instruments designed specifically to aid the working poor. Yet, the income-related allowances serve an

---

[57] Dutch tweede kamer, *Kamerstukken II* 2004/05, 29764, nr 3, zoek.officielebekendmakingen.nl/kst-29764-3.html (last accessed 8 May 2023), 2; Bouwmeester, Brink and Vonk (n 14) 316.

[58] Bouwmeester, Brink and Vonk (n 14) 317; Morel, Touzet and Zemmour, 'Fiscal Welfare in Europe: Why Should We Care and What Do We Know So Far' (n 1) 550–51.

[59] Bouwmeester, Brink and Vonk (n 14) 314; Caminada et al (n 56) 17.

[60] Ministry of Finance of the Netherlands, *IBO Toeslagen Deelonderzoek 1 – Eenvoud of Maatwerk: uitruilen binnen het bestaande toeslagenstelsel* (2019), archief.rijksbegroting.nl/system/files/12/eindrapport-toeslagen-deel-1.pdf (last accessed 8 May 2023), 22; Ministry of Finance of the Netherlands (n 53) 27; P Koot and M Gielen, *Naar eenvoudigere inkomensafhankelijke regelingen* (2019), esb.nu/events/overig/20056905/naar-eenvoudigere-inkomensafhankelijke-regelingen (last accessed 8 May 2023).

[61] Bouwmeester, Brink and Vonk (n 14) 311.

[62] Ministry of Finance of the Netherlands (n 53) 16, 26; Bouwmeester, Brink and Vonk (n 14) 313.

[63] N Barr, *Economics of the State* (Oxford, Oxford University Press, 2012) 408–09; Bouwmeester, Brink and Vonk (n 14) 317.

important function in reality in providing income supplements to this specific vulnerable group of working poor, having become more and more dependent on the system.[64] With state-funded allowances becoming more important in supporting the working poor, there is a risk of employers being relieved of the responsibility to provide a liveable wage. To counter this scenario, Bouwmeester, Brink and Vonk plead for a strict monitoring of minimum wages, to avoid wage erosion and more households being pushed into poverty.[65]

iii. On the Border between Fiscal Measures and Social Measures, but not STEs

The Dutch system of income-related allowances cannot be classified as either strictly fiscal or strictly social measures.[66] While there is a tendency to identify the allowances as an element of the fiscal system (especially in international literature), they do not appear in the form of tax breaks and their distribution is disconnected from the collection of income taxes. Another break from the Dutch fiscal system is the use of the household as a barometer for deservingness, instead of assessment of the individual needs.[67] This secession from fiscal procedures was a policy choice, and very much intentional.[68] In the same vein, when drafting the legal base of the income-related allowances, it was explicitly stated that the allowances should not be regarded as a social security measure. The reasoning was that social security measures are a further supplement to income intended to ensure a livelihood, while the allowances simply offer monetary support for certain costs.

Bouwmeester, Brink and Vonk argue that this is a reductionary view of social security, narrowing the definition into something equating the subsistence minimum. The same authors categorise the allowances as a part of social security rather than the fiscal system and label them as 'income-dependent targeted welfare in the sphere of social amenities'.[69] They also note that due to the dependence that the allowances have on both systems, they might appear to exist in the periphery of socio-fiscal welfare.[70] However, since one of the characteristics of STEs is that they take the form of a tax provision that deviates from standard taxation, the allowances cannot be classified as such. When utilising the proposed typology of socio-fiscal welfare as a collection of various STEs, the Dutch income-related allowances do not fall within its scope.

---

[64] See also the contribution by De Becker in this book (ch 7).

[65] Bouwmeester, Brink and Vonk (n 14) 317; Marchal, Marx and Verbist (n 53) 14.

[66] Bouwmeester, Brink and Vonk (n 14) 311; see also S Klosse and G Vonk, *Hoofdzaken socialezekerheidsrecht* (Den Haag, Boom juridisch, 2020).

[67] Bouwmeester, Brink and Vonk (n 14) 314–15.

[68] Dutch tweede kamer, *Kamerstukken II* 2004/05, 29764, nr 3, zoek.officielebekendmakingen.nl/kst-29764-3.html (last accessed 8 May 2023) 2; Bouwmeester, Brink and Vonk (n 14) 316.

[69] Bouwmeester, Brink and Vonk (n 14) 311, 319.

[70] Bouwmeester, Brink and Vonk (n 14) 311; see also Klosse and Vonk (n 66).

E. Further Developing a Typology of Socio-Fiscal Welfare

Contrary to common belief, a closer analysis shows us that the discussed income-related systems do not in reality qualify as socio-fiscal welfare measures. They do not fit the criteria to be regarded as such. (See Figure 10.2.)

Figure 10.2 Current model of socio-fiscal welfare based on existing legal literature, providing no categorisation for multiple European systems

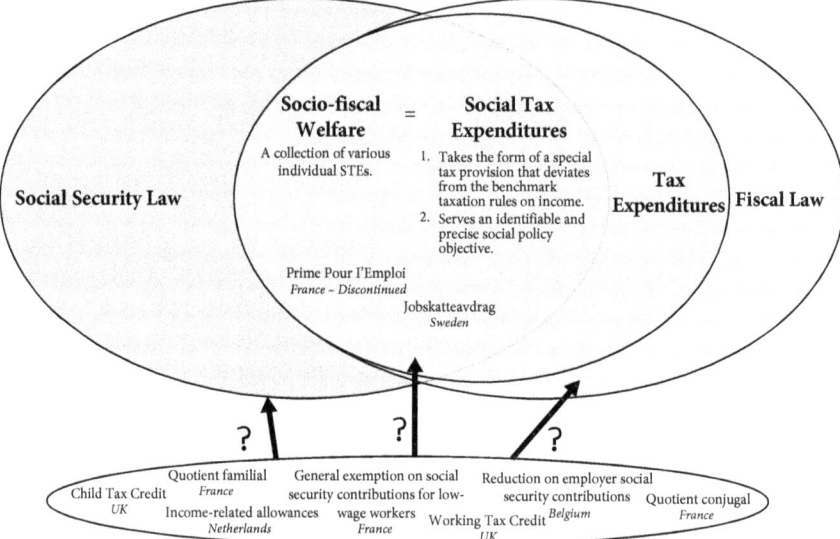

Tax measures such as tax exemptions do however develop over time, as do the underlying techniques used to shape socio-tax welfare measures. On the one hand, socio-fiscal welfare seems to be used as a catch-all term for legal structures that lean into both fiscal and social instruments or that have policy goals traditionally associated with either of these branches. On the other hand, there have been efforts to create a strict typology for social tax expenditures, which is fundamentally connected to the overarching concept of socio-fiscal welfare. Yet, even scholars who have written about the subject in detail apply a definition of STEs that may evolve over the years (see above). The examples of the employment (tax) bonuses discussed above already show that STEs present themselves in much more diverse forms than the original 'tax provisions that deviate from the benchmark taxation'; yet we consider all these benefits as part of the scope of socio-fiscal welfare.

While the aforementioned theoretical approximation of socio-fiscal welfare – proposed by Morel, Touzet and Zemmour – serves as a solid basis, there is room to further develop it. As such, we suggest disconnecting the concept of STEs from the concept of socio-fiscal welfare. If our understanding of STEs remains unchanged, but the concept of socio-fiscal welfare is broadened, this allows us to facilitate comparative studies of all of these systems without being constrained by the narrow definition assigned to STEs. At the same time, however, STEs would still fall under the umbrella of socio-fiscal welfare. Socio-fiscal welfare and STEs both serve an identifiable and precise social policy objective, yet they differ in as much that STEs take the form of a specific tax provision that deviates from the benchmark taxation rules on income whereas socio-fiscal welfare may rely on (broader) structures or calculation methods established by fiscal law. This does not preclude that the latter serve social policy objectives indirectly. (See Table 10.3.)

Table 10.3 Schematic Overview – Part III

Socio-fiscal welfare	(1) Relies on structures or calculation methods established by fiscal law.
	(2) Serves an identifiable and precise social policy objective.
Social tax expenditures	(1) Takes the form of a special tax provision that deviates from the benchmark taxation rules on income.
	(2) Serves an identifiable and precise social policy objective.

Consequently, reductions of social security contributions fall strictly speaking outside the scope of STEs, since they are not formally considered to be tax measures. However, social security financing by contributions can be considered as a parafiscal measure and by reducing monetary contributions to the social security systems it may very well serve social policy objectives in specific instances; in that sense it can be understood as a social security (financing) rule that belongs to socio-fiscal welfare in the broad sense (see Figure 10.3).

Figure 10.3 Proposed alternative model of socio-fiscal welfare

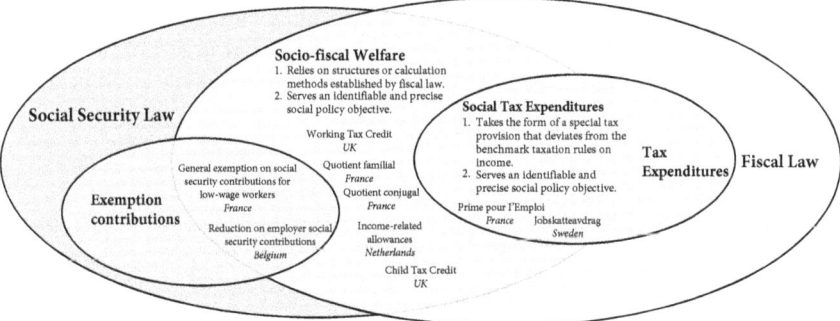

V. Concluding Remarks: Relevance for the Working Poor in the EU?

The hidden welfare state as it exists in Europe appears not only horizontally – across a multitude of European legal systems – but vertically as well. It runs deep into family, employment and health policies, and influences states' budgets to a severe extent. Having a theoretical approach towards the phenomenon which is based mainly on US (legal) literature, is not sufficient, nor is settling for a working definition of socio-fiscal welfare that is not attuned to the practical applications of many of the systems that are supposed to fall under its definition. The label of 'socio-fiscal welfare' has little point if it does not stick to anything. Limiting socio-fiscal welfare strictly to STEs does not serve the discussion either.

European socio-fiscal welfare is only recently beginning to be understood. Besides being structurally part of social welfare systems, it also has an important impact on our social security systems. A clear understanding of the concept is primordially important both from a legal and (social) policy point of view. It may also help to come to a better analysis of the social situation of the working poor across the European Union.

Socio-fiscal welfare in general and STEs in particular lie on the division line between social (security) and tax law. A well-defined concept of STEs and good (European) understanding of socio-fiscal welfare is important for the application of EU law. If the socio-tax measure can be considered as an advantage granted to the (migrant) worker, non-discrimination provisions foreseen under Article 45 of the Treaty on the Functioning of the European Union (TFEU) and Article 7(2) of Regulation 492/2011[71] will apply (non-discrimination of social and tax advantages). However, it might be just as important to establish whether the concerned measure is to be considered as social security or as a tax measure, as the relevant transnational measures indicating the competent national state are different (ie Regulation 883/2004 with regard to social security,[72] respective bilateral tax treaties). In that sense a better understanding of the concept of socio-fiscal welfare from a European perspective and a more precise delineation of STEs for the application of both EU law and national law is part of the specific legal literature that focuses on the crossroads between social law and tax law of moving persons.[73]

---

[71] Regulation (EC) No 883/2004 of the European Parliament and of the Council of 29 April 2004 on the coordination of social security systems [2004] OJ L 166/1.

[72] Regulation (EU) No 492/2011 of the European Parliament and of the Council of 5 April 2011 on freedom of movement for workers within the Union [2011] OJ L 141/1.

[73] D Pieters, 'Taxation and Social Security: Non Co-ordinated Taxes and Co-ordinated Social Contributions' in P Schoukens (ed), *Prospects of Social Security Co-ordination* (Leuven, Acco, 1997) 113; D Pieters, 'What Is a Social Security Contribution and What Is a Tax?' in W Boecken, F Ruland and HD Steinmeyer (eds), *Sozialrecht und Sozialpolitik in Deutschland und Europa* (Neuwied/Friftel, Hermann Luchterhand Verlag, 2002) 515; D Pieters, P Schoukens and B Zaglmayer, *Cooperation*

Beyond the legal sphere, it is also relevant to better understand social policies consequences of socio-fiscal measures that affect the fabric of our welfare states. The effects of these measures, especially when applied through tax expenditures, are not easy to grasp. They are indirect, often hidden, and can serve, from a social welfare perspective, very opposing objectives, which may undermine goals pursued by other social policies. As mentioned in the introduction, many of the original tax exemptions served in the first place the interest of middle and higher incomes, especially when combined with policy goals to direct persons and families towards the consumption of certain goods or services. The tax deduction of premiums paid for certain private pension products, targeting medium/higher incomes, may eg outnumber the budgets spent directly on poverty alleviation. The example of the Dutch tax allowances – although not an STE in the very strict sense – showed us the strong potential impact it may have had on combating poverty for the (working) poor. However, these effects have not been quantified in detail and much still remains to be said about the impact of these measures on (combating) social exclusion. Also from a monitoring perspective, the EU has an interest in better understanding socio-fiscal measures, among other things by defining more clearly concepts such as tax exemptions and STEs when applied in tax systems. Furthermore, it can help to make the lens clearer when assessing neighbouring domains such as family, tax and/or employment policies regarding their (in)direct impact on poverty. The goals behind these policies do not always coincide: a policy focusing strongly on familialism does not necessarily serve fully the overall objective of poverty reduction, nor is the granting of employment bonuses through the tax system always beneficial to the financing of social protection schemes.

Re-evaluating the meaning of socio-fiscal welfare allows for legal researchers to use the concept thereof more consistently, which would help it becoming entrenched in the application of EU law. Additionally, it would also contribute to a clearer idea of which national systems fall under the definition and how such systems apply which kinds of STEs. This in turn can result in better reporting and more effective data gathering, and hopefully more consistent monitoring across the various fields that affect social security systems. From the VUPs we could learn that working poor are by definition at the crossroads of these different policies; that sometimes tax or family policies may have bigger impact on reducing poverty levels of working poor than social security policies targeting poverty in the strict sense. If flexibilisation of work is the continuing norm for the coming decades, inevitably socio-fiscal measures and STEs will grow in importance in the policy debate on working poor, both at a national and EU level. More than ever, it is time to develop a clear vision on the phenomenon of conducting social policy through tax measures; preferably an EU vision reflecting its social model.

Between Social Security and Tax Agencies in Europe (IBM Center for the Business of Government, 2005) 55; E Bakirtzi, D Pieters and P Schoukens, *Merging the administrations of social security contribution and taxation* (European Institute of Social Security and IBM, 2010) 132.

11

Structural In-Work Poverty and its Antidotes

LUCA RATTI

L'existence, ça vous tord et ça vous écrase la face. À elle aussi ça lui avait écrasé la face mais moins, bien moins. Les pauvres sont fadés. La misère est géante, elle se sert pour essuyer les ordures du monde de votre figure comme d'une toile à laver. Il en reste.

Louis-Ferdinand Céline, *Voyage au bout de la nuit*
(Denoël et Steel, Paris, 1932) 270

I. Introduction: Labour Laws against Poverty

The law of work is rooted in industrialism and was born to emancipate working people, providing them with enforceable rights vis-à-vis both their employers and public authorities.[1]

Appearing with increasing frequency and intensity, labour laws crafted private parties' ability to regulate their own interests, by restricting their capacity and freedom to contract, limiting property rights, and ultimately regulating their powers and prerogatives towards each other.[2] Still, in many respects, labour laws contributed to preserve such freedoms, property rights and prerogatives, albeit to a lesser extent than in other fields of law.[3] This constraining effect on contractual freedom came as a natural consequence of labour laws being consistently tailored on subordination, a concept (and status) implying by definition a relation of power and inequality between an employer and a worker.[4]

---

[1] B Veneziani, 'The Evolution of the Contract of Employment' in B Hepple (ed), *The Making of Labour Law in Europe. A Comparative Study of Nine Countries up to 1945* (London and New York, Mansell Publishing, 1986) 31.

[2] H Collins, 'Against Abstentionism in Labour Law' in J Eekelaar and J Bell (eds), *Oxford Essays in Jurisprudence* (Oxford, Clarendon Press, 1987) 86.

[3] K Pistor, The Code of Capital: How the Law Creates Capital and Inequality (Princeton, Princeton University Press, 2019).

[4] O Kahn-Freund, 'A Note on Status and Contract in British Labour Law' (1967) 30(6) *Modern Law Review* 635.

Yet, a closer observation of the many facets of in-work poverty and economic inequalities across the EU allows us to reflect more attentively on the actual role of labour laws in perpetuating, or at least not adequately addressing, power and economic inequalities in contemporary societies.

The aim of this chapter is to draw some lessons from the legal research conducted so far on in-work poverty – in the chapters of this book and beyond – by questioning the ultimate function of legal norms in relation to the societal problem of lifting working people out of poverty. The main argument is that instead of counteracting the rampant resurgence of poverty amongst workers – a facet of poverty relatively uncommon during the twentieth century in Western Europe and the US – labour laws partially contributed to the worsening of some working and employment conditions, thus transforming in-work poverty into one of the most evident diseases of contemporary labour markets. As most diseases that become structural and increasingly constant, in-work poverty should not be underestimated and requires a careful consideration on possible antidotes to treat its spread amongst workers. Existing literature on the legal determinants that contribute to structuralising forms of precarity, vulnerability and ultimately social injustice, is used to reinforce the claim that the enactment of labour laws and especially their legal interpretation should be addressed to combat in-work poverty as much as to protect other individual rights of workers. In-work poverty should thus become a yardstick to benchmark labour legislation and its concrete effects.

To assess the structuralisation of in-work poverty and its countermeasures, this chapter proceeds as follows. In section II, EU social policy's strive against poverty is diachronically situated. Section III zooms in on the emergence of inequality and in-work poverty as endemic features of modern economic environments. Section IV portrays four situations of in-work poverty, corresponding to the four groups of vulnerable and under-represented persons (VUP Groups) analysed throughout this book. Section V addresses potential antidotes to structural in-work poverty, questioning how the human rights and the EU law perspectives may help counter the increase of in-work poverty. Section VI concludes with the way forward that can be envisaged against a background of fundamental societal transformations.

II. Working, Yet Poor in Europe: Dialectical and Yet Coexistent

The very title of this book evokes the contradictory coexistence between the activity or status of 'working' and the condition of being (considered as) 'poor'.

While at first glance, received narratives seem to challenge this apparent contradiction, reality shows an increasing polarisation of incomes and a slow but steady trend towards pushing those on the lower end of European societies below a social minimum, thus exposing them to social and material deprivation and other manifestations of what is currently identified as multidimensional poverty.[5]

Accounts of the effects of recent economic trends confirm the tangible worsening of living and working conditions of vast sectors of the population, in the US as well as across the EU.[6] Poverty emerges as the main consequence not of personal choices, but rather of a more structural double deficiency: of labour markets to provide individuals with adequate working opportunities, and of welfare states to support and develop education, housing and healthcare services.[7] Such double deficiency articulates along different trajectories, bringing people towards impoverishment, disempowerment and exclusion from the society.[8] Specific segments of the labour population suffer more than others, with vertical and horizontal disparities between women and men marking the reality of contemporary employment relations, and potentially influencing pension outcomes and wealth accumulation in the future.[9] All this has been dramatically worsened by the Covid-19 pandemic,[10] which inter alia amplified the (already evident) divide between essential and non-essential workers, and emphasised the need to provide the former with better working and employment conditions after the lift of pandemic-related restrictions.

Working, yet being poor, however, has not always characterised labour-related income earners, at least not in Europe. In fact, the approach taken by European institutions since the 1970s has been focused primarily on poverty as a societal issue which characterises specific clusters of the non-working population, hence marking a clear divide between working and poor.

Since 1975, targeted European anti-poverty programmes funded a number of projects and comparative research aimed at supporting those who were in a condition in which resources were 'so small as to exclude them from the minimum acceptable way of life of the member state in which they live'.[11] With the late 1980s and the 1990s, the activism of the then President of the EC Commission Jacques Delors helped to turn the concept of (and the policy initiatives on) 'poverty' into that of 'social exclusion', which paved the way to the more structured

---

[5] Oxford Poverty and Human Development Initiative, Global Multidimensional Poverty Index 2022, *Unpacking Deprivation Bundles to Reduce Multidimensional Poverty* (Oxford, University of Oxford, 2022), available at ophi.org.uk/wp-content/uploads/G-MPI_Report_2022_Unpacking.pdf.

[6] M Burt, *Who Owns Poverty?* (Chicago, Red Press, 2019); D McGarvey, *Poverty Safari. Understanding the Anger of Britain's Underclass* (Edinburgh, Luath Press, 2017); L Tirado, *Hand to Mouth. The Truth about Being Poor in a Wealthy World* (New York, Penguin Books, 2014).

[7] M O'Hara, *The Shame Game. Overturning the Toxic Poverty Narrative* (Bristol, Policy Press, 2020).

[8] B Hvinden and R Halvorsen, 'Who Is Poor? Linking Perceptions of Poor People and Political Responses to Poverty' in R Halvorsen and B Hvinden (eds), *Combating Poverty in Europe. Active Inclusion in a Multi-level and Multi-actor Context* (Cheltenham, Edward Elgar, 2016) 33.

[9] Annabelle Williams, *Why Women are Poorer than Men and What We Can Do About It* (New York, Penguin Books, 2022).

[10] S Hennigan, *Ghost Signs. Poverty and the Pandemic* (Hebden Bridge, Bluemoose Books, 2022).

[11] Council of the European Communities, Council Decision of 22 July 1975 concerning a programme of pilot schemes and studies to combat poverty (75/458/EEC).

interventions on social policy inaugurated in 2000 with the Lisbon Council and culminated with the statistical indicators on poverty approved in 2001 during the Laeken Council.[12]

Based on the clear mandate enshrined in Articles 151 and 153 of the Treaty on the Functioning of the European Union (TFEU), after Lisbon the combating of poverty and social exclusion became a primary objective of the EU and Member States' action. As a result, with the launch of the European platform against poverty and social exclusion in 2010, financial resources were allocated to reach the innovative and ambitious targets set in the Europe 2020 strategy, in particular the headline initiative of lifting some 20 million EU citizens out of poverty by 2020.[13] Member States were monitored on the basis of the Social Scoreboard in the context of the European Semester, which since 2013 has featured a specific focus on the impact of public policies to reduce poverty.[14]

The separation between working poverty (based on a relative evaluation) and material deprivation poverty (based instead on absolute measurement) emerged relatively late in EU social policy. Despite the early 2000s adoption of statistical indicators to carefully monitor both forms of impoverishment, it was only very recently that in-work poverty was found as one of the main objectives of EU's action in the social domain. This happened in November 2017 with the proclamation of the European Pillar of Social Rights ('EPSR' or the 'Pillar'). Not by chance, the EPSR deals with in-work poverty in relation to the right to receive an adequate remuneration from work, by including the prevention of in-work poverty in its Principle 6(b). The proclamation of the Pillar prompted a revised version of the Social Scoreboard, which thereafter included new indicators marking precarity and income insecurity, such as the share of involuntary temporary employees, the median at-risk-of-poverty gap, and the housing cost overburden.[15]

The EPSR implementation through the 2021 Action plan further mirrored the EU Commission's activism in addressing in-work poverty as a standalone societal issue. The legal instrument most evidently showing this attitude is Directive 2022/2041 on Adequate Minimum Wages, which considers in-work poverty within

---

[12] For a detailed account on such historical evolution see M Ferrera and M Jessoula, 'Poverty and Social Inclusion as Emerging Policy Arenas in the EU' in R Halvorsen and B Hvinden (eds), *Combating Poverty in Europe. Active Inclusion in a Multi-level and Multi-actor Context* (Cheltenham, Edward Elgar, 2016) 67, 74.

[13] M Daly, 'Paradigms in EU Social Policy: A Critical Account of Europe 2020' (2012) 18(3) *Transfer* 273.

[14] J Ryszka, 'Protection of Social Rights as a Permanent Challenge for the European Union' (2021) 46 *Review of European and Comparative Law* 109; J Zeitlin and B Vanhercke, 'Socializing the European Semester: EU Social and Economic Policy Co-ordination in Crisis and Beyond' (2018) 25(2) *Journal of European Public Policy* 149.

[15] S Garben, 'The European Pillar of Social Rights: An Assessment of its Meaning and Significance' (2019) 21 *Cambridge Yearbook of European Legal Studies* 101, 115.

its main objectives and draws a causal link between granting adequate minimum wages and the reduction of in-work poverty.[16]

Despite the aforementioned policy initiatives, across the European continent working poverty did not stop increasing. Moreover, the EU's target to reduce poverty by 20 million individuals before 2020 was not achieved. As the previous chapters of this book make evident, the many social and economic factors aggravating in-work poverty grew to such an extent as to question the very ability of EU law and policy to tackle it. The quasi-permanent crisis of European economies not only made it impossible to lift people from absolute poverty, but also increased the number of working people falling below the relative poverty line.

Given the persistence of the (only apparent) contradiction between 'working' and 'poor', it seems necessary to raise a broader question, namely whether the steady (and worrying) growth of in-work poverty across EU countries is exceptional or rather must be taken as a given, being an essential, endemic component of contemporary societies. The question interrogates the very role of labour laws – and of the law more generally – to reduce or rather amplify and structuralise in-work poverty, and requires courage and imagination to envisage how such structuralisation can be counteracted.

III. Current Times: The Rise of Inequalities and In-work Poverty

Writing in 1913, Richard Tawney famously remarked that 'what thoughtful rich people call the problem of poverty, thoughtful poor people with equal justice call the problem of riches'.[17] On that basis, a growing (and nowadays impressive) body of literature has been focusing on the unequal distribution of income and wealth,[18] especially in terms of income derived from work, at least since the emergence of labour movements demanding higher wages and better working conditions for their affiliates.[19] In what follows I will try to emphasise that the connections between income inequality and in-work poverty are intuitively evident but not always measurable. Yet, the spread of inequality tends to increase the clustering of vulnerabilities and in-work poverty.

---

[16] See L Ratti, 'The Sword and the Shield: The Directive on Adequate Minimum Wages in the EU' (2023) *Industrial Law Journal*. For a contextualisation of the directive within a broader set of instruments see the contribution by Marchi in this book (ch 6).

[17] R Tawney, 'Inaugural Lecture on Poverty as an Industrial Problem' in *Memoranda on the Problems of Poverty* (London, William Morris Press, 1913).

[18] A Atkinson, *Inequality. What can be done?* (Harvard, Harvard University Press, 2015); O Galor, *The Journey of Humanity. The Origins of Wealth and Inequality* (New York, Penguin Books, 2022).

[19] T Piketty, *A Brief History of Equality* (Harvard, Harvard University Press, 2021).

The globalisation and financialisation of economies have contributed to concentrating wealth and amplifying the divide between particularly high- and particularly low-income earners. Large portions of those at the lowest end of the spectrum became incapable of improving their living conditions through work, thus hindering social mobility. While this phenomenon triggers broader political and democratic questions – related to the concentration of power and the creation of a wide typology of shields to perpetuate the status quo[20] – important labour law-related questions also arise from the spread of inequalities.

On a historical level, Thomas Piketty has demonstrated how labour rights in a broad sense have been negatively affected by the rise of income inequalities. Increased disadvantage in bargaining power and the concentration of decision-making in the hands of few big corporations have made it more difficult for workers to organise and advocate for their rights, which in turn has led to a decline in social cohesion. While Piketty's core argument is on progressive taxation as a means to redistribute wealth and reduce income inequality – as happened during the 'grande redistribution' between 1914 and 1980[21] – in the field of labour rights measures such as minimum wages, collective bargaining rights and an effective enforcement of labour laws are seen as important tools to share the benefits of economic growth.[22]

On a more normative level, the post-globalisation disappearance of the social contract bridging the state, capitalism and democracy has led to claim for a proper rethinking of capitalism. According to Adalberto Perulli, against a background of increased inequalities, new conditions for the regulation of economic life of humanity should be conceived along the axes of a rebalance of power between capital and labour, a renewed centrality of the nation state (with a view to de-globalising markets), and a stricter conditionality in international trade agreements, centred on the essential role of social sustainability.[23]

Inequalities have spread not only between areas and countries across the globe, but also within the same country, both vertically – ie between the rich and the poor in a given societal context – and horizontally – ie between different groups or categories.[24] The rise of inequality in its many aspects, however, does not fully explain the increase of in-work poverty. They are in fact two distinct concepts, and so is their measurement, therefore a strict causality between the former and the latter cannot be empirically established. In-work poverty, contrary to

---

[20] R Reich, *Supercapitalism. The Transformation of Business, Democracy, and Everyday Life* (New York, Vintage Publishing, 2008); T Piketty, *Capital and Ideology* (Harvard, Harvard University Press, 2020), in particular chapter 13.

[21] Piketty, *A Brief History of Equality* (n 19), in particular chapter 6.

[22] T Piketty, *Capital in the Twenty-First Century* (Harvard, Harvard University Press, 2013), in particular chapter 10.

[23] A Perulli, 'Social Justice and Reform of Capitalism' in B Langille and A Trebilcock (eds), *Social Justice and the World of Work. Possible Global Futures* (Oxford, Hart Publishing, 2023) 23, 32.

[24] World Bank, Poverty and Shared Prosperity 2022: Correcting Course (Washington DC, World Bank, 2022).

income inequality, is a bi-dimensional construct which assumes an individual (a single worker earning a work-related income) as embedded in a collectivity (the household).[25] When only the individual element is considered, the main reasons driving workers into poverty are related to the type of employment, how much income such employment can generate, personal characteristics including age, sex or migrant background, and level of education. By contrast, when considering the household context, other factors such as the number of dependent children or the overall characteristics of the labour-related income produced by the household are determinant.[26] It is not always the same reasons identified as drivers of in-work poverty that can bring individuals, or more generally societies, towards inequality. The contrary tends, however, to hold true. In fact, inequalities fuel in-work poverty, in that high levels of income inequality tend to slow down poverty reduction. As recognised by the International Labour Organization (ILO), 'achieving the SDG [Sustainable Development Goal] on ending poverty (Goal 1) will be possible only if that Goal is pursued in conjunction with efforts to achieve the Goal on reducing inequality (Goal 10). Reducing poverty most effectively would require a combination of higher economic growth and decreased levels of inequality.'[27]

A 2021 Resolution of the European Parliament[28] considers inequalities and in-work poverty in a relationship between 'genus' and 'species', so that in-work poverty is seen as a specification of inequality. In particular, gender inequality, job precarity, low wages and the decrease in collective bargaining coverage are identified as the main factors worsening living and working conditions, thus leading to in-work poverty.[29]

What is only sketchily delineated in the European Parliament's Resolution – but has become clear in recent years – is that the aforesaid economic, societal and institutional determinants do not play an equivalent role, as working poverty is unevenly distributed across the labour market. The increasing inequalities and rates of in-work poverty in Europe have amplified this uneven distribution by creating, perpetuating or worsening the living and working conditions of specific groups of people, who risk finding themselves trapped and not being sufficiently supported by labour laws and welfare state institutions. This requires a careful consideration of the way these groups are studied, and the relevant regulatory responses articulated.

---

[25] See the contribution by García-Muñoz in this book (ch 1). See also L Bardone and A-C Guio, 'In-work poverty. New commonly agreed indicators at the EU level' (2005) *Statistics in Focus. Population and Social Conditions* 2005–5, Eurostat.

[26] M Filandri and E Struffolino, 'Individual and Household In-work Poverty in Europe: Understanding the Role of Labor Market Characteristics' (2019) 21(1) *European Societies* 130; E Crettaz and G Bonoli, 'Worlds of Working Poverty: National Variations in Mechanisms' in N Fraser, R Gutiérrez and R Peña-Casas (eds), *Worlds of Working Poverty: National Variations in Mechanisms* (New York, Palgrave Macmillan, 2011).

[27] ILO, *Inequalities and the World of Work* (Geneve, ILO, 2021) 10, 11.

[28] EU Parliament, Resolution of 10 February 2021 on Reducing Inequalities with a Special Focus on In-work Poverty (2019/2188(INI)).

[29] ibid.

IV. Portraits of Clustered In-work Poverty

Throughout this book – mirroring the scientific journey conducted by the Working, Yet Poor (WorkYP) Consortium from February 2020 to January 2023 – we have focused on several aspects of in-work poverty, starting with its main social and economic determinants.

We did this on the basis of a conceptual assumption: that in-work poverty particularly affects some specific clusters of working people in the labour market.[30] This assumption is not only empirically, but also philosophically supported by the concept of 'disadvantage' unfolded by Wolff and de Shalit. By arguing that the central components of disadvantage are risk and insecurity, they claimed that the law may contribute to the 'clustering of disadvantage'. This led them to identify the exposure to such disadvantage as grouped and magnified whenever more causes of risk and insecurity intersect, giving rise to 'corrosive disadvantage' situations.[31]

By using the concept of VUP Groups as a valuable proxy for clusters of people more intensely experiencing in-work poverty,[32] we can identify how the law of selected EU Member States and EU law itself address the clustered disadvantages of these vulnerable and under-represented persons.[33] This section provides an overview on how the legal framework at the domestic level actually contributed crystallising or even increasing in-work poverty amongst the four VUP Groups.[34]

A. Low-skilled Employees with Standard Employment Contracts Employed in Poor Sectors (VUP Group 1)

Across the seven jurisdictions investigated by the WorkYP consortium,[35] the majority of working people are employed under standard employment contracts, with lower levels in the Netherlands and higher in Luxembourg. Some factors are considered as directly influencing in-work poverty of VUP Group 1 workers and are supposedly tackled by labour laws. Their concrete application and enforcement, however, may prove at times problematic, thus magnifying rather than alleviating the causes of in-work poverty.

---

[30] See the contribution by García-Muñoz in this book (ch 1).

[31] J Wolff and A de Shalit, *Disadvantage* (Oxford, Oxford University Press, 2007).

[32] See the contribution by Garcia-Muñoz in this book (ch 1) and L Ratti (ed), *In-Work Poverty in Europe. Vulnerable and Under-Represented Persons in a Comparative Perspective*, Bulletin of Comparative Labour Relations 111 (London, Wolters Kluwer, 2022).

[33] See the contributions in this book by Hiessl (ch 2) and Houwerzijl (ch 3).

[34] This section builds on Deliverable D5.1 of the Working, Yet Poor project, prepared by K Duffy and F Tornincasa (EAPN Europe) and available at workingyetpoor.eu/deliverables.

[35] Namely Belgium, Germany, Italy, Luxembourg, the Netherlands, Poland and Sweden.

Antidiscrimination laws are important to ensure equal working conditions between male and female workers, as well as to integrate migrant workers in the labour market adequately. However, focusing on what can be identified as 'poor sectors' – ie sectors where more than two-thirds of the working population are low-wage workers – the share of women and people with a migrant background is more prominent, especially in Italy and Poland.

The role of Vocational and Educational Training (VET) policies is also crucial, as there is correlation between the level of education and professional specialisation and the levels of in-work poverty. The obsolete system of VETs in some Member States (eg Italy) surely contributes to increasing the spread of in-work poverty among standard employees and hinders the efficacy of other labour law instruments. Research shows a rise in the proportion of jobs classified as highly skilled, and, until recently, a decline in the proportion of jobs classified as low skilled, at least by reference to occupation. Currently, almost all labour markets across EU Member States are experiencing unfilled vacancies for highly skilled jobs, suggesting greater competition for the remaining low-skilled jobs.[36] Education also plays a role, as in-work poverty is more visible amongst the less educated workers. Germany shows a relatively small proportion of graduates from tertiary education, more attention to upskilling, and vocational training, but a large low-wage sector (over 20 per cent of the workforce in Germany and Poland, but lower than 4 per cent in Sweden).[37] Data from EU-SILC show that the majority of workers in occupations classified as 'low skilled' have a medium level of education (this rises to 80 per cent in Poland), and diachronically highly educated workers are more and more represented in low-skilled occupations, as well as in 'poor sectors'.

VUP Group 1 is particularly affected by the level and distribution of wages, where national legislation still maintains a pivotal role (even after the enactment of Directive 2022/2041 on adequate minimum wages).[38] The low level of wages may increase the risk of in-work poverty, although the number of low pay earners is typically concentrated in certain sectors (eg logistics, construction, tourism). Wage inequalities are more visible in some countries than in others, with sectoral low pay ranging between 0.74 per cent and 11.46 per cent (excluding the public sector) in Sweden and from 1.44 per cent and 66.09 per cent in Germany. Overall, Swedish and Polish workers on full-time permanent contracts are largely protected from poverty, except for the youngest workers.[39]

Social security transfers typically contribute to shield standard workers from in-work poverty. This is particularly evident when decoupling relative and absolute

---

[36] C Hiessl, 'Working, Yet Poor: A Comparative Appraisal' in L Ratti (ed), *In-Work Poverty in Europe: Vulnerable and Under-Represented Persons in a Comparative Perspective* (London, Wolters Kluwer 2022) 313 ff.
[37] ibid.
[38] See the contribution by Marchi in this book (ch 6).
[39] Duffy and Tornincasa (n 34).

poverty amongst VUP Group 1 workers. Standard employees have about half of the monetary poverty levels and two-thirds of the rate of severe material deprivation of the general workforce, which also includes all those working less than full-time for a full year and all forms of non-standard work. Even those standard employees in low-skilled occupations have below average monetary (AROP) poverty rates, except in Luxembourg where already high rates are even higher for this group.[40] Monetary poverty rates for low-skilled employees in poor sectors range from 20 per cent in Luxembourg (the vast majority working under standard employment contracts), to 4.4 per cent in the Netherlands (more prone to non-standard employment). In 2019, low-skilled standard employees were just 14.4 per cent of the Netherlands workforce, demonstrating a greater problem of in-work poverty amongst non-standard employees.[41]

B. Solo and Dependent Self-employed Persons and Bogus Self-employed (VUP Group 2)

The self-employed cover about 7 per cent of the EU workforce, with fluctuating trends since the 2000s. The self-employed is a very heterogeneous group, which constantly changes its internal composition, therefore interpreting its in-work poverty levels and characteristics is particularly problematic. The same comparison between EU Member States proves difficult. Data show that in Italy and Poland, the self-employed account for around 20 per cent of the workforce. Germany, Luxembourg and Sweden, on the contrary, feature much lower levels, all below 10 per cent. The Netherlands saw a rising share of self-employed in the last 15 years, reaching around 12 per cent of the active labour force.

Labour laws typically abstain from regulating self-employment relations. However, in recent years several Member States have introduced either specific protections targeting the self-employed or an extension of historical protections to some segments thereof. A notable example is Italy, where since 2015 those workers whose activities are organised by an employer who decides where and when they should work, are granted the application of all labour laws.[42]

While women account for about one-third of the self-employed as an EU average, across the seven countries investigated self-employed women represent around 40 per cent of the total self-employed in four Member States (Germany, Luxembourg, the Netherlands and Poland). Older people (over age 50) represent a larger share of the self-employed than younger people; this proportion varies

---

[40] Duffy and Tornincasa (n 34).

[41] Hiessl (n 36).

[42] See E Villa, G Marchi and N De Luigi, 'In-Work Poverty in Italy' in L Ratti (ed), *In-Work Poverty in Europe: Vulnerable and Under-Represented Persons in a Comparative Perspective* (London, Wolters Kluwer 2022) 121 ff.

significantly in the investigated Member States, from 26.6 per cent in Luxembourg, through 36.9 per cent in Italy, to 55 per cent in Germany. Solo self-employed, who are the most exposed to the risk of in-work poverty, account for three-quarters of the self-employed and appear to be less well-educated and more likely to be non-nationals of the country in which they work. One in five of the solo self-employed have just one dominant client, which may hide the fact that they could be considered as bogus/false self-employed.[43]

The self-employed show lower levels of median income than employees at EU level, though the difference is smaller in the Netherlands and Sweden. Receiving a lower income exposes this group to a higher risk of in-work poverty, so that for instance in Belgium, Germany, Poland and Sweden, the monetary poverty rate of the self-employed is three times higher than that of the general workforce, and even higher focusing on the solo self-employed only. The 2017 Eurostat Labour Force Survey (LFS) – which featured an ad-hoc module on the self-employed – found that only 5 per cent of the solo self-employed had a second job. However, in some countries, having a second job is much more common amongst the self-employed (eg in Poland around 31 per cent, in Germany 16.6 per cent). In contrast to their higher monetary poverty levels, the solo self-employed at EU level have only slightly higher levels of severe material deprivation.[44]

C. Flexibly-employed Workers (VUP Group 3)

VUP Group 3 includes fixed-term, temporary agency and part-time workers. The share of temporary work (thus including the first two contractual forms) is around 15 per cent at EU level, with a slight decrease during the Covid-19 pandemic.

A small but significant share of the EU's workforce (between 1.25 and 4.4 per cent of all employees) consists of involuntary part-timers, with Italy having a much higher level (around 12 per cent). In 2020, as a share of all EU part-time employment (LFS measurement), involuntary part-time employment was below 25 per cent, having declined in the years that followed the financial crisis. Across the Member States investigated in this book, there is a very wide range for involuntary part-time employment, from below 5 per cent of all part-time employment in Belgium, to a much higher two-thirds of all part-time employment being involuntarily part-time working in Italy.

As argued by Duffy and Tornincasa,[45] 'the size of the involuntary part-time subgroup is heavily affected by what is included in the definition of involuntary and whether a threshold number of hours is defined for "part-time". Three notions are commonly used to define what is involuntary. Involuntary part-time occurs

---

[43] Duffy and Tornincasa (n 34).
[44] ibid.
[45] ibid.

when workers: (a) cannot find full-time work (LFS); (b) would work more hours –
a broader definition but then narrowed by the qualification that the respond-
ent must be currently available to work more hours (Organisation for Economic
Cooperation and Development, OECD); (c) cannot work more hours due to caring
responsibilities (EU Statistics on Income and Living Conditions, EU-SILC).[46] As
correctly pointed out by Houwerzijl,[47] the exclusion of casual workers from the
Part-Time Work Directive results in limiting minimum protection for a considerable part of the workforce. Furthermore, the absence of any regulatory distinction
between involuntary and voluntary part-time employment and the lack of an anti-
abuse clause in the Part-Time Directive substantially undermine the opportunities
of part-time workers to make a decent living.

D. Casual and Platform Workers (VUP Group 4)

VUP Group 4 includes a vast array of contractual arrangements leading to the
performance of casual and platform work, ie work performed through digital
labour platforms. While data on the overall numbers and the characteristics of this
group are lacking, it seems reasonable to assume that intermittent and unpredictable work is unlikely to result in stable incomes above the poverty line, which may
directly influence the rate of in-work poverty at the individual level. Moreover,
while there seems to be no evidence of such a strong causal link at the household
level, the loss or reduction of such forms of top-up income may plunge households
into poverty. Since employers often use casualised workers to meet fluctuating
demand, this is highly likely to occur.

Labour laws tend to tackle casual and platform workers' vulnerabilities by
favouring their classification as subordinate employees. This may happen either
through the activism of case law (as is the case almost everywhere in the EU) or by
extending or creating specific legislation for such contractual arrangements. Hiessl
argues that workers belonging to VUP Group 4 are in fact for the most part either
dependent (and potentially bogus) self-employed or fixed-term and/or part-time
employees, along with a very few ordinary employees, who are 'very likely to be
low-skilled'.[48]

The main problem, however, remains avoiding an excessive casualisation of
work, which at times happens regardless of the type of contract in question and
depends much more on the overall work-intensity at the household level. The
combination of involuntary part-time jobs and casual assignments, oftentimes
distributed through online platforms, renders VUP Group 4 workers inextricably
bound to in-work poverty risks.

---

[46] ibid.
[47] See the contribution by Houwerzijl in this book (ch 3).
[48] Hiessl (n 36).

V. Searching for Antidotes to Structural In-work Poverty

When describing in-work poverty as structurally embedded in contemporary societies and to some extent facilitated by the law, one might get the impression it is inevitable. Being identified as an endemic characteristic of EU labour markets, the spread of in-work poverty may look like an insurmountable obstacle and yet an inexorable consequence of current economic and legislative developments.

Yet, nothing should lead to considering in-work poverty as unavoidable or irreducible. On the contrary, research shows how much has been and can be done from a legal perspective to effectively address the major causes of in-work poverty and reduce its levels across EU countries.

A. Adopting a Human Rights Approach: The Debate on the 'Social Minimum' and Structural Injustice

Human rights studies suggest a number of valuable research trajectories which deserve attention. Courts have in fact deployed constitutional rights in an effort to achieve greater economic justice relying precisely on specific human rights.[49]

Katie Boyle identified two main approaches to the constitutionalisation of the so-called 'social minimum', ie the minimum standard to achieve a dignified life.[50] On the one hand, a substantive approach might be translated into the recognition of a specific right to a given outcome or the right to a policy to achieve an outcome (such as a public policy to get decent housing). On the other hand, a procedural approach would lead to demanding procedural fairness from public authorities while adopting certain decisions that affect individuals. Both approaches, Boyle suggests, would require considering absolute and relative thresholds, so that not only is the bare minimum achieved, but also extreme inequalities are reduced at societal level.[51]

A human rights approach is particularly promising in axiological terms, and it can also bring methodological insights on how to look at structural inequalities in contemporary labour markets. This has been recently outlined by Virginia Mantouvalou in her reflection on structural injustice.[52] Building on the concept

---

[49] M Versteeg, 'Can Rights Combat Economic Inequality?' (2020) 133(6) *Harvard Law Review* 2053.
[50] K Boyle, 'Constitutionalising a Social Minimum as a Minimum Core' in T Kotkas, I Leijten and F Pennings (eds), *Specifying and Securing a Social Minimum in the Battle Against Poverty* (Oxford, Hart Publishing, 2019) 273, 276.
[51] ibid 280.
[52] V Mantouvalou, *Structural Injustice and Workers' Rights* (Oxford, Oxford University Press, 2023).

of structural injustice coined by Iris Marion Young,[53] Mantouvalou's approach to the working poor relies on a notion of 'disadvantage' which largely coincides with the idea of VUP Groups as clusters of people more visibly exposed to the risk of in-work poverty.[54] She claims that welfare-to-work measures altered their typical function – of activating people with a view to (re)integrating them in the labour market – by changing this function from supporting workers to forcing and trapping workers into low-paid jobs.[55] Conditionality systems and over-bureaucratisation of welfare-to-work schemes did not simply penalise jobseekers, but also and especially deteriorated the situation of those who are already employed but earn low incomes.[56] The main argument maintained by Mantouvalou is that legal rules aimed to remedy labour market vulnerabilities in fact contributed to amplify them, putting welfare recipients in front of the alternative of whether to be out of work (thus still benefiting from welfare measures) or working poor. This happened not only through activation policies, but also by allowing fragmentation and casualisation of work relations.[57] Mantouvalou's solution to address this situation is to seriously adopt a human rights perspective – one which brings the right to work, the prohibition of inhuman and degrading treatment, and the right to a subsistence minimum and to social assistance to the forefront. With a view to identify the (unintended but determinant) role of the legal systems in exacerbating in-work poverty, Mantouvalou identifies the state as responsible and the role of human rights monitoring bodies (including courts) as crucial, while reserving additional functions to the European Committee of Social Rights (ECSR), the ILO and the UN Special Rapporteur on Extreme Poverty and Human Rights.[58]

Further developing this perspective, Olivier De Schutter has argued that poverty in general – and in-work poverty in particular – could be strictly considered as a prohibited ground of discrimination,[59] often intersecting with other recognised grounds including gender, nationality and ethnic origin. While this line of reasoning has not yet found proper recognition in court, it may unfold further avenues to enforce human rights related to a situation of in-work poverty vis-à-vis the state, which is responsible for not fulfilling the goals of shared prosperity and equality enshrined in supranational declarations and national constitutions.

---

[53] IM Young, *Responsibility for Justice* (Oxford, Oxford University Press, 2011). On this (now affluent) literature see M McKeown, 'Structural Injustice' (2021) 7 *Philosophical Compass* 16; and more recently M McKeown (ed), *With Power Comes Responsibility: The Politics of Structural Injustice* (London, Bloomsbury Academic, forthcoming).

[54] Mantouvalou (n 52) 74.

[55] ibid.

[56] See also D Seikel and D Spannagel, 'Activation and In-work Poverty' in H Lohmann and I Marx (eds), *Handbook on In-Work Poverty* (Cheltenham, Edward Elgar, 2018) 245.

[57] Mantouvalou (n 52) 87, 88.

[58] Mantouvalou (n 52) 171, 173.

[59] O De Schutter, 'A Human Rights-Based Approach to Measuring Poverty' in M Davis, M Kjaerum and A Lyons (eds), *Research Handbook on Human Rights and Poverty* (Cheltenham, Edward Elgar, 2021) 5, 7.

From an ILO perspective, Keith Ewing and Lord Hendy KC have maintained that achieving a just minimum, including a fair minimum remuneration, is only possible through establishing procedural justice (ie a process in which employers and trade unions freely negotiate on working conditions) coupled with substantive justice, aimed at recognising both 'equal remuneration for work of equal value' and 'fair remuneration for work of different value'.[60] As a result, getting the 'just share of the fruits of progress'[61] would be legally achieved by counteracting wage disparities and thus preventing excessive differences between the highest and lowest ranges of wage scales.[62]

The many ways human rights law and supranational adjudication may support in-work poverty claims leave legal remedies largely uncharted. The rise of structural inequalities and vulnerabilities renders it necessary to unveil the potential of existing tools aimed to identify specific responsibilities of the state.[63] Yet, the road seems still long, not least because the penetration of human rights in the public discourse and, ultimately, the efficacy of its main principles on concrete changes in policymaking is contested and still unexplored.[64]

B. Expanding the Interpretation of Minimum Wage Rules to Include the Household Dimension

An alternative direction towards a more effective legal response to in-work poverty lies at the level of legal interpretation of existing policies and principles. Pivotal in this sense are the principles governing minimum wages, stemming from the international, the EU and the national level, all of which seem to stress the importance of the household dimension.

The Universal Declaration of Human Rights (1948) proclaims the right of everyone to 'just and favourable remuneration ensuring for himself and his family an existence worthy of human dignity, and supplemented, if necessary, by other means of social protection' (Article 23(3)). The two ILO Minimum Wage Conventions on minimum wage machinery (1928 and 1970) aim to ensure a level of minimum wages that is appropriate with due regard inter alia to 'the needs of

[60] KD Ewing and KC Lord Hendy, '"A Just Share of the Fruits of Progress": What Does It Mean?' in B Langille and A Trebilcock (eds), *Social Justice and the World of Work. Possible Global Futures* (Oxford, Hart Publishing, 2023) 66, 70.

[61] See K Ewing, 'A Just Share' – *The Case for Minimum Wage Reform* (Liverpool, Institute of Employment Rights, 2021).

[62] I Katsaroumpas, 'A Right Against Extreme Wage Inequality: A Social Justice Modernisation of International Labour Law' (2021) 32 *King's Law Journal* 260; H Collins, 'Fat Cats, Production Networks, and the Right to Fair Pay' (2022) 85(1) Modern Law Review 1, 24.

[63] Mantouvalou (n 52).

[64] See S Moyn, *Not Enough: Human Rights in An Unequal World* (Cambridge, Harvard University Press, 2018). Critically, on the claim that human rights approaches have not led to the expected outcomes see: Versteeg (n 49) 2059–60.

workers and their families, taking into account the general level of wages in the country, the cost of living, social security benefits, and the relative living standards of other social groups'" (Article 3(1)(a), ILO Minimum Wage Fixing Convention, 1970 (No 131)). In a similar vein, the (revised) European Social Charter (1996) (ESC) provides that workers 'have the right to a fair remuneration sufficient for a decent standard of living for themselves and their families' (Article 4). Finally, in the EPSR the reference point for anchoring the adequacy of minimum wages (as per Principle 6) is identified with 'the needs of workers and their families according to national economic and social conditions', thus building on the constitutional traditions of some European Member States.

Despite their heterogeneous origin and fabric,[65] supranational sources seem to already encompass the two main dimensions of in-work poverty – individual and household-related. So far, the legal interpretation of the right to an adequate wage has been limited to consider only the individual level, focusing on the employment relation between an employee and an employer. While this is certainly in line with the legal nature of the 'fair exchange' embedded in employment contracts,[66] the societal (and macroeconomic) dimension of the right to an adequate minimum wage should suggest considering the needs of the worker's household as a compelling element in the fixation of remuneration. Of course, such consideration should not lead to wage differentials paid directly by the single employer, who cannot bear the costs of individual aspects related to the household dimension and composition. However, these aspects should be considered by the state while imposing taxation and social contributions on wages – and correspondingly while delivering family-related benefits – thus reaching a more progressive and differential treatment depending on the effective needs of the household. Against the objection that the labour laws should not perturbate the individual setting of mutual interests between a worker and their employer, it is easy to reply that the law already does so whenever it considers individuals eligible to receive social security benefits or other financial transfers or services from welfare states.

When questioning whether the aforesaid supranational sources have in fact been operationalised by concrete legislative measures, the text of Directive 2022/2041 comes to the forefront.[67] Despite being directly linked to Principle 6 of the EPSR,[68] the Directive fails to recognise the household dimension in its stipulations. Recitals 4 and 5 of the Directive's preamble merely quote the European Social Charter where the family dimension is contemplated. Households are never mentioned throughout the text of the Directive, nor is the household dimension

---

[65] For a contextualisation of economic and social rights in the Universal Declaration of Human Rights, see: N Bhuta, 'Recovering Social Rights', IILJ Working Paper 2023/1, 20, 21.

[66] M Freedland and S Deakin, 'The Exchange Principle and the Wage-Work Bargain' in M Freedland (ed), *The Contract of Employment* (Oxford, Oxford University Press, 2016) 52, 72.

[67] For a contextualisation of the directive and its main objectives see Ratti (n 16).

[68] Which, as mentioned earlier, considers 'the needs of workers and their families according to national economic and social conditions' as an integral part of the right to a fair remuneration.

cited by Article 5 when focusing on the procedures to ensure adequacy of minimum wages. Against this background – and given the importance of supranational references in the field of remuneration[69] – a possible interpretation of Directive 2022/2041, and specifically of its Article 5(1) focused on the goals 'promoting social cohesion and upward social convergence, and reducing the gender pay gap', cannot avoid considering the needs of the worker's household as a necessary criterion to achieve those goals.

Not only is in-work poverty an issue for welfare states,[70] but it is also (and particularly in a European context) an issue for the systems of labour law. The need to adequately consider the situation of the worker's household can therefore emerge as a specific obligation for the single Member State which, in order to successfully meet the targets established by the Directive, should design its taxation and social contribution policies in a way to relieve those workers living in households in danger of falling below the poverty line.

Whether this conclusion is partially contradicted by the narrow legal basis chosen by the EU legislator to articulate Directive 2022/2041 on adequate minimum wages depends on how the heated debate preceding the final approval of the directive is read. An option would be complementing the legal basis of Article 153(1)(b) TFEU on 'working conditions' – which remains controversial due to an alleged contrast with Article 153(5) TFEU[71] – with the more 'reassuring' legal basis of Articles 174 and 175 TFEU on social and territorial cohesion. In reality, the fact that such alternative or complementary legal basis – which provides inter alia for Commission reporting on the progress made towards achieving economic, social and territorial cohesion every three years[72] – was not chosen does not seem to run against still considering social cohesion as a guiding principle to interpret the same Directive 2022/2041. The combat of social inequalities, therefore, derives from an overall consideration of the EU's objectives in the social sphere as enshrined in Article 3 of the Treaty on European Union (TEU) and Articles 9 and 151 TFEU.

C. Revisiting Labour Law's Horizon to Tackle the Vulnerability of the Self-Employed and Precarious Workers

The received approach on how to reduce in-work poverty levels usually centres on the deployment of public policy (in particular fiscal and/or welfare) measures, together with an efficient guarantee of work-related incomes. Indeed,

---

[69] Including the ILO, ESC, Charter of Fundamental Rights (CFR) and other international covenants.
[70] L Simmons (ed), *Welfare, The Working Poor, and Labor* (London and New York, Routledge, 2004).
[71] See CJEU, Case C-19/23, *Denmark v European Parliament and Council of the European Union*.
[72] See the latest one approved in 2022: European Parliament resolution of 15 September 2022 on economic, social and territorial cohesion in the EU: the 8th Cohesion Report (2022/2032(INI)).

this reflects an attitude to in-work poverty from a redistributive perspective, which tends to prioritise *ex post* measures as an effective way to reduce negative externalities.

Recent studies in private law challenge this approach, (re)discovering how labour law may also serve as an *ex ante* driver of emancipation. It is argued that 'a concern for poverty, properly defined, is integral to relational justice and, consequently, bears on the morality of private law'.[73] Worker's protections, therefore, should be anchored to a contractual approach instead of fully relying on the logics of public law.[74] Reflecting the relational measurement of in-work poverty, those who are in a more precarious situation – regardless of their status, the duration of their assignments, and the quantity of hours performed – may well benefit from a labour law approach. As the analysis in this book has revealed, casual, non-standard, and self-employed workers are among the most exposed to the vulnerabilities typical of the working poor precisely because established levels of treatment do not apply or are practically unenforceable. The persistence of in-work poverty among standard employees, however, suggests that it may not be enough to extend typical labour law guarantees to all types of employment.[75] What those workers claim, in fact, is not only to gain access to (some parts or the whole) labour legislation, but also to overcome their situation of vulnerability and under-representation.

Yet, labour laws were generally unable to address the wide spread of casual working arrangements,[76] including involuntary part-time, casual work, and even zero-hours contracts.[77] In the European context, Directive 2019/1152 on transparent and predictable working conditions marks a clear change and provides some useful tools, making the use of 'on-demand or similar employment contracts, including zero-hour contracts' conditional upon the obligation of Member States to ensure that 'effective measures to prevent their abuse are in place'.[78] More specifically, among the 'complementary measures for on-demand contracts', the Directive provides for 'a rebuttable presumption of the existence of an employment contract or employment relationship with a guaranteed amount of paid

---

[73] H Dagan and A Dorfman, 'Poverty and Private Law: Beyond Distributive Justice' (2023) *American Journal of Jurisprudence*.

[74] H Dagan and M Heller, 'Can Contract Emancipate? Contract Theory and The Law of Work' (2021) 24(1) *Theoretical Inquiries in Law* 49 ff.

[75] As it is the case for instance to the hetero-directed self-employed workers in Italy. See for further details: Villa, Marchi and De Luigi (n 42); M Del Conte, E Gramano, 'Looking to the Other Side of the Bench: The New Legal Status of Independent Contractors Under the Italian Legal System' (2018) 39(3) *Comparative Labour Law & Policy Journal* 579.

[76] ACL Davies, 'Regulating Atypical Work: Beyond Equality' in N Countouris and M Freedland (eds), *Resocialising Europe in a Time of Crisis* (Cambridge, Cambridge University Press, 2013) 244.

[77] For a discussion on how zero-hours contracts cannot be seen as employment contracts in common law see: P Elias, 'Changes and Challenges to the Contract of Employment' (2018) 38(4) *Oxford Journal of Legal Studies* 869, 880.

[78] Preamble 35, Directive 2019/1152 of the European Parliament and of the Council on transparent and predictable working conditions in the European Union.

hours' (Article 11). Directive 2019/1152 also features provisions on the maximum duration of probationary periods (Articles 4(2)(g) and 8) and requirements for predictable working patterns (Articles 4(2)(m) and 10).[79] These provisions seem to suggest that a correct implementation of the Directive should oblige Member States to effectively increase the protections for casual workers and reduce their risk of in-work poverty.

Mirroring what has been already done with Council Recommendation (2019/C 387/01) of 8 November 2019 on access to social protection for workers and the self-employed, in the field of labour law, casual, non-standard and self-employed workers should also become part of the policy discourse. Status, social protection and collective representation may therefore become the three testbeds to realise a proper emancipation to tackle their insecurity, income discontinuity and, eventually, in-work poverty.[80]

VI. Conclusion: Societal Transformations and the Way Forward

This chapter provided an overview of existing issues at EU and Member State level – including policy initiatives – concerning the wide spread of in-work poverty across Europe. Years of studies and reflection on the many determinants and internal components of in-work poverty helped outline important regulatory instruments that may and should be refined or modified. Still, a number of societal transformations question the very ability of such instruments to be really fit for purpose in the years to come.

A first challenge that regulatory measures aimed to combat in-work poverty will need to address concerns the variations in *demographic* structures of European societies. Van Winkle and Struffolino, for instance, have provided an interesting observation on the US labour market, claiming that the age-specific effects of family demographic processes are 'considerably larger compared to the average effects of traditional stratification factors reported in the literature'.[81] As a consequence, the risk of belonging to the working poor is 'relatively stable

---

[79] For an overall assessment of the Directive's impact see B Bednarowicz, 'Delivering on the European Pillar of Social Rights: The New Directive on Transparent and Predictable Working Conditions in the European Union' (2019) 48 *Industrial Law Journal* 604 ff; JM Miranda Boto, 'Much Ado about Anything? The New Directive (EU) 2019/1152 on Transparent and Predictable Working Conditions in the European Union' in F Marhold and others (eds), *Arbeits- und Sozialrecht für Europa. Festschrift für Maximilian Fuchs* (Baden Baden, Nomos, 2020) 157 ff.

[80] A Perulli, 'A Critique of Self-Employment' (2022) 13(2) *European Labour Law Journal* 307, building on R Semenza, F Pichaud (eds), *The Challenges of Self-Employment in Europe. Status, Social Protection and Collective Representation* (Cheltenham, Edward Elgar, 2019).

[81] Z Van Winkle and E Struffolino, 'When Working Isn't Enough: Family Demographic Processes and In-work Poverty across the Life Course in the United States' (2018) 39(12) *Demographic Research* 365 ff.

over individual life courses', while a 'wider prevalence of in-work poverty during defined phases characterized by care responsibility (typically when small children are present in the household)' can be identified.[82] Furthermore, examining how the household composition affects the structure and persistence of in-work poverty, Thiede, Sanders and Lichter have observed that single-parent families expose the household to major risks of in-work poverty that are not adequately addressed by specific family-oriented policies.[83] Variations may occur cross-country even in the European context, as welfare state models largely remain regulated at Member State level. This may explain why an increase in household resources may prove an effective remedy to protect the household from in-work poverty only in some jurisdictions.[84] The increase in life expectancy and the progressive ageing of European population – regularly certified by Eurofound[85] – still deserve to be thoroughly analysed for their effects on any proposed measure to reduce in-work poverty levels, as it may well be that some policy options are more practicable than others precisely considering the demographic composition of the workforce. In countries where intergenerational dependence is more structural, typically located in the south of Europe, the family may keep young people out of poverty (being supported by family resources) but this may also increase the risk of poverty for older people (because they have also the needs of the young adults to meet). Conversely, in the Nordic countries where inter-generational dependency is weak and young people leave home early, in-work poverty is more common among young people but has been historically a transitory phenomenon.[86]

A second important aspect which deserves attention is how the law addresses the *longitudinal* trajectory of in-work poverty. The way people enter and exit in-work poverty is dramatically important from a policy perspective, as it makes it possible to distinguish whether the law has been effective or not in improving working and living conditions. Also, this aspect needs to be understood against the background of very diverse welfare models in Europe.[87] Considering the composition of the labour force, both horizontally and from a longitudinal perspective, Hick and Lanau have found that labour market events, such as a decrease in the hours worked both at the individual and the household level, trigger the majority of in-work poverty entries. On the contrary, exits from in-work poverty are

---

[82] ibid.

[83] B Thiede, S Sanders and D Lichter, 'Demographic Drivers of In-work Poverty' in H Lohmann and I Marx (eds), *Handbook on In-Work Poverty* (Cheltenham, Edward Elgar, 2018) 109 ff.

[84] See A Polizzi, E Struffolino and Z Van Winkle, 'Family Demographic Processes and In-work Poverty: A Systematic Review' (2022) 52 *Advances in Life Course Research* 15.

[85] See at last Eurofound, *Demographic Outlook for the European Union* (Brussels, European Union, 2022).

[86] H Lohmann, 'Welfare States, Labour Market Institutions and the Working Poor: A Comparative Analysis of 20 European Countries' (2009) 25(4) *European Sociological Review* 489 ff.

[87] R Layte and C Whelan, 'Moving in and out of poverty: The impact of welfare regimes on poverty dynamics in the EU' (2003) 5(2) *European Societies* 167, 191.

typically due to household-related events, including an increase of income, number of income earners, and hours worked in the household.[88] Their conclusion – referred to the UK – is that most of the working poor population departs from situations of in-work poverty by exiting poverty in general. This suggests the importance not only of stabilising the working situation and increasing the number of jobowners in the household, but also of guaranteeing basic welfare tools like housing, childcare, healthcare and transport, as crucial preconditions to favour exiting trajectories from in-work poverty.[89]

A third significant societal transformation which requires specific policy attention relates to the structural *casualisation* of labour relations. Unpredictable working schedules and uncertain employment prospects lead to low work-intensity at the household level, which has been clearly outlined as one of the most serious causes of in-work poverty in Europe. This raises the broad question of adapting existing indicators to the current reality of employment relations. Since the threshold of in-work poverty is identified considering those who are 'in-work' – ie have worked for more than half of the reference period (a year) – current indicators may be too rigid and fail to capture all those casual and intermittent work assignments that are not continuous enough to meet the threshold. As already flagged in the 2019 European Social Policy Network (ESPN) study on in-work poverty across Europe,[90] there is ample margin for improvement of current statistical indicators, as several determinant factors are not adequately considered and could make the dynamic situation of current labour relations more visible to policy makers.

The formulation of specific antidotes against in-work poverty leaves us with the impression that the complex and changing nature of the phenomenon is still not entirely acknowledged. This is in spite of the current social policy framework at EU level, as solemnly enshrined in the interinstitutional proclamation of the EPSR. A literal and contextual interpretation of Principle 6 of the Pillar, in fact, should lead to concluding that in-work poverty is not something which must be merely 'reduced' – as happens at UN level with SDG 1 on absolute poverty – but something which must be prevented,[91] avoided[92] and combatted.[93] An obligation of result in terms of policy output, therefore, can be derived from that Principle, which requires that not only the EU and its institutions, but also the Member

---

[88] R Hick and A Lanau, 'Moving In and Out of In-work Poverty in the UK: An Analysis of Transitions, Trajectories and Trigger Events' (2018) 47(4) *Journal of Social Policy* 661 ff.

[89] This conclusion is in line with what have been identified as 'indirect measures' to combat in-work poverty. See ESPN, *In-work Poverty in Europe. A Study of National Policies* (Brussels, European Commission, 2019). See also the contribution by R Peña-Casas, D Ghaliani and K Kominou in this book (ch 7).

[90] ibid.

[91] Principle 6(3) EPSR, English, German and Italian versions.

[92] Principle 6(3) EPSR, French, Dutch and Spanish versions.

[93] Principle 6(3) EPSR, Portuguese version.

States (equally bound by the EPSR at Council level) are called to introduce specific policies aimed at achieving that result. The absence of any reference to an overall approach to combat in-work poverty in the 2021 EPSR Action plan requires to be filled by an overall strategy on in-work poverty, intended to direct efforts and coordinate policies. The regulatory capabilities to prevent in-work poverty are all but fully developed. The EU and its Member States must do more and better, and scholars too.

INDEX

Milton Keynes UK
Ingram Content Group UK Ltd.
UKHW031538160224
437875UK00003BA/88